WHITEHALL HISTORIES: NAVAL STAFF HISTORIES

Series Editor: Capt. Christopher Page

ISSN: 1471-0757

THE EVACUATION
FROM DUNKIRK

NAVAL STAFF HISTORIES

Series Editor: Capt. Christopher Page

ISSN: 1471-0757

Naval Staff Histories were produced after the Second World War in order to provide as a full an account of the various actions and operations as was possible at the time. In some cases the Histories were based on earlier Battle Summaries written much sooner after the event, and designed to provide more immediate assessments. The target audience for these Naval Staff Histories was largely serving officers; some of the volumes were originally classified, not to restrict their distribution but to allow the writers to be as candid as possible. These histories have been in the Public Record Office for some time, and are here published for the first time.

The Evacuation from Dunkirk: 'Operation Dynamo', 26 May–4 June 1940
Edited and with a preface by W. J. R. Gardner

Naval Operations of the Campaign in Norway, April–June 1940
Edited and with a preface by David Brown

THE EVACUATION
FROM DUNKIRK

'Operation Dynamo'
26 May–4 June 1940

Edited and with a Preface by

W. J. R. GARDNER
Naval Historical Branch, Ministry of Defence

FRANK CASS
LONDON · PORTLAND, OR

First published in 2000 in Great Britain by
FRANK CASS PUBLISHERS
Newbury House, 900 Eastern Avenue
London, IG2 7HH

and in the United States of America by
FRANK CASS PUBLISHERS
c/o ISBS, 5804 N.E. Hassalo Street
Portland, Oregon, 97213-3644

Website: www.frankcass.com

British Library Cataloguing in Publication Data

The evacuation from Dunkirk: Operation Dynamo, 26 May–4
June 1940. – (Naval staff histories)
1. Great Britain. Royal Navy – History – World War,
1939–1945 2. World War, 1939–1945 – Naval operations,
British 3. Dunkerque (France), Battle of, 1940
I. Gardner, W. J. R.
940.5'45941

ISBN 0-7146-5120-6 (cloth)
ISBN 0-7146-8150-4 (paper)
ISSN 1471-0757

Library of Congress Cataloging-in-Publication Data

The evacuation from Dunkirk: Operation Dynamo, 26 May–4 June 1940 / edited with a
preface by W.J.R. Gardner.
    p. cm. – (Whitehall histories, Naval Staff histories)
    Originally prepared by the Historical Section of the Admiralty in 1949 as Battle
Summary No. 41.
    Includes bibliographical references and index.
    ISBN 0-7146-5120-6 – ISBN 0-7146-8150-4 (pbk.)
    1. Dunkerque (France), Battle of, 1940. 2. World War, 1939–1945 – Naval operations,
British. I. Gardner, W. J. R. II. Great Britain. Admirality. Historical Section. III. Series.

D756.5.D8 E93 2000
940.54'21428–dc21   00-031707

Published on behalf of the Whitehall History Publishing Consortium.
Applications to reproduce Crown copyright protected material in this
publication should be submitted in writing to: HMSO, Copyright Unit,
St Clements House, 2–16 Colegate, Norwich NR3 1BQ. Fax: 01603
723000. E-mail: copyright@hmso.gov.uk

Typeset by Regent Typesetting
Printed in Great Britain by
Bookcraft (Bath) Ltd, Midsomer Norton, Somerset

CONTENTS

LIST OF ILLUSTRATIONS

All photographs reproduced by permission of the Imperial War Museum, London

Foreword by Admiral Sir Michael Boyce GCB OBE ADC
First Sea Lord and Chief of Naval Staff

This year marks the sixtieth anniversary of the traumatic events of 1940, which saw the collapse of the Allied armies in France and the Low Countries and the subsequent evacuation of well over 300,000 servicemen from the Dunkirk area. The success of 'Operation Dynamo' and the other, less-publicized, evacuations from various French ports enabled this country to retain the vital military skills and core competences upon which the British Army could base its plans for the recapture of the European mainland and the eventual defeat, in concert with our Allies, of the most formidable enemy.

The Royal Navy has a long-standing tradition of supporting our troops ashore and, when all else fails, of providing an escape route to allow them to fight again. However, the ability to undertake such operations depends on sea control: we were able to effect the withdrawal of our troops from Norway, France, Greece and Crete during the Second World War only because of the ability of the Royal Navy to command the seas within those theatres. By contrast, the loss of Singapore in early 1942 provides a stark lesson on the results of not having won sea control. And later in the war, it was precisely this ability to use the sea for our own purposes that enabled the Allies to launch the dozens of separate assaults which finally defeated the Japanese and German enemies.

Dunkirk was a major defeat, of that there is no doubt, and a costly exercise for the Royal Navy and the hundreds of small vessels which participated in the evacuation. More than 170 vessels were sunk and a further 50 damaged including 1 anti-aircraft cruiser, 23 destroyers and 13 minesweepers. These figures do not include large numbers of unnamed boats lost or damaged. But, as always in such circumstances, there was much that was praiseworthy: the brilliance of the improvised organization; the excellent inter-service cooperation, and the behaviour of the sailors and troops under the most demanding conditions.

All aspects of the operation, good and not so good, are comprehensively and frankly covered in this History. I am delighted that it is now available to the general public and whole-heartedly recommend it to casual and serious readers alike.

Ministry of Defence
March 2000

PREFACE TO THE NEW EDITION

At the blackest point of the Second World War, the British people and the free world was saved not by the exertions of its armed forces but by a flotilla of small craft manned by amateur yachtsmen, fishermen and the like who spontaneously took themselves across the Channel in their own boats and rescued a whole army from the beaches of Dunkirk, thus thwarting the ambitions of an evil Axis . . .

The above is not a literal quote but it does give a fairly good idea of the popular view of what happened at Dunkirk at the end of May and beginning of June 1940. Although not entirely untrue, the above statement has, it would be correct to say, taken on the status of a myth; a myth because it conveys neither an accurate nor a balanced account of the real achievement of evacuating a considerable body of troops under very difficult conditions. Clearly, from the angle of human interest, the mythical interpretation has an appeal which has accounted for its creation and perpetuation. But now, some 60 years after the event, it is time for less mythical and more factual material to become more clearly visible. There could be no better candidate for doing this than the Naval Staff History written in 1949 and bearing the prosaic heading of Battle Summary No. 41. This account was produced in that year by the Historical Section of the Admiralty (now the Naval Historical Branch of the Ministry of Defence), drew directly on contemporary reports and was originally intended for purely internal consumption, so it pulls few punches. Produced largely for naval use, it is mostly about seaborne operations but it does take account of what was happening on land, in both the events that led up to the necessity of evacuating the British Expeditionary Force (BEF) from France and the more immediate movements on land in the Dunkirk area. Nor are air operations neglected where these are relevant.

But perhaps the first point to be dealt with is the wider picture, taking in most of north-western Europe in the first months of the Second World War. The high drama of the declaration of war in September 1939 had not made any significant difference to the Poles whose national fate was the immediate cause of the wider war. However, these events were to have an effect on the early German conduct of the world war. It is now generally accepted that Hitler hoped to bluff his way through the Polish operations in the same way as he had with the re-militarisation of the Rhineland in 1936, the *Anschluss* with Austria in 1938 and the annexation of Czechoslovakia in 1939. The short Polish war of September 1939 nevertheless resulted in a significant check on immediate German operations, because of a lack of worked-out plans for further warfare and marked casualties to German forces. What then ensued on land – if not in the air and, in particular, at sea – was a stalemate which lasted several months over the winter. Known variously as 'The Phoney War' (Britain), '*Sitzkrieg*' (Germany) and '*drôle de guerre*' (France), this ended abruptly in April 1940 with the start of German operations against Norway and Denmark. On 10 May, an offensive against the Netherlands, Luxembourg and Belgium began. This could only be described as wildly successful for the Germans and disastrous for the Allies, as the Germans swept across the Low Countries and then France.

Contrary to much popular belief, the Germans at this point were not equipped with vast numbers of greatly superior tanks and other equipment; but they were experienced, well led and also made good use of co-ordinating land and air forces. This helped them achieve early breakthroughs, especially against the southern-sector French forces. By continuing to move quickly thereafter, the Germans made it very difficult to mount organised resistance against them. Further, it could not be said that the Allied effort was fully co-ordinated, and failure in one sector affected others which had themselves come under significant pressure; by 23 May, not a fortnight after the start of their offensive, the Germans were within 20 miles of the Channel coast. Various Allied forces were forced into pockets around Dunkirk, other places in the Channel area and elsewhere in France. Clearly, this was a rapid and disastrous outcome.

During the long buildup over the relatively quiescent winter, there had been little consideration given to the prospect of the sudden withdrawal that was now necessary, although the many requirements of the multi-division BEF would have necessitated the use of a considerable amount of shipping. All this now had to change; the majority of the BEF was concentrated around Dunkirk and initial interest was focused there.

The operation that was about to take place in France was on a scale well beyond any individual having precise control over all levels at all times, but it was still important that it be properly led and conducted. It was the nation's good fortune to have the then Vice-Admiral Sir Bertram Ramsay at Dover. Strictly speaking a retired officer, he had received a temporary appointment as Flag Officer, Dover, in 1938, during the Munich crisis. He quickly realised that the headquarters was in a poor condition and was responsible for having it equipped more fully, a very useful preparation for 1940. Ramsay has sometimes been considered as the supreme organiser of set-piece operations, but Operation Dynamo indicates very clearly that he also had improvisational skills of a very high order.

Many people appear in the Naval Staff History, especially those who displayed merit at Dunkirk itself, but it is worth mentioning two more who worked at Dover but go unrecorded in this volume. One was the Staff Officer Operations, Commander F. J. Walker, who was later to become nationally famous as the most successful and best-known escort group commander in the Battle of the Atlantic. The other was Vice-Admiral Sir James Somerville, who periodically relieved Ramsay. Such an arrangement would have been difficult to envisage in that era and the fact that it worked so well with two officers of such strong character says a great deal for the fundamental soundness of Ramsay's organisation.

In the early years of the twenty-first century, when a great deal of emphasis is being laid on the doctrine and reality of services operating together – joint operations – and co-operating closely with other nations – combined ones – it is sometimes easy to forget that this was far less marked at the outset of the Second World War. Clearly, doctrine cannot be invented on the spot and transmitted instantly to all participants, but closer co-operation can be improvised to some extent. At Dunkirk this was greatly hampered by problems with communications-material difficulties, very much a commonplace of the period, with scanty numbers of (unreliable) radio sets and procedures to use them that did not always stand up to the stress of operations under pressure. The solution lay in a good deal of effort being put into personal contacts, with various naval-shore parties being deployed and communications often having to be improvised. It may not have been quite all done by runners with cleft sticks, but often this was what was used in effect.

There were, however, failures of communication and practice, and the Staff History is frank on this, noting such things as the wastage of small boats which went from beaches to offshore ships full of troops, but for which no boat-keepers were detailed – the boats thus became lost to any further operations as they were cast adrift as every soldier vacated them. The study also nails one of the great misperceptions of Dunkirk: namely, that the Royal Air Force (RAF) abandoned the Army to its fate on the beaches. Certainly, there were instances where troops awaiting embarkation were bombed, and the loss of warships and personnel vessels to aircraft was significant, being the cause of the greatest losses. However, part of the RAF's role lay in preventing more *Luftwaffe* aircraft reaching the coastal area and in that it succeeded.

The popular perception of Dunkirk has it that the majority of the troops evacuated went from the beaches, but this was not so. As is made clear in Table 3 at the end of the Staff History, a much greater number – a proportion of over two times greater – were in fact evacuated from Dunkirk harbour. This should not really be surprising. Despite a fair amount of attention being turned by the Germans on to the harbour area, its capacity was very much greater than that of the beaches, where even destroyers could not get close enough to permit direct embarkation. The beaches, therefore, were very much a second choice, although sometimes they had to be used. As a result, during the 10 days of operations, the beaches had no embarkations on two days and fewer than 10,000 on four. There was one day only, 30 May, when the numbers embarked from the beaches (29,512) exceeded those from the harbour (24,311) – this was a tremendous figure for the beaches. On 1 June the harbour peaked at 47,081. According to the Staff History, over 338,000 British and Allied troops were evacuated during Operation Dynamo. although the War Office figures suggest a lower figure of some 308,000, split approximately in the ratio of two British troops to one Allied troop. The numbers issue is explored thoroughly and fairly in John Winser's recent book *B.E.F. Ships: Before, At and After Dunkirk* (Gravesend, World Ship Society, 1999). What is not in dispute, however, is that over 300,000 British and Allied servicemen were evacuated, an important asset for the five years of war that lay ahead.

Winser's book is useful from another viewpoint. The Staff History does not cover the subsequent evacuation operations, which extended as far south as the Spanish border. Operation Cycle was mounted to evacuate forces from St Valery and Le Havre, and by 13 June some 15,000 British and French troops had been evacuated. This was succeeded by Operation Aerial from the rest of France and the Channel Islands, and accounted for some 186,000 British and Allied troops, nearly half the Dunkirk total. The locations were Nantes, Brest, Cherbourg, St Malo, La Pallice, St Nazaire, the Channel Islands, the River Gironde and St Jean de Luz close to the

Spanish border. In total, these accounted for a further 140,000 British and 47,000 Allied troops, as well as some guns and over 2,000 pieces of motor transport. It was Aerial, however, that was to result in the worst incident of all the evacuations, at St Nazaire, when the heavily loaded passenger liner *Lancastria*, at anchor to take troops on board, was attacked by bombers. She was hit by four bombs, caught fire and rolled over. Little more than half an hour elapsed between the attack and her sinking. Nearly 4,000 were rescued, but many were not. Confusion over the numbers on board meant that the exact numbers lost were not known and are now never likely to be. However, the figure of more than 4,000 gives some idea of the scale of the loss.

Nevertheless, despite this and other lesser losses which occurred during the evacuation operations, the achievement remains considerable. At the lowest accounting, over 500,000 British and Allied troops were brought from Europe to the United Kingdom in less than a month with little notice and under very difficult circumstances. Operations Dynamo, Cycle and Aerial were successes.

The Naval Staff History provides a clear and authoritative guide to Operation Dynamo, using accounts written by those who planned and executed the operation, and set down very soon after the events, as its source materials. Inevitably, there are gaps consequent on improvisation, information deficiencies at the time and the sometimes fragmented nature of the operations. What comes across vividly despite all this is the professionalism and determination of those who effected this operation. Largely, and properly, this should be credited to the Royal Navy, although the book makes it very clear that there was a considerable contribution by those who had not been long-time career Royal Navy men, including those in the various reserves, the merchant service and others.

Operation Dynamo was not a victory: no evacuation can ever be considered as such. What it did mean, however, was that a substantial body of troops in dire difficulty on land and pressed from the air were firstly sustained, then delivered from this situation because of the utility and flexibility of sea power. In comparable circumstances, such as in 1944, when German troops were cut off in the Crimea, the inability of the Germans to conduct naval operations sealed the fate of significant numbers of men. Admittedly, geography, has a part to play in whether operations such as Dynamo begin to be feasible, but it is clear that, even when this does occur, the tools of seapower are an essential adjunct to being able to conduct land operations. This is not merely a matter of owning enough shipping and support forces at sea to conduct the lift, but also of being able to have sufficient command of the waters between points of embarkation and disembarkation to give a reasonable assurance of free movement in these areas. This the Royal Navy was able to do in late May and early June 1940, allowing the operation to happen.

Operation Dynamo did not win the war, but it was an essential step in Britain's being able to stay in it until a proper alliance of strength could be forged some 18 months later.

W.J.R. Gardner
Naval Historical Branch, Ministry of Defence, March 2000

ADDENDUM TO SOURCES

The original list of sources uses the old numbering system. As a guide to further research, the existing PRO references set out below embrace the documents from the original list, where they still exist.

The principal sources on which this account of 'Operation Dynamo' is based are as follows:

ADM 1/12441	Evacuation from Dunkirk: awards to personnel of Norwegian SS *Hird*.
ADM 199/96	Blocking of French and Belgian ports: operation orders, narratives and reports.
ADM 199/667	Operations off French, Belgian and Dutch coasts.
ADM 199/786–794	'Operation Dynamo': evacuation of troops from Dunkirk.
ADM 199/795	Operations off Dutch, Belgian and French coasts: reports.
ADM 199/796	'Operation 'Dynamo': evacuation of troops from Dunkirk; German attacks on Holland.

ABBREVIATIONS

A/A	Anti-Aircraft	M.L.	Motor Launch
A.B/V	Armed Boarding Vessel	M/S.	Mine Sweeper
A.L.C.	Assault Landing Craft	M.S.F.	Mine Sweeping Flotilla
A.P.	Auxiliary Patrol	N.C.S.O.	Naval Control of Shipping Officer
A/S	Anti-Submarine, also Admiral Superintendent	N.O.I.C.	Naval Officer In Charge
B.L.O.	British Liaison Officer	P.S.T.O.	Principal Sea Transport Officer
B.N.L.O.	British Naval Liaison Officer	P/V	Personnel Vessel
C.K.	Blocking of Dunkirk Harbour (Operation C. K.)	(R)	(Of signals), repeated to. Modern version is information addressee
C.M.S.	Captain, Minesweepers	R.O.I. – VI	Documentary reference – see Sources
D.M.O.	Director of Military Operations (Army)	S.N.O.	Senior Naval Officer
D.N.I.	Director of Naval Intelligence	S-boat	*Schnellboot* (German – fast boat) – light fast enemy craft, often referred to by British as E-boats
D.R.	Operation Dynamo Report of Proceedings (documentary reference)		
D. of S. T.	Director of Sea Transport	S.T.N.	See Sources
D.S.V.P.	Director of the Small Vessels Pool	S.V.P.	Small Vessels Pool
E-boat	Common British term for light fast enemy craft; see also S-boat	T.B.D.	Torpedo Boat Destroyer – more normally Destroyer
		T.O.D.	Time of Despatch (of signal)
F.A.A.	Fleet Air Arm	T.O.R.	Time of Receipt (of signal)
F.O.I.C.	Flag Officer in Command		
H/C	Hospital Carrier	V.C.I.G.S.	Vice-Chief, Imperial General Staff (Army)
H.E.111	Heinkel 111 – German bomber	V/S	Visual Signalling
LL	Magnetic minesweeping gear	W/T	Wireless Telegraphy – radio
L/V	Light Vessel	X	Class of Admiralty lighters
M.A/S. B.	Motor Anti-submarine Boat	X.D., also XD	Demolitions at Dunkirk (Operation XD)
M/B	Motor Boat	Y.C.	Class of Admiralty lighters
Me. 109	Messerschmidt 109 – German fighter aircraft		

B.R. 1736 (32)
BATTLE SUMMARY No. 41

THE EVACUATION FROM DUNKIRK

OF THE

BRITISH EXPEDITIONARY FORCE AND FRENCH TROOPS

Operation "Dynamo"
26th May — 4th June 1940

The contents of this book are based on information available up to and including September, 1947.

T.S.D. 64/48.
TACTICAL AND STAFF DUTIES DIVISION (HISTORICAL SECTION)
NAVAL STAFF, ADMIRALTY, S.W.1.

CONTENTS

CHAPTER I

Preliminary Events, 10th to 18th May, 1940

CHAPTER II

The week before Operation "Dynamo", 19th to 25th May, 1940

CHAPTER III

Operation Dynamo is commenced, Sunday, 26th May, 1940

CHAPTER IV

Monday, 27th May

CHAPTER V

Tuesday, 28th May

CHAPTER VI

Wednesday, 29th May

CHAPTER VII

Thursday, 30th May

CONTENTS

Page

CHAPTER X.

The night of 1st-2nd June and from daylight to dusk on 2nd

CHAPTER XI

The night 2nd-3rd June : B.E.F. Evacuated 2330/2

CHAPTER XII

The Final Night, 3rd-4th June

CHAPTER XIII

Analysis of the Operation

APPENDICES

Page

TABLES

Notes to Tables 1–3

1. An analysis of the allied ships which took part in Operation "Dynamo", and of the recorded numbers of troops lifted by them from Dunkirk harbour and the beaches ... *Facing page* 210

2. An analysis of the recorded numbers of troops lifted daily from Dunkirk harbour and the beaches ... ...

3. Troop and Ship Summaries—
   (a) Ships taking part—summary.
   (b) Allied ships—summary of troops transported
   (c) Disembarkations—summary

ix

PLANS

SOURCES

The principal sources on which this account of Operation "Dynamo" is based, are as follows :—

M.011883/40	Operation "Dynamo." Report of Proceedings. (Report of Vice-Admiral Ramsay, F.O.C. Dover, referred to in this narrative as D.R.)
M.020721/40	List of ships which took part in Operation "Dynamo," 26th May to 4th June (From F.O.C. Dover, 26/10/40).
M.017681/40	Ships lost during Operation "Dynamo" – Report (From F.O.C. Dover, 5/9/40).
M.017978/41	Report of Rear-Admiral Wake-Walker on the evacuation from Dunkirk, 29th May to 4th June, 1940. (Rear-Admiral Dover's Report).
C.W.29685/40	Operation "Dynamo." Recommendations for Honours and Awards. (From F.O.C. Dover, July 1940).
Case 5458 [6 volumes] Admiralty Record Office	Operation "Dynamo." Evacuation of troops from Dunkirk, May to June 1940. (Contains reports of individual ships, "Dynamo" Maintenance Officer, S.N.O. Dunkirk, etc.) Referred to as "R.O.I – VI."
Enclosure Box No. 370 Admiralty Record Office	Contains signals connected with the operation.
	Admiralty War Diary. (Signals).
M.011431/40	Blocking of Dunkirk Harbour (Operation C.K.)
M.010977/40	Demolitions carried out at Dunkirk (Operation X.D.)
Case 6256 Admiralty Record Office	H.M. Ships lost during the evacuation of troops from Dunkirk.
H. & A.8/42	Evacuation from Dunkirk Norwegian S.S. *Hird*. Recommendations for awards.
M.016146/40	Dutch coasters. List of commissioned for "Dynamo," etc.
M.010932/40	Report of Proceedings of Riflemen landed to cover Demolition Party at Boulogne on 23/5/40.
M.010824/40	Evacuation of Boulogne. Report by Major C. F. L. Holford, Royal Marines (with M.010932/40).
M.3422/40	Particulars of [Belgian] men and craft from the Dartmouth area who assisted in Dunkirk evacuation. (From C. in C. Western Approaches, 14/7/40).
M.011882/40	Operation "Dynamo" Work of Personnel Vessels. (From F.O.C. Dover, 18/6/40).
M.014793/40	Reports of Operations off Dutch, Belgian and French Coasts [Evacuation of Boulogne.]

M.013316/40 — Operations conducted by F.O.C. Dover during period 10th-15th May on Dutch, Belgian and French Coasts.

T.O.9436/40 — Operation "Dynamo" Small Craft. (Ministry of Shipping 5/6/40).

T.M. 6213/40 — Voyage reports by Masters or crews of ships and small craft which took part in the evacuation of the B.E.F. from Dunkirk. (From Ministry of Shipping, Sea Transport Dept., 2/8/40).

T.O.9144/41 (part I) — (Small craft taken up for "Dynamo" Operation). Letters received giving account of operations. (Ministry of Shipping, Sea Transport Dept., 17/11/41).

T.O.9144/40 — Provision of certain small craft for special service (pooled at Sheerness) " E " Scheme. (Ministry of Shipping, Sea Transport, Dept., 27/5/40).

T.O.9436/40 — Operation "Dynamo" – small craft. Procedure for settlement of claims.

N.L.5097/40 — Compulsory reporting of small craft – Proposed order. (From small vessels pool, 16/4/40).

S.T.N.4B — (Director of Sea Transport). Vessels dealt with by S.T.N.4B which took part in " Dynamo."

D.Y./1/01 — Operation " Dynamo " (from Commodore in Charge Sheerness). (Pack of signals and letters).

R.E./2/014 — Operation "Dynamo". (Reports and Recommendations. From Commodore in Charge Sheerness).

R.A.F. Narrative. The Campaign in France and the Low Countries, Sept. 1939 – June, 1940. (Air Historical Branch (1) Air Ministry).

The following sources contain some first-hand information which is not in Official Records :

Statements made by Masters of tugs engaged in the evacuation from Dunkirk (From William Watkins Ltd., Steam tug owners, London).

Account by the R.N.L.I. of their work in the evacuation of the B.E.F. from Dunkirk.

Reports made by crews of vessels engaged in " Dynamo " operation. (From Pickfords' Ltd.)

" Little ships of Dunkirk)" [in manuscript]. (Reports of small craft collected by Mr. J. D. Casswell, K.C.)

Statements made by Masters of tugs engaged in Operation "Dynamo." (From W. H. J. Alexander Ltd., tug owners, London).

French Admiralty records of French ships at Dunkirk.

The following books provide a background to the operation :

Dunkirk. By A. D. Divine, D.S.M. London. Faber & Faber Ltd. (Mr. Divine took part in the operation).

The Epic of Dunkirk. By E. Keble Chatterton. London. Hurst & Blackett Ltd. (Contains some vividly illustrative photographs).

INTRODUCTION

The Dunkirk evacuation looms large in the history of the war. It involved the dual problem of lifting a mass of hard-pressed troops from a continually shrinking perimeter under uncertain conditions of wind and sea, the menace of heavy attacks by air, and the onrush of a great hostile army ; and then of transporting them to England in the face of air attacks, shore bombardments, torpedoes, mines, and the dangers of unlit shoals and wreck-strewn channels.

Despite the heavy losses suffered from all these perils, no less than 239,000 troops were embarked from the shattered quays of a wreck-encumbered harbour ; while some 99,000 more were lifted from the 10 miles stretch of shoaling beach north-east of the harbour. This was no light task. The evacuation from the beaches was performed by many hundreds of shallow-draught motor boats, fishing craft, lighters, barges, sailing and pulling boats, manned partly by civilian volunteers – which ferried the weary troops to the destroyers, mine-sweepers, skoots, personnel vessels, tugs and other ships lying off in deeper water.

Operation " Dynamo " was essentially a combined operation, requiring the devoted co-operation of the Royal Navy and the Royal Air Force, and the cheerful courage and steadiness of an exhausted Army waiting on the beaches with hardly anything to eat or drink.

It must at once be said that the stupendous success which crowned Operation " Dynamo," in the face of the determined onslaught of numbers of hostile bombers, could not have been achieved without the air cover provided by Fighter and Coastal Command,[1] which performed its task almost invariably against superior numbers, and with the serious handicap of having no base nearer than England. In spite of the most strenuous efforts, however, the inadequate numbers of aircraft available precluded the possibility of continuous cover, and it is significant that the losses of ships by air attacks were greater than the aggregate of losses from all other enemy action, while their severity varied proportionately with the strength of our fighter cover at the time.

[1] The following five naval aircraft squadrons also operated under Coastal Command :

| 801 } Skuas | 815 } Swordfish | 826 Albacore |
| 806 } | 825 } | |

These aircraft were the only available British *dive* bombers They carried out attacks on tanks, transport, batteries, gun emplacements, enemy positions in the Calais and Dunkirk areas, and E-boats. In spite of their relative inadequacy for the purpose the Skuas were also detailed for fighter escort for ships. (M.011883/40)

The incidence of losses by enemy action is given in the two following tables :

	AIR ATTACKS	E-BOATS OR S/MS	MINES	SHORE GUNS
Destroyers	5[1]	3[1]		1[2]
Gunboats	1			
Minesweepers	5			
Armed boarding vessels	1			
Trawlers	6[5]	2	5[1]	1[3]
Special Service vessels	1			
Drifters	2			1
Yachts			1	
Skoots	1			1[4]
Personnel vessels	6		1	
Hospital carriers	1			
Seaplane tender	1			
Tugs	2			
Cockle Bawley boat			1	
Total	32	5	8	4

Ships Damaged and put out of Action

	AIR ATTACKS	E-BOATS OR S/MS	MINES	SHORE GUNS
Destroyers	8	1[6]		
Sloops	1			
Minesweepers	2			
Trawlers				1
Personnel vessels	2			2
Hospital carriers	2		1	
Total	15	1	1	3

[1] Including 1 French.
[2] French. Driven on to Allied minefield where she struck a mine.
[3] Driven on to Allied minefield where she struck a mine.
[4] Damaged and had to be abandoned.
[5] Including 3 French.
[6] French.

Something must now be said of the Army movements.

The *active* operations of the British Expeditionary Force in northern France and Belgium began on 10th May, 1940, when Germany invaded the Low Countries. The first phase of these operations (see Plan 1) was the advance to the River Dyle, from 10th–16th May ; the second-phase, from 17th–26th May (see Plan 2), the withdrawal from the Dyle to the River Escaut, the defence of the Belgian frontier, and of the southern and western flanks ; and the third and final phase was the withdrawal into the Dunkirk perimeter and the embarkation of the B.E.F., from 26th May – 4th June.[1]

In the following day-by-day account may be discerned, first, the rapid sequence of events which resulted in the desperate task imposed on the Royal Navy on 26th May, and second, the supreme difficulty of co-ordinating naval measures with an ever-changing military situation. That situation it is not intended to present in detail, but only so far as the sudden onrush of military events affected the course of naval dispositions.

[1] Lord Gort's Second Despatch, para. 1.

CHAPTER I

PRELIMINARY EVENTS

10TH–18TH MAY 1940 *(See Plan 1)*

10TH MAY

Germany Invades Holland and Belgium

On the 10th May, following the invasion of Holland and Belgium, the Franco-British forces under General Georges, commanding the French Front of the North East, crossed the Belgian frontier and began their advance to the River Dyle,[1] according to plan.

11TH MAY

Allies reach River Dyle

During the afternoon and evening of the 11th May the leading infantry brigades reached the Dyle.

The news from the Belgian Army, of which King Leopold had assumed command on the outbreak of war, was not good. At Maastricht the Belgians had been unable to demolish important bridges over the Albert Canal and the river Meuse, and the enemy had begun to move across them; whilst the Belgian anti-tank obstacle eastward had been reconnoitred by the French Cavalry Corps and found to be not only badly sited but unfinished.[2]

12TH MAY

German thrust on French 9th Army Front

The Allied advance to the Dyle was successfully completed by the 12th May. The B.E.F. was in position between Wavre and Louvain, with the French 7th Army (General Giraud) on its left and the French 1st Army (General Blanchard) on its right. On the right of the French 1st Army was the French 9th Army (General Corap) of the French Southern Command. Disquieting news was, however, received from the south, where a German thrust with at least two armoured divisions[1] was reported as developing on the front of the French 9th Army.

This thrust eventually proved to be the beginning of the German breakthrough and their sweep westward, which cut off the Allied northern forces from the main French forces in the south, led to the capture of Boulogne and Calais, and culminated in the evacuation of Dunkirk.

General Billotte was in command of the French First Group of Armies, which included the French 1st Army (with the French Cavalry Corps), and the French 7th Army. Between these two armies lay the Belgian Army (under the independent command of their King), and the B.E.F., which, though under the command of General Georges, was not under that of General Billotte. On this day, however, it was agreed to co-ordinate the action of the British, French and Belgian forces, and General Billotte was appointed to perform this task.[3]

---

[1] Lord Gort's Second Despatch, para. 18.
[2] Lord Gort's Second Despatch, para. 19.
[3] Lord Gort's Second Despatch para. 22.

13TH MAY

Occupation of Walcheren and Zuid Beveland imminent

Movements of the main bodies of the French 1st and 7th Armies continued in accordance with their plans, and by the 13th May, units of the latter were north of Antwerp on the Dutch border. It was, however, becoming increasingly evident that they would be unable to prevent the enemy occupation of Walcheren and Zuid Beveland, which was developing from the north-east.[1]

During the day and the following night the Belgians were withdrawing their northern forces to the general line Louvain-Antwerp.[1]

14TH MAY

Germans cross Meuse

May the 14th was crucial, for on that day the enemy penetrated the French 9th Army front, and crossed the Meuse between Sedan and Mézières.[1] (See *Plan 1*).

15TH MAY

Dutch Army surrenders

On the 15th May the Dutch Army laid down its arms. The immediate effect of this on the operations of the B.E.F. was small, but "I anticipated . . . " says Lord Gort, "that this would come as a shock to the Belgian Army".[2]

The French 7th Army withdrew its advanced formations to the neighbourhood of Antwerp, and the French divisions on the B.E.F.'s left flank were ordered to move across the British rear to fill the gap which had been created on the French 9th Army's front. This move did not, however, actually take place till some 3 days later,[2] and it then left the Belgian Army responsible for the security of the British left flank.

On the British front the day passed quietly on the whole. The 1st Corps [Lt.-Gen. M. G. H. Barker] was not attacked in strength ; 3rd Division [Maj.-Gen. B. L. Montgomery] of 2nd Corps [Lt.-Gen. A. F. Brooke] was attacked north-west of Louvain, and its forward positions were penetrated, but a counter-attack successfully restored the original line.[3]

At about 1800, however, the enemy penetrated the French 1st Army's front, and, in spite of British support, some ground was lost.

16TH MAY

Allies withdraw to river Escaut

By the 16th May it became clear that a prolonged defence of the Dyle position was impracticable,[3] because the French 1st Army on the B.E.F.'s right flank were unlikely to make good the ground lost on the previous day and a further withdrawal seemed likely to be forced on them by events in the south.[3]

It was therefore decided to withdraw to the River Escaut, spending one day on the River Senne and one day on the River Dendre. Accordingly, on the night of 16th–17th May, the 15 to 20 miles withdrawal to the Senne positions began.

---

[1] Lord Gort's Second Despatch para. 22.
[2] Lord Gort's Second Despatch, para. 23.
[3] Lord Gort's Second Despatch, para. 24.

17TH MAY

French 9th Army front broken

By the early morning of the 17th May, the situation on the French 9th Army's front had become grave. The French line was broken, and enemy armoured and mobile forces had crossed the river Oise. East of St. Quentin, there was a gap of at least 20 miles in which there appeared to be no organised resistance.[1] The enemy break-through was now offering an imminent threat to the British rear G.H.Q. at Arras, to the communications over the Somme at Amiens and Abbeville, and to the base areas. To meet this, every available man and weapon were collected. A mobile bath unit, for example, took part in the defence of St. Pol; General Construction Companies of the Royal Engineers, and many units of the Royal Army Service Corps, set to work to place their localities in a state of defence, and manned them until overwhelmed, relieved or ordered to withdraw.

These numerous delaying actions, though small in themselves, all contributed to gain the time required for the withdrawal of the main forces.[2] A force was also organised to guard against a more immediate threat to the B.E.F.'s right flank; and, as a further precaution against the risk of being out-flanked on the right, the withdrawal to the Dendre and thence to the Escaut was continued without pause.[3]

18TH MAY

Allied rail communications severed

By the morning of the 18th May the Belgians had effected a junction with the B.E.F. left flank at Alost, on the Dendre. From the B.E.F.'s right flank the French line ran through Mons and Maubeuge.

During the day, the enemy, pounding westward, had penetrated as far as Amiens in sufficient strength to sever rail communications with the Allies' bases.

On the night of the 18th–19th May, the 1st, 2nd and 3rd Corps of the B.E.F. completed their withdrawal to the line of the Escaut without interference, and prepared to defend the line of that river. (The French 1st Army completed its withdrawal by the following day and was in touch with the right of the British 1st Corps).

Meanwhile, inundations were being carried out southward by the French; unfortunately however, without regard to the front of the B.E.F.,[4] where it was soon found that the level of water in the Escaut was becoming so low that the river was fast ceasing to form a serious obstacle.

After a conference that night with General Billotte, Lord Gort formed the opinion that there was an imminent danger of the forces in the north-eastern area – that is the French forces next to the sea, the Belgian Army, the B.E.F. and the bulk of the French 1st Army on its right – being irretrievably cut off from the main French forces in the south.[4] The event three days later showed this opinion to have been fully justified.

---

[1] Lord Gort's Second Despatch, para. 24.
[2] Lord Gort's Second Despatch, para. 25.
[3] Lord Gort's Second Despatch, para. 26.
[4] Lord Gort's Second Despatch, para. 30.

CHAPTER II

THE WEEK BEFORE OPERATION "DYNAMO,"
19TH – 25TH MAY, 1940

19TH MAY

Compulsory withdrawal of B.E.F. foreseen

A crisis was now approaching. After considering various alternatives, Lord Gort was forced to the conclusion that the possibility of a compulsory withdrawal of the B.E.F. from the Continent must be faced, and so his Chief of the General Staff, Lieut-General H. R. Pownall, telephoned to the Director of Military Operations and Plans at the War Office and discussed this possibility.[1]

On this 19th day of May communications by road and rail over the Somme at Abbeville were still holding, but there was little doubt that enemy armoured forces in that area would shortly break through to the coast. The force could then no longer be supplied through the ports south of the Somme, and the great bulk of the reserves, which were in the rearward areas, would shortly cease to be available for maintaining replacements.[1]

R.A.F. Component begins return to England

The growing failure of communications had now made it impracticable for the British air organisation to function, and by the evening orders had to be given for a large proportion of the R.A.F. Component of the B.E.F. (Air Vice-Marshal C. H. B. Blount) to return to England.

Equally serious was the fact that, by the evening, German troops had arrived in Amiens. The picture was no longer that of a line bent or temporarily broken, but of a besieged fortress.[2]

Vice-Admiral, Dover, represented at War Office conference

Meanwhile, in London, following the receipt of General H. R. Pownall's message, a meeting had been held at the War Office at which Vice-Admiral B. H. Ramsay (Vice-Admiral, Dover), was represented.

This meeting discussed the temporary maintenance of the B.E.F.—and the evacuation of its personnel through Dunkirk, Calais and Boulogne. Among other questions considered was the possiblity of "the hazardous evacuation of very large forces." So little, apparently, was the true military situation then known in London that this problem was regarded as "unlikely," though only seven days later it developed into Operation "Dynamo". "The main decision of this meeting," says Vice-Admiral Ramsay, "was that the control must be delegated to the Vice-Admiral Dover, and available shipping placed at his disposal."

Channel ports the German objective

On the 20th May the breach south of Arras deepened and widened; the enemy armoured forces appeared to be directed on two main objectives – one down the valley of the Somme on Abbeville, the other doubtless making for the Channel ports.[3]

---

[1] Lord Gort's Second Despatch, para. 30.
[2] Lord Gort's Second Despatch, para. 31.
[3] Lord Gort's Second Despatch, para. 32.

1.   Bertram Ramsay, Vice-Admiral Dover, seen later in the war as an Admiral. [A23443]

2. Dover. The Wireless Room. The generally inadequate nature of communications is indicated. [A9927]

3. Dover. The office of the Staff Officer (Intelligence). [A9917]

4. Soldiers boarding the destroyer *Vivacious*. [HU37128]

5. HMS *Vivacious* alongside the Mole at Dunkirk immediately after an air attack. The trawler alongside had less luck, having taken a direct hit.
    [HU1149]

6. Double-banked destroyers delivering troops. [H1645]

7. Troops aboard unidentified destroyer. [H1628]

8. Not just the BEF. French troops, having waded to sea, are evacuated on a fishing vessel. Note the bare feet and fishing gear, suggesting recent requisition. [PL7042]

9. French troops being evacuated by the minesweeper *Queen of Thanet.* [HU50403]

10. Evacuation conditions. This photograph may not be of Dunkirk but the atmosphere is well indicated. Note the hospital ship alongside. [F4869]

11. Taken some four miles east of Dunkirk, the photograph shows rough offshore and surf conditions and many ant-like troops awaiting embarkation [C1718]

12. Evacuated personnel on quarterdeck of Isle of Man steamer. [c1751]

13. Evacuated soldiers on deck of ship returning them from France. [C1748]

14. The minesweeper *Brighton Belle* sinking after hitting a submerged wreck during an air attack on 28 May. [HU3252]

15. HMS *Grenade* sinking alongside at Dunkirk on 29 May. [HU46179]

16. The French destroyer *Foudroyant* in happier days. She was sunk in two and a half minutes by two salvos of bombs on 1 June, having earlier evacuated 1,250 troops. [HU70044]

17. The destroyer *Havant*, her decks crowded with soldiers, prepares to berth. She delivered 2,432 troops before her loss on 1 June. [H1665]

Block out Background (censor's handwritten note)

18. An unidentified destroyer shows its Dunkirk scars: damage to bridge, many splinter and small arms holes. Note censor's marks and instructions. [Album 16 No 15]

19. German photograph showing a beach after the operation. The row of black objects along the beach is an improvised pier of trucks. [HU43956]

20. Some of the Dunkirk 'little ships' are returned to the Thames. Approaching the Hungerford bridge, 9 June 1940. [HU3384]

General Weygand directing Allied operations

During this day also, Lord Gort became aware that Allied operations were actually being directed by General Weygand (successor to General Gamelin), who announced later, on 23rd May, that he was Commander-in-Chief in all theatres of war.[1]

The first move in this so-called "Weygand plan," (see under 23rd–24th May), now became apparent when General Sir Edmund Ironside, the Chief of the Imperial General Staff, arrived at Lord Gort's G.H.Q. with instructions from the British Cabinet that the B.E.F. was to move southward upon Amiens, attacking all enemy forces encountered and taking station on the left of the French Army.[1] This move, Lord Gort pointed out, was impracticable because it would involve the disengagement of seven British divisions which were actually in close contact with the enemy on the Escaut, and would be immediately followed up by the enemy. In any case, owing to the prospective interruption by the enemy of the B.E.F.'s line of supply, imminent at any moment, it was unlikely that the B.E.F. could undertake sustained offensive operations.

Lord Gort had, however, already made plans to counter-attack with two divisions southward of Arras, and now proposed that they should make this attack on the following day. The C.I.G.S. agreed with this action.[1]

R.A.F. Component to set up rear H.Q. at Hawkinge

Meanwhile, the evacuation of the R.A.F. Component was proceeding, and it was decided to set up its rear headquarters at Hawkinge, in England.[2]

Naval Staff at Dover considers large-scale evacuation

At Dover, the possiblity of a large-scale evacuation was now definitely fore-seen for a meeting of the Naval Staff was held there during the day to consider the emergency evacuation across the channel of very large forces. This meeting, which was attended by Liaison Officers from the War Office Movement Control and the Ministry of Shipping, considered the number of personnel vessels and small craft available ; it agreed that the air protection of sailings, embarkations and disembarkations was to be arranged by Vice-Admiral, Dover, direct with Fighter Command ; and it called attention to the necessity, in the event of evacuation, for a large number of small boats to carry the troops from the very gradually shoaling beaches to the off-shore ships. Furthermore, as it was considered extremely doubtful whether the whole of the troops to be evacuated could be lifted from the beaches, it was urged that " if at all possible, *the ports must be used as well* "[3]. It is evident that, at this date, it was not yet realised that the only port available for the evacuation would be Dunkirk.

Provision of small craft considered

After this meeting at Dover, a long series of telephone conversations took place between the V-A. Dover, the Admiralty, the Ministry of Shipping and the C. in C. Nore, as to the provision of small craft for the final evacuation and the provision of naval personnel for manning the skoots[4] and small boats required for transport and ferrying.

---

[1] Lord Gort's Second Despatch, para. 32.
[2] R.A.F. Narrative.
[3] D.R.
[4] Dutch schuyts or coasters.

Counter-attack south of Arras

The counter-attack with 2 divisions south of Arras planned by Lord Gort was begun this day under the command of Major-General H. E. Franklyn. He had the co-operation of the French Cavalry Corps and a French Light Mechanised Division, but the movements of the latter " did not develop so widely to the flanks as General Franklyn had hoped"[1]. The hope that two divisions of the French 5th Corps would also attack southward from Douai, did not materialise. Furthermore, serious mechanical troubles developed in the British overworked tanks, whose tracks were now beginning to break through wear[1].

Although the objectives of the day were therefore reached, it became clear that the attack would not maintain its momentum unless it was reinforced and supported by the French on its left[1].

During the 22nd May General Franklyn held his ground, but on the 23rd enemy pressure compelled the Allied force to withdraw – and in an easterly direction.[1] " Thus concluded the defence of Arras," said Lord Gort, " . . . It had imposed a valuable delay on a greatly superior force against which it had blocked a vital road centre".[1]

Germans approach Boulogne

In the meantime, the 21st May had marked a still more serious change in the military situation, for, in the afternoon, an enemy column of all arms was approaching Boulogne.[2] The military situation was rapidly deteriorating; the Germans were across the Somme[2] and had cut the railway at Abbeville, completely severing our line of communications.[3] A quarter of a million Allied troops now lay north of the Somme, cut off from the daily flow of 2,000 tons of ammunition and supplies essential to their maintenance. " The decision to maintain the force through the northern ports", said Lord Gort, " was finally taken on 21st May and the headquarters of a Base Sub-Area established at Dunkirk. . . ."[3]

A conference of the Allied Commanders was essential, and at 2000 Lord Gort went to Ypres where he met the King of the Belgians and General Billotte.[4] He explained the situation developing on the Escaut, where the water in the river was so low that it no longer formed a tank obstacle. It was thereupon decided that the Escaut should be abandoned on the night of 22nd–23rd May, and the line be withdrawn to the Belgian frontier defences.[5]

As it was evident that sooner or later the Belgian Army would have to swing back to a line in rear, General Billotte asked the King of the Belgians whether, if he were forced to withdraw from the positions on the Lys, he would fall back on to the line of the Yser so as to continue to maintain touch with the left of the B.E.F.[5] His Majesty agreed that no alternative line existed, but five days later the Belgian command decided that the idea of the withdrawal to the Yser " must be ruled out".

---

[1] Lord Gort's Second Despatch, para. 33.
[2] Lord Gort's Second Despatch, para. 36.
[3] Lord Gort's Second Despatch, para. 37
[4] General Billotte was fatally injured in a motor accident returning from this conference. General Blanchard succeeded him in command of the French First Group of Armies.
[5] Lord Gort's Second Despatch, para. 35.

Organisation of the Canal line

On the 21st May, also, steps were taken to defend the south-western flank of the Allied force by organising the defence of the canal line from the Escaut to La Bassée, and to continue it to St. Omer and the sea at Gravelines.[1]

From this date all arrangements for air co-operation with the B.E.F. were made by the War Office in conjunction with the Air Ministry, the air liaison work being carried out in England at Hawkinge.[2]

Emergency evacuation again considered at the War Office

Meanwhile, in London, a meeting was held at the War Office at which, once again, the emergency evacuation across the channel of very large forces, now looming close ahead, was under consideration.[3]

22ND MAY

Canal line occupied

By the 22nd May the 85 miles of canal line from Gravelines, through St. Omer and Aire, to the Escaut (west of St. Amand) had been occupied, so far as was possible, with the 10,000 men available. This line was divided into sectors, for each of which a British commander was responsible,[1] but the number of anti-tank weapons was barely adequate to cover all the crossing places, and no effective watch could be kept against small parties of infantry crossing the canal between the bridges.[1]

Boulogne cut off, Calais threatened

The ports of Boulogne and Calais were now no longer working and consequently the supply situation had grown worse than ever. It was found too that, at such short notice, the port of Ostend could not be adapted to military requirements.[4]

Boulogne was, in fact, by this time completely cut off, and by the evening enemy armoured forces were within 9 miles of Calais.[5] At Merville, the last remaining advanced landing ground available for the R.A.F. Component was abandoned.

On the night of 22nd/23rd May, according to plan, the Allied withdrawal to the Belgian frontier defences was carried out.[6]

" The operation . . . will be known as ' Dynamo ' "

Meanwhile, the Admiralty had begun to make definite preparations for an evacuation from the Continent. There were at this time, lying at Poole and in the Port of London, some 50 Dutch skoots (*schuyts*), 200 ton-motor coasters which had escaped from Holland. On the 22nd May the Admiralty, after allocating 8 of these vessels to the War Office for use as supply ships, directed the Commanders-in-Chief Portsmouth and the Nore to take over and man the remainder, arrange for their organisation and assembly, and report the names of the vessels as they became ready for service. At the same time it was intimated that, when ready, the skoots would be placed at the disposal of V-A.

---

[1] Lord Gort's Second Despatch, para. 34.
[2] Lord Gort's Second Despatch, para. 29.
[3] D.R.
[4] Lord Gort's Second Despatch, para. 37.
[5] Lord Gort's Second Despatch, para. 36.
[6] Lord Gort's Second Despatch, para. 39.

Dover.[1] It was added that the operation for which these ships were being prepared would be known as " Dynamo "[2], the first mention of the now famous word.

As a result of this direction, 40 skoots in all were commissioned ; of these, 18 lying at Poole were commissioned by the C. in C. Portsmouth on the 25th May, and 22 lying at London were commissioned by the C. in C. Nore between the 25th and 27th May.

23RD MAY

Enemy within 20 miles of Dunkirk

Over in France, the situation on the canal line deteriorated during the 23rd May (see *Plan 2*), and the enemy established bridgeheads at Aire, at St. Omer (" which seems to have changed hands twice during the day")[3], and near Watten. German tanks were reported harbouring in the forest of Clairmarais (immediately east of St. Omer), and, during the day, hostile armoured fighting vehicles came within 3 miles of Hazebrouck ; and though by the evening these movements had been checked,[3] the enemy was then within some 20 miles of Dunkirk.

Calais cut off

Calais was now finally cut off, and, said Lord Gort, " the remainder of the gallant defence of Calais was conducted under the orders of the War Office".[3]

Dunkirk, though its water supply was destroyed,[4] was by this time the only port available for unloading supplies. Even the small supply by air of rations and small arms ammunition now ceased, as it had become impossible for aircraft to land. Accordingly, on the advice of the Quarter-Master-General (Lieut.-General W. G. Laidsell), Lord Gort put the B.E.F. on half rations.[4] During the day the evacuation of the R.A.F. Component of the B.E.F. was completed.

Naval demolition parties were ready at the Nore, and one was landed at Dunkirk during the day to prepare the locks for demolition. (Operation X D (E)).

Boulogne evacuated

Early on the same day a demolition party (Operation XD (G)), under Lieut.-Comdr. A. E. P. Welman, D.S.O., D.S.C., R.N., (Retd.), was also despatched, in the destroyer *Vimy*, to Boulogne, together with a force known as " Force Buttercup", to restore control of the docks area and cover the demolition party ; Major C. F. L. Holford, R.M. was in command of this force, and it consisted of 4 platoons of seamen, 2 Marine platoons with a section of machine guns and a medical party. Two battalions of Irish Guards and an anti-tank battery had been sent on the previous day.

When " Force Buttercup" arrived, the town was under shell fire and being attacked by enemy tanks and infantry, and the Army forces were being withdrawn to the jetty in readiness for evacuation, although the War Office sent orders during the afternoon that the troops were to stay and fight it out[5].

---

[1] Appendices F.1 and F.2.
[2] Appendix F.3.
[3] Lord Gort's Second Despatch, para. 39.
[4] Lord Gort's Second Despatch, para. 37.
[5] Admiralty Message 1422/23, *War Diary* 23.5.40, p. 356.

Communication with England was cut, and all messages had to be sent by destroyers.

By 1530 the Germans had occupied the whole of Boulogne except a bridgehead, all anti-tank guns were out of action, and half of Major Holford's force were estimated to be casualties.   The destroyers *Keith* (D. (19), Captain D. J. R. Simson) and *Whitshed*[1] went over to Boulogne during the afternoon, and were followed later by the *Venetia, Venomous, Vimiera, Wild Swan* and *Windsor*. The arrival of the first two destroyers was followed by an enemy air attack, together with close range mortar, machine gun and rifle fire, which caused damage and casualties, including Captain D. (19) who was killed, and necessitated breaking off the work of evacuating wounded and withdrawing temporarily from the port.   Fortunately, No. 92 Squadron of the R.A.F. (12 Spitfires) soon encountered the large enemy formation and, with some loss to themselves and much to the enemy, gained a measure of control of the situation; and by 1955 the destroyers were back in harbour and carrying out the evacuation of the Welsh Guards.   The *Keith* had received a signal at 1749 ordering all troops to be evacuated.

About 2000, while Lieut.-Comdr. Welman was on the point of firing the last of the demolition charges, German tanks towing field guns appeared over the hill north of the harbour and opened heavy fire at the three destroyers coming in to take off " Force Buttercup."   An amazing engagement, described by eye-witnesses as magnificent, ensued between the German field guns and the destroyers.   The *Venetia* was hit while in mid-channel, but she was got under control and out of the harbour, thus avoiding blocking in the *Venomous* and *Wild* who were embarking " Force Buttercup " and the Irish Guards while engaging the enemy tanks and field guns with every gun they had.

It was low water when the destroyers eventually backed out of harbour, loaded down with troops.   When the *Venomous* backed out her wheel jammed and she had to steer with her engines ; the *Wild Swan*, following her, grounded for a moment, but both ships got off and both reached Dover safely.   When, at 2234 some 3,000 troops had been brought off, the *Wild Swan* reported that although a considerable number remained further evacuation was impracticable.

The *Windsor*, however, which had been ordered at about 2030 to help in the evacuation, arrived after the rest of the destroyers had left ; she entered the harbour after dark, filled to capacity and sailed again without damage or much difficulty.   On clearing the harbour, the *Windsor* informed V.-A. Dover that further evacuation under cover of darkness was still possible and that two more destroyers could lift all the soldiers still left at Boulogne.

Vice-Admiral, Dover, therefore, despatched the *Vimiera* at 0015 on the 24th to try to bring off the remaining troops.   She arrived at Boulogne at 0130, and found all silent.   At length the Commanding Officer's hail was answered, and it was found that there were more than 1000 troops waiting for a ship. Going alongside the jetty, the destroyer was crowded to the tiller flat by 0230, the only space left being round the guns ; and when she slipped at 0245 she was compelled to leave some 200 men behind.   Five minutes later shore batteries opened fire on the jetty, and at 0255 a bomber passed close and a bomb exploded 20 yards away.   The *Vimiera* was so over-loaded that even five degrees of helm made the ship list unpleasantly.   She reached Dover safely at 0355 and landed some 1400 men, including Belgian and French troops and some

---

[1] The *Whitshed* had been at Boulogne helping to evacuate wounded from 0630 to 1045 when she left with two transports for Calais.

refugees who got on board. The numbers evacuated by the destroyers concerned were approximately :—

Keith	...	...	...	180
Vimy	...	...	...	150
Whitshed ...	...	...	...	580
Vimiera	...	...	...	1955 (in two trips)
Wild Swan	...	...	...	403
Windsor	...	...	...	600
Venomous	...	...	...	500
	Total	...		4368

The *Venetia*, damaged, did not get alongside a quay. During the night
22/23rd May, before the evacuation under fire, the *Verity* took off two General
Officers and some 150 troops.

In addition to the *Venetia*, the *Wild Swan*, *Whitshed*, *Keith* and *Venomous*
all received damage during the evacuation. The *Keith* lost Captain D. (19) and
7 ratings killed, and had 28 wounded ; the *Vimy* had one officer killed and her
Commanding Officer, Lieut.-Comdr. C. G. W. Donald R.N. was seriously
wounded and died subsequently ; the *Whitshed* lost one officer killed and had
12 ratings wounded ; the *Venetia* had 20 ratings killed or missing and 11
wounded ; the Commanding Officer of the *Verity*, Lt. Cdr. A. R. M. Black R.N.
was wounded and subsequently died.

23RD - 24TH MAY

The " Weygand " Plan

In the midst of this changing panorama of events, on the 23rd May, General
Weygand became " Commander-in-Chief in all theatres of war ". He had,
however, previously formulated the " Weygand plan ". This plan contem-
plated a counter-offensive on a large scale[1] and, briefly, it consisted of 3
operations :—

(a) An attack south-westward from the north, by the French 1st Army
    and the B.E.F., with the Belgian Cavalry Corps supporting the
    British right.
(b) An attack northward from the line of the Somme, which line the newly
    formed Third French Army Group was *reported* to be organising.
(c) Operations on the line of the Somme west of Amiens, by a new Cavalry
    Corps which was assembling south of the river near Neufchatel.

On the 23rd May Lord Gort received a telegram from the British Prime Minister
to the French Prime Minister, M. Reynaud, of which the following is an
extract :—

> "Strong enemy armoured forces have cut communications of Northern Armies.
> Salvation of these Armies can only be obtained by immediate execution of Wey-
> gand's plan. . ." [1]

Not feeling sure that the situation developing for the Allied armies in the
north could be accurately appreciated except on the spot, Lord Gort telegraphed
to General Sir John Dill asking him to fly over that day.[1]

---

[1] Lord Gort's Second Despatch, para. 38

On the following day (24th May), however, the Prime Minister again conferred with M. Reynaud and General Weygand in Paris ; an extract is quoted below from the telegraphic report of this conference which Lord Gort received from the Secretary of State for War :

> "Both are convinced that Weygand's plan is still capable of execution and only in its execution has [?lies] hope of restoring the situation. Weygand reports French VII Army is advancing successfully and has captured Péronne, Albert, and Amiens . . . It is essential that you should make every endeavour to co-operate in this plan. Should however, situation on your communications make this at any time impossible you should inform us so that we can inform French and make Naval and Air arrangements to assist you should you have to withdraw on the north coast"[1].

Lord Gort says that he " fully appreciated the importance of attacking early, before the enemy could bring up his infantry in strength, but facts had to be faced "[1].   These were some of the facts :--

(a)   General Weygand's report of the recapture of Péronne, Albert and Amiens was, says Lord Gort, " inaccurate "[1].   None of these three towns on the line of the Somme had been recaptured.

(b)   Two British divisions were still closely engaged with the enemy, and three others were awaiting relief by the French and Belgians, and would not become available for a further 48 hours.[1]

(c)   Only about 300 rounds per gun were immediately available to the B.E.F., and with communications cut the prospect of further supply was remote.[1]

(d)   Serious losses in Allied tanks had already been suffered and could not be replaced.[1]

(e)   The Belgian cavalry was unlikely to be able to engage, at short notice, in a battle 40 miles away, and on French soil.[1]

Nevertheless, after consultation with General Blanchard, Lord Gort agreed that in order to implement their share of the Weygand plan they should attack southwards with 2 British divisions, one French division and a French Cavalry Corps.   The attack however, could not take place till the 26th May at the earliest, owing to the reliefs in progress and the need to assemble the 2 British divisions which were still closely engaged with the enemy.[1]   Furthermore, Lord Gort emphasised, both to the Secretary of State and to General Blanchard, that the principal effort must come from the south, and that the operation of the northern forces could be nothing more than a sortie.

It will be seen therefore that the British and the French Governments were both urging a counter offensive on a large scale, barely 48 hours before the Dunkirk evacuation became a desperately urgent necessity.

24TH MAY

The Allied position on the canal line was considerably strengthened during the 24th May.   On this day also Lord Gort prepared for the proposed counter-attack southwards on the 26th May, with the ultimate objective Plouvain – Marquion – Cambrai.   In effect, this attack was never carried out.

Fighting troops hold on at Calais

In the meantime the evacuation of Boulogne was completed.   At Calais evacuation was limited to non-fighting personnel.   The fighting troops held on, and a supply ship [the *Benlawers*][2] with stores and transport unloaded for them at Calais.

---

[1] Lord Gort's Second Despatch, para. 38.
[2] T.M. 6213/40.

Defences of Dunkirk

It was now obvious that if the B.E.F. was to be evacuated the only port available would be Dunkirk[1]. Its local defences were under the Amiral du Nord, Admiral Abrial, whose command included Boulogne, Calais and Dunkirk, but on this day (24th May) he delegated the command of military forces in these areas to General Fagalde.

The French defences of Dunkirk extended only as far as the Belgian frontier, and comprised an inner and an outer sector ; the inner on the line of the Mardyck Canal to Spyker, thence to Bergues to the frontier and so to the sea ; the outer on the line of the river Aa to St. Omer, thence by Cassel and Steenvoorde to the frontier.[1]

The French now took over the British posts on the Aa and began to operate the inundations which formed part of the defence scheme of Dunkirk.[2]

Belgian line penetrated

In the late evening the enemy attacked the Belgian line on the Lys, penetrating to a depth of $1\frac{1}{2}$ miles on a 13 mile front[3] and endangering the security of the British left flank.

It had become a matter of vital importance to keep open the B.E.F.'s line of communication to the coast through a corridor of withdrawal which was hourly narrowing. The penetration of the Belgian line made it certain that before long the whole area east of the Yser canal would be in the hands of the enemy, with the serious risk of the Belgian right becoming separated from the British left at Menin, and of the Belgian Army being forced to fall back in a northerly, rather than a westerly direction.[3]

25TH MAY

Enemy pincer attack

On the 25th May enemy activity intensified. He was across the canal at St. Venant, and was developing the bridgeheads between that place and Aire and also at St. Omer, while further north the situation on the river Aa remained obscure.

During the day the Belgians continued to withdraw in a north-westerly direction under enemy pressure.

General Sir John Dill, who had now succeeded General Sir Edmund Ironside as C.I.G.S., visited Lord Gort in the morning. He then informed the Prime Minister and the Secretary of State for War that there could be no disguising the seriousness of the situation.[3]

By 1800, says Lord Gort, " I was convinced that the steps I had taken to secure my left flank would prove insufficient to meet the growing danger in the north.

" The pattern of the enemy pincer attack was becoming clearer. One movement from the south-west on Dunkirk had already developed, and was being held ; the counterpart was now developing on the Belgian front. The gap between the British left and the Belgian right which had been threatening

---

[1] D.R.
[2] Lord Gort's Second Despatch, para. 41.
[3] Lord Gort's Second Despatch, para. 42.

the whole day, might at any time become impossible to close ; were this to happen, my last hope of reaching the coast would be gone".[1]

In order to secure the British northern flank Lord Gort decided to issue orders for the occupation, as quickly as troops could be made available, of the line of the Ypres – Comines canal and the positions covering Ypres. In the absence of General Blanchard, who was visiting the Belgian G.Q.G. at Bruges, Lord Gort communicated this decision that evening to the Headquarters of the French First Group of Armies.[1]

The necessity of evacuation was becoming a matter of paramount immediacy.

British destroyers bombard suburb of Calais

Meanwhile, on the 25th May, the trawler *Lord Howe* sailed to Calais with a cargo of ammunition[2]. She entered the port and discharged part of her cargo in the face of heavy enemy fire from the dunes to the southward. In view of the risk involved, Commodore W. P. Gandell, R.N. (P.S.T.O., French Ports), who was on the quay, then ordered the *Lord Howe* to sail.

Outside Calais the destroyer *Greyhound* closed the *Lord Howe*, which was carrying a request for bombardment support of the town. At the same time, the *Greyhound* received a signal from the Vice-Admiral, Dover, ordering the bombardment of the Calais suburb of St. Pierre. The *Greyhound* opened fire, and at 2000, an H.A. battery east of Sangatte registered a hit on her, killing 2 and wounding 3. About this time the destroyer *Grafton* arrived and also opened fire. The 2 destroyers returned to Dover as darkness set in.[3]

Evacuation of Calais countermanded

At 2130 a force of seven trawlers[4], three yachts[5] and two drifters[6], sailed for Calais road, ready to evacuate troops from Calais, the moment an order was received to do so. Five of the trawlers towed motor boats. Commander W. V. H. Harris, R.N. (Commander M/S, Dover), in the *Grey Mist*, was in command. The destroyers *Windsor* and *Verity* left Dover at 2300, to cover the withdrawal of this force.

On arrival off Calais, two of the motor boats were ordered into Calais harbour. At about 0300/26, a signal was received that Calais was to be held at all costs ; furthermore, it was ordered that this signal was to be sent by hand to the Brigadier commanding on shore. The *Conidaw* went in to deliver the signal.

All ships were then ordered back to the Downs, but the *Botanic* and *Maretta* remained behind until the two motor boats and the *Conidaw* returned.[7]

The *Botanic* and *Maretta* were damaged by gunfire when returning on the 26th May, and were unable to take part in Operation "Dynamo".

---

[1] Lord Gort's Second Despatch, para. 43.
[2] Lieut. L. C. Whittle, R.N.R., in the *Lord Howe*, says it was the 24th May.
[3] Vice-Admiral, Dover's 1907/25/5.
[4] The *Botanic, Fyldea, Maretta, Arley, Polly Johnson, Brock* and *Calvi*.
[6] The *Grey Mist, Conidaw* and *Chico*.
[5] The *Playmates* and *Willing Boys*.
[7] Report by Commander M/S, Dover (R.O. II, p. 497).

CHAPTER III

OPERATION "DYNAMO" IS COMMENCED,

SUNDAY, 26TH MAY, 1940

Allied decision to withdraw

In the morning of Sunday, 26th May, Lord Gort was able to visit General Blanchard at his H.Q. The French general shared his view as to the impending collapse of the Belgian Army and felt that the time for the proposed combined French and British counter-attack southwards was past. It was agreed to withdraw the Allied main bodies behind the line of the Lys, subject to there being no further deterioration in the Belgian situation, and with this decision there vanished the last opportunity for a sortie.[1]

The disposition of the B.E.F. was beginning to take its final shape. Starting from what might be described as a normal situation with Allied troops on the right and left, there had developed an ever-lenghtening defensive right flank. This had then become a semi-circular line with both flanks resting on the sea, manned by British, French and Belgians. Finally it had assumed the form of a corridor, with its southern end blocked by the French 1st Army, and each side manned, for the greater part of its length, by British troops ; next to the sea were French troops on the west, and French and Belgian troops on the eastern flank.[1]

The Franco-British forces were now holding a front of 128 miles, of which 97 miles were held by British troops, though some of its sectors were held jointly with the French. The immediate problem was to shorten this front, and Lord Gort issued orders, in accordance with the agreement reached with General Blanchard that morning, for withdrawals north-westward to take place in successive stages, on the three coming nights.[1] These withdrawals would have the effect of shortening the Franco-British front by 58 miles, but *there would still remain the possible necessity of having to occupy the 25 miles front from Ypres to the sea, at present the responsibility of the Belgian Army.*[1]

H.M. Government authorises withdrawal to the coast

So far Lord Gort had not discussed with General Blanchard a further withdrawal to the sea, and although he (Lord Gort) had foreseen the possibility of being forced to make this move, " up to now " he says, " no instructions had been given authorising me to undertake such an operation".[2] The tempo of events was, however, increasing rapidly, for at 1030 on 26th May, on returning to his H.Q., Lord Gort received a telegram from the Secretary of State for War which said, *inter alia*, " . . . information . . . goes to show . . . French offensive from Somme cannot be made in sufficient strength . . . only course open to you may be to fight your way back to west where all beaches and ports east of Gravelines will be used for embarkation. Navy will provide fleet of ships and small boats and R.A.F. would give full support. . .[2]" This was the first intimation to Lord Gort that evacuation must be seriously considered.

Lord Gort replied that a plan for withdrawal north-westward had been agreed with the French that morning. He added that the news from the Belgian front was " disquieting," and concluded, " I must not conceal from

---

[1] Lord Gort's Second Despatch, para. 43.
[2] *Ibid*, para. 44.

you that a great part of the B.E.F. and its equipment will inevitably be lost even in best circumstances".

Later in the day Lord Gort received a further telegram from the War Office which said, *inter alia*, " . . . not . . . possible for French . . . to effect junction with Northern Armies . . . no course open to you but to fall back upon the coast . . . you are now authorised to operate towards the coast forthwith in conjunction with French and Belgian Armies".[1]

It will be remembered that on the evening of the 21st May the King of the Belgians had agreed that, if forced to abandon the Belgian positions on the Lys, he would withdraw to the Yser, maintaining touch with the left of the B.E.F. Now, however, late on the morning of the 26th May, a note was received from General Michiels, the Chief of the Staff of the Belgian Army, which said, *inter alia* " . . . the Belgian Army is being attacked with extreme violence . . . and . . . the lack of Belgian reserves makes it impossible to extend our boundaries . . . we have no longer any forces available to fill the gap in the direction of Ypres. As regards the withdrawal to the Yser, the idea must be ruled out since it would destroy our units more quickly than the battle. . ."[2]

The Belgian collapse was impending, if it had not actually taken place, and the *task of defending the Allied line as far as the sea had fallen on the British and French troops.*[2]

Dunkirk perimeter organised

Faced with this critical situation Lord Gort, on the evening of the 26th May, put in hand his plans for withdrawing in to the bridgehead at Dunkirk[3]. Orders had already been given for the embarkation of certain key personnel, and now all units not required for battle were being withdrawn. It was possibly at this juncture that, " owing to a misunderstanding, the personnel of certain anti-aircraft units had been embarked instead of being retained for the defence of the port of Dunkirk".[4] The task of organising a bridgehead at Dunkirk was delegated to Lieut.-General Sir Ronald Adam, Bt., Commander of the 3rd Corps.[5]

The Admiralty signals, "Operation 'Dynamo' is to Commence"

Meanwhile, in the morning of 26th May, a meeting had been held at the Admiralty to give further consideration to the provision of small craft, and the crews for manning both them and the ex-Dutch skoots. The meeting also examined the number of craft available for the evacuation. The port of Dunkirk had already been so damaged by air attacks as to be no longer available for unloading supplies, which would now have to be landed on the beaches to the eastward.

Long before the operation was ordered, the Admiralty fully realized that large numbers of small craft would be required for a beach evacuation ; but such was the secrecy of even the possibility of evacuation, that steps could not yet be taken to collect craft for the purpose.

During the afternoon of the 26th May, under the pressure of the acute military situation, the Admiralty informed the Vice-Admiral, Dover, that " it was imperative for *Dynamo* to be implemented with the greatest vigour,

---

[1] Lord Gort's Second Despatch, para. 44.
[2] Lord Gort's Second Despatch, para. 45.
[3] Lord Gort's Second Despatch, para. 47.
[4] Lord Gort's Second Despatch, para. 55.
[5] He handed over command of the 3rd Corps to Maj.-Gen. S. R. Wason.

with a view to lifting up to 45,000 of the B.E.F. within two days, at the end of which it was probable that evacuation would be terminated by enemy action".[1]

A further step was taken when, at 1800, Captain W. G. Tennant, M.V.O., R.N., was ordered by the Vice-Chief of the Naval Staff, Vice-Admiral T. S. V. Phillips, C.B., to proceed to Dunkirk to take control of the naval shore embarkation parties. Captain Tennant's appointment as S.N.O., Dunkirk, was promulgated, his duties to commence the following day[2], and beach masters and pier parties were ordered to proceed from the Nore to Dover.

Then, at 1857, there went out from the Admiralty, by teleprinter, the historic signal, " Operation Dynamo is to commence "[3], which was to save our Army in France, and to have the most momentous results for the Nation, the Empire and the World.

Mona's Isle makes the first round trip

Except for the destroyer *Wolsey*, which left Dover at 1930 to act as W/T link ship, the first ship to sail on this great mission was the armed boarding vessel *Mona's Isle*, which left the Downs at 2116. After some delay with a fouled propeller she berthed at the Quai Félix Faure during an air attack, and embarked 1420 troops. On the return journey, she was straddled by shore guns off Gravelines, and shortly after, was heavily machine-gunned from the air ; these attacks caused 83 casualties, including 23 dead. She reached Dover at noon on the 27th May escorted by the destroyer *Windsor*, which had put her doctor on board and landed her troops. *Mona's Isle* was the first ship to complete the round trip in Operation " Dynamo".

Mona's Queen first ship back on 27th May

This, however, was not the first passage on 26th May. Even *before the Admiralty signal*, the despatch of personnel vessels to Dunkirk had begun, a flow of 2 vessels every 4 hours having been accepted by the B.E.F.[4]. The armed boarding vessel *King Orry* had sailed at 0930, and the *Mona's Queen* at noon. The *Maid of Orleans* had sailed at 1100 (with 6,000 two-gallon cans of water), but arriving off Dunkirk during an air attack was " unable to effect an entrance and returned to Dover " ; she was sailed again at 1726, escorted by the destroyer *Wild Swan*, which had also taken out the *Canterbury* at 1728, and escorted her part of the way.

The *Mona's Queen* (carrying 1200 troops) was the first of these ships to arrive back from Dunkirk, reaching Dover shortly after midnight on the 26th/27th May ; the *Canterbury* arrived at 0309/27 (with 1,340 troops), the store ship *Ngaroma* at 0500/27 (with a hundred troops), the *Maid of Orleans* at 0600/27 (with 980 troops), and the *King Orry* at 1100/27 (with 1,131). As a result of these sailings on the 26th May 6,083 troops were landed in England on the 27th May, of which *Mona's Isle* had contributed 1,420 towards the tentative Admiralty target of " lifting up to 45,000 of the B.E.F. within two days".

Hospital carriers

The work of the hospital carriers was specially hazardous ; their immunity under the Hague Convention was ignored, and their conspicuous white hulls

---

[1] D.R. page ii.
[2] Appendix M. 2.
[3] Appendix M. 1.
[4] D.R.

and blazing lights made them an easy target. On the 26th May the hospital carriers *St. Andrew* and *St. Julien* sailed at 1054 for Dunkirk, but coming under fire from the guns of Gravelines, they returned to Dover in company with the P/V *Maid of Orleans*.

The hospital carriers *Isle of Guernsey* and *Worthing* sailed from Dover at noon and were bombed when off Calais ; nevertheless, that night, flood-lit by the fires which raged in the docks and town of Dunkirk, they each embarked about 300 stretcher cases.

Admiralty call for cutters and whalers

All these troops and casualties, it should be noted, were lifted from the quays of Dunkirk harbour. Evacuation from the beaches did not commence until 24 hours later, and then only in a very small way, using ships' boats. On the 26th May, says Vice-Admiral Ramsay, " the only inshore craft available . . . were 4 Belgian passenger launches and the naval small craft of the Dover Command such as drifters, and motor boats from the Contraband Control Base at Ramsgate ; the only ones capable of lifting personnel direct from a beach being the boats from Ramsgate." The Admiralty had been asked for a supply of small boats, especially whalers and cutters, but there remained the difficulty of arranging for the personnel to man them[1]. This request led at 2028, on 26th May, to an Admiralty signal to the Home Ports asking how many cutters and whalers could be made available for immediate service under Vice-Admiral, Dover.[2]

Sea and air patrols

Meanwhile, at 1937, C. in C. Nore had been requested to use all available forces to cover Operation " Dynamo " that night.

In conformity with these directions Allied fighters maintained continuous patrols, from 1700 to 2130, on the line Calais–Dunkirk.[3]

Germans occupy Calais

That very night, however, the gallant defence of Calais came to an end. The yacht *Gulzar* had gone there with water and stretchers, to bring back wounded. She secured alongside the Gare Maritime and sent a party on shore to investigate. The town was found to be in German hands, and the *Gulzar* made a hasty departure under fire. On the way out, however, in response to a hail, she stopped, and brought off 3 officers and 48 men from the end of the breakwater.[4]

---

[1] D.R. p. 1, para. 2.
[2] Appendix G. 1.
[3] R.A.F. Narrative, p. 315.
[4] R.O. II, p. 513.

CHAPTER IV

MONDAY, 27TH MAY

(See Plan 3)

The Dunkirk perimeter

On the morning of 27th May, Lieut.-General Sir Ronald Adam commenced the organisation of the Dunkirk bridgehead. Its perimeter was to extend from Gravelines, south-eastward to the Canal de la Colme, along the canal to Bergues and thence by Furnes and Nieuport to the Belgian coast. In fact, however, the French were already evacuating Gravelines and the western part of the perimeter, and were falling back to the line of the Mardyck Canal, from the sea, to Spyker on the Canal de la Colme. The French were to be responsible for the defence of the western half of the perimeter as far as Bergues inclusive, and the British for the eastern half. The position of the Belgian Army was now so obscure that its inclusion in the bridgehead was not taken into account.[1]

The British sector of the Dunkirk perimeter had its right at Bergues, whence it followed the canals to Furnes and Nieuport. Immediately north of this line were the inundations ; to the north of the inundations was low-lying land, and then the Dunkirk-Furnes Canal and the main lateral road from Furnes to Dunkirk ; finally, there was the narrow strip of dunes giving way to a wide open beach running the whole length of the position and shelving very gradually to the sea. There were no quays or piers whatever, except those at Dunkirk itself. At intervals of from 3 to 4 miles along the shore (from east to west) lay the seaside resorts of Coxyde, La Panne, Braye-Dunes, and Malo-les-Bains (adjoining Dunkirk).

During the day troops and their transport began to withdraw into the perimeter on the fronts of all three British Corps. Where the troops had received the necessary orders, vehicles were disabled and abandoned in the assembly areas ; but owing to the shortage of troops for traffic control a great number of British and French vehicles were able to enter the perimeter and the town of Dunkirk[2], causing grave congestion on the roads. Beaches were organised at La Panne, Bray-Dunes and Malo-les-Bains, one beach being allotted to each of the 3 British Corps.[3]

Dunkirk had been bombed for some days, but the town and port received their most serious damage on 27th May. At least 12 attacks were made on Dunkirk and the sea approaches between 0825 and 2000[4]. Lorry columns had been set on fire in the town and a pall of black smoke from the burning oil tanks hung continuously over the town and docks, impeding the air defence. Dunkirk was therefore cleared of all troops and they were sent to the dunes east of the town to await embarkation.[3]

The Belgian armistice

During the 27th May Lord Gort received a further telegram from the Secretary of State for War which read, ". . .want to make it quite clear that sole

---

[1] Lord Gort's Second Despatch, para. 47.
[2] Lord Gort's Second Despatch, para. 49.
[3] Lord Gort's Second Despatch, para. 50.
[4] R.A.F. Narrative, p.320.

task now is to evacuate to England maximum of your force possible."[1] No policy had yet been laid down by French G.Q.G., or any other French higher authority, for a withdrawal northward of the Lys, and, says Lord Gort, " I had no idea what plans either he [General Blanchard] or Admiral Abrial had in mind".[1]

Lord Gort failed to contact General Blanchard either at La Panne, or at the French naval headquarters, situated at Bastion No. 32, Dunkirk.   While at the Bastion, however, at 2300, he was informed in the course of conversation with General Koeltz (General Weygand's deputy) that the King of the Belgians had asked for an armistice from midnight that night.   The British Commander-in-Chief thus found himself suddenly faced with an open gap of 20 miles between Ypres and the sea, through which enemy armoured forces might reach the beaches[2].

Owing to congestion on the roads Lord Gort was unable to reach his head-quarters at Houtkerque until 0430 on 28th May ; he then found that a telegram had been received from the War Office at 0130/28 saying that the King of the Belgians was capitulating at midnight, 27th/28th May.[3]

This was the derelict situation facing Lord Gort in the early hours of the morning.

Dunkirk locks prepared for demolition

On the 27th May, on the orders of Admiral Abrial, the Royal Naval demolition party which had arrived at Dunkirk on the 23rd May placed demolition charges at the New, the Trystram and the Guillain locks in Dunkirk harbour.

Route Z under fire : Route Y adopted : Route X prepared

Owing to the great lack of inshore craft for beach work the main naval effort during the day had been confined to maintaining the flow of personnel vessels to Dunkirk at the rate of 2 every $3\frac{1}{2}$ hours.   Even this limited transport service had been seriously interrupted by the fire of shore batteries between Les Hemmes (east of Calais) and Gravelines.   At 0623 the *Biarritz* and *Archangel*, en route for Dunkirk escorted by the destroyer *Verity*, were shelled 6 miles E.N.E. of Calais.   The *Biarritz* was hit several times and had 1 killed and 2 wounded.   The *Archangel* was also apparently damaged, and neither ship took any further part in " Dynamo".   At 0640, the M/V *Sequacity* and the freighter *Yewdale* were also shelled off Calais.   The *Sequacity* was hit four times, and at 1020, when north of Dunkirk channel, after the crew had been transferred to the *Yewdale*, the *Sequacity* went down by the head and sank. At 0750 the armed boarding vessel *Mona's Isle*, loaded with troops, suffered severe casualties and damage from shore guns off Gravelines, and also from an air attack shortly afterwards, and had to go into dock for repairs.   At 0800 the H/C *Isle of Thanet* was shelled off Calais and returned to Dover.   At 0900, the A.B/V *King Orry*, returning from Dunkirk loaded with troops also suffered casualties and damage from the Calais guns.

As a result of these happenings the Vice-Admiral, Dover, reported to the Admiralty that the normal or southern route, Dover to Dunkirk (later known as Route Z), was impracticable in daylight.   Another, more northern route (later known as Route Y), via the Dyck Whistle buoy, Middelkerk buoy, and Zuydcoote Pass, was accordingly adopted.   This, however, increased the

---

[1] Lord Gort's Second Despatch, para. 51.
[2] Lord Gort's Second Despatch, para. 49.
[3] Lord Gort's Second Despatch 50.

round trip from 80 to 172 miles, and the route had to be swept before it could be used.   Orders were therefore given for the establishment of a third, shorter route (the middle Route X), from the North Goodwin to the Ruytingen Pass, and thence into the Dunkirk road, and at 1140 work on this new route was commenced by the destroyer *Impulsive*, the minesweepers *Skipjack* and *Halcyon*, and the Trinity House Vessel *Patricia*.   This route X had the great advantage of shortening the round trip from 172 to 108 miles.

Among the earliest ships to use the northern Route Y were the P/V's *St. Helier*[1] and *Royal Daffodil*, which left Dover at 1054 under escort of the destroyer *Vimy* ; in company was the destroyer *Anthony*, escorting the S.S. *Kyno*.[2] The convoy was joined *en route* by the hospital carriers *St. Andrew* and *St. Julien*.   Route Y was certainly, at that time, out of range of gunfire, but two bombing attacks were made on the hospital carriers between the West Hinder and Kwint Bank buoys, and when the convoy arrived off Dunkirk heavy air attacks were in progress there.   The *Royal Daffodil* and the *St. Helier* entered the harbour, but the latter was ordered to withdraw, and she and the 2 hospital carriers returned empty to the Downs under escort of the *Vimy*.   The *Royal Daffodil* embarked 840 troops before returning to Dover.

Sea and Air Patrols

The principal patrol line covered in the morning of the 27th May by Fighter Command, was Calais-Dunkirk, as it was not known that the Calais garrison had ceased fire.   From 1450 onwards, however, Calais fell out of the picture, and it became possible to concentrate fighter protection more exclusively on the work of evacuation[3].   Sixteen squadrons, varying in strength from 9 to 20 aircraft, were engaged on these activities from 0500–2130 ; patrols were, however, limited to squadron strength.   Most squadrons carried out 2 patrols, and 287 sorties in all were flown during the day.[4]

To cover the passage of ships between Dunkirk and the Downs destroyer patrols had been established to the northward during the forenoon, and Vice-Admiral, Dover, asked for 6 additional destroyers to strengthen the Dover forces.   The Admiralty immediately ordered 4 destroyers from the Western Approaches Command, and 2 from the Portsmouth Command, to proceed to Dover.[5]

Ex-Dutch skoots for Dunkirk

Other vessels were on their way to Dunkirk during the day, among them being 15 skoots[6].   Of these the *Lena*, *Hebe II*, and later the *Oranje*, arrived off the beaches and embarked troops during the night of 27th/28th May ; the *Abel Tasman*, *Alice* and *Kaap Falga*, loaded with ammunition and food, arrived off La Panne early in the morning of 28th May ; the *Hilda* and *Doggersbank* reached Dunkirk by noon the 28th May, and were sent to the beaches ; while the remainder[7], in error, returned to the Downs, after having got within a few miles of Dunkirk.

---

[1] Eleven of the *St. Helier's* crew had been replaced by naval ratings.
[2] Off R buoy the *Anthony*, with the *Kyno*, was ordered back to the Downs and subsequently to Portsmouth.   The *Kyno* took no further part in Operation "Dynamo".
[3] R.A.F. Narrative, p. 319.
[4] R.A.F. Narrative, p. 320.
[5] Appendices D. 1 and D. 2.   The *Wakeful, Mackay, Worcester, Montrose, Shikari* and *Scimitar* were sent.
[6] See Appendix F.
[7] The *Bornrif, Brandaris, Hondsrug, Jutland, Patria, Tilly,* and *Twente.*

The " build-up " of small craft commences

Early on the 27th May, the Ministry of Sea Transport had been asked by the Admiralty to find between 40 and 50 small craft, which were to assemble at Sheerness " for a special requirement". The Director of the Small Vessels Pool (Vice-Admiral Sir Lionel Preston, K.C.B.) supplied a list of what were thought to be suitable vessels, but it was soon found that a great number of these were not in a fit state for service. A meeting was therefore held at the Admiralty which was attended by a representative of the Director of Sea Transport, Mr. H. C. Riggs. On Mr. Riggs' suggestion, Admiral Preston agreed to send some of his officers to the various boat-yards from Teddington to Burnham and Brightlingsea, to inspect and send to Sheerness all vessels fit for service[1]. Forty motor boats or launches were thus obtained, and arrangements made for them to reach Sheerness by 28th May.[2] Very few of these reached the Dunkirk beaches by the 29th May, but they were the forerunners of nearly 300 small craft, which were destined to play an important part in the embarkation from the beaches of some 99,000 troops, by ferrying them to off-lying ships.

In the evening of the 27th the Naval Officer-in-Charge, Ramsgate, assumed by arrangement the duty of fuelling and despatching all small power boats with the attendant pulling boats forming the inshore flotilla.

Some delays occurred in the assembly at Ramsgate or in the Downs of small craft despatched from other commands, owing to many of them being routed to Dover in error, instead of to the Downs. Once despatched by the authorities no communication with these small vessels was possible until they arrived at their destination ; this resulted in delays of up to 24 hours or more before assembly, because during the night misfortune befell many tows that came adrift owing to the moderate weather or collisions, and the business of rounding them up could not be effected until daylight.

" Dynamo Maintenance Officer " appointed

To take charge of these small craft, Rear-Admiral, A. H. Taylor, O.B.E., (with the acting rank of Commodore), after getting final instructions from the Vice-Admiral, Dover, proceeded to Sheerness on the 27th May to act as " Dynamo Maintenance Officer." He was responsible for the preparation of various vessels, small motor craft, and pulling boats, for service in Operation " Dynamo " ; his staff comprised Cdr. H. R. Troup, R.N., and Lt. Cdr. D. E. Holland-Martin, R.N. The type of machinery fitted in many of the vessels and its defective state presented the Fleet Engineer Officer, Captain T. E. Docksey, R.N., and Sheerness Dockyard with some difficult problems ; but within a week, under Commodore Taylor's general direction, no less than 100 motor boats, 10 self-propelled lighters, 7 skoots, 1 oil tanker, 6 paddle steamers, and numerous pulling boats, were prepared for service and sent out from Sheerness.

S.N.O. Dunkirk assumes duty 1900/27

Meanwhile, at 1315, Captain Tennant left Dover for Dunkirk in the destroyer *Wolfhound*, with a naval beach and pier party of 12 officers and 160 ratings. A communications staff was also taken, as it was intended that the *Wolfhound* should relieve the *Wolsey* at Dunkirk as W/T link. The *Wolfhound* was

---

[1] T.O. 9144/40.
[2] Appendix G. 3.

attacked twice by dive-bombers *en route*, receiving some damage from near misses, and, on arrival at Dunkirk at 1655, found an air attack by 21 aircraft was in progress.

Captain Tennant proceeded ashore to the Bastion Naval Headquarters to investigate the local situation. The whole area of the docks and town was enveloped in a vast pall of smoke from the oil depots and refineries. The town was blazing, air raid casualties were lying about the streets, which were littered with masses of wreckage.

On arrival at the Bastion, Captain Tennant held a meeting with Brigadier Parminter ; Colonel Whitfeld, Sub-Area Commandant ; and Commander H. P. Henderson, R.N., the B.N.L.O. It was decided that the harbour was untenable, and that it was impracticable to retain the *Wolfhound* at Dunkirk as a W/T link.

At 1900 Captain Tennant assumed the duties of S.N.O. Dunkirk, and ordered the *Wolfhound* and *Wolsey* to proceed to the beach east of Dunkirk and embark troops, using their own boats. This they proceeded to do, but did not get away unscathed ; the *Wolfhound* grounded as she left Dunkirk harbour and received further damage from a bomb which struck the jetty six feet away. She made no more trips to Dunkirk, but on that evening she and the *Wolsey* became the pioneers of beach evacuation.

Beach evacuation begins

Meanwhile, during the afternoon, four personnel vessels and two hospital carriers had sailed for Dunkirk[1]. Of these, the personnel vessels *Queen of the Channel* and *St. Seiriol* left Dover at 1330, by Route Y, and entered Dunkirk harbour at about 1930, during an air raid. The *Queen of the Channel* had barely embarked 50 troops when both ships were diverted to the beaches. At 2230, however, before the *St. Seiriol's* boats had started ferrying, S.N.O. Dunkirk signalled the *Wolfhound* to send a personnel ship to the east pier, Dunkirk, to embark 1,000 men. The *Wolfhound*, then with the *Wolsey* off the beaches passed this order to the *St. Seiriol* by megaphone and commandeered her boats, which were manned as necessary by naval ratings or towed by the destroyers' motor boats. The *Queen of the Channel*, using her own boats, embarked about 150 troops from the beach and then, returning to Dunkirk harbour, picked up a further 700 troops. She was the first ship, except the destroyers *Wolfhound* and *Wolsey*, to embark troops from the beaches, though she was unfortunately sunk by aircraft early next morning (May 28th) shortly after leaving Dunkirk.

" Evacuation tomorrow night is problematical "

By 1958, on 27th May, only an hour after he had assumed the duties of S.N.O. Dunkirk, Captain Tennant had arrived at a very serious view of the local situation, and he sent this dramatic signal to the Vice-Admiral, Dover :

> " Please send every available craft to beaches east of Dunkirk immediately. Evacuation tomorrow night is problematical. T.O.O.1958."

This signal, delayed in transmission, was not received until 2055, but in the

---

[1] The *Queen of the Channel*, *St. Seiriol*, *Canterbury*, *Maid of Orleans*, *Isle of Thanet* and *Worthing*.

meantime at 2025, the Vice-Admiral, Dover, received another signal sent only a few minutes later :

> " Port continuously bombed all day and on fire. Embarkation possible only from beaches east of harbour A.B.C.D.[1] Send all ships and passenger ships there to anchor. Am ordering *Wolfhound* to load there and sail. T.O.O.2005."

To the Vice-Admiral, Dover, the situation must have appeared critical when, later that evening, he received a report from two military officers from G.H.Q., that the plight of the B.E.F. was precarious and that the enemy might, indeed, succeed in cutting it off from Dunkirk.[2]

All ships diverted to the beaches

Such was the grim picture presenting itself to the Vice-Admiral, Dover, that night – the B.E.F. in grave and very real danger of being cut off altogether from Dunkirk, and possibly only a bare 24 hours available for its evacuation. Admiral Ramsay reacted to these dire tidings with characteristic drive and energy, and a period of intense activity ensued. Every effort was concentrated on sending as many craft as possible to the beaches without delay[2]. Order followed order in rapid succession. Personnel ships were diverted to the beach, code letters A, B, C and D (i.e. Malo beach). Four paddle minesweepers[3] were sailed from the Downs to La Panne beach. Destroyers were rushed to the beaches and urged to embark as many British troops as possible, as this was the " last chance of saving them " ; the *Gallant*, and *Vivacious*, then on patrol, the *Windsor*, *Vimy*, *Anthony*, *Impulsive*, *Sabre* and the cruiser *Calcutta*, were all ordered to proceed with the utmost despatch to the beach at Malo-les-Bains and the beach at Zuydcoote, just east of it ; the *Grafton* and *Greyhound*, on patrol between Fairy Bank and Kwint Bank buoys, and the *Wakeful*, just arrived at Dover from Plymouth, were hurried to the beach at La Panne.

The wording of some of the signals[4] conveying these orders reflects the desperation felt that night, a desperation which, in spite of the course of subsequent events, was at the time only too well-founded. " Had the situation appeared less critical," observes Admiral Ramsay, " an organised flow of large and small craft, working in reliefs, would have been arranged."[5]

Yet a further batch of vessels arrived off the beaches that evening ; the 17 available flare-burning drifters of the Dover Auxiliary Patrol[6] had sailed for Dunkirk during the afternoon, and on arriving were diverted to the beaches by the *Wolfhound*, in accordance with a signal from the Vice-Admiral, Dover[7], and anchored close inshore. The boats from the *Wolfhound* and *Wolsey*, and

---

[1] These letters refer to an arrangement, whereby at the commencement of " Dynamo " the Dunkirk beaches were described by a letter code referring to Map G.S.G.S. 4040, Sheet 29, 1/50,000. The lengths of beach lying in each 1000 metre map square were lettered, west to east, commencing with " A " at square 2686 in sequence to " O " at square 3990. (Appx. N. 10). Under this arrangement, A.B.C.D. actually refers to the beach at Malo-les-Bains.
This arrangement appears to have fallen into disuse on and after 29th May, when the stretch of beach, one mile east of Dunkirk to one mile east of La Panne, was divided into 3 equal parts, referred to as *La Panne*, *Bray* and *Malo*, from east to west, with a mile gap between each part. (Appendix O. 11).
[2] D.R. page 3, para. 8.
[3] The *Sandown*, *Medway Queen*, *Brighton Belle* and *Gracie Fields*.
[4] See Appendices D. 3, D. 4, D. 5, D. 7, and D. 8.
[5] D.R., p.3, para. 38.
[6] They were the *Netsukis*, *Lord Howard*, *Lord Howe*, *Golden Sunbeam*, *Midas*, *Golden Gift*, *Girl Pamela*, *Paxton*, *Boy Roy*, *Eileen Emma*, *Girl Gladys*, *Forecast*, *Ut Prosim*, *Yorkshire Lass*, *Young Mun*, *Shipmates* and *Torbay II*.
[7] Appendix D.6.

from the *St. Seiriol* and *Queen of the Channel*, in addition to the drifters' own dinghies, enabled these drifters to lift some 2,000 troops from Malo and Bray beaches during the night of the 27th/28th May.

Results of S.N.O. Dunkirk's 2005/27

As a result of the action taken on S.N.O. Dunkirk's signals, there were assembling off the beaches on the night of 27th/28th May the *Wolfhound*, *Wolsey* and 6 other destroyers[1], 1 cruiser, 4 paddle-minesweepers, 17 drifters, 3 skoots (the *Lena*, *Hebe II* and *Oranje*) and 2 transports (the *Queen of the Channel* and the *St. Seiriol*). All these ships were ordered to use their own boats for ferrying, as no other small power boats, cutters, whalers or other pulling boats, were yet available.

S.N.O. Dunkirk's signals had therefore a big result ; but owing to the difficulty of passing orders at night in a shattered harbour his decision to divert vessels to the beaches had unforeseen repercussions, and it was associated with a false report that Dunkirk had fallen, and the failure of one personnel vessel and 7 skoots to reach the beaches that night. The circumstances are described below.

The P/V *Canterbury*, which had entered Dunkirk harbour at 2000, left at 2058 with 457 troops, including 140 stretcher cases. Before leaving, she was ordered by the " Sea Transport Officer "[2] " to turn back ships attempting to enter Dunkirk " ; the order, evidently intended to divert ships to the beaches, was misunderstood. In the Dunkirk road, the *Canterbury* passed the order to the P/V *Maid of Orleans* and to the H/C's *Isle of Thanet* and *Worthing*, and those vessels thereupon turned back to Dover. Later the order became definitely garbled, for the skoot *Tilly* (which was in company with the 4 skoots *Hondsrug*, *Jutland*, *Patria* and *Brandaris*) met the *Canterbury* (in company with the 2 hospital carriers) 8 or 9 miles from Dunkirk, and received from her the signal " Dunkirk is in enemy hands. Keep clear." This signal was variously recorded by some of the other skoots, as " Dunkirk has fallen. Return " ; and all five of them, as well as the skoots *Bornrif* and *Twente*, did in fact return to the Downs, although the *Jutland* and the *Patria* first closed Nieuport Bank buoy in an unsuccessful endeavour to obtain more definite information. Some of the skoots, in turn, promulgated this false report to other ships, notably to the P/V *Dorrien Rose* ; this ship, which received the signal, " unsafe to approach Dunkirk," did at first alter course to the northward, but, shortly after, again set course for Dunkirk. It was subsequently thought by some of the vessels concerned that the false information had been passed by " fifth columnists," though there is very little proof of this.[3]

" Chronic shortage " of beaching boats

Such was the beginning of the great build-up of ships[4] and of the inauguration of beach evacuation. The successful development of the latter was necessarily dependent on the continuation of fine weather, and the making good of the " chronic shortage " of beaching boats[5]. A wind of any strength in the northern sector between south-west and north-east would have made

---

[1] The situation having changed by the time they arrived, the *Gallant* and *Wakeful* went into Dunkirk. The *Windsor* remained on patrol. The *Anthony* had not yet returned from Portsmouth whither she had escorted the S.S. *Kyno*.
[2] *Canterbury's* report.
[3] See Appendices H.30 and H.32.
[4] Appendices D, E and F.
[5] D.R. page 3, para. 11.

beach evacuation impossible; at no time did this happen, but it was not until the fifth day of the operation (May 30th) that small power boats and beach craft began to become available in adequate numbers.[1]

The reason for this is to be sought mainly in the need for secrecy enjoined by the British and French Governments, even after the operation had been ordered. The necessity for avoiding any action that might have given rise to talk rendered the collection of small craft slow. It was not until 31st May that the British public learnt from the press that evacuation had begun.

Disembarkation ports designated

In these early days the limiting factors seemed likely to be the scale of enemy attacks at Dunkirk and on the beaches, and the difficulty of concentrating the ships and the troops at a common point or points[2].

Meanwhile, in order to ensure air protection, Blenheims maintained a patrol by single aircraft over the Dunkirk area during the night.[3]

At 2330, the Vice-Admiral, Dover, promulgated the names of ports for the disembarkation of troops in England as follows : –

> The *Calcutta* at Sheerness ;
> destroyers at Dover ;
> drifters, minesweepers, ⎱ ⎰ At Margate or Ramsgate as directed
>   skoots and coasters ⎰ ⎱   by N.O.I.C. Ramsgate ;
> personnel vessels at Folkestone.

Throughout the whole course of the operation the despatch of troops from the points of disembarkation in England was directed by the War Office Movements Control Organisation, and proceeded with great smoothness[4].

Summary of troops evacuated

The ships which had sailed for Dunkirk on the 26th May brought back 6,183 troops and 646 stretcher cases next day.

During the 27th May only two personnel vessels actually made the round trip, viz. : the *Royal Daffodil*, which brought back 840 troops from Dunkirk, and the *St. Helier*, which was ordered back before she could embark any troops. The destroyers *Wolsey* and *Wolfhound*, which embarked 206 and 130 troops respectively from Malo beach on the evening of 27th May, did not sail for England until shortly after midnight.

Thus, the total number landed in England from the commencement of Operation "Dynamo" to midnight 27th/28th May was :

> 26th May – Nil ;
> 27th May – 7,669, all of whom were lifted direct from Dunkirk harbour.

---

[1] D.R. covering letter, No. A.14/0/876/40, page 2, paras. 3 and 5.
[2] D.R. page 3, para. 11.
[3] R.A.F. Narrative, p. 320.
[4] D.R. covering letter No. A.14/0/876/40, page 2, para. 6.

CHAPTER V

TUESDAY, 28TH MAY

First supplies reach the beaches

This was a day of tension. The first supplies of food, water and ammunition from England arrived at the beaches, and in spite of many losses by enemy action considerable quantities were landed at La Panne and at Coxyde to the north of it.[1]

Germans reach Nieuport

Early on the 28th May the leading enemy mobile troops and tanks reached Nieuport, but the danger that the enemy forces, released by the Belgian armistice, might forestall the B.E.F.'s occupation of the perimeter had been foreseen[2], and the measures taken by Lord Gort to meet a desperate situation and to delay the enemy proved successful.

At 1100 General Blanchard visited Lord Gort at his headquarters at Hout-kerque. It then transpired that General Blanchard, having received no instructions from his Government regarding the evacuation of French troops, declined to contemplate any such operation. Later in the day, however, he consented, and orders were given for part of the French 1st Army to withdraw so as to arrive within the Dunkirk perimeter on 30th May.[3]

Lord Gort's Headquarters move to La Panne

Meanwhile, during the afternoon, Lord Gort moved his headquarters from Houtkerque to La Panne, which was in direct telephonic communication with London. There he received from Lt.-Gen. Sir Ronald Adam and the Quarter-Master-General, Lt.-General W. G. Laidsell, a very unfavourable report : " No ships could be unloaded at the docks at Dunkirk, and few wounded could be evacuated. There was no water in Dunkirk and very little on the beaches. The Naval plans were not yet in full operation, and some 20,000 men were waiting to be taken off the beaches, 10,000[4] having been taken off in the last 2 days, chiefly from Dunkirk." Also, they stated it as their opinion that " given a reasonable measure of immunity from air attack, troops could be gradually evacuated. . . If, however, intensive air attacks continued the beaches might easily become a shambles within the next 48 hours".[5]

Possibility of surrender is visualised

Lord Gort informed the C.I.G.S. of the gist of this report, and asked that H.M. Government should consider the policy to be followed if a crisis arose, " as well it might." He received this telegram in reply :

" . . H.M. Govt. fully approve your withdrawal to extricate your force in order to embark maximum number possible of B.E.F. If you are cut from all communication from us, and all evacuation from Dunkirk and beaches had, in your judgment, been finally prevented after every attempt to re-open it had failed, you would become sole judge of when it was impossible to inflict further damage to enemy".[2]

---

[1] Lord Gort's Second Despatch, para. 50.
[2] Lord Gort's Second Despatch, para. 53.
[3] Lord Gort's Second Despatch, para. 52.
[4] Some of these had been taken off before operation " Dynamo " commenced.
[5] Lord Gort's Second Despatch, para. 54.

While a situation that could only mean surrender was now visualised in England as possibly a stark necessity, General Weygand sent an urgent telegram to Lord Gort appealing to him personally to ensure that the British Army took a vigorous part in any counter-attack thought necessary; the situation, said General Weygand, made it essential to hit hard.

Lord Gort, who saw the situation more clearly, observes, " when he [General Weygand] sent this message, he could have had no accurate information of the real position or of the powers of counter-attack remaining to either the British or French."

Germans take Ostend

That evening, at 2030, the Admiralty informed the Vice-Admiral, Dover, that Ostend was reliably reported to be captured. Dunkirk was the only port left in Allied hands.

Situation at Dunkirk becomes easier

Nor were the prospects at Dunkirk very hopeful. When the *Wolfhound* and the *Wolsey* left Malo beach for Dover just after midnight on the 27th May the whole of the port appeared to be ablaze[1].

At 0125 the cruiser *Calcutta*, en route for La Panne, was missed by a torpedo 100 yards astern fired from an E-boat. No further attack took place, and the *Calcutta* arrived off La Panne beach an hour later to find that the destroyers *Grafton*, *Greyhound* and *Impulsive*, and the paddle-minesweepers *Sandown* and *Gracie Fields*, were already there.

Ever since 0030 destroyers making their first trip to the evacuation area had been arriving off the beaches, and only two – the *Gallant* and the *Wakeful* – went to Dunkirk. The *Vivacious* and the skoot *Hebe II* reached Malo beach at about 0030, and the *Sabre* at 0120. The *Hebe II*, unable to find any troops, entered Dunkirk harbour and embarked 150 from the east pier; the *Sabre* embarked troops from two drifters. At 0320 the *Vimy* arrived off the beach at Zuydcoote, 3 miles east of Dunkirk, and sent her boats to assist in filling up the minesweeper *Brighton Belle*, which was embarking troops with the assistance of the ex-Belgian canal boat *Yser* and a small pulling boat. The skoot *Lena* had been off Zuydcoote since the previous evening and in the early hours of the 28th May transferred the 120 troops she had embarked to a destroyer; the minesweeper *Medway Queen*, off La Panne since 2300/27, sailed with 600 troops on board.

By 0400 the situation in Dunkirk harbour appears to have eased, and at 0436 S.N.O. Dunkirk was asking for all vessels to go alongside the east pier. At 0445 the *Vimy*, leaving her boats with the *Brighton Belle*, went into Dunkirk harbour and embarked 613 troops. At 0955 the destroyer *Mackay* reached Dunkirk from the Irish Sea, and picked up 600 troops in an hour from the seaward end of Dunkirk east pier, giving up her berth to the destroyer *Montrose*. The *Sabre*, which had in the meantime returned to Dover with a load of 158 troops from Malo beach, berthed outside the *Montrose*. An hour later, the destroyers *Worcester* and *Anthony* arrived, and berthed ahead of the *Montrose*. The pier was crammed with troops and several aircraft, attempting to bomb it, were driven off by the destroyers' gunfire. Vast columns of smoke were drifting westwards from the burning oil tanks ashore, and houses on the sea front were bursting into flames from time to time[2].

---

[1] Report by the *Wolfhound*.
[2] Report by the *Montrose*.

The destroyers *Codrington*, *Jaguar* and *Javelin*, diverted from patrol, arrived off Dunkirk at 1315. They had picked up 33 survivors that morning from the S.S. *Abukir*, which had been torpedoed by an E-boat while returning with about 200 evacuees from Ostend to the United Kingdom; these survivors were transferred to the destroyer *Grenade* which subsequently went on to Dunkirk. The *Codrington* went into Dunkirk harbour, while the *Jaguar* and *Javelin* using their own boats, embarked troops from Bray beach. At 1730 the *Grenade* left Dunkirk with 1,000 troops on board.

Between 1230 and 1815 the *Vivacious*, making her second trip, embarked 359 troops from Zuydcoote, assisted by ships' boats, the *M.T.B.16*, and the skoot *Lena*. The *Vimy* also made a second trip, embarking 591 troops from Dunkirk harbour.

More ships were on the way. From 1230 onwards 19 minesweepers were sailed from Harwich, from Dover and the Downs, for Dunkirk and the beaches. By 2130 five of them had arrived off Bray beach [1], and four off La Panne [2]; three reached Dunkirk by 2140 [3].

Four other minesweepers arrived off the beaches late on the night of 28th/29th May [4], and two more reached the beaches at 0600/29 [5].

Early on the 28th May the eight ships of the 7th and 8th minesweeping flotillas had been ordered from Rosyth to Harwich, to work under the orders of the Vice-Admiral, Dover [6]; they could not, however, reach the beaches until about 72 hours later.

During the forenoon and afternoon of the 28th May the call went out for more and more destroyers, and seven reached the evacuation area next day [7]. In the signals from the Admiralty and the Vice-Admiral, Dover, summoning them there sounds the same note of extreme urgency, traceable to S.N.O. Dunkirk's message [8] declaring that evacuation on the night of 28th/29th May was problematical. "If the older class destroyers and other vessels cannot compete with the situation " signalled the Admiralty, " destroyers of all classes are to be used for bringing men off" [9]. " Every available destroyer " in the Western Approaches and Portsmouth Commands was to be sailed to Dover [10]. Destroyers on patrol or on escort duty were to be diverted to Dunkirk or the beaches [11].

Vulnerability of personnel vessels

The vulnerability of the personnel vessels, with their large troop-carrying capacity, was a cause of anxiety. On the 27th May the *Biarritz* and *Archangel*, the *Mona's Queen*, *King Orry*, *Sequacity*, *Yewdale*, and the *Isle of Thanet* [12],

---

[1] The *Albury*, *Gossamer*, *Leda*, *Kellett* and *Sutton*.
[2] The *Salamander*, *Halcyon*, *Skipjack* and *Waverley*.
[3] The *Ross*, *Pangbourne* and *Lydd*.
[4] The *Hebe*, *Sharpshooter*, *Duchess of Fife* snd *Emperor of India*.
[5] The *Oriole* and *Marmion*.
[6] A.M.0163/28.
[7] The *Verity*, *Harvester*, *Esk*, *Malcolm*, *Express*, *Shikari* and *Scimitar*.
[8] Appendix M.4.
[9] A.M.0754/28.
[10] A.M.1229/28.
[11] Appendices D.4, D.5 and D.7.
[12] At 0254, on 28th May, shortly after leaving Dover for Newhaven, the *Isle of Thanet* collided with the Examination Service Vessel *Ocean Reward*, which sank immediately. Assisted by the tug *Lady Brassey*, a search was made for survivors, but none was found.

had all come under fire from the shore guns at Calais and Gravelines. At 0415 on the 28th May the *Queen of the Channel*, loaded with 904 troops, was attacked by one aircraft ; 3 or 4 bombs were dropped, which straddled the ship abaft the mainmast and broke her back, the starboard propeller shaft and the rudder. By good fortune the *Dorrien Rose, en route* for Dunkirk, was in the vicinity and rescued the troops : the *Queen of the Channel* sank about ½ hour later. The *St. Seiriol*, which left Dunkirk at about 0415 with 494 troops, reached Folkestone in safety.

Civilian crews feel the strain

Some 45 personnel vessels were used during operation "Dynamo"[1]. Of these eight were sunk, at least six were so damaged by bombing or gunfire as to render them unfit for further use during the operation, and two were damaged in collision. Nine of the largest of these personnel vessels had been engaged prior to "Dynamo" in operations at Dunkirk, Calais and Boulogne, and their Captains and crews were beginning to feel the strain when Operation "Dynamo" started.

Thus it was that the Master of the *Canterbury*, which had already completed 2 round trips to Dunkirk in operation "Dynamo", reported, on the 28th May, that he was too worn out to make a third trip. The P.S.T.O. went on board and explained the gravity of the situation to the Master, and the *Canterbury* sailed at 0930 the next day. On her return voyage from Dunkirk she was bombed and damaged, and after landing her 1960 troops went into dock for repairs. In the 3 trips she made the *Canterbury* brought back 4,416 troops ; her Master, Captain C. A. Hancock, was awarded the D.S.C.

Personnel vessels not to be employed during full daylight

On the 28th May, however, it had become apparent that development of the German air threat over the evacuation area, and the increasing artillery fire from shore batteries covering the sea approaches to Dunkirk, prohibited the employment of personnel and similar vessels during daylight, until the position was restored, and that evacuation from Dunkirk by day must for the moment be confined to warships and small vessels[2].

It was not, therefore, until later in the day, that the P/V *Royal Daffodil* sailed for Dunkirk, and eight other personnel vessels and a hospital carrier[3] received their sailing orders during the afternoon and evening.

The northern Route Y was by this time in general use[4], but ships proceeding from Dover to Dunkirk were ordered to use the southern and shorter Route Z, if the passage from Calais Bell buoy to Dunkirk could be made in darkness.

N.O.I.C. Ramsgate responsible for servicing skoots

In these circumstances some 20 skoots reached Dunkirk, or arrived off the beaches during the day and evening of the 28th May ; others were on the way. Their speed varied, but most of them were very slow. Eight of them went into Dunkirk harbour[5], and four to Bray beach[6]. The *Abel Tasman*, loaded with ammunition, the *Alice* and *Kaap Falga*, loaded with food, and three

---

[1] This number includes 3 store ships, 3 motor vessels and a few freighters, coasters and tramps.

[2] D.R. p. 4, para. 13.

[3] The *Scotia, Malines, Prague, Manxman, Royal Sovereign, Tynwald, Lochgarry, Killarney* and the H.C. *Paris.*

[4] Appendix K.1.

[5] The *Caribia, Fredanja, Friso, Jutland, Tilly, Patria, Sursum-Corda,* and *Twente.*

[6] The *Amazone, Doggersbank, Hilda,* and *Oranje.*

others[1] were off La Panne beach. The *Alice* which arrived in the early morning, was put aground to facilitate unloading ; a few hours later, however, after she had been refloated, her engines seized up as a result of damage during an air attack, and she was abandoned.

At this stage began the running of a continuous service of skoots between Margate and Ramsgate and the beaches, whose servicing was performed by N.O.I.C. Ramsgate.

Evacuation plan for the night 28th-29th May

The full significance of this rapidly growing armada of ships became apparent in the numbers of troops lifted the following day. By midday on the 28th May, approximately 12,000 troops had been transported since the commencement of Operation " Dynamo " ; about 1,000 were en route to the U.K., and about 5,000 were embarking in 5 destroyers. Nine more destroyers were on the way to Dunkirk, and a total force of 16 destroyers would be maintaining a continuous ferry service during the day.

The plan for the night of 28th/29th May, was to sail all available ships, small craft and boats, so as to develop the maximum effort at 2200. The details of the plan were signalled by V. A. Dover to S.N.O. Dunkirk at 1555. Briefly, 3 hospital carriers, 7 personnel vessels and 2 destroyers were to embark troops at the east pier Dunkirk ; while some 20 destroyers, 19 paddle and fleet sweepers, 17 drifters, 20 to 40 skoots, 5 coasters, 12 motor boats, 2 tugs, 28 pulling cutters and lifeboats, were to work along the 10 mile stretch of beach from Dunkirk to La Panne.

Fighter Command patrols strengthened

Meanwhile, at Dunkirk, conditions had proved easier during the day ; enemy air activity over the port was restricted, probably by the heavy pall of smoke from the burning town, and increased fighter activity was keeping the enemy in check[2]. Fighter Command patrols were strengthened from an average of one squadron to an average of 2 squadrons, and Coastal Command maintained a continuous daylight patrol (usually of 3 aircraft at a time) on the line North Goodwins – Gravelines – Ostend. About 320 sorties were flown on Continental patrols during the day, and severe losses were inflicted on the enemy. Nineteen Me. 109's and 4 bombers were definitely destroyed for a loss of 13 British fighters.[3]

Windsor damaged

At 1000 some 40 Me. 109's were engaged by our fighters, and at 1040 they encountered a German force of nearly 150 bombers and fighters[3]. At 1125, the destroyer *Anthony* observed 40 to 50 planes in aerial combat over Dunkirk. At 1145 the destroyer *Windsor*, which was on patrol, was attacked near the South Goodwin Light Vessel by 15 dive-bombers supported by 10 fighters ; she suffered considerable damage from near misses and m.g. fire and had 30 casualties.

---

[1] The *Reiger, Pacific* and *Pascholl*.
[2] Appendix L.3.
[3] R.A.F. Narrative, p. 323.

Boy Roy and *Paxton* damaged and beached

At 1215 German fighters in strength were encountered by our fighter patrols ; during the rest of the day there was no further air fighting[1], but the mine-sweeper *Sandown* was bombed off the Gull Light buoy at 1230, and Bray beach was bombed at 1420[2].   In an air raid off Dunkirk channel at about 1800, the prifters *Boy Roy* and *Paxton* were damaged by near misses and had to be beached ; there were, however, no casualties.

Difficulty of synchronising arrival of ships with flow of troops

Meanwhile, at 0935, 2,000 troops were on Malo beach and 7,000 more were on the sand dunes, waiting anxiously for ships to come[3].   An hour after mid-day, 6,000 troops were reported to be on Bray beach, 7 miles east of Dunkirk pier, and 4 minesweepers were sailed from the Downs to embark them.   When they arrived at 2130, however, conditions had changed, and three of them, the *Salamander*, *Fitzroy* and *Skipjack*, went to La Panne ; the fourth, the *Sutton*, went to the beach at Zuydcoote 4 miles east of Dunkirk[4].   Throughout the whole operation it was never found possible to adjust the arrival of ships, either at Dunkirk or opposite the beaches, to synchronise with the ebb and flow of troop concentrations.

Shortage of drinking water.

At this time the troops were sorely in need of drinking water ; joint naval[5] and military measures were taken to provide it in tanks and cans, and ships off the beaches were directed to do what they could from their own resources. There was, however, inevitably some delay before all requirements could be met, and as late as the 30th May no water or food had yet reached Malo beach[6].

Brighton Belle sunk

Meanwhile, at 1230, the *Brighton Belle*, returning to Ramsgate with the 350 troops she had picked up from the beach at Zuydcoote, struck a submerged wreck off the Gull Light buoy during an air attack and sank.   All the crew and troops were transferred to the *Sandown*, *Medway Queen*, and *Yser*.   Pay-master Sub.-Lieut. W. J. Butler, R.N.V.R., of the *Sandown* was killed and 2 ratings were wounded.

Shortage of boats

At 1420, when Bray beach was bombed, S.N.O., Dunkirk, ordered some of the troops there to march to Dunkirk in spite of the congestion in the port. By 1830, however, there were still several thousand troops at Bray and more were arriving.   At this time the *Grafton* reported that she was off Bray beach

---

[1] R.A.F. Narrative, p. 323.
[2] Report by S.N.O. Dunkirk, (R.O. III p. 346).
[3] Appendix N.2.
[4] It is not always possible to record precisely the beaches off which ships were lying. The 10-miles stretch of beach had arbitrarily been divided up into 3 *sections*, Malo, Bray and La Panne.   In the confusion of the times, and particularly in the darkness of the night, it is not surprising that ships in company sometimes gave different names to the particular section of beach off which they were lying.
[5] The *Maid of Orleans* had landed 6,000 two-gallon cans of water at Dunkirk on the 26th May.   The motor boat *Glitter* II went over with water for the beaches on the 29th May and the lighter *Seine* took 5,000 cans of it ; the *Friso* and the *Mona's Queen* also went over on the 29th with water, but the latter was mined and sunk before she could unload it.
[6] Appendix P.1.

with the *Calcutta*[1], the *Gallant, Wakeful, Verity,* two skoots the (*Doggersbank* and *Hilda*), two power boats and a tow of pulling boats ; at 2115 this force was joined by the minesweepers *Kellett* and *Leda,* but there were insufficient boats and motor launches to cope with the number of troops on the beach.

Off La Panne, at 2157, the *Calcutta,* assisted by the skoot *Reiger,* embarked 70 wounded (cot cases) ; heavy surf made embarkation difficult and the *Calcutta* had already lost one of her two whalers[2].

By the 28th May beach evacuation had become a vitally essential part of Operation " Dynamo ". It was, however, severely restricted by the almost complete lack of small beaching craft, other than ships' boats – aftermath of the wish, already noticed, to prevent early information of the operation becoming known to the enemy ; and an urgent and persistent cry for boats arose from the ships off the beaches.[3]

Beach craft are sailed for Dunkirk

Steps had already been taken, however, to begin the provision of small boats. At 0800 on the 28th May, 8 motor boats were sailed from the Thames for the South Downs. At noon the tug *Sun V* with 8 cutters and 2 whalers in tow, and the tug *St. Clears* with 11 cutters in tow, left Sheerness for Ramsgate, and both tugs sailed for Dunkirk late in the evening. Of these two tows, however, only 7 cutters reached the beaches, the remainder being lost *en route*.[4]

At 1500 the tug *Java* left Ramsgate for Dunkirk, in company with four drifters[5] and 5 motor launches[6]. They arrived off Bray at 0100 on 29th May, and were the first arrivals of small motor craft off the beaches. With them, at 1500 on the 28th May, 5 drifters of the 1st Mine Recovery Flotilla left Ramsgate for Dunkirk[7], and at 1845, 18 motor boats with 17 whalers left Sheerness for Dover.[8]

Supply of small craft is accelerated

These supplied only a portion of what was required. There was still a lack of small craft, and at 2002 V.A. Dover asked that *every available shallow draft power boat* should be sent to the beaches[9]. The Admiralty's vigorous reaction to this request became fully evident on the following day, the 29th May, when the Portsmouth and Nore Commands, the Thames estuary and the Port of London Authority were combed for motor boats, lighters and barges[10]. To accelerate the journey arrangements were made to route them direct to the beaches, provided they had charts, food, fuel etc.[11], though some difficulty was experienced in providing the large number of charts required. Indeed, on the 31st May the Master of the coaster *Hythe* states that he was given an " army road map " to navigate on.

---

[1] The *Calcutta* reported she was off La Panne.
[2] Appendix H.2.
[3] Appendices H.1 and H.2.
[4] The *Sun V's* tow was lost early next morning in a collision with the destroyer *Montrose.* Five of the *St. Clears'* cutters were lost *en route* to Dunkirk next day, as the result of enemy gunfire from Gravelines and Nieuport ; one of the 5 was, however, subsequently picked up by the Sp. Serv./V. *Crested Eagle.*
[5] The *Lord Rodney, Lord Keith, Lord Collingwood* and *Lord St. Vincent.*
[6] The *Walker I, Walker II, New Britannic, Nayland,* and *Angler II.*
[7] The *Lord Cavan, Fidget, Jacketa, Silver Dawn* and *Fisher Boy* (Appendix G.5).
[8] Appendix G.6.
[9] Appendix G.7.
[10] Appendices G.13 to G.18.
[11] Appendix G.9.

In spite, however, of every effort as more and more ships were drawn into Operation "Dynamo", the pressing demand for beaching craft grew, almost hourly, more insistent. A climax was reached on 1st June[1], when, in spite of the number sent over, the "inshore flotilla" – crippled by weather, accidents, mechanical breakdowns, exhaustion of crews and enemy action – was still unable to meet requirements, and the minesweeper *Gossamer's* urgent request for boats received the curt reply "It is now impracticable to send more boats. You must do your utmost with yours[2]. A perusal of the "Dynamo" signals brings sharply to notice the great driving force of the Vice-Admiral, Dover ; the clamorous signals for "more boats" were an indication of the great strain to which he was being subjected.

Beach and harbour evacuation compared

There can be little doubt that had not valid reasons prevented more beach ferrying craft from being made available for the first 5 days of the evacuation, a greater number of troops could have been evacuated. "The initial problem", says the Vice-Admiral, Dover, "called for a maximum effort over a limited period, regardless of the future, and accordingly all resources in the way of small boats were thrown on the beaches, before adequate provision had been made for their maintenance off the coast in such matters as relief of the personnel and the provision of large beach parties.

"It was only due, to the foresight of the Admiralty in making arrangements for a continued flow in ever increasing numbers of small power boats and beach craft, *which became available on the fifth day onwards*, that the continued evacuation from the beaches remained a reasonable proposition after the initial crisis had passed.

"A perusal of the signals that passed between Dover and the French coast here reveals the many occasions on which the responsible officers stationed on the coast considered so little had been achieved from the beaches that they advocated restriction of evacuation to Dunkirk harbour. Many complaints of 'no boats', 'no ships' might lead a detached observer to the conclusion that the great effort that was being made was proving abortive.

"At Dover, where the whole operation could be viewed in truer perspective because the number and origin of the troops being landed in England was always to hand, it was clear that the evacuation from the beaches required by the military situation was, in fact, achieving a considerable success."[3] Admiral Ramsay's view is borne out by these recorded figures : Of the 251,000 troops landed in the United Kingdom between May 28th and June 1st inclusive – the period during which Dunkirk and the beaches eastward were available day and night except for enemy interference – 90,000 *were lifted from the beaches*, while 55,000 were lifted by personnel ships and hospital carriers, and 106,000 by other vessels, direct from Dunkirk harbour (see Table 2).

Anti-submarine patrols are maintained

While the lifting of troops from Dunkirk and the beaches was progressing with ever-increasing speed, anti-submarine patrols had been maintained from the North Goodwin to Kwint Bank ; but on the 28th May all destroyers except

---

[1] Appendices H.17 to H.25.
[2] Appendix H.22.
[3] Letter from V. A. Dover (A.14/0/876/40 of 18/6/40) covering his Report on Operation "Dynamo". Italics not in original.

the *Vega* and the Polish *Blyskawica* were diverted from them to the beaches[1]. On patrol this day with these two destroyers were the corvettes *Mallard, Widgeon, Sheldrake, Shearwater* and eleven A/S trawlers[2]. Of the latter, the A/S trawler *Thuringia* was sunk by a mine early in the day, and her Captain, Chief Skipper D. W. L. Simpson, D.S.C., D.S.M., R.N.R., was not among the 4 survivors.

Owing to a misunderstanding the LL trawlers *Our Bairns, Inverforth* and *Thomas Bartlett*, which were in company, carried out a sweep in Dunkirk roads instead of sweeping the war channel. These vessels were shelled off Calais ; and the *Thomas Bartlett*, while endeavouring to get out of range of the guns, ran on to a British minefield, and, striking a mine at 1017, sank with the loss of 8 of her crew[3].

During the night of 28th/29th May, to strengthen this patrol, all available M.T.B.'s of the Nore and Dover Commands were ordered to patrol north-east of the line Wandelaar L/V and Whistle Buoy.

Summary of troops landed in England

The figures for May 28th gave grounds for hope. 17,804 troops were transported to England[4] (of which 11,835 were transported by destroyers). Of these, 11,874 were lifted from Dunkirk east pier, and 5,930 from the beaches. (See Table 2).

Ships lost or damaged on 28th May

Lost	Damaged
The A/S trawler *Thuringia*	The destroyer *Windsor*.
The drifter *Ocean Reward*	
The M/S *Brighton Belle*	
LL trawler *Thomas Bartlett*	
P/V *Queen of the Channel*	
The skoot *Alice*	
The H/C *Isle of Thanet*	

---

[1] The *Windsor* had returned to Dover after being damaged in an air attack at 1145.
[2] The *Cayton Wyke, Kingston Alalite, Kingston Andalusite, Kingston Galena, Saon, Spurs, Stella Dorado, Westella, Blackburn Rovers, Lady Philomena* and *Thuringia*.
[3] Report by C.M.S., Dover (R.O. II, p.498). See also Appx. J.12
[4] D.R. gives 14,409, but this figure is not confirmed by the recorded numbers of troops disembarked by the various ships, as shown in Tables 2 and 3.

CHAPTER VI

WEDNESDAY, 29TH MAY

FIRST HEAVY ENEMY AIR EFFORT

German bridgehead in Nieuport

Throughout the 29th May, the enemy attempted to cross the canal between the Franco-Belgian frontier and Nieuport – and, indeed, succeeded in establishing a bridgehead in the town of Nieuport, although everywhere else he was driven back. Some of the enemy attempted to cross in rubber boats ; others, disguised as civilians, with the refugees, horses and cattle. The few vital hours gained made it possible, against all expectation, to embark practically the whole British force[1].

Two-day traffic block in perimeter

Large numbers of French troops arriving in the perimeter brought a mass of transport which caused such traffic congestion that for two days the main road between La Panne and Dunkirk became totally blocked with vehicles three deep[2].

French evacuation not yet ordered

Admiral Abrial (whose headquarters were at Bastion No. 32, near Dunkirk Mole) had apparently received no orders from his Government that the whole of the British troops were to be embarked, and he professed great surprise when he heard of Lord Gort's intentions. He imagined that British troops would stay and defend the perimeter to the last, side by side with the French[2].

Meanwhile, the French troops were expecting to embark along with their British comrades, notwithstanding that only two French ships had so far been provided[3]; the beaches were becoming crowded with French soldiers, and difficulties might have occurred at any time.[2] Later in the day, however, three French torpedo boats and one minesweeper sailed to Dunkirk harbour to evacuate troops.[4]

Dunkirk perimeter established

On the evening of the 29th May the organisation of the perimeter was complete, and General Sir Ronald Adam, his task accomplished, embarked for England that night.[5]

Mackay and *Montrose* out of action

The story of the 29th May is largely one of ships sunk or damaged. Our losses were very heavy and began very early. At 0005, the destroyer *Mackay* (*en route* to Bray beach with the destroyer *Harvester*) ran aground at the western

---

[1] Lord Gort's Second Despatch para. 53.
[2] Lord Gort's Second Despatch, para. 55.
[3] So far, the French torpedo boat *Cyclone* had brought back 460 troops, and the minesweeper *Commandant Delage* 520 – both on 29th May, from Dunkirk harbour.
[4] The torpedo boats *Cyclone*, *Mistral* and *Sirocco* and the minesweeper *Commandant Delage*.
[5] Lord Gort's Second Despatch, para. 57.

end of Zuydcoote Pass. Eight minutes later, about 1 mile W.S.W. of No. 2 Buoy, the destroyer *Montrose*, en route to Dunkirk, ran into a patch of fog and collided with the tug *Sun V*, which was towing 11 naval cutters. The *Sun V* put her helm hard to starboard, but she received a severe glancing blow, and narrowly escaped sinking; the 11 cutters were lost in the darkness. The *Montrose* had to be towed, stern-first, to Dover by the tug *Lady Brassey*. Neither the *Mackay*, the *Montrose* nor the tug were able to take any further part in the evacuation.

The *Harvester* reached Bray beach at 0050, and sent in her motor boat in charge of Sub-Lieut. E. C. Croswell, R.N., who found about 4,000 soldiers awaiting embarkation... There was a strong cross sea and sand bars made the launching of boats difficult. During the course of the night the *Harvester* managed to evacuate about 700 which included some 100 wounded. At 0400, however, the supply of boats for embarkation ceased. There had been considerable wastage of boats through overcrowding, which was difficult to control as the embarkation beach extended for over one mile. At 0500, the *Harvester* moved to La Panne.[1]

Wakeful sunk

In the meantime, at 0045, there occurred the only two E-boat successes against British destroyers. The destroyer Wakeful, returning from Bray beach with about 650 troops on board, was $\frac{1}{4}$ mile west of Kwint Whistle buoy when 2 parallel torpedo tracks about 30 yards apart were seen approaching, 150 yards away on the starboard bow. They had been fired by the S-boat *S 30*.

Avoiding action was taken, and one torpedo missed ahead, but the other hit the *Wakeful* in the forward boiler room. The *Wakeful* broke in half and the two portions sank within about 15 seconds, each portion remaining upright with the bow and stern standing about 60 feet above the water.

Most of the guns' crews floated clear, 30 men and an officer remaining on the stern portion. All the troops were asleep below, and all except one went down with the ship. All the *Wakeful's* engine room department, except one or two, were lost. The Captain, Cdr. R. L. Fisher, R.N., floated clear of the bridge.

After about half an hour, the danlayers *Nautilus* and *Comfort*, which were en route to La Panne, arrived and began to pick up those still swimming. The *Nautilus* picked up 6 and the *Comfort* 16, including Cdr. Fisher. Then the minesweeper *Gossamer*, returning from Dunkirk harbour with 420 troops, arrived, lowered her boats, and picked up a further 15 survivors.

Cdr. Fisher directed the *Comfort* to go alongside the wreck and take off the men clinging to the stern. The *Nautilus* continued on her way to La Panne, where she was lost during the afternoon in an air attack.

Grafton torpedoed

It was now 0220, and the minesweeper *Lydd* arrived on the scene bringing 300 troops from Dunkirk harbour. By the light of an Aldis lamp, she sighted the bow and stern portions of the *Wakeful* with men clinging to them. The *Lydd* lowered her boats, but was ordered by the *Gossamer* to put out her Aldis lamp and drop a depth charge; the latter order could not, however, be carried

---

[1] Sub-Lieut. Croswell, who remained at La Panne until 1st June, says in his report, "Except during the first day of evacuation, the bearing of the B.E.F. at La Panne was magnificent." (C.W.23187/40).

out because of the men in the water. By the time the *Lydd* had picked up 10 survivors, the destroyer *Grafton,* loaded with about 800 troops from Bray beach, also arrived and ordered the *Lydd* to circle round her. The *Gossamer* went on to Dover.

In the meantime, the *Comfort* had reached the stern portion of the wreck of the *Wakeful,* and finding that it had fallen over[1], went alongside the *Grafton* to warn her of the danger of torpedoes. It was then about 0240, and the *Grafton* having first sighted a small darkened vessel about 3 cables on the port quarter, signalled it to pick up survivors. Almost at once a torpedo hit the *Grafton's* port side and exploded; a second explosion followed, thought to be a shell or grenade hit, which wrecked the *Grafton's* bridge killing her Captain, Cdr. C. E. C. Robinson, R.N., and 3 others. The torpedo blew off the *Grafton's* stern, abaft the after magazine bulkhead, and broke her back, but she still floated on an even keel. A German submarine, U.62 had fired the torpedo.

The torpedo explosion almost swamped the *Comfort;* she rose, and Cdr. Fisher was washed overboard. He seized a rope's end, but with the *Comfort* going full speed ahead soon had to let go. The *Comfort* came round in a wide circle until within about 50 yards of the stricken *Grafton,* whereupon the *Grafton* and *Lydd,* mistaking her in the darkness for an E-boat, opened a heavy raking fire with 4-inch and Lewis guns.[2]

Comfort cut in half

When the firing ceased Cdr. Fisher, who had reached the bow of the *Comfort,* endeavoured to get abord ; but the *Lydd,* having circled round to finish off the supposed E-boat, bore down at full speed and, ramming the *Comfort* amidships (it was then about 0307), cut her in half. Some of the *Comfort's* crew attempted to spring aboard the *Lydd,* but the *Lydd,* mistaking them for boarders, opened up with rifle fire. Two men were, however, taken off the rammed vessel and it was then discovered that she was the *Comfort.* Altogether, the number saved from this most tragic occurrence, shrouded in the darkness of the night, were only 5, of which 4 were survivors from the *Wakeful.* As the *Grafton* then appeared able to look after herself, the *Lydd* set course for Ramsgate.

When the *Comfort* went down Cdr. Fisher again sank, but he came to the surface and, after swimming about until 0515, was picked up by a boat lowered from the Norwegian S.S. *Hird,* which was *en route* from Dunkirk to England with about 3,500 troops and refugees on board.

Grafton sunk

In the meantime, at 0400, the personnel ship *Malines,* which was returning empty from Dunkirk, heard S O S signals ; she placed herself alongside the torpedoed *Grafton* and transferred the destroyer's 800 troops. "The Master . . . handled his ship with extreme skill," reported the acting Captain of the *Grafton,* Lieut. H. C. J. McRea, R.N.

It was now 0430, just before sunrise, and the destroyers *Javelin, Icarus, Vanquisher, Intrepid* and *Ivanhoe, en route* from Dover to Dunkirk, sighted the sinking *Grafton.* The *Ivanhoe* went to her assistance and embarked the

---

[1] On the 30th May the corvette *Sheldrake* was ordered to destroy the *Wakeful's* asdic apparatus. She found the *Wakeful* completely capsized with her stern resting on the bottom. As, by then, information was received that the area had been mined, the *Sheldrake,* to minimise the risk, sank the wreck by gunfire and a pattern of depth charges.

[2] Later the *Grafton's* fire was shifted to another vessel further away on the port quarter, which was observed to blow up with a bright flash. This may well have been the E-boat.

seriously wounded. The *Grafton* was by then listing heavily, and had her after end awash; the *Ivanhoe* fired 3 shells into her at 500 yards range and then proceeded to Dunkirk, where she berthed alongside the east pier and embarked troops.

Following the loss of the *Grafton*, destroyers were ordered not to stop to assist ships in distress.[1]

Mona's Queen sunk by mine

In the meantime the *Javelin* and *Icarus* had entered Dunkirk harbour, and the *Vanquisher* had anchored off Malo beach. The *Intrepid*, waiting for a berth, anchored off the harbour, ahead of the personnel vessel *Mona's Queen*, which was loaded with fresh water for the troops. Then, at about 0530, the *Mona's Queen* blew up on a magnetic mine and sank in two minutes. The *Vanquisher's* whaler and the *Intrepid's* motor boat picked up the Master, Captain A. Holkham and 31 of the crew.

The German minelaying effort

Minelaying by the enemy during the dark hours probably took place during the night 28th/29th May, and was maintained with great intensity during the following two nights. Not only was the Dunkirk road mined, including the Zuydcoote Pass, but also Route X and the area round the Kwint buoy. Folkestone and Dover Harbour entrances were also mined. In spite of the large number of mines laid, only one British ship other than the *Mona's Queen* was known for certain to have been sunk by magnetic mines – the Fleet Air Arm yacht *Grive* which was sunk on 1st June. On that date, also, the hospital carrier *St. David* was damaged at anchor off Dover when a mine was exploded by a LL. trawler sweeping close at hand. The A/S trawlers *Thuringia*, *Westella* and *Blackburn Rovers* were believed at the time to have been sunk by moored mines laid by a U-boat, although at first it was thought that the last two at any rate had been torpedoed. If the enemy had been able to lay moored contact mines by aircraft, instead of magnetic mines, the results would have been very different[2].

Allied air cover, 29th May

The remainder of the long list of naval losses on this day was caused by hostile bombers. The odds which our fighters had encountered on the 27th and 28th May, led on the 29th to a further strengthening of the fighter patrols up to 4 squadrons; actually the largest number of fighters on any one patrol was 44, the smallest 25. All fighter patrols were concentrated within a radius of 10 miles of Dunkirk, except for a Hurricane patrol at midday covering a line Dunkirk – Furnes – Cassel[3].

The Dunkirk area was covered during the day by fighter patrols at approximately the following times : 0440 – 0610, 0720 – 0925, 1030 – 1200, 1300 – 1400, 1450 – 1620,   1700 – 1800,   1930 – 2030,   2000 – 2110[3]. Coastal Command patrols covered the line North Goodwins – Gravelines – Ostend throughout the day; all three aircraft of one of the Coastal Command patrols were shot down by Me. 109's at about 1130[3].

---

[1] Appendix 0.6.
[2] V. A. Dover's letter, No. A.14/0/876/40, p.3, paras. 7(a) and 7 (c).
[3] *R.A.F. Narrative*, p.326.

Gallant put out of action

The destroyers *Jaguar*, *Gallant* and *Grenade*, *en route* for Dunkirk by the new middle Route X with instructions to test it for opposition by shore batteries, were attacked at 1155 off Snouw Bank by about 17 dive bombers. The attack was concentrated on the *Gallant* which was damaged by a near miss and had to retire ; she was unable to take any further part in Operation " Dynamo ". " One dive-bomber, was seen to be hit by pom-pom, and while losing height " observes the *Jaguar*, " was despatched by a fighter ". This attack appears to have taken place " just when one of our main [fighter] patrols had turned for home."[1]

On arrival at Dunkirk, the *Grenade* reported that there had been no interference from shore batteries. Shipping was thus able to make use of the route directly it had been swept. The minesweepers completed this work late on the same afternoon, and the route was taken into use within a few hours of both the other routes, Y and Z, being rendered unsafe for use by day owing to the German shore gunfire.

Bombing of Dunkirk and beaches commences

At 1358 the S.N.O., Dunkirk reported to V.A. Dover that the bombing of the beaches and of Dunkirk pier had commenced without fighter opposition. This attack occurred while Hurricanes were sweeping inland to Cassel.[1]

At 1250 the *Grenade* berthed alongside the east pier in Dunkirk outer harbour (the *Nouvel Avant-Port*), the *Jaguar* securing alongside her. The *Grenade* was ordered by S.N.O., Dunkirk, to remain at his disposal and not to embark troops. Between 1400 and 1525, the *Jaguar* embarked about 1,000 ; level bombers were being held off by fighters and A/A fire during this period, and two patterns of heavy bombs which were dropped close to the pier did no damage to ships.[2]

Fourteen ships lying at Dunkirk

In the meantime, at 1330, six Oropesa trawlers of the Dover M/S Command, viz. : the *Fyldea* (Lieut. R. Bill, R.N., S.O.), the *Arley*, *Brock*, *Calvi*, *John Cattling* and *Polly Johnson*, arrived off Dunkirk harbour and the *Fyldea* and *Arley* were ordered inside to pull the personnel vessel *Lochgarry*, which had embarked over 1,000 troops, away from the east pier[3]. By 1420 when they had done this, the six trawlers, triple-banked, occupied the *Lochgarry's* berth. Ahead of the six trawlers were the *Grenade* and *Jaguar* ; astern of the trawlers was the personnel vessel *Canterbury*, and astern of her, at the *Quai Félix Faure* in Dunkirk inner harbour (the *Avant-Port*), was the French destroyer *Cyclone*.

On the opposite side of the outer harbour, at the west Quay, lay the French destroyers *Mistral* and *Siroco*. Outside the harbour, on the seaward side of the east pier opposite the *Grenade*, was the P/V *Fenella*, and at 1430 the Special Service Vessel *Crested Eagle* berthed astern of her (see Diagram p.40). Off Malo, Bray and La Panne beaches were numbers of destroyers, minesweepers, skoots, personnel vessels, trawlers, tugs and small craft.

---

[1] R.A.F. Narrative, p.326.
[2] *Jaguar's* report.
[3] See *Fyldea's* report.

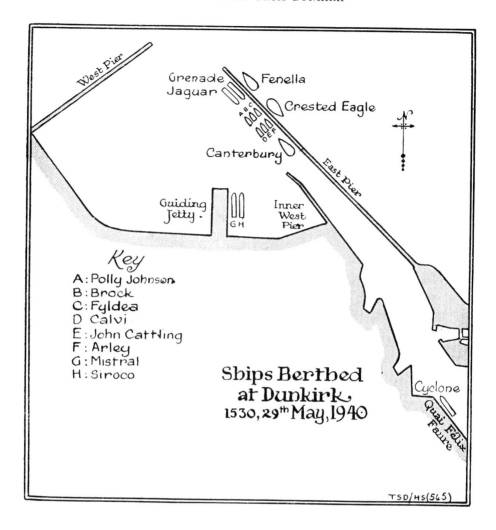

Ships Berthed
at Dunkirk
1530, 29th May, 1940

Key

A: Polly Johnson
B: Brock
C: Fyldea
D: Calvi
E: John Cattling
F: Arley
G: Mistral
H: Siroco

This was the first occasion on which a massed target of ships had been presented in Dunkirk harbour, and the scene was thus set for one of the most disastrous air onslaughts of the operation ; indeed, it was only by good fortune that the vital Dunkirk harbour channel was not blocked by sinking ships at this early date.   The air onslaught, which took place between 1530 and 2000, appears to have comprised 4 separate air attacks ; the manner of it was as follows : —

Air onslaught begins

The *first air attack* over Dunkirk commenced at 1530, and was made by 12 bombers[1].   The 20 or 30 bombs which were dropped on the harbour fell mostly wide, but the *Polly Johnson* was severely damaged by a near miss (*see* p.44). One bomber was shot down by fighters[2].

---

[1] See *Mistral's* report.
[2] *Fyldea's* report.

Mistral damaged

At 1555 a bomb struck the west quay and damaged the *Mistral*, killing 3 and seriously wounding 4, including her captain.

Jaguar severely damaged

Meanwhile, at 1550, the *Jaguar* was ordered out of Dunkirk harbour, to act as escort to the *Lochgarry* then waiting outside. While taking station ahead of the *Lochgarry* at about 1630 the *second air attack* over Dunkirk took place[1]. Dive-bombers attacked with salvoes of 4 bombs. About 14 salvoes were aimed at the *Jaguar* and one at the *Lochgarry*. A near miss severely damaged the *Jaguar*, holing her near the waterline and putting her engines and steering gear out of action ; a list to port developed. The destroyer drifted helplessly until, at 1645, she was in danger of drifting on to a wreck 50 yards away. The destroyer *Express* then sighted her and taking her in tow alongside transferred some of her troops. The skoot *Rika, en route* for La Panne beach, although she had been severely shaken by bombs off Middelkerke buoy, closed the *Jaguar* and took off 295 troops. The *Jaguar* eventually reached Dover at 2350 (in spite of further high level bombing attacks at 2014 and 2026), making the last part of the passage under her own power. She was unable to take any further part in " Dynamo."

Clan Macalister sunk

In the attack which damaged the *Jaguar*, the *Lochgarry* was also damaged by a near miss ; she was, however, able to proceed, and did so unescorted. Near 6 W buoy, she passed the S.S. *Clan Macalister* which, after having hoisted out 6 motor landing craft earlier in the day and subsequently embarked troops, had just been bombed and was on fire and sinking. The destroyer *Malcolm* had already taken off the wounded members of the *Clan Macalister's* crew and some of her troops, and the minesweeper *Pangbourne* had embarked the remainder. The *Clan Macalister* settled on the sea bed on an even keel with her upper works above water, and remained on fire for days. For days also, she acted as a target for enemy airmen, who thought she was still afloat.

Gracie Fields abandoned

Continuing on her way near Kwint Bank buoy, the *Lochgarry* saw the paddle-minesweeper *Gracie Fields* (which was carrying about 750 troops from La Panne beach) hit amidships by a bomb. The *Gracie Fields*, unable to stop her engines, and with her upper deck enveloped in clouds of steam, continued underway at 6 knots with her helm jammed with 15° starboard wheel. on. Nevertheless, the skoot *Twente*, which was on her way to La Panne beach, secured alongside the circling *Gracie Fields* and transferred as many injured and others as she could. The skoot *Jutland*, returning from La Panne beach with 275 French troops, also secured alongside the *Gracie Fields'* disengaged side and took off some more of her troops.

Later, at about 1830, the minesweeper *Pangbourne* (which had just been holed on both sides above and below the waterline and had had 13 killed and 11 wounded by near misses off Bray beach) went alongside the *Gracie Fields*, transferred about 80 British troops, and took her in tow. The M/S *Kellett*, carrying 550 troops from Bray beach, led the *Pangbourne*, whose compasses had been put out of action by bomb blast. At 0130 next morning the *Gracie*

---

[1] " At 1630 hours, a renewed spell of Luftwaffe activity began, . . . when none of our fighters was on the line. . . ." (*R.A.F. Narrative*, p.327).

Fields (in approx. position 51° 20′ N., 02° 05′ E) reported that she was sinking. The *Pangbourne* slipped the tow, took off the *Gracie Fields'* ship's company and abandoned her.

Grenade damaged

Meanwhile, at about the time that the *Jaguar* had left Dunkirk harbour, the *Express* (with 500 troops she had picked up from Bray beach) entered it to berth alongside the *Grenade* and embark more troops. Before she could do so, however, the previously mentioned second air attack took place, and the *Express* was near-missed ahead and astern. Only splinters came on board the *Express*, but the *Grenade* was damaged and had some casualties. The *Express* thereupon cleared out of the harbour.

Greyhound severely damaged, *Nautilus* sunk

The bombing between 1530 and 1600 was widespread[1]. The destroyer *Anthony*, which left La Panne for Dover at 1525 with 550 troops, was bombed at 1555 (and 1645), but the bombs fell wide. Off La Panne, at about 1600, a high level bombing attack was made on the destroyer *Greyhound*, on the mine-sweepers *Sutton* and *Salamander*, and on the paddle-minesweeper *Sandown*. The *Sutton* was straddled but no damage was done. In the dive-bomb attack which followed, however, the *Greyhound* was severely damaged by 2 near misses, and had 90 casualties, 20 of which were fatal. The Sp. S/V *Royal Eagle*, which was assisting in rescue work, escaped damage, but the trawler *Nautilus*, which had already ferried some 600 troops from the beach, was straddled by bombs and had her engines and steering gear put out of action. Making water rapidly, she managed to get alongside the *Greyhound* and transfer to her the 150 troops she was carrying. The *Nautilus*, already 6 feet down in the water and sinking, was then abandoned and set on fire.

The *Greyhound* limped back to Dover carrying 506 troops, but for 4 hours of the passage she was in tow of the Polish destroyer *Blyskawica* which had been on patrol with the destroyer *Vega* in the vicinity of the West Hinder buoy. The *Greyhound* took no further part in " Dynamo."

Waverley sunk

Meanwhile, at about 1630, the *Cyclone* left the harbour with 500 troops on board en route for Dover. Near Kwint Bank buoy she saw the minesweeper *Waverley* sinking ; a bomb had struck her on the port quarter and passed right through her bottom, leaving a hole about 6 feet in diameter. Four of the 600 troops she had embarked from La Panne beach were killed and a number wounded. When the *Waverley* sank, many of her troops were left swimming or trying to keep afloat, but the numbers thinned out considerably within 15/20 minutes[2]. The *Cyclone* picked up 158. About an hour later the Sp. S/V *Golden Eagle* picked up 285 and, guided by a plane, the tug *Java* and 2 drifters picked up a few more.

Canterbury damaged

While these air attacks had been going on the *Canterbury* had embarked 1,960 troops from the east pier. During a brief lull in the bombing, at about

---

[1] " From the vessels off-shore there came a series of signals, between 1545 and 1555 hours, to the effect that the anchorages at Bray and La Panne were being bombed. These attacks seem to have begun at about 1430 . . . when none of our aircraft were on the line. . ." (*R.A.F. Narrative*, p.327).

[2] Report by the Captain of the *Waverley*.

1650, she left the harbour, but soon after was damaged by a near miss. She was able to reach Dover, but took no further part in " Dynamo." At 1720 the berth vacated by the *Canterbury* in Dunkirk harbour was taken by the destroyer *Verity*.

Intrepid severely damaged

Meanwhile, at 1700, the *Intrepid*, hurrying back to Dunkirk from Dover (where she had disembarked 661 troops), was bombed between Middelkerke Bank and La Panne. A near miss caused severe damage, started fires, and killed 2 and wounded 19. The *Intrepid* had to return to Dover, and took no further part in Operation " Dynamo."

Hospital ship deliberately bombed

At 1700 also, the H/C *St. Julien, en route* for Dunkirk harbour, was deliberately bombed " for a considerable period " in the vicinity of Nieuport Bank buoy[1]; she was slightly damaged by near misses. The *St. Julien* lay off Dunkirk harbour for about $\frac{1}{2}$ an hour waiting for an opportunity to enter; when air attacks recommenced, however, she sailed for Dover without having entered the harbour.

At 1730 the *Siroco* sailed from Dunkirk harbour with 500 troops and a little later was joined outside by the *Mistral* which had only embarked 4 troops. Both the French destroyers proceeded to Dover. The *Mistral* took no further part in " Dynamo."

Grenade hit, *Calvi* and *Fenella* sunk

At about 1750 *the third air attack* was made over Dunkirk harbour by waves of bombers; some 100 bombs were dropped. Allied fighters, being engaged by enemy fighters, were unable to interfere with the bombing[2]. A near miss blew a hole in the *Grenade's* side; the trawler *Calvi*, lying outside the *John Cattling*, received a direct hit and sank immediately. Her masts and funnel were above water, and her ensign remained flying from the foremast. The personnel vessel *Fenella*, which by then had 650 troops on board, was hit on the promenade deck; a second bomb hit the pier, and blew some concrete through the *Fenella's* side below the waterline; a third bomb, falling between the pier and the *Fenella's* side, wrecked the engine room. The *Fenella's* troops were disembarked on to the pier and re-embarked in the *Crested Eagle*. The *Fenella* was abandoned while sinking. The P/V *St. Seiriol*, which shortly before had secured alongside the outer east pier, astern of the *Crested Eagle*, cast off and shifted eastward to the beaches.

Grenade hit, set on fire, and abandoned

Then five minutes after the third air attack had begun the *Grenade* received two direct hits; her engines were put out of action and she caught fire. As she swung round, some of her ships company were able to step on board the damaged trawler *Polly Johnson*. The *Verity* (which had been continuously

---

[1] Reports by *Pangbourne* and *Lydd*.

[2] According to the *R.A.F. Narrative*, p.327, two Hurricane squadrons which arrived at 1710 were attacked by large numbers of Me. 109's; one Spitfire squadron was attacked from above and behind at 1715, and another was in combat with enemy fighters at 1740. " None of our squadrons encountered enemy bombers, and the attacks on our shipping between 1630 and 1745 hours (resulting, amongst other casualties, in the *Crested Eagle* being hit and beached off Bray) can thus not have been interfered with by our patrols ". *R.A.F. Narrative*, p.327).

straddled by bombs for 35 minutes), seeing that traffic all along the east pier had ceased, cast off, and skirting the burning *Grenade* and the sunken *Calvi*, proceeded out of harbour, grounding slightly on a sunk drifter in the entrance.

The troops now began climbing out of one ship into another ; but, acting on the instructions of the Piermaster Cdr. J. C. Clouston, R.N., Lieut. Bill (*Fyldea*) restored order.

At 1815 the *Grenade* was abandoned and her Captain, Cdr. R. C. Boyle, R.N., having made arrangements with the Piermaster to tow her clear of the fairway, embarked with some of his ship's company in the *Crested Eagle*.

Polly Johnson sunk

The burning wreck of the *Grenade* did, in fact, commence to drift down on to the five remaining Oropesa trawlers. The *John Cattling* was instructed to attempt to pull her clear, and the remaining 4 trawlers, with troops and survivors on board, proceeded out of the harbour towards the beaches. A little later, near Nieuport Bank buoy, the *Polly Johnson*, leaking badly as a result of the damage caused by a near miss in the first air attack, and with damaged engine, was abandoned ; the *Arley* embarked her crew and troops and sank her by gunfire.

Grenade blown up

The *Grenade* was guided into a pocket to the westward of the main channel. She burned fiercely for some hours and then blew up.

Crested Eagle blazing, is beached

Meanwhile, when the *Verity* left the harbour at 1755, the *Crested Eagle* swung clear of the east pier and proceeded on an easterly course. Shortly afterwards, however, she was hit by 4 bombs and caught fire ; out of control, she continued under way. The *Verity* instructed the *Crested Eagle* to stop so that she might transfer her troops ; but the *Crested Eagle* could not stop. At about 1830, blazing fiercely fore and aft (she was a wooden ship) the *Crested Eagle* ran aground west of Bray beach. The 200 survivors, who could be seen in the water, were heavily machine-gunned from the air, and the ships that came to the rescue were bombed. Some of the survivors, several with severe burns, were picked up by the minesweepers *Hebe* and *Lydd* ; others, including the Captain and other survivors of the *Grenade*, by the minesweeper *Albury*. Among those picked up by the *Sabre* was the Second Engineer of the *Crested Eagle* and a stoker from the *Grenade*.

Normannia sunk

In the course of this third air attack the personnel vessel *Normannia* was hit by a bomb off 11 W buoy. She was towed clear of Dunkirk channel by the gunboat *Mosquito*, then began to sink. The *Mosquito* and the minesweeper *Ross* took off the crew and the few troops that were on board. The *Normannia* sank off 11 W buoy at about 0245 the following day.

Saladin severely damaged, *Lorina* sunk

The fourth air attack, which was widespread, took place between about 1830 and 2000. Ships returning to England were bombed. There were continuous attacks off Bray beach and its vicinity ; the destroyers *Sabre*, *Verity* and *Saladin* in company there were attacked ; the *Saladin*, attacked 10 times, was so severely damaged in the engine room by a near miss that she had to return to Dover at 15 knots, and could take no further part in "Dynamo." The personnel vessel *Lorina* was bombed and sunk at about this period, but no details are forthcoming.

Icarus damaged

The destroyer *Icarus*, which had been embarking troops off Zuydcoote, and in addition had embarked about 470 from the skoot *Doggersbank*, was attacked by 10 dive bombers at 1830. She received only slight damage from near misses but had 1 killed and 25 wounded.

King Orry sunk

The armed boarding vessel *King Orry* arrived at Dunkirk harbour at about 1900, to find it apparently occupied only by burning and sinking ships. She herself was immediately subjected to a bombing attack which put her steering gear out of action and shattered all her instruments. Further air attacks, and damage by near misses ensued. Realising the risk of the ship blocking the channel, S.N.O. Dunkirk instructed her Captain, shortly after midnight, to take her out of harbour. She struggled out at 0230/30, but when clear of the harbour entrance the *King Orry* foundered. Several ships, including the drifter *Vivacious*, the trawler *Lord Grey*, and a D.C./M.B., picked up survivors.

Isle of Guernsey deliberately bombed

At about the same time that the *King Orry* was being bombed, the M/S *Halcyon* witnessed the deliberate bombing of the hospital carrier *Isle of Guernsey*. She was bombed by 10 planes off Dunkirk harbour while attempting to pick up an airman. The airman was subsequently picked up by the *Halcyon*. Although damaged by near misses, the *Isle of Guernsey* entered the harbour after dark and embarked 490 wounded in the early hours of 30th May. She then proceeded to Newhaven, but was not repaired in time to make another trip to Dunkirk.

Bideford's stern blown off

The air onslaught had not yet, however, come to an end. The sloop *Bideford* had arrived off Bray beach at 1730. At 1750 the first boat loads of troops (mostly French) came alongside. "The boats," says her Captain, Lt. Cdr. J. H. Lewes, R.N., "were dangerously overcrowded and several swamped on the way off from the shore. On arrival alongside, the men would all jump on board and let their boats drift off on the tide. Paddles were lost overboard, rendering the boats useless. *Bideford's* M/B was lowered and ordered to collect and tow inshore any empty boats. The whaler was lowered and 2 officers and a signalman were sent in to endeavour to take charge on the beach . . . . this was next to impossible. The men rushed the boats and capsized them in shallow water, and then left the boats without making any attempt to right them and use them again. There were only 2 motor landing craft in the vicinity. One [A.L.C.17] had one engine out of action; the other [A.L.C.16] was blown up subsequently when lying alongside the ship."

Dive-bombing attacks commenced on the *Bideford* at about 1915. She was then machine-gunned by low flying aircraft. At 2007 four bombs were dropped; one landed 30 yards away; one hit the quarter deck; and one hit or near missed the stern, detonating a depth charge. About 40 feet of the *Bideford's* stern was blown away completely; a further 40 feet was reduced to a tangled mass of metal; the mainmast fell in 3 pieces on the searchlight and machine gun platforms, wrecking them both ; the bridge superstructure was severely shaken, a bulkhead was dished, and several frames cracked.   Of the ship's company, 3 officers and 13 men were killed, 1 officer and 18 men wounded ; of the passengers, 2 officers and 10 men were killed and 2 officers wounded.   Then a fire broke out, and orders were given to flood the magazine and burn the signal books.   A further dive bomb attack took place, but the bombs fell wide.   The *Bideford* anchored.

The M/S *Kellett* came alongside the *Bideford*, and took off about 300 troops, and the tug *St. Clears* endeavoured to take the *Bideford* in tow ; she was, however, fast aground, and the tow parted.   The dr. *Havant* then tried to take her in tow, but again the tow parted.

Bideford towed to Dover

During the night of 29th–30th May, 350 French and 50 British troops embarked in the *Bideford*.   Near dawn, the gunboat *Locust*, carrying 620 British and French troops from La Panne beach, passed a tow to the *Bideford*, and at daylight she floated – in tow.   At less than 2½ knots course was set for Dover ; *en route*, during the first 3 miles, the tow parted 3 times.   Throughout the 30th May the *Locust* struggled on with her burden.   During the night a French soldier jumped overboard, fully equipped.   The tow was stopped, a buoy was dropped and a boat lowered ; but, in spite of good visibility and a calm sea, the unknown soldier was not recovered although a search was made for 30 minutes.   In spite of the tow again parting, the *Bideford* reached Dover at 1130 on the 31st May and disembarked 436 troops.

The momentous issues at stake in Operation " Dynamo " were not to be attained without grievous losses, but the *Bideford's* heroic voyage to safety marked a momentary respite from the rapidly mounting toll of lives and ships.

Twelve hundred troops wade out to a skoot

At about 2300 on the 29th May the skoot *Patria* arrived off Bray from Ramsgate and, in the glow of the still burning *Crested Eagle*, saw troops on the beach. The Captain of the *Patria*, who decided to ground his ship, records that " The troops, holding hands, waded out and clambered on board by nets, ladders and ropes' ends.   The sight of two solid phalanxes of men, delineated by phosphorescence in the water and steadily advancing to the ship, will be memorable. . . . Over 1,000 men were embarked in just over two hours."   Among them were naval ratings – casualties with severe burns from the *Grenade*, the *Crested Eagle* and the *Fenella*.

Dover unaware of losses

Little information of the disastrous losses of the afternoon and early evening filtered through to Dover, except that it was known that Dunkirk was under heavy bombardment and that destroyers there were being hit soon after 1600.[1]

Lord Gort and 3rd Corps at La Panne

Earlier in the day other important information had, however, come through to Dover, and at 0127 the Vice-Admiral, Dover, informed the *Calcutta* that Lord Gort and the 3rd Corps of the B.E.F. were at La Panne, and that every effort was to be made to concentrate destroyers and light craft at that end of the beach and embark the force.

---

[1] D.R.

Calcutta contacts Lord Gort

On receipt of this signal at 0345 the *Calcutta*, which had already been embarking troops from La Panne beach, sent her boats in again, in charge of Mr. F. J. March, Gunner. Mr. March made personal contact with Lord Gort about 8 miles inland, and placed the *Calcutta* at his disposal for his or his staff's evacuation. Lord Gort, however, " courteously refused " to be evacuated at this stage[1].

La Panne beach cleared of troops

Meanwhile the *Calcutta* was proceeding with the embarkation, having enlisted the assistance of the minesweepers *Sutton* and *Salamander*, the tug *Java*, five drifters[2], and three motor launches[3]. By 1357 the *Calcutta* had embarked 1200 troops, with whom she proceeded to Sheerness.

In addition to the ships assisting the *Calcutta*, 7 minesweepers[4], 4 skoots[5], and 5 destroyers[6] also embarked troops from La Panne beach. Of the destroyers, the *Greyhound* was bombed and severely damaged (see p.42). The minesweepers embarked, in all, 3415 troops, the skoots 1137 and the destroyers 2100. The tramp *Yewdale* and the motor vessels *Beal* and *Bullfinch* between them brought off 1,854. The assault landing craft *A.L.C.15* ferried about 750 troops from the beaches to off-lying ships, and finally transported 25 to Dover ; the *A.L.C.5* also ferried troops throughout the day.

The paddle-minesweeper *Oriole* had beached herself at La Panne at about 0600, thus permitting about 2,500 troops to pass over her decks to be embarked by other ships before she refloated at about 1800. In this connection, Sub-Lieut. Croswell, who had been landed at La Panne at about 0600 with a small beach party in the *Harvester's* motor skiff, says : " On the beach we found 14 boats which we launched. A line ferry was established from a paddle-steamer [the *Oriole*] which was aground close inshore, and this steamer served as a pier alongside which other boats were able to come. . . . Throughout the day embarkation continued."

Later in his report, Sub-Lieut. Croswell says : " About 1400 . . . . bombing commenced – there were no casualties though 8 heavy bombs fell within 100 yards of the place of embarkation. A supply ship [the danlayer *Nautilus*] to the right of the beach was fired and destroyed by a near miss, and a destroyer [the *Greyhound*] was hit by an incendiary bomb [in fact she was severely damaged by a near miss] but continued in action. I joined up with the Army Staff controlling evacuation – there were no other naval officers at La Panne.[7] About 2300 . . . . I requested that piers should be built but was told nothing could be done that night. . . . Lord Gort arrived on the beach on Thursday morning [30th May] and asked what could be done to assist. I again suggested erection of piers, and under Colonel Porter's direction this was begun, the pier at La Panne being ready and in use by 1400".

---

[1] *Calcutta's* report.

[2] The *Golden Sunbeam*, *Lord Rodney*, *Lord Keith*, *Lord St. Vincent*, and *Lord Collingwood*.

[3] The *Angler II*, *Nayland* and *New Britannic*.

[4] The *Emperor of India*, *Gracie Fields*, *Halcyon*, *Hebe*, *Oriole*, *Princess Elizabeth* and *Waverley*.

[5] The *Reiger*, *Doggersbank*, *Jutland* and *Oranje*.

[6] The *Shikari*, *Harvester*, *Anthony*, *Sabre* and *Greyhound*.

[7] Sub. Lt. Croswell was not given orders by his commanding officer to remain ashore. He says " as at La Panne there was no liaison between Army and Navy, I realised I could do a much more useful job by remaining there," and he stayed there until 1st June. Commenting on this, Lt. Cdr. M. Thornton, R.N., Captain of the *Harvester* says : " This young officer wisely accepted responsibility of missing his ship and then took charge of the beaches and embarkation. . . ." (C.W.23187/40.)

More Personnel ships feel the strain

In the early hours of 29th May information was received at Dover that the personnel vessels (manned by Mercantile Marine crews) were having difficulty in making the entrance to Dunkirk harbour in the face of the navigational difficulties caused by the heavy pall of smoke over the entrance, and the bombing and shelling encountered *en route* to, and off, Dunkirk. After completing one round trip during the previous 24 hours, the Captain of the *St. Seiriol* felt unable to sail and an officer, (Lt. A. R. MacKewn, R.N.R.) took the ship over and sailed at 1100.   On her return voyage the ship was bombed and damaged[1], and did not sail again.

Parties to supplement ships' crews were lent to three personnel vessels and a hospital carrier[2] and to various drifters and motor boats.[3]

Commodore E. G. de S. Jukes-Hughes, R.N., who was Principal Sea Transport Officer at Dover during "Dynamo," says that on two occasions Sea Transport Officers took the place of Officers in personnel ships and proceeded to sea in them. "The effect of the personality of the Master," he says, "was very noticeable. A strong Master carried his crew with him and imbued them with his spirit. A weak Master only succeeded in disturbing his crew."[4]

Surf. More ships sent to Dunkirk

S.N.O., Dunkirk, and other Senior Officers on the French coast reported during the early hours of 29th May that surf on the beaches was retarding boat-work[5]. At 0709 S.N.O., Dunkirk, reported that embarkation from Dunkirk was going on at the rate of 2,000 an hour and asked for all ships to go to Dunkirk harbour[6]. An increased number of H.M. ships was therefore sent to the harbour, in spite of the danger that an accumulation of ships alongside the east pier at Dunkirk by day might well invite an intensive air attack – and, as has been seen, it actually did so.   In view, however, of the military situation the limitations of Dunkirk harbour (with its narrow gangway along the east pier), and the probability of the surf reducing as the tide rose, the Vice-Admiral, Dover, continued to send a proportion of ships to the beaches.[7]

Route Y under gunfire

Meanwhile, at 1100, enemy troops were reported north-east of Nieuport, and shortly after noon enemy shore batteries near Nieuport brought the Zuydcoote Pass (on Route Y) under spasmodic gunfire. The southern Route Z was already under fire from the guns at Calais and Gravelines, so that Route X would soon be the only practicable *daylight* approach to Dunkirk and the beaches. By 1606 Route X was fully swept, and all ships were ordered to use it ; ships from Dover, however, were instructed to use Route Z, provided the passage between Calais Bell Buoy and Dunkirk could be made in darkness.

Route X passed some 26 miles to the south-west of the extreme north-east point of Route Y, the locality in which E-boat attack threatened, and the

---

[1] Authority for this is V. A. Dover's *Report on Personnel Vessels*, M011882/40. No report by the officers or owners of the *St. Seiriol* mentions that she was damaged. She apparently did not sail again because her crew were in an overwrought state. (R.O.III, p.213, – 219).

[2] The *Canterbury, Lady of Mann, Princess Maud* and the H/C *St. Julien.*

[3] Report by officer in charge of No. 3 Party (R.O.III, p.416).

[4] R.O.III, p.564.

[5] See Appendix 0.1.

[6] Appendix 0.2.

[7] D.R., p.6, para. 24.

route was shielded by the French minefields in the Ruytingen and Dyck channels. The E-boat Command apparently failed to appreciate this withdrawal of traffic to the south-west, and did not follow up.[1]

Barge piers impracticable

The considerable alarm as to the immediate safety of the B.E.F. felt during the night of 27th/28th and the forenoon of 28th May, which caused all available resources to be immediately concentrated on the French coast, eased during the 29th. But emergency measures taken late on the 28th had an adverse effect on the orderly organisation for evacuation so necessary if effective measures were to be devised and put in force[2]. On the 29th, for instance, the practicability was considered of building piers on the beaches to facilitate embarkation, using lines of barges[3]; but reports from ships that worked off the beaches showed that the very gradual shoaling of the water at all states of the tide would necessitate such piers being inordinately long, and beyond the resources available. A much needed Medical Party was shipped in the *Verity* for use on the beaches, and a Naval Medical Party was sent to Dunkirk.

Captain Howson sails for Dunkirk

As the result of a report of an Army Officer recently evacuated it was decided that a party of Naval officers was required on the beaches between La Panne and Dunkirk. Accordingly, Captain J. M. Howson R.N., with Commanders H. G. Gorton and R. J. O. Otway-Ruthven, R.N., Lt. Cdrs. Cockburn, R.N. and R. G. Wardrop, R.D., R.N.R., and Lieuts. Whalley, Nettle and Jones sailed at 1600 in the *Sabre* for Dunkirk.[4] Captain Howson arrived at Dunkirk at 1815 to find that S.N.O., Dunkirk, had been away at La Panne since noon on a visit to Lord Gort. Captain Tennant returned to Dunkirk at about 2140, and at 2300 Captain Howson was able to have a consultation with him. Captain Howson then divided the beach party into two; 3 officers under Cdr. Gorton proceeded to the beach east of Bray, and two officers under Cdr. Otway-Ruthven to the beach at Bray. Captain Howson went with the latter party. These appointments appear to have had good results, for embarkations at the beaches reached peak next day.

Rear-Admiral, Dover sails for Dunkirk,

Captain E. W. Bush, D.S.C., R.N., had also taken passage in the *Sabre* at 1600, to act as " S.N.O. afloat off the beaches " in the *Hebe*[5]; but an hour and a half later, the Admiralty appointed Rear-Admiral W. F. Wake-Walker, O.B.E. as *Rear-Admiral, Dover*, " for command of sea-going ships and vessels off the Belgian coast ", and left it to the Vice-Admiral, Dover, to decide in which ship the R.A., Dover, should fly his flag[6]. Rear-Admiral Wake-Walker, who was to take over from Captain Bush[7], sailed in the destroyer *Esk* at 2000 for Dunkirk. With him on board were Vice-Admiral (acting Commodore) G. O. Stephenson, C.B., C.M.G., and Vice-Admiral (acting Commodore) T. J. Hallett, C.B., C.B.E. Also on board were 12 officers and 60 ratings to act as beach parties. On the way over he arranged that Commodore Stephenson

---

[1] D.R. p.9, para. 29.
[2] D.R. p.7, para. 27.
[3] Appendix G.
[4] Captain Howson's report. (R.O.III, p.394).
[5] D.R. p.9, para. 30, and R.O.III, p.394.
[6] Appendix O.4.
[7] D.R. p.11, para. 36.

should take charge off La Panne and Commodore Hallett off Bray. It was then thought, says Rear-Admiral Wake-Walker, that the embarkation could hardly go on for more than a day or two, and each day was expected to be the last. At this time, he says, he had very little idea of what it was going to be possible to do, or how to set about it.[4]

As early as 1321 V.A. Dover had informed " Ships and Authorities, Nore and Dover Forces," and S.N.O., Dunkirk, that all vessels arriving at Dunkirk were to report for orders to Captain Bush, S.N.O.(A), in *Hebe*. Following the Admiralty's appointment of Rear-Admiral Wake-Walker, however, V.A. Dover sent a further signal, at 1943, informing S.N.O., Dunkirk and *Hebe* that R. A. Wake-Walker was proceeding to the *Hebe* to carry out the duties of S.N.O., Dunkirk, in charge of all embarkation arrangements[2]. On the next day, the 30th May, presumably to clarify the situation, the Vice-Admiral Dover sent the following signal[3] to all authorities concerned :

" . . . . Authority for Operation Dynamo under V.A. Dover is as follows :
R.A. Wake-Walker has been appointed as R.A. Dover, for command of seagoing ships and vessels off the Belgian coast.
R.A. Dover has hoisted his flag in *Hebe*. Captain Tennant has been appointed as S.N.O. Dunkirk, and is responsible under R.A. Dover for all shore organisation. T.O.O. 1328/30."

Plan for the night 29th/30th May

Meanwhile, at 1906, the Vice-Admiral, Dover promulgated the plan for the night by signal[4] as follows :

"Evacuation of British troops to continue at maximum speed during the night. If adequate supply of personnel vessels cannot be maintained to Dunkirk east pier destroyers will be sent there as well. All other craft except hospital carriers to embark from beach which is extended from one mile east of Dunkirk to one mile east of La Panne. Whole length is divided into 3 equal parts referred to as La Panne, Bray, Malo, from east to west with a mile gap between each part. La Panne and Bray have troop concentration points each end and in middle ; Malo at each end. These points should be tended by inshore craft. Pass this message by V/S to ships not equipped W/T as opportunity offers. 1906".

Dunkirk harbour reported blocked

Almost at the same time he received (through the War Office and the Admiralty) a telephone message from La Panne military headquarters to the effect that Dunkirk harbour was blocked by damaged ships, and that all evacuation must therefore be effected from the beaches.[5]

" Pier undamaged", but " impossible. . . embark. . . troops "

About the same time as this telephone message came through a corrupt message from S.N.O., Dunkirk, was received, stating : " continuous bombing, one destroyer sinking, one transport with troops on board damaged and impossible at present to embark more troops, though pier undamaged".[6]

---

[1] M.017978/41, p.3.
[2] It was not until 0100/30 that Admiral Wake-Walker found the *Hebe*, and he took over from Captain Bush at 0400. (Report by Admiral Wake-Walker).
[3] Appendix O.5.
[4] Appendix O.11.
[5] " Apparently incorrect information as to the blocking of Dunkirk harbour had been telephoned by Cdr. Dove from La Panne." (S.N.O. Dunkirk's report, R.O.III, p.350).
[6] D.R. p.10, para. 33. The destroyer was presumably the *Grenade*.
Note : S.N.O. Dunkirk went to La Panne by motor boat at 1200 (R.O.III, p.348). He did not return to Dunkirk until about 2100 (Report by Capt. Howson – R.O.III, p.394). The corrupt message referred to by V.A. Dover was therefore sent in his absence.

No contact with S.N.O. Dunkirk

At 2057 the Vice-Admiral, Dover, asked the *Verity* and the S.N.O., Dunkirk, whether the harbour *was* blocked[1]. At 2120 the *Verity* replied that the eastern half of the channel was blocked, and that on leaving the harbour she had grounded slightly on a sunken drifter in the entrance. S.N.O. Dunkirk replied at 2150 that the harbour was *not* blocked, but that it was doubtful whether much more could be done during daylight hours[2]. It is not known if or when this reply was received, because as late as 2357 V.A. Dover signalled *Admiral Abrial*, " I cannot get in touch with Captain Tennant. Can you inform me whether it is still possible for transports to enter harbour and berth alongside."

It is noteworthy that *reception* on the Naval W/T set at Dunkirk was not established until 2300 on the 30th May, and *full communication* with Dover was not established on the set until daylight on the 31st May.[3]

Vice-Admiral, Dover, diverts all ships to the beaches

Indeed, already at 2128, the situation, as it could be seen by the staff at Dover, was confused, and it seemed probable that the use of Dunkirk harbour would be denied to us except possibly for small ships[4]. Consequently, the Vice-Admiral, Dover, ordered all ships approaching Dunkirk not to close the harbour, but to remain off the eastern beach and collect troops from the shore[5]; drifters and minesweepers which were about to be despatched to Dunkirk harbour were also diverted to the beach[6].

A good opportunity at Dunkirk missed

In the event, only 4 drifters and a yacht[7] entered Dunkirk during the hours of darkness, and as only 2 bombing attacks were made a good opportunity was missed. It is probable that about 10,000 troops could have been lifted from the harbour during the night with little reduction of the numbers embarked from the beaches[8]. Nevertheless, it was only by good fortune that the vital Dunkirk channel was not blocked by sinking ships at this early date[9].

Admiralty's urgent call for small craft

Meanwhile, during the forenoon of the 29th May, in response to the insistent call for beaching craft, the Admiralty called on the C's in C. Portsmouth and the Nore " to investigate as a matter of urgency " the provision of additional small motor craft and X and other self-propelled lighters, which could be made available within 48 hours from all ports in their Commands[10]. Thereafter, the supply of beaching craft increased rapidly.

The A.L.C.'s arrive off the beaches

On this day, however, only the first trickle of the anxiously awaited small motor craft began to arrive off the beaches. The most important arrivals

---

[1] S.N.O. Dunkirk's report. (R.O.III, p.350).
[2] Appendix O.12.
[3] See p. 67.
[4] D.R. p.10, para. 34.
[5] D.R. p.10, para. 34.
[6] D.R. p.10, para. 34.
[7] The 4 drifters of the 1st M/R Flotilla – the *Fidget, Fisher Boy, Jacketa* and *Silver Dawn* – and the yacht *Bystander*.
[8] D.R. p.10, para. 35.
[9] V.A. Dover's letter No. A 14/0/876/40 of 10th June 1940 (covering his report on Operation Dynamo), para. 7(b).
[10] Appendix G.14.

were the 8 assault landing craft (A.L.C.'s), under the command of Cdr. R. A. Cassidi, R.N., which had been loaded into, and brought over by, the S.S. *Clan Macalister*. They were *A.L.C.'s 3, 4, 5, 8, 15, 16, 17* and *18*. While *A.L.C.4* was being hoisted out, off No. 6 W buoy, at about 1030, the dr. *Vanquisher* passed at speed, causing the *Clan Macalister* to roll heavily ; *A.L.C.4* crashed down on *A.L.C.18* and both craft were rendered unfit for service. The remaining six A.L.C.'s however, did valuable work ferrying some thousands of troops from the beaches.

French troops rush *A.L.C.5*.

Cdr. Cassidi, who was in *A.L.C.5* proceeded some way up the coast and then carried on inshore ; his craft was " immediately rushed on all sides by French soldiers, so many of them got on board that the boat was grounded."[1] Some of the troops had to be forced off the boat before she could be got off the beach. The second attempt to embark French troops failed, so *A.L.C.5* proceeded to La Panne beach[1]. Thence, British troops were ferried to off-lying ships at the rate of about 3 trips an hour, 50 men per trip, throughout the day, except for interruptions by frequent air attacks. The *A.L.C.5* made 15 trips.

A.L.C.16 is sunk

The *A.L.C.16* (S/Lt. R. O. Wilcoxon, R.N.V.R.) made 7 trips, after which " she was boarded by French soldiers, who overwhelmed the boat to such an extent that she became partially swamped, the starboard battery was flooded and both engines failed. Eventually sufficient French were evicted to enable *A.L.C.16* to be floated off and the port engine started"[2]. In going astern, however, the port stern tube was damaged and water poured into the boat ; nevertheless, continually pumping and bailing, *A.L.C.16* continued ferrying for a further 1½ hours. She then went alongside the sloop *Bideford* to transfer a load of troops. S/Lt. Wilcoxon went on board the *Bideford* to arrange for a tow back to England. Then came the dive-bomb attack in which the *Bideford's* stern was blown off. S/Lt. Wilcoxon was mortally wounded. *A.L.C.16* was heavily damaged, and sank in a few minutes ; she had ferried about 600 troops.

French troops rush *A.L.C.17*

A.L.C.17 followed *A.L.C.5* up the coast towards Bray beach. " On approaching the beach she was promptly boarded by a crowd of French troops who so overloaded the boat that she grounded"[3]. With a falling tide she remained stranded for 3 hours. As the tide rose, " the French. . . . again attempted to rush the boat [but] the cox'n of *A.L.C.17* procured the assistance of some British troops, who, drove off the French "[3]. Ferrying was continued all day and throughout the night from La Panne, until the *A.L.C.17's* engines broke down ; she was towed by a drifter to England next day for repairs. *A.L.C.'s 3*, and *8* also ferried troops, and transported 20 and 10 troops respectively to Dover, where they arrived at 0400 next day.

M/B *Minikoi* sunk

One of the earliest of the privately owned M/B's to start for the beaches was the *Minikoi*. Unfortunately, at 0015/29, while still in the Downs, she was rammed and sunk by the *M.A./S.B.6*, which picked up her crew of three.

---

[1] Report by *A.L.C.5*.
[2] Report by *A.L.C.16*.
[3] Report by *A.L.C.17*.

M/B *Sceneshifter* swamped and lost

The M/B *Silver Moon*, from Ramsgate, arrived off the beaches at 0800 and ferried troops to ships at anchor. Without charts or compass she returned to Ramsgate that night. The M/B *Sceneshifter*, on arrival, was rushed by French troops, swamped, and became a total loss.

M/B *Viewfinder* dragged aground and lost

The six motor yachts, *Advance, Bobeli, Elizabeth Green, Hanora, Reda* and *Viewfinder* sailed from Dover for La Panne beach and were machine-gunned from the air off Gravelines. They arrived off La Panne beach at about 1500/29, and at once began towing whalers full of troops to off-lying ships. At 1830, the *Viewfinder* was dragged aground by Belgian soldiers and became a total loss.

M/B's *Hanora* and *Bobeli* abandoned

At 1900, the *Hanora* fouled her propeller and was abandoned; her crew transferred to the *Elizabeth Green* and thence to the minesweeper *Lydd*. At 1900 also, the dr. *Sabre* requisitioned the *Advance* and embarked in her a W/T transmitter and 2 operators for transportation to G.H.Q. at La Panne. The *Reda*, having ferried troops, sailed for Ramsgate at 2200 with 21 troops on board. The *Bobeli* having received some damage while alongside a destroyer which suddenly went full ahead on account of an air attack, subsequently fouled her screw and rudder; she made fast to the minesweeper *Albury*, but was abandoned when the *Albury* departed and became stranded on the beach. The *Elizabeth Green* and *Advance* sailed in company that night for Ramsgate.

M/B *Glitter II* brings drinking water

The *Glitter II* arrived off Bray beach at 1600 on the 29th May, loaded with tins of fresh water. She then ferried troops. Next day she lost her rudder and was towed to Dover by a drifter.

M/B *Queen of England* sunk

A number of other small motor craft left Southend, Sheerness or Dover for the beaches on the 29th May, but did not arrive until 30th May. Among them was the *Shamrock*, and in company with her were the *Princess Maud, Canvey Queen* and *Queen of England*. On the way over on the night of the 29th/30th May the *Queen of England* was rammed amidships by the skoot *Tilly* and sank immediately; her crew were picked up by the *Shamrock* and transferred to the *Tilly*[1]. The remaining three motor boats were all abandoned and lost next day after ferrying troops to various destroyers, among them the *Anthony*; the *Canvey Queen* and *Shamrock* fouled their propellers, and the *Princess Maud* went aground.

The *Mirasol*[2], alongside Dunkirk mole, was damaged by a near miss. She was taken in tow by a trawler, but later sank.

Other M/B's that sailed for the beaches on 29th May

The *Triton* and *Silver Queen*, with 6 motor launches in company, sailed for La Panne at 2200. Three of the motor launches broke down on the way over

---

[1] *Shamrock's* report, unconfirmed. The name of the vessel is in doubt; the matter is not referred to in *Tilly's* report.
[2] Commonly, but erroneously referred to in reports as the " *Marasole*."

and returned to harbour ; the remainder reached La Panne at 0500/30. The Dutch eel-boats *Johanna* and *Chantecler* and the M.B. *Golden Lily* also left Ramsgate at 2200/29. The *Chantecler* was only capable of 4 knots, and her " compass which was situated over the engine. . . . revolved slowly round and and round"[1]. She reached the beaches, however, at 0900 on the 30th May, and brought back 30 troops. The *Johanna* did not get over on this trip ; she had no charts, lost her way in the Downs in the darkness, and returned to Ramsgate on the morning of the 30th May. Later on that day she was towed to the beaches by the skoot *Jutland*.

Troops transported on 29th May

The 29th May closed with a formidable list of ships lost or damaged, a marked reduction in the number of destroyers available and with failure to achieve the high rate of evacuation hoped for. The effect of the day's occurrences was even more marked next day, when instead of the 50,000 to 60,000 British troops which had been calculated as the probable achievement, only 48,000 odd were in fact transported.[2]

Nevertheless, 47,310 troops (including some 2,000 casualties) were landed in England on the 29th May (see Table 2), 13,752 having been lifted from the beaches and 33,558 from the harbour. Only about $1\frac{1}{2}$ per cent of these were French troops[3], whose organised evacuation had not yet begun. (See Appendices Y.[2] to Y.[5]).

During the morning and forenoon of the 29th May, when there was no bombing of Dunkirk harbour, 10 personnel vessels[4] lifted 14,760 troops from the east pier ; during the afternoon, in spite of the bombing, the *Canterbury* lifted a further 1,960.

The development of beach evacuation is indicated by the fact that nearly $2\frac{1}{2}$ times the number of troops were lifted from the beaches on 29th May as compared with the number lifted on the previous day. Seventeen destroyers[5] each made one *round trip* during the 24 hours of the 29th May and an eighteenth destroyer, the *Icarus*, made two such trips. On these trips the 18 destroyers embarked and transported to England 10,694 troops of which 6,198 were lifted from the beaches and 4,506 from Dunkirk harbour. Nine minesweepers[6] together lifted 2,426 troops from the beaches although one of them, the *Albury* did not land her troops in England until the next day.[7] Among other ships which brought back troops from the beaches was the cruiser *Calcutta* with 1,200.

The record of troops landed in England now stood as follows :—

			From the beaches	From the harbour	Total for the day
26th May	.....	.....	Nil	Nil	Nil
27th May	.....	.....	Nil	7,669	7,669
28th May	.....	.....	5,930	11,874	17,804
29th May	.....	.....	13,752	33,558	47,310

---

[1] Report by *Chantecler*.

[2] D.R. p.11, para. 38.

[3] D.R., which incidentally puts the total of troops and casualties landed on 29th May as 40,724. This figure probably does not include troops carried by foreign ships (See Table 2).

[4] The *Côte d'Argent*, *Killarney*, *King George V*, *Maid of Orleans*, *Manxman*, *Prague*, *Royal Daffodil*, *Royal Sovereign*, *Scotia*, and *Tynwald*.

[5] The *Anthony*, *Codrington*, *Esk*, *Express*, *Greyhound*, *Harvester*, *Intrepid*, *Ivanhoe*, *Javelin*, *Malcolm*, *Sabre*, *Scimitar*, *Shikari*, *Vanquisher*, *Verity*, *Wolsey* and *Worcester*.

[6] The *Albury*, *Duchess of Fife*, *Emperor of India*, *Fitzroy*, *Halcyon*, *Hebe*, *Leda*, *Marmion* and *Sharpshooter*.

[7] See Table 3, *in conjunction with the reports of ships' proceedings in Vol. II.*

Ships lost or damaged on 29th May

H.M. SHIPS SUNK

The destroyers *Wakeful, Grafton* and *Grenade.*
The armed boarding vessel *King Orry*[1].
The Special Service Vessel *Crested Eagle.*
The Paddle Minesweepers *Waverley* and *Gracie Fields.*[1]
The Personnel Vessels *Normania,*[1] *Lorina, Fenella* and *Mona's Queen.*
The trawlers *Polly Johnson* and *Calvi.*
The danlayers *Comfort* and *Nautilus.*
The drifter *Girl Pamela*[2].

H.M. SHIPS DAMAGED AND PUT OUT OF ACTION.

The destroyers *Saladin, Greyhound, Intrepid, Montrose, Mackay, Gallant* and *Jaguar.*
The sloop *Bideford.*
The minesweeper *Pangbourne* (required dockyard repairs).
The personnel vessel *Canterbury.*
The hospital carrier *Isle of Guernsey.*

OTHER VESSELS

SUNK *A.L.C.16* , the S.S. *Clan Macalister* (6,900 tons), the M/B's *Minikoi, Viewfinder, Bobeli, Hanora, Sceneshifter* and *Queen of England.*

DAMAGED AND PUT OUT OF ACTION   The tug *Sun V.*

Destroyers of the " H," " I " and " J " Classes withdrawn

As a result of the heavy casualties and losses amongst the destroyer force, particularly the misfortunes which befell those of the larger and more modern types, a consultation was held between the Admiralty and the Vice-Admiral, Dover, on 29th May, which led to a decision to withdraw the 7 destroyers of the " H", " I" and " J" Classes from " Dynamo"[3]; they were the only modern destroyers remaining with Vice-Admiral, Dover. All destroyers of the "G" class[4] were already out of action.

There remained available for " Dynamo " 15 destroyers :—

Esk	*Malcolm*	*Verity*
Express	*Whitehall*	*Vanquisher*
Anthony	*Winchelsea*	*Sabre*
Keith	*Worcester*	*Scimitar*
Codrington	*Windsor*	*Shikari*

Excluding any casualties, this number of destroyers might be expected to maintain a flow of one destroyer per hour to the coast and would lift 17,000 troops in 24 hours[5]. It is noteworthy that in spite of their unsuitability for the work of *troop carrying*, the 39 destroyers so employed in " Dynamo " brought off more troops—96,000—than any other type of ship (see Table 1). The 45 personnel vessels brought off 87,000 ; the 36 minesweepers 46,000 ; the 39 skoots 22,000 ; and among the smaller vessels, the 51 drifters brought off 12,000.

---

[1] Actually sank on 30th May, as a result of damage received on 29th May.
[2] In collision with the *Lydd* off Dunkirk harbour on the night of 28th/29th May.
[3] The *Icarus, Impulsive, Intrepid, Ivanhoe, Harvester, Havant* and *Javelin.*
[4] The *Gallant, Grafton, Grenade* and *Greyhound.*
[5] D.R. p.11, para. 37.

CHAPTER VII

THURSDAY, 30TH MAY

French and British troops to embark in equal proportions

By the 30th May Lord Gort estimated the British troops remaining in the area at 80,000, and he set about completing his plans for their final withdrawal. He had received the following telegram from the Secretary of State for War :—

> "Continue to defend present perimeter to the utmost in order to cover maximum evacuation now proceeding well. . . . If we can still communicate with you we shall send you an order to return to England with such officers as you may choose at the moment when we deem your command so reduced that it can be handed to a Corps Commander. You should now nominate this commander. If communications are broken you are to hand over and return as specified when your effective fighting force does not exceed equivalent of three divisions. This is in accordance with correct military procedure and no personal discretion is left to you in the matter. . . . The Corps Commander chosen by you should be ordered to carry on defence and evacuation with French whether from Dunkirk or beaches. . . ."

The problem, as Lord Gort saw it, was to thin out the troops, while maintaining a proper defence of the perimeter, with a force which could be embarked finally in one lift.[1]

Meanwhile Lord Gort had received orders from home that French and British troops were to embark in equal proportions, and early next morning this policy of H.M. Government was also promulgated by the Admiralty to the V.A. Dover, R.A. Dover Straits (i.e. Rear-Admiral Wake-Walker), and S. N. O. Dunkirk.[2]

The adoption of this policy, desirable as it was, made Lord Gort's problem more difficult, and necessitated a prolongation of the time that the existing perimeter, or a smaller one, must be held, to enable all the troops to embark. " Yet the enemy pressure was increasing and there was no depth in our position. A line on the dunes could only be held during the hours of darkness to cover the final phase of the withdrawal".[1]

After discussing the situation with the Commanders of the 1st and 2nd Corps, Lord Gort came to the conclusion that the eastern end of the perimeter could not be held much longer, as the enemy had already begun to shell the beach at La Panne. He therefore motored to Dunkirk to inform Admiral Abrial of his views and to assure himself that the arrangements for embarking British and French troops in equal proportions were working smoothly. Admiral Abrial assured Lord Gort of his agreement about the evacuation of the sector, and the problem of embarkation was discussed.[1]

Judging that it would be imprudent to continue to maintain the British position on the perimeter, outside the permanent defences of Dunkirk, for more than another 24 hours, Lord Gort decided to withdraw the 2nd Corps on the night of 31st May/1st June, and the necessary moves began to take place on the morning of the 31st May.[1]

Naval situation

So far as the Navy was concerned it was not easy to appreciate the situation at Dunkirk and off the beaches. As an example of the difficulty of doing so,

---

[1] Lord Gort's Second Despatch, para. 57.
[2] Appendix Y.3.

Admiral Ramsay records that, at 0030/30[1], the S.N.O. on the French coast (Rear-Admiral Wake-Walker) reported that he had no destroyers, though in fact, at that time, all available destroyers (namely ten) in the Dover Command were either on the coast, or on passage, while the remaining 5 were at Dover discharging troops embarking ammunition, fuelling, etc., and were to sail within the next 4 hours. Simultaneously, says Admiral Ramsay, " the V.C.I.G.S. reported[2] that the beaches were well organised, the troops in good heart, and there had been no bombing since dark, but that there was still a great shortage of small craft which were urgently required. " This last fact", says Admiral Ramsay, " was well known to the Vice-Admiral, Dover "[3].

In fact, on practically every occasion when officers on and off the coast complained of the lack of ships, investigation of ship's reports goes to show that all ships were working to their utmost capacity and that the only reason for their absence in any one place was that they could not be in two places at once. The sharp rise in the numbers of troops landed in England on consecutive days—e.g., from 17,000 troops on the 28th May, to 47,000 on the 29th, 53,000 on the 30th, and 68,000 on the 31st May—indicates the remarkably effective effort which was being made in spite of the occasional shortage of ships at Dunkirk or off the beaches.

It was the constantly changing situation which invariably made abortive any attempt—by the authorities either in England or in the evacuation area—to centralise the conduct of the operation except in its broadest aspects. Rear-Admiral Wake-Walker (Rear-Admiral, Dover), states that La Panne was in telephonic communication with England and sometimes he received messages by W/T from Dover about the situation there [i.e. at La Panne]—as for instance one timed 1749 saying that ships were urgently wanted off La Panne though actually at 1900 there were 4 destroyers and one minesweeper there and the situation was constantly changing.

Further, he pointed out that G.H.Q. was in touch with the Admiralty and Vice-Admiral, Dover, and were constantly presenting their own views and criticisms of what was happening which probably accounts for a signal from the First Sea Lord on the 30th May, asking if boats were distributed along the beaches to the best advantage[4]. Actually at the time whalers were the only boats that could get inshore, (except the pontoons and a few local craft), and their distribution was entirely dependent on the position of their parent ship[5].

Rear-Admiral, Dover, takes over his Command

Rear-Admiral Wake-Walker points out that where incidents are so crowded it is difficult not to give a confused picture. "The picture *was*, however, confused, and so far as operations off the beaches were concerned organisation was not possible. The most that could be done was to exercise some control and direction".[6]

This is a just appreciation of the situation, and it provides an explanation of the not infrequent occasions when officers—both senior and junior and whether on or off the beaches—considered that, from their own particular view point, things were going awry. " Dynamo", though termed an operation, was in the nature of a desperate improvisation ; but it was carried out with

---

[1] Error for 0039/30. (See Appendix H.7.)
[2] Appendix H.8.
[3] D.R. p.13, para. 40.
[4] Appendix G.21.
[5] R.A. Dover's report (M.017978/41).
[6] R.A. Dover's report of Proceedings. (R.O.III, p.373).

such courage, energy and single-mindedness, and in the face of such incredible and unpredictable difficulties, that it has since come to be spoken of as a miracle.

By 0100 Rear-Admiral Wake-Walker found the *Hebe* off Bray, and, transferring to her from the *Esk*, he took over the duties of S.N.O. (Afloat) from Captain Bush. From him, Rear-Admiral Wake-Walker heard more of the situation, and "of the ghastly sight of the shore, black with men standing in the water up to their waists." He had had "to watch the terribly slow progress of embarkation", says Rear-Admiral Wake-Walker, "which I had not then seen, but I did not feel that I could accept the note of despair which I seemed to detect in his voice".[1]

Commodores Stephenson and Hallett were transferred to drifters, the former proceeding to take charge off-shore at La Panne, and the latter off-shore at Bray.

By dawn the *Hebe* was off La Panne, and in the growing light Rear-Admiral Wake-Walker was able to glimpse for the first time the environment in which he had to work. He saw a dark line of men at the water's edge, and large groups of men all over the beaches. Off Bray the *Bideford* was ashore with her stern completely blown off and the *Locust* was trying to take her in tow. Nearer Dunkirk the *Crested Eagle* was high and dry on the beach—burnt out. Lying off the beaches were destroyers, sloops, drifters and other craft, while men were making their way off in whalers, motor boats and pontoon craft. There was a slight swell which made landing difficult, and many boats were lying broached-to and stranded by the tide.

As daylight illumined the scene Rear-Admiral Wake-Walker saw that the beaches were packed with troops, who were orderly and under proper control. To anyone with an appreciation of the practical difficulties of embarking in small boats with a long pull to seaward, the sight of that beach black with troops was indeed almost dismaying. The numbers increased steadily as more men filed down the sand dunes, and "at the back of our minds all the time", says Rear-Admiral Wake-Walker, "was the question of how long the defence line could hold and the weather remain fair." The crux of the matter was boats.[2]

Twice during the day Rear-Admiral Wake-Walker went to Dunkirk in unsuccessful efforts to contact Captain Tennant. With his staff he transferred from the *Hebe* to the *Windsor* and thence to the *Worcester*, as these ships in turn filled up with troops. Captain Bush took passage home in the *Hebe* "to stress the vital necessity for boats and crews if any large numbers were to come off the benches".[3]

There was great difficulty in exercising control off the beaches. The Rear-Admiral was hampered "by lack of means of getting about quickly". Ships would arrive at beaches and start loading; and a redistribution, though desirable, would be impracticable. The urgency of the moment governed everything[4].

At 2000 on the 30th May Rear-Admiral Wake-Walker landed at La Panne where he met Lord Gort and Captain Tennant. The situation was discussed and arrangements were made for Lord Gort's embarkation from La Panne at 1800 next day, and Commodore Stephenson was put in charge of it.

On this evening a method of identifying the beaches from seaward was

[1] M.017978/41, p.4.
[2] R.A. Dover's report (M.017978/41).
[3] R.A. Dover's *Report of Proceedings.* (R.O.III, p.374).
[4] R.A. Dover's Report (M.017978/41).

established—two lights being shown at La Panne and one at Bray—and Dover was informed accordingly.[1]

Later that night Rear-Admiral Wake-Walker transferred from the *Worcester*, by that time full of troops, to the *Express*—his fourth transfer in twenty-four hours.

Captain Howson, N.O.I.C., Beaches

On the beaches the progress was better than appeared at the time. Captain Howson, Naval-Officer-in-Charge of beaches, making his first acquaintance with conditions there, says that on the 30th May, off Bray, " in the lightening dawn, a number of destroyers, sloops and skoots were seen to be lying off, and embarkation was proceeding in such boats as were available. Several boats were aground, others were holed, and some had no oars. . . . By about 0600, all destroyers, sloops, etc., had cleared for England and there were no further ships available . . . ."

Before leaving Dover he had understood that there would be 24 signal ratings along the beaches adequately supplied with Aldis lamps, but he never saw any of them[2]. " Communication along so many miles of flat beaches was very difficult, if not impossible, with so many troops on the shore. . . . there was no communication until Thursday afternoon [30th May] between La Panne and Bray[3], and never any between Bray and Dunkirk[4]".

At about 0600 Captain Howson went to Corps Headquarters in a house at Bray, where he met one of his party, Commander Gorton, and also some naval officers " who had apparently been working on the beaches for some time before our arrival".

" About 0800", continues Captain Howson, " I proceeded on a motor bicycle to La Panne where I met Commander J. S. Dove, R.N., who . . . . took me to see Q.M.G. [Lieut. General Laidsell] with whom I discussed the position. . . . off La Panne " there were 2 or 3 destroyers and sloops, and embarkation appeared to be proceeding satisfactorily. . . . On the return to Bray an hour later the sky was . . . . overcast and a Scotch mist prevailed which was a Godsend, for throughout the forenoon vast masses of French troops, quite apart from British troops, were proceeding along the beaches, and had aircraft attacked the carnage would have been dreadful. No further ships arrived during the forenoon off Bray or La Panne and a great opportunity was missed for embarking troops undisturbed. . . . "

" During the forenoon . . . . on my way to Dunkirk I found the water lighter *Claude*[5] high and dry, but with ample supplies of water, and on my return . . . . arranged with the military aurhorities for lorries and cans to collect and distribute this sorely needed requirement".

Meanwhile, during the forenoon also, the sappers and troops of the First Division had built a long pier of lorries off Bray into the sea[6] with plank decking. This was an excellent piece of work, and though not strong enough for use by

---

[1] Report by S/Lt. E. C. Croswell, R.N. (C.W.23187/40).
[2] See p. 67.
[3] S/Lt. E. C. Croswell, R.N., on shore at La Panne, says, " Lt. Cdr. McCullough [?L. Cdr. J.W. McClelland R.N.] and signal staff " arrived at La Panne on the evening of 30th May. (C.W.23817/40). The *Gossamer* reports that she embarked a party of signalmen for La Panne on 30th May, and arrived there at 1930.
[4] 1st Corps had a H.Q. at Bray.
[5] She had been towed over to Dunkirk on 25th May by the tug *Fairplay I*.
[6] This was done at the suggestion of Cdr. H. du P. Richardson R.N., who was in charge of a section of Bray beach. (R.O.III, p.369).

heavy craft, nor even by small craft in a lop, it was invaluable later for embarking troops into small boats. A similar pier was commenced on the morning of the 30th May at La Panne, and was completed and in use by 1400 the same day (See p. 47).

Captain Howson goes on to say that in the afternoon one or two skoots and 2 or 3 motor yachts and paddlers arrived and anchored to the westward of Bray ; none proceeded east of the Bray pier, where the First Division had waited many hours patiently. One or two destroyers or sloops passed from the westward to La Panne, and he tried without success with a lamp to tell them to anchor off the pier. Eventually he managed to get a signal to Rear-Admiral Wake-Walker asking him to arrange for this. Captain Howson also sent an officer to Dunkirk to represent the urgent need for destroyers off Bray. It was not until 2 days later that he learned that all the destroyers, etc., had been given specific instructions as to which beach they were to anchor off. Later a certain number of destroyers, sloops and skoots anchored off Bray and the embarkation proceeded satisfactorily. Unfortunately, time after time, owing to a lack of naval ratings, he saw a procession of boats going off loaded with troops, only to be cast adrift and left floating empty out to seaward[1].

Later that evening Captain Howson got in touch with Rear-Admiral Wake-Walker, then in the *Worcester*, and obtained permission to embark the following day in a motor boat off the beaches so as to prevent a recurrence of this waste of beaching craft[2].

In spite of the difficulties and shortcomings emphasised in the above reports great progress was being made. In fact, beach evacuation reached its peak on this day; 29,500 troops were lifted from the beaches (as against 24,300 from the harbour) ; and some 50 ships, including destroyers, minesweepers, skoots, trawlers, drifters, personnel and special service vessels, were engaged continuously in the arduous work.

The armada grows, but service of ships to Dunkirk is slowed up

Meanwhile the build-up of ships continued, and some 31 additional craft reached Dunkirk and the beaches this day. They included two minesweepers of the 8th M.S.F.[3], the Fleet Air Arm training vessel *Grive*, 4 yachts and a drifter of the Dover M/S Command[4], the corvette *Kingfisher*, (with the ex-Belgian canal boat *Sambre* in tow), the Yarmouth Examination Service yacht *Laroc*, the M/V *Scottish Co-operator*, the S/M tender *Dwarf*, the drifters *Fair Breeze* and *Ocean Breeze*, the ex-Belgian canal boats *Ambleve* and *Escaut* (in tow of the minesweeper *Skipjack*), the motor coasters *Seine* and *Lady Sheila*, the coasting barge *Viking*, the ex-Dutch eel-boat *Johanna* (in tow of the skoot *Jutland*), the oyster dredging smacks *Seasalter* and *Vanguard*, the steam hopper *W.24*, the sailing barge *Beatrice Maud*, and the dumb barges *Sark* and *Shetland*. The Ramsgate (R.N.L.I.) lifeboat *Prudential* (towing 7 wherries loaded with fresh water, and the punt *Carama*), and the Margate (R.N.L.I.) lifeboat *Lord Southborough*, were manned by their own crews, but naval ratings manned the wherries. The trawler *Olvina*, which should have been on A/S patrol, went to Bray beach in error and picked up 244 troops. Another important contingent appeared on the scene. At long last a dozen of the long awaited motor boats[5]

---

[1] R.O.III, p.396.
[2] R.O.III, p.397.
[3] The *Glen Avon* and *Glen Gower*.
[4] The danlaying yachts *Gulzar* and *Sargasso*, the echo sounding yachts *Chico* and *Conidaw* and the danlaying drifter *Starlight Rays*.
[5] The *Constant Nymph*, *Bonny Heather*, *Adventuress*, *Black Arrow*, *Sunshine*, *Reda*, *Triton*, *Silver Queen*, *Cordelia*, *Golden Lily*, *Pauleter* and *Ma Joie*.

reached the beaches, and by retrieving the abandoned and drifting pulling boats they were able to do much to increase the rate of lifting[1].

Many more were on the way. The destroyers *Basilisk* and *Venomous* from the Western Approaches Command were making for Dover, and the mine sweepers *Niger* and *Dundalk* were coming down from the Humber. The attempt to maintain an adequate rate of lift with only the older destroyers soon proved unavailing, and all the modern destroyers of the H, I and J classes which had been withdrawn on the 29th May were ordered back to Dunkirk on the 30th[2].

Small craft were hastening up from Portsmouth, Newhaven and Sheerness; six tugs were plodding along from Tilbury (towing 23 motor and 46 rowing lifeboats), and five others had left Gravesend (towing barges). Yachts, drifters and trawlers; launches, lighters and steam hopper barges; car ferries, coasters and cockle boats; train ferries, speed boats and picket boats; seaplane tenders, fishing craft and pleasure craft; steam pinnaces, sailing craft and a Thames fire float—a host of vessels—were heading in ever-increasing numbers[3], for Dover, the Downs, or Dunkirk direct, while the cry " more ships, more boats ", still went up off the French coast.[4]

Set-backs were inevitable, but this concourse of ships, big and little, fast and slow, manned by willing and eager crews fired by one purpose of saving the British Expeditionary Force, continued to grow until it assumed the proportions of an armada.

Late on the previous evening the *Bideford* had sent a call for large quantities of rope for towing to be sent, and within a few hours 9 coils (1080 fathoms) of 4-inch grass hawser were speeding by lorry from Chatham dockyard to Ramsgate to help the skoots to haul boats off the beaches, thus speeding up the boat work and compensating for the shortage of boats, " which would continue ", says Vice-Admiral, Dover " for at least another 24 hours "[5].

Undoubtedly as a result of the messages and signals received on the 29th May by V.A. Dover with regard to the harbour at Dunkirk, the number of ships sent there on the 30th May was curtailed, with a corresponding reduction in the volume of embarkation. After V.A. Dover's signal to Admiral Abrial late on the 29th May, asking whether it was possible for transports to berth alongside, further signals to the same effect were sent to the *Vanquisher* and the *Codrington* and to Rear-Admiral Wake-Walker. Finally, at 1020, the *Wolsey* was called upon for a detailed report of conditions alongside the east pier; and by 1524 V.A. Dover was able to inform destroyers that " a good berth with bollards exists 400 yards from end of east . . . . pier ".

In the meantime signals were coming in from Rear-Admiral Wake-Walker and from the *Vivacious* stating that the beaches were filling up rapidly and more ships and boats were urgently required there.[6] Although it was known that the destroyers could use Dunkirk, it appeared, says V.A. Dover, that the best division of transport was to send the great majority of destroyers to the beaches, where urgent demands could not be ignored, and the personnel vessels to Dunkirk harbour, only an occasional destroyer being sent to Dunkirk from the reduced number available.[7]

---

[1] D.R. p.15, para. 49.

[2] Appendices D.9, D.10. Except the *Intrepid* and *Jaguar* (in need of repairs) and the *Javelin*.

[3] Appendices G.20, G.27, G.28.

[4] Appendices H.7 to H.10.

[5] D.R. p.13, para. 41.

[6] Appendices H.7, H.9 and G.22.

[7] D.R. p.13, para. 43.

In pursuance of this decision, during the forenoon and early afternoon only seven destroyers went to Dunkirk[1], although later in the afternoon four of them, the *Vanquisher, Malcolm, Vimy* and *Wolsey* made a second trip to the east pier.

There was delay in the sailing of personnel vessels, while enquiries about the harbour were being made, and this resulted in only one of them—the *Royal Daffodil*—reaching Dunkirk during the forenoon.   The store ship *Dorrien Rose* arrived there at 0650, and unloaded part of the provisions she was carrying; then, in view of the number of troops awaiting transport, she was filled up with 590 and sailed.   The *Dorrien Rose* had not brought any of the much needed fresh water, but some was obtained from the destroyers.

The only other ships arriving at Dunkirk harbour during the forenoon were the drifters *Girl Gladys, Golden Sunbeam* and *Yorkshire Lass*[2].

It was this restricted service of ships during a day of quiet (because of mist and low visibility) and a night of little enemy activity during which only 4 drifters and a yacht had entered Dunkirk[3], that called forth the reproachful comment from the harassed Naval Staff, in their dug-out at the shore end of the east pier[4], "a great opportunity . . . . again lost".[5]

At 1257 the P/V *Princess Maud*, en route for Dunkirk, was fired on when 3 miles west of Gravelines, by a shore battery and received 3 hits, one being six inches above the water line.   Three of the crew were killed and three wounded, and the ship had to return to Dover for repairs.

French ships arrive in larger numbers. *Bourrasque* sunk

The contribution of French ships had so far been negligible.   On Friday (May 30th), however, some 15 ships went to Dunkirk harbour, including 2 destroyers and 3 torpedo boats[6], the minesweepers *Arras* and *L'Impétueuse*, 4 trawlers[7] the tug *Lutteur*, and 3 motor fishing vessels[8].

The participation in "Dynamo" of one of these French reinforcements was unfortunately very short-lived, for an enemy battery at Nieuport was instrumental in sinking the torpedo boat *Bourrasque*.   She had sailed from Dunkirk at 1530 loaded with over 600 French troops of all descriptions—officers without troops, a mixture of artillerymen, Moroccan troops, air force personnel, sailors from barracks, fleet air arm personnel, naval recruiting officers, crews of sunken ships, etc. . . . even one woman ("I did not notice her presence until at sea," says Capitaine de Frégate R. Fouque, "or she would have been one of the first to be saved").   The troops had few arms ; on the other hand the decks were encumbered with baggage and there were even some bicycles.   An attempt to make an approximate count of the passengers had to be given up, because of the congestion in the gangways and spaces.

At about 1600, after passing Nieuport buoy, the *Bourrasque* came under the fire of a battery at Nieuport, the salvoes falling regularly at about 3½ minute intervals.   To open the range more rapidly and so avoid this bombardment, course was set closely to the edge of an adjacent French minefield and speed was increased.   The crowded decks made it dangerous to return the fire of the

---

[1] The *Vanquisher, Vimy, Malcolm, Wolsey, Sabre, Express* and *Scimitar*.
[2] Reports by Captain A/P, Dover, and S.N.O., Dunkirk.
[3] See Section 139, footnote [8].
[4] M.017978/40, p.7.
[5] S.N.O. Dunkirk's report.
[6] *Foudroyant, Branlebas, Bourrasque, Bouclier, Siroco.*
[7] *Louise Marie, Chasse-Marée, Angèle Marie* and *Jeune France.*
[8] *Du Guesclin, Surcouf* and *Thérèse Louis.*

German battery. When the *Bourrasque* was about 5 miles north of Nieuport buoy a shock was felt, followed by one more violent ; smoke rose from the torpedo firing platform and there was a big escape of steam. The ship stopped and the electricity failed. It was difficult to say if the ship was seriously damaged ; there was a breach in the deck and water was entering some compartments, but it was not possible to get to the engine room to assess the damage there. During this time, not unnaturally, a certain degree of panic, which had to be controlled, reigned among this mixed crowd of passengers ; some of them threw themselves into the water, while others lowered the boats and threw themselves into them in such numbers that they sank, even the rafts. Order was, however, restored. The *Branlebas* was approaching. It soon became evident, however, that the *Bourrasque* was doomed, and " abandon ship " was ordered[1].

At 1625 the French torpedo boat *Branlebas*, which had been 4 cables astern of the *Bourrasque*, saw a heavy explosion take place in the *Bourrasque* which disappeared from view in a column of smoke and water. When the column subsided the *Bourrasque* appeared to have broken in two and was sinking rapidly. She had apparently struck a French mine. The *Branlebas*, which had already embarked 300 troops from Dunkirk picked up 100 survivors, the drifter *Ut Prosim* 250, and the drifter *Yorkshire Lass* (assisted by an English motor launch) 194. At 0530 next morning the motor vessel *Bat*, en route for Dunkirk, took off 15 naked and oil-covered survivors from the capsized wreck of the *Bourrasque*.

It is officially considered by the French Admiralty that the *Bourrasque* was sunk by a mine, but her Captain was of the opinion that her sinking was the result of one or more shell hits.

Troops embark at the double

Following the disastrous air attacks on massed shipping on the 29th May S.N.O., Dunkirk, decided on the 30th May that only one destroyer at a time should enter Dunkirk and secure alongside the east pier. This policy was adhered to throughout the forenoon and early afternoon.

At about 1700 Captain Tennant turned over the duties of S.N.O., Dunkirk, to Commander G. O. Maund, R.N., and went by car to G.H.Q. at La Panne to confer with Lord Gort.

Cdr. Maund says : " Towards the close of the day [i.e. the 30th] a great number of ships had arrived, and I accordingly decided to accept the risk of further losses, and ordered the vessels waiting in the roads to proceed alongside and embark troops. Strong air attacks were launched by the enemy, but fortunately they were mostly concentrated against wrecks in the roads. Time and again they sent waves of bombers and directed their attack, not against our ships loading troops, but only against these wrecks in the roads. We got a great deal of amusement and satisfaction from this, for loading was proceeding apace with no casualties. At the same time, I decided that the rate of embarkation must in some way be speeded up as the capacity of the ships now alongside was more than adequate for the rate of the flow of troops. This laid our vessels open to attack from the air. . . . I therefore went down to the Eastern Arm and rigged up a loud speaker[2] and addressed the troops in the following terms : ' Remember your pals, boys. The quicker you get on board, the more of them will be saved.' " This ", continues Cdr. Maund, " worked like a miracle. The

---

[1] Report by Capitaine de Frégate R. Fouque (French Admiralty Record, Folio 4).
[2] A portable loud speaker equipment had been brought to Dunkirk on 30th May.

thousands of troops, tired, depressed, and without food or water for days, broke into a double and kept it up for the whole length of the Eastern Arm for more than two hours.   During that period I estimate that more than 15,000 troops were embarked.   The Army certainly responded splendidly".[1]

Cdr. Maund's estimate was triumphantly confirmed : between 1802 and about 2100, eight destroyers[2] embarked from the east pier an aggregate of 8,528 troops ; four personnel vessels[3] embarked an aggregate of 5,694 troops ; and other vessels, including the skoots *Reiger* and *Doggersbank*, also embarked troops, while the hospital carrier *Dinard*, well down the pier, embarked a number of wounded.

Anthony and *Sabre* damaged

Of the eight destroyers referred to above, one, the *Anthony*, when returning to Dover was attacked by a single aircraft which dropped 5 bombs, which extinguished her lights, stopped her engines, and put her compasses and W/T out of action.   She was subsequently able to proceed, steering by her engines, and the *Keith* escorted her into Dover.

Earlier in the day another destroyer, the *Sabre*, when near No. 6 Calais buoy, on her way to Dunkirk by Route Z, came under fire from shore batteries and received several hits on the bridge and upper works.   A shell went through the gyro-compass, an oil fuel tank was pierced, the magnetic compass put out of action, and she had to return to Dover for repairs.

The destroyer crews, who had hardly slept since the operation began, were beginning to show signs of exhaustion, and at 2341 (May 30th) the Admiralty ordered a spare destroyer's crew to be sent to Dover to provide temporary reliefs.

Air patrols

In the air low visibility checked the enemy's activity, but as on the previous day patrols were again carried out by Fighter Command at three—or four—squadron strength, the largest number of aircraft on the line at any one time being 44, and the smallest 26.   Sixteen squadrons again operated, the total number of sorties amounting to 265.   Small Coastal Command patrols operated as before throughout the day along the line North Goodwins—Gravelines—Ostend, and at night the patrol over Dunkirk by single Blenheims continued ; but the governing factor of the air operations over Dunkirk on the 30th May was the low visibility, which restricted the enemy's activities.[4]

Summary of troops landed in England

Thus the day was one of reviving hope.   It ended with the numbers going up, and a record number were embarked from the beaches.   (See table p. 65).

Arrangements for evacuation of B.E.F. rearguard

Meanwhile, during the forenoon, representatives of the Commander-in-Chief of the B.E.F. had attended a conference with the Vice-Admiral, Dover.

The Commander-in-Chief's plan was explained ; it gave daylight on Saturday, 1st June, as the latest reasonable date up to which the B.E.F. might be expected to hold the eastern perimeter with an available force of about 4,000.

---

[1] Cdr. Maund's report (R.O.III, p.443).
[2] The *Anthony* (1137), *Codrington* (1100), *Esk* (1041), *Vimy* (948), *Impulsive* (1112), *Keith* (1200), *Winchelsea* (925) and *Wolsey* (1065).
[3] The *Prague* (1039), *Royal Sovereign* (1502), *St. Helier* (2000) and *Tynwald* (1153).
[4] R.A.F. Narrative, p. 331.

SUMMARY OF TROOPS LANDED IN ENGLAND

	From the beaches	From the harbour	Total for the day
26th May	Nil	Nil	Nil
27th May	Nil	7,699	7,669
28th May	5,930	11,874	17,804
29th May	13,752	33,558	47,310
30th May	29,512	24,311	53,823

By that date and time the Vice-Admiral knew that he would have available ocean-going tugs, ships' lifeboats and ships' power lifeboats which he could specially reserve for the climax of this critical operation.

The conference made the following decisions :

(a) That evacuation should proceed with the utmost vigour to ensure that by 0130 on 1st June the British forces ashore should have been reduced to the rearguard of 4,000.

(b) That special boats and tugs should be accumulated and held aside to ensure them being available in the early hours of 1st June.

(c) That the plan should provide for lifting the rearguard of 4,000, plus R.N. beach parties, in one or more flights between 0130 and 0300 on 1st June.

(d) Final decision, based on the progress of the evacuation of the main body to be made by the Vice-Admiral at 1400 on Friday, 31st May, as to the possibility of adhering to the plan.

Other technical details were settled at the meeeting, and the Military staff were assured that the ever increasing rate of lifting made it probable that an affirmative decision would be reached at the critical hour of 1400 on the 31st May. In the event, the Military plan was changed on the 31st May, as it was found to be impossible to hold the original covering position with 4,000 troops and then withdraw them to the beaches for embarkation by boat.

CHAPTER VIII

FRIDAY, 31ST MAY

EVACUATION REACHES ITS ZENITH

Lord Gort hands over his Command to Major-General Alexander

Orders had been issued on the 30th May for the 3rd, 4th and 5th Divisions (2nd Corps) to withdraw to the beaches and Dunkirk. The 50th Division was to fall back to the French defences on the Belgian frontier and, together with the British Base staff at Dunkirk, to come under the 1st Corps. These moves began to take place on the morning of 31st May.[1]

This meant that the remnant of the B.E.F., on being withdrawn inside the area of the French defences, came under the orders of Admiral Abrial; the time had therefore arrived for Lord Gort to hand over his command in accordance with the instructions he had received.[2] He selected Major-General the Hon. H. R. L. G. Alexander to remain in France in command of the 1st Corps, now numbering less than 20,000 men in all; and, on taking over command of the 1st Corps, Major-General Alexander handed over command of the 1st Division to Brigadier M. B. Beckwith-Smith.

Lord Gort agreed with Major-General Alexander that a provisional date for evacuating his force was to be the night of 2nd/3rd June.

On the 31st May therefore, Lord Gort's headquarters closed at 1800, and, after handing over command to Major-General Alexander, Lord Gort embarked with his A.D.C. in the *Hebe's* whaler, which had been towed in by the motor yacht *Lahloo* to a point a little west of La Panne beach. He proceeded to the *Lahloo* and thence to the *Hebe*. During the embarkation an enemy attack was made by about 40 aircraft and considerable shelling was directed on to La Panne beach itself. With Lord Gort on board, the *Hebe* proceeded to La Panne beach and continued to embark troops.

It was not, however, till about midnight, that the motor yacht *Bounty* with Cdre. Stephenson on board proceeded to transfer Lord Gort from the *Hebe* to the *Keith*. At about the same time, however, the *M.A/S.B.6*, having embarked Lord Gort's chief staff officer General Leese from the *Keith*, was sent to the *Hebe* with orders from Rear-Admiral Wake-Walker to embark Lord Gort. On finding that he had left the *Hebe*, the *M.A/S.B.6* returned to the *Keith*, embarked Lord Gort, and sailed at 0304 on the 1st of June for Dover which she reached at 0547 the same evening.

It had been the intention of the Admiralty that Lord Gort and his staff should be embarked in M.T.B.'s and at 1522 V.A. Dover had informed Rear-Admiral Wake-Walker by signal that 4 of these vessels would be available for this purpose[3]. *Unfortunately, V.A. Dover's signal did not reach R.A. Dover*[4], and the 4 M.T.B.'s were put to other uses; and indeed were all four back at Dover by 2315. Speaking of the non-receipt of V.A. Dover's signal, Rear-Admiral Wake-Walker says, " The signal informing me of this, like many others, never reached me "[5]. At 1543/30 Rear-Admiral Wake-Walker had asked that he

---

[1] Lord Gort's Second Despatch, para. 57.
[2] Lord Gort's Second Despatch, para. 58.
[3] M.T.B's. *67, 107, 68* and *102*. (See Appendix G.30).
[4] R.A. Dover—Report of Proceedings (R.O. III. para. 19).
[5] M.017978/41, p.18.

be embarked in a ship capable of keeping 2 wireless lines for communication purposes, and at 0645/31 he embarked in such a ship, viz. the flotilla leader *Keith*, and thereafter (until she was sunk 24 hours later) kept her free from troops so that his movements should be unrestricted[1].

One of the four M.T.B.'s, viz: *M.T.B.67*, had been ferrying troops to the gunboat *Mosquito* at 1915 from La Panne beach, and her commanding Officer, Lieut. C. C. Anderson, R.N., says, " It is desired to express appreciation of an unknown soldier, who, although severely wounded about the face and head and on the point of collapse, remained quietly in the water watching *M.T.B.67* draw away because he thought we looked full up and might not want him. This man was of course taken on board".

Meanwhile anxiety was felt at Dover at the non-appearance of Lord Gort and at 2336, the Admiralty sent a peremptory signal to Rear-Admiral Wake-Walker demanding an explanation. Rear-Admiral Wake-Walker says, " About 2300 I received an urgent signal from Admiralty asking where Lord Gort was and why I had detailed the M.T.B.'s sent for him to other work. As the M.A./S.B. [i.e. *M.A/S.B.6*] had just returned with [Lt. Cdr.] C. J. Wynne-Edwards[2], I sent it off at once to *Hebe* to collect Lord Gort .... it came back almost at once to say that Lord Gort had just left *Hebe* in a motor launch. It was very dark and *Hebe* could not be seen though we knew where she was, and I waited anxiously for the boat to arrive. Presently out of the dark a boat appeared and came alongside, still not the right one, and I had a bad moment thinking of the boat getting lost. However, to my relief, after what appeared about half an hour, the right boat, in charge of [Commodore] Stephenson once more, found us at last. Apologising to Lord Gort for keeping him waiting so long, I transferred him to the M.A/S.B. and sent him off to Dover with General Leese".[3]

In the meantime, a little before 1800, Lord Gort's staff had been embarked during an air attack by the *Keith's* boats at a point 2 miles west of La Panne.

Signal communication established between Dunkirk and Dover[4]

At daylight on the 31st full signal communication was at length established between Dunkirk and Dover.

On the 26th May the destroyer *Wolsey* had been despatched to Dunkirk to act as W/T link. The S.N.O., Dunkirk, on arrival next day, decided, however, that conditions in the port made it impossible for a destroyer to lie there. On the morning of the 27th May Commander M. O. D. Ellwood, R.N., who had been placed in charge of communications in Operation " Dynamo", proceeded to Dunkirk in the *Wolfhound* that afternoon with a signal party consisting of one yeoman of signals and 24 signalmen, who were distributed between Naval headquarters at Dunkirk (one yeoman and 8 signalmen) and the beach parties (2 signalmen each). The only equipment available other than hand flags was one Aldis lamp, which was taken over from the British Naval Liaison Officer and made to function with the help of a battery acquired from a French motor car.

A Headquarters signal station was established at the shore end of the East Pier for communication with ships arriving, but until 30th May, when one Naval wireless set arrived, there was no means of communication between

---

[1] R.A. Dover – Report of Proceedings (R.O.III, p.374, para. 19).
[2] He had been engaged in directing the then arriving tows of boats to the beaches.
[3] M.017978/41, page 21.
[4] R.O. Case 5458, Vol. III, p.417.

Headquarters and the various parties, nor between one party and another, except by despatch riders, for the distances were too great for the effective employment of semaphore. Beach parties improvised signalling arrangements as best they could with the help of lamps of commandeered motor cars. Messages for transmission to Dover by W/T were either sent through the French station at the Bastion or, for the sake of greater secrecy as well as convenience, taken by hand down the pier for transmission by destroyers. This was done because the coding of messages sent through the French Station was a laborious business which first necessitated the translation of the message into French, and decoding the type of code (the Anglo French) in use at that date was a very slow business.

Reception on the naval W/T set which arrived on the 30th May was established by 2300 on that day, but owing to a defective transmitter full communication was not established with Dover until daylight on the 31st. Transmission broke down altogether on the evening of 1st June, probably on account of sand in the generator.

On the 1st June the Royal Corps of Signals established a W/T station in a lorry by the Bastion, as well as telephone communication between the Bastion and the Headquarters Signal Station. The intense bombing and shelling by the Germans that day severed the line more than once.

In view of the possibility of the arrival of enemy forces on the 2nd June all signal forms and records were destroyed on that day.

British Sector to be held till midnight 1st/2nd June

Meanwhile, on taking over command of the 1st Corps, Major General Alexander proceeded to Dunkirk to interview Admiral Abrial who informed him that he intended to hold the perimeter till all the troops were embarked. A French Corps on the right was to hold the sector from Gravelines to Bergues (though Gravelines had not apparently been in French hands for some days) and a mixed French and British Corps under command of Major General Alexander was to hold a line from Bergues to Les Moeres and thence to the sea[1].

Major General Alexander at once told the Admiral and General Fagalde that in his view this plan did not take account of the true naval and military situation which was serious and deteriorating rapidly. The fighting condition of the troops was now such that prolonged resistance was out of the question, and the present front could not in his opinion be maintained after the night of 1st/2nd June; furthermore, the line to be held was so close to the beach and to Dunkirk that the enemy might soon stop all further evacuation by short range artillery fire[1].

Major General Alexander gave the same opinion to the Secretary of State for War, and received a reply that the British force should be withdrawn as rapidly as possible on a basis of British and French troops being embarked in equal numbers from that time onward. This he showed to Admiral Abrial and General Fagalde, stating that he would hold the sector allotted to him till midnight 1st/2nd June, and then withdraw under cover of darkness, which they agreed was the only plan feasible[1].

Cyclone damaged by torpedo

Day and night our patrols were maintaining their vigil northward, but on this day two French destroyers were subjected to E-boat attacks. One, the

---

[1] Appendix to Lord Gort's Second Despatch.

Cyclone, was on her way to Dunkirk when, apparently between T buoy and the West Hinder, the track of a torpedo was seen at 0121 crossing from port to starboard 10 yards ahead ; a minute later another track was seen to port, and although avoiding action was taken the torpedo struck forward and considerably damaged her, but the *Cyclone* was still able to steam and she proceeded back to Dover at 4 knots escorted by an English vessel ; later, the French torpedo boat *Bouclier* and then the French minesweeper *Arras* took over the duty of escort. The *Cyclone* reached Dover at 1600, having transferred two serious casualties to an English M/B while on passage. She took no further part in " Dynamo ".

Siroco sunk

At 0145, some 20 minutes after this attack, the French destroyer *Siroco*, on her way to Dover with 770 troops from Dunkirk, was hit near T buoy by 2 torpedoes fired by an E-boat which had stopped and was unseen in the darkness ; the destroyer *Vega*, on patrol 4 miles to the south-east, saw a column of flame 200 feet high. The *Siroco* capsized shortly after. Survivors to the number of 252 were picked up, 50 by the trawler *Wolves*, 21 by the trawler *Stella Dorado*, 166 by the corvette *Widgeon* and 15 by the Polish destroyer *Blyskawica*.[1]

At 0700, the *Vega*, which had been on patrol since noon 28th May, was relieved by the destroyer *Jackal*.

It was on this morning that clear evidence of the presence of enemy submarines was obtained, for the *Vimy*, en route to Dunkirk, sighted the periscope and conning tower of one between the North Goodwin buoy and the North-West Goodwin buoy. A depth charge was dropped, and a hunt began in which the trawlers *Westella* and *Spurs*, the corvette *Sheldrake*, and the *Jackal* joined, but without success.

Conditions on the beaches

Meanwhile, conditions on the beaches were by no means favourable. Already at 0400 a lop had started. At about 0600 the R.N.L.I. life boat *Lord Southborough* was ferrying troops to the destroyer *Icarus* off Bray. " There was a nasty surf," said the coxswain of the life boat. " Troops were rushing out to us from all directions and were being drowned close to us and we could not get to them. . . . it seemed to me we were doing more harm [than good] by drawing the men off the shore, as with their heavy clothing, the surf was knocking them over and they were unable to get up. . . . The whaler from the destroyer. . . . was swamped, so was the motor pinnace that was working with the whaler, and so it was all along the sands as far as I could see, both sides of us, and there was not a boat left afloat ".

At 0600 also, Lt. Col. R. L. Hutchins, M.C., Grenadier Guards, in command of the War Department motor launch *Swallow*, arrived off Dunkirk, and described the situation as follows : " Dunkirk was under a pall of smoke from fires which appeared to be mainly to the south and west of the port. There were numerous wrecks outside the harbour, and along the beaches. There were large numbers of troops on the shore as far as it was possible to see to the eastward, and the beach was strewn with all forms of motor transport. Along the foreshore were a very large number of pulling boats, aground, capsized or damaged, and abandoned. There were also a considerable number of motor

---

[1] Appendix J.2.

boats, motor launches and yachts aground and, in most cases, abandoned, and several wrecks close inshore.   About one mile out in the Dunkirk roads were numerous destroyers and other vessels waiting to embark troops, but scarcely any boats were running between the shore and these ships. . . . the beaches were quiet except for occasional shelling and intermittent bombing. . . .'' Nevertheless between 0800 and 1315 Lt. Col. Hutchins ferried about 450 troops to the *Impulsive* off Malo, and thereafter, about 250 troops to the *Winchelsea* off Bray. The *Swallow* sailed for Ramsgate at about 1800 with 30 troops on board.

At 1035 Rear-Admiral Wake-Walker informed V.A. Dover that the majority of pulling boats were broached-to and had no crews ; that conditions on the beaches were very bad owing to a freshening on-shore wind ; that only small numbers were being embarked even in daylight ; that motor boats could not get close in, and that under present conditions any large scale embarkation from the beaches was quite impracticable.   He considered that the only hope of embarking any number was at Dunkirk, but that he would attempt to beach a ship to form a lee and so improve conditions[1].

Sailing of personnel vessels suspended

Simultaneously with this bad news came a signal from S.N.O., Dunkirk, to the effect that Dunkirk was being continuously and heavily bombarded ; that the enemy artillery were gradually finding the range of the loading berths ; and that only ships necessary for the flow of troops should enter[2].   This signal confirmed the V.A. Dover in a decision he had made to suspend the sailing of personnel vessels to Dunkirk until the number of those *en route* had been reduced.   There were at this time no less than 9 personnel vessels and 3 hospital carriers known to be on the round trip U.K.—Dunkirk and back, and one other personnel vessel had been ordered to sail during the night but her whereabouts was unknown.   In addition, 3 other personnel vessels were under orders to sail between 0900 and 1030.

Military plan changed

The plan, arranged between V.A. Dover and representatives of the C.-in-C., B.E.F. on the 30th May, was to lift the B.E.F. rearguard of 4,000, plus R.N. beach parties, on the night of 31st May/1st June; and naval arrangements had been made[3].   The minesweepers had received their orders[4] ; instructions had been issued for the special tows to leave Ramsgate at 1300/31 for Dunkirk via Route X ; and C.-in-C. Nore, and F.O.I.C. Harwich, were requested to provide all available M.T.B.'s to escort this convoy for as much of the outward passage as possible.   Speed of advance 6 knots[5].   A party of Naval officers assembled at Dover to embark in these tows were given detailed instructions on the plan. At 1000 the *Hebe* arrived off La Panne beach carrying the plans for this evacuation.

In the afternoon of the 31st May, however, Dover was informed that the Military plan had been changed, as it was no longer possible for the original covering position to be held by 4,000 troops who were finally to withdraw to the beaches for embarkation.   Instead, the easternmost Division was to be withdrawn westward from the La Panne area, and the special flight of boats was to be used to lift this force from the beaches.   At the same time the troops

---

[1] Appendix Q.6.
[2] Appendix Q.7.
[3] Appendices Q.1, G.29.
[4] Appendix Q.1.
[5] Appendix G.29.

in the Bray and Malo sectors were being thinned out by movements westward towards Dunkirk iteslf.   This change of plan involved concentrating the special tows and the minesweepers to which they were to transfer the troops, into the stretch opposite the beach between Zuydcoote Sanatorium and one mile east of La Panne[1], and also advancing the commencement of the operation by one hour[2].

A risk was involved in this change of plan as the boat tows were not in communication with the Vice-Admiral, and it would therefore be necessary for minesweepers to see that the escorting M.A./S.B.'s shepherded the tows to the new positions   It had been explained to the Naval officers in each tow that the minesweepers would be anchored so as to serve as guiding marks[3].

" It was always impossible for me to do more than deal with the situation of the moment", says Rear-Admiral Wake-Walker.   " I did not know what ships were coming or when—except for the pre-arranged plan of the sloops.   Nor was it possible for Dover to give me much information.   Ships got back there, unloaded, and were off again, the stream was constant but irregular and it was not possible to see any way ahead.   My policy was always to keep only sufficient ships off the beaches and send all the others into Dunkirk, but the situation changed continually."[4]

Small craft arrive in hundreds

It was in such circumstances that, at about 1900, Rear-Admiral Wake-Walker had proceeded to Dunkirk in the *Keith* to see how the boat situation was getting on.   There he saw for the first time that strange procession of craft of all kinds the story of which was to become famous—tugs, towing dinghies, life-boats and all manner of pulling boats[5]—small motor yachts, motor launches, drifters, Dutch skoots, Thames barges, fishing boats, pleasure steamers[6].   This was indeed the first time that the small craft had come over in hundreds[7].   Since noon Lt. Cdr. C. J. Wynne-Edwards, R.N. (of R.-A. Dunkirk's staff), embarked in *M.T.B.68*, had been directing the tows to the various beaches.

---

[1] See Appendix Q.18, observing that D.R. p.20, para. 61 says " the beach between *Bray* and 1 mile east of La Panne."

[2] Appendix Q.19.

[3] D.R. p.20, para. 61.

[4] M.017978/41, p.17.

[5] The following 14 tugs (their tows are shown in brackets) reached Dunkirk that evening : The *Racia* (12 life-boats), *Sun VIII* (12 life-boats), *Sun XV* (6 life-boats), *Vincia* (3 life-boats), *Sun IV* (9 boats), *Tanga* (6 boats), *Ocean Cock* (6 M/B's), *Sun VII* (seaplane tenders *243, 254, 276, 291* and *A.M.C.*3), *Foremost* 87 (two sailing barges), *Fairplay I* (sailing barge *Barbara Jean*), *Empire Henchman* (sailing barge *Aidie*), *Crested Cock* (a lighter), *Sun XI* (a lighter), and the *Sun XII* (sailing barges *Tollesbury* and *Ethel Everard*).
In the early hours of 1st June 4 other tugs arrived.   The *St. Fagan* (auxiliary barges *Pudge* and *Lady Rosebery*, and the sailing barge *Doris*), *St. Abbs* (auxiliary barge *Thyra* and sailing barges *H.A.C.* and *Duchess*), *Cervia* (sailing barge *Royalty*), and the *Persia* (sailing barge *Glenway* and *Lark*).

[6] M.017978/41, p.19.

[7] New arrivals off Dunkirk and the beaches on 31st May included the following : The yachts *Amulree, Aronia, Glagla, Caleta, Christobel II* and *Llanthony*, the nine yachts of the Portsmouth Inner Patrol, viz : the *Ahola, Ankh, Bounty, Caryandra, Eilla II, Lahloo, Noneta, Seriola* and *Thele* ; and from the R.N. Air Station, Ford, the yacht *Andora*.
The drifters *Ben and Lucy* (towing 4 boats), *Dorienta* (towing boats), *Monarda, Renascent* and the 13 drifters of the Yarmouth Base, viz : *Alcmaria, Feasible, Genius, Gula, Jeannie MacIntosh, John and Norah, Lord Barham, Lord Hood, Overfalls, Reed, Rewga, Swift Wing* and *Taransay*.   The drifters *Fair Breeze* and *Ocean Breeze* were again over, the former towing a motor life-boat and 3 life-boats.
The steam hopper barges *Foremost 102* (towing the *Excellent's* 35 ft. fast motor boat and

Typical of the urge which characterised this movement of small craft was the trawler *Strathelliot*, which sailed from Ramsgate at 0205 on the 31st May escorting motor boats, 8 of which were disabled and in tow of various vessels ; the M/B *Skylark*, disabled, was in tow of *Strathelliot*. At 0640 the *Skylark's* towing bollard tore away and she was taken in tow stern first. Then the M/B *Mary Rose*, which had been in tow of the M/B *Rapid I*, was damaged. Her crew were transferred to the *Strathelliot* and the *Mary Rose* was sunk. Later, the *Skylark* also became damaged, and she was sunk after her crew had been embarked in the *Strathelliot*. Shortly after this the M/B *Malden Annie IV* had to be taken in tow—and later taken in tow stern first—and she arrived off Dunkirk beaches with her pumps choked, bilge full of rubbish and making water fast, and drifting on to the beach she was abandoned. She fulfilled some useful purpose, however, by being used as a pier.

It is impossible to give the story of every ship, although each ship has its story. Here, for instance, is the unvarnished history of the M/B *Marsayru* which went over on the 31st May in company with the lighters *X. 217* (S/Lt. R. A. W. Pool, R.N.) *X. 213* and *X. 149*. They arrived off Malo beach at about 1600. During an air attack *X. 213* and *X. 149* were sunk. The *Z. 217* was beached and, assisted by the dinghy, embarked 95 troops which were transferred to the yacht *Llanthony*. The *X. 217* continued to embark troops using the *Marsayru* and a cutter. At about 2100 that evening, with the *Marsayru's* skipper and crew and about 200 British and French troops on board, the *X. 217* left for home towing the *Marsayru* and a cutter.

Shortly after sailing the *Marsayru* broke adrift, and in darkness could not be found. Next day, the 1st June, however, at 1400, S/Lt. T. E. Godman, R.N.V.R. in a Naval steam pinnace, off La Panne, sighted the *Marsayru* drifting with the tide and unoccupied. She was found to be in working order ; the engine was started up and Sub-Lieut. Godman took an A.B. and a soldier as crew. He left Petty Officer Morrison in charge of the steam pinnace with orders to lay off and wait for the return of the *Marsayru*.

With the dinghy in tow the *Marsayru* proceeded to the western end of the beach and anchored ; the dinghy ferried 19 troops to her, which filled her to capacity.

In the meantime the crew of the steam pinnace had embarked in the skoot *Doggersbank* and had left the steam pinnace anchored near Dunkirk harbour. Sub-Lieut. Godman decided to leave her there and sailed in the *Marsayru* for England ; he overtook the *Doggersbank* on the way and obtained some fuel from her.

At 2330 on the 1st June the *Marsayru* made fast to a conical flashing buoy and waited for daylight. At 0430 on the 2nd June a trawler took the *Marsayru* in tow to Ramsgate, which was reached at 0800, and the 19 troops were disembarked.

---

the pleasure launches *Enterprise* and *Wave Queen*), the *Foremost 101*, *Lady Southborough*, *Queen's Channel*, *Gallion's Reach* ; and the hopper barge *W.26*. The M/B's. *Minotaur*, *White Heather*, *Westerley*, *Naiad Errant*, *Lansdowne*, *Balquhain*, *Tigris I*, *Rapid I*, *Marsayru*, and *Mermaiden*. The *Excellent's* A/A M/B, the *Dolphin's* power boat, the *Nelson's* picket boat and the motor coaster *Hythe*.

The X lighters *95*, *149*, *209* (towing a boat), *213*, and *217*. The motor barge *Sherfield*, the motor launch *Nanette II* the lighter *Y.C.63*. The War Department's seven 30 knot motor launches *Grouse*, *Haig*, *Kestrel*, *Marlborough*, *Swallow*, *Wolfe* and *Vulture ;* an eighth, the *Pigeon*, went over on 1st June.

The skoot *Hilda* towed over the motor boats *Moss Rose*, *Rose Marie*, *Lady Haig*, *Britannic Gipsy King*, *Golden Spray II* and two life-boats.

Three more of Pickford & Co. Ltd.'s motor vessels went over, viz : the *Chamois*, *Hound* and the *M.F.H.*

Later on 2nd June, on instructions from the N.O.I.C., the original crew took charge of the *Marsayru*, but *she did not, apparently, make a second trip to Dunkirk.*[1] Her skipper (G. D. Olivier) received the D.S.M. for his services, and her engineer (C. Coggins) a mention in despatches.

The Cockle Bawley boats

Of the small craft that went over on this day, Admiral Ramsay speaks in the following terms of the Cockle Bawley boats[2]:

> "The conduct of the crews of these cockle boats was exemplary. They were all volunteers who were rushed over to Dunkirk in one day, probably none of them had been under gunfire before and certainly none of them under Naval discipline. These boats were Thames estuary fishing boats which never left the estuary, and only one of their crews had been further afield than Ramsgate before. In spite of this fact perfect formation was maintained throughout the day and night under the control of a Sub-Lieutenant R.N.V.R.[3] in command of the Unit, and all orders were carried out with great diligence even under actual shell fire and aircraft attack."

One of these cockle boats, the *Renown*, was blown up by a mine while returning to England disabled and in tow of the drifter *Ben and Lucy*. Her skipper, W. H. Noakes, and his crew[4] were killed. The *Ben and Lucy* had been towing the drifter *Feasible* (disabled by a shell hit), 3 life-boats and the cockle boat *Letitia*. At 0115 on the 1st June the *Renown*, by then disabled, attached herself to this tow, but an hour later she was blown to pieces and a hail of wood and splinters came down on the *Letitia's* deck. The *Letitia's* skipper (A. J. Dench) says, "In the pitch dark we could see nothing, and after the explosion we hard nothing and we could do nothing, except pull in the tow rope, which was just as we passed it to the *Renown* about ¾ hour before. . ."

French and Belgian ships arrive

Early on the 31st it became known that the Belgian Government were anxious that several small Belgian fishing craft lying at Brixham should take part in the evacuation and steps were taken to arrange this.

At 1335 the French destroyer *Léopard* routed from the Downs to Dunkirk two French trawlers[5], three French motor fishing vessels[6], and ten Belgian trawlers[7].

The Belgian trawlers were under the orders of *Pilote* Malet; the remainder of the ships under *Lieutenant de vaisseau* Drogou.

Other Allied ships that sailed for Dunkirk on this day were the French cargo ships *Ingénieur Cachin* and *Margaux*, the trawlers *Pierre et Marie*, *Emma* and *Duperre*, and the patrol vessel *Diligente*; the Belgian trawlers *Lydie Suzanne* and *Yvonne*, and the drifters *Gerard-Léon* (H.64), *Anne Marie* and *Thérèse Compas*. On her return journey the *Pierre et Marie* picked up 3 English sailors from a drifting motor boat.

---

[1] The *Marsayru's* skipper says that throughout 31st May, "and the days and nights that followed (its all a complete jumble in my mind) we were . . . under constant fire . . . but the ship was not hit by anything." It seems, however, that Mr. Olivier was only in the evacuation for 5 hours, i.e. from 1600 to 2100, 31st May.

[2] *Defender, Endeavour, Letitia, Reliance, Renown* and *Resolute*.

[3] S/Lt. M. H. B. Solomon, R.N.V.R.

[4] L. V. Osborne, Mate, and F. W. Osborne, Engineer.

[5] *Chasse-Marée* and *Angèle Marie*.

[6] *Margaux* (D.692), *Jeune France* (Di.1213) and *Du Guesclin* (D.G.910).

[7] *Indépendence* (0.308), *Victor-Erna* (H.63), *Louise-Irène* (H.80), *Pharailde* (H.42) *Raphael-Raymonde* (H.43), *O.L.V. Van Vlaanderen* (N.49), *John* (O.210) *Anna Marguerite* (Z.2), *Buffalo Bill* (Z.4) and the *M.41*.

The French trawlers *Marie* and *Pierre* carrying munitions, and the *Ste. Isabelle* carrying food, also went to Dunkirk. While unloading under shell fire the *Pierre's* munitions were hit and exploded and the ship caught fire. She was still on fire when her consorts left Dunkirk at 1100.

Captain Howson returns to Dover

Meanwhile the enemy made the last of his three major air attacks of the day ; the other two having been made at 1415–1500 and 1700–1715[1]. Off Bray at about 1930 some 30 bombers escorted by fighters appeared overhead. Most went on to bomb Dunkirk, others bombed the *Mosquito*, destroyers, sloops and small craft[2].

The yacht *Ankh*, which Captain Howson was using as his headquarters, received some damage from a near miss and started making water forward and also through the stern glands. Being of opinion that the *Ankh* would be unlikely to stand up to further " rough treatment", Captain Howson decided to return to Dover, ordering the yacht *Amulree* to keep company. Being then some 2 to 3 miles to seaward, in the failing light Captain Howson was unable to signal to Rear-Admiral Wake-Walker in the *Keith*. The yachts *Eilla II* and *Caryandra* closed the *Ankh* ; the former reported that she was short of fuel and the latter that she was damaged and short of lubricating oil, so they returned in company with the *Ankh* to Dover.

It was at about this time, 2000, that the yacht *Glagla* (which was standing by to tow the boats of the *Vivacious* from the beach) found that her tiller wire was reduced to a single strand. Her Commanding Officer said, " The bombing and shelling which had been going on continuously, became intense. A Captain R.N. in yacht No. 1 of the Solent Patrol [i.e. Captain Howson in the *Ankh*], ordered us to make for the open sea, and all the smaller craft followed him out."

It was in the above circumstances that a number of power boats started a withdrawal to Dover, and that at 0611 on the 1st June Rear-Admiral Wake-Walker found it necessary to report to V.A. Dover that all craft used for towing boats had left during the night, and to urge that they be sent back[3].

At about 0145 on the 1st June the yacht *Amulree*, which was escorting the *Ankh*, was rammed and sunk by the *Vimy* in the vicinity of the Gull. Her crew were picked up. The Commodore-in-Charge, Sheerness, Captain H. R. Marrack, R.N., D.S.C., in a report to V.A., Dover, says that it was " a matter for regret that this vessel [the *Amulree*] was diverted from the very valuable work which she was performing in towing out pontoons from the beaches, to carry out a seemingly minor administrative duty which indirectly resulted in her being rammed and sunk by a British destroyer in the Downs".[4]

The *Ankh* arrived at Dover at 0815 on the 1st June.

Casualties to towing craft

Of the motor boats lost this day, 2 were lost by enemy action. The M/B *Commodore* ferried troops to the *Worcester* off Malo. She was eventually machine gunned, holed and abandoned. Her crew embarked in the M/B *Eastbourne Queen*. The M/B *New Prince of Wales* was damaged by a shell from a shore battery. Two able-seamen were killed, and S/Lt. P. H. E. Bennett, R.N. and 2 of the crew were wounded. The vessel was abandoned and the crew embarked in the M/B *Triton*.

---

[1] R.A.F. Narrative, p.336.
[2] Captain Howson's Report (R.O.IV, p.119).
[3] Appendix H.26.
[4] R.O.III, p.551.

At least fourteen other motor boats[1] were lost by misadventure, e.g. engine failure, grounding, swamping, damaging rudders and/or propellers on floating or submerged wreckage, or breaking adrift and being lost when on tow. The seaplane tender *No. 291* managed to get back to England in spite of the damage she had sustained, but was unable to take any further part in " Dynamo".

Conflicting news of La Panne

Meanwhile, as the tows of boats (which Rear-Admiral Wake-Walker now saw for the first time at 1900 on the 31st May), arrived off Dunkirk they were directed to the beaches by Lt. Cdr. Wynne-Edwards, first from *M.T.B.68* and later at about 2100, from *M.A/S.B. 6.* It was found, however, that in the growing darkness, and with no lights to help them, there was a tendency for the boats to stop at the first place they came to where other craft were assembled. At about 1930 the *Codrington*, then off Bray, was warned by Rear-Admiral Wake-Walker to send on the boats detailed for La Panne, but the bulk of them did not get further than Bray.

The night was dark, and Rear-Admiral Wake-Walker stayed off La Panne, " wondering how things were going. Everything was black, ships and boats and shore showed no lights", although arrangements had been made for a light to be shown to seaward to guide boats inshore. Shelling was continuous and seemed to be falling among the ships at the anchorage. News was conflicting ; a message from the shore said that thousands of men were waiting but there were no boats, while messages came from ships that their boats could find no one on the beach."…. the ships and the boats were there, and the troops ashore, and one could do no more…. I do not know to this day", says Rear-Admiral Wake-Walker, " what really took place there".[2]

La Panne beach 31st May/1st June

It is not easy to discover what happened at La Panne, but the following account, based on a report by Lt. Cdr. J. W. McClelland, R.N., who with a party of signalmen reached La Panne in the minesweeper *Gossamer* at 1930 on the 30th May, gives the main course of events. He was S.N.O., La Panne, for the seven hours prior to its abandonment as a place of embarkation at about 0200 on the 1st June.

About 1600 on May 31st Captain Tennant, who had been visiting Lord Gort at La Panne, decided to return to Dunkirk, but he first instructed Lt. Cdr. McClelland to arrange for the evacuation of Lord Gort and his staff, to carry out the duties of S.N.O., La Panne[3], and to join Major General B. L. Montgomery, then in command of 2nd Corps.

At that time, says Lt. Cdr. McClelland, an enemy battery near Nieuport, assisted by 2 kite balloons, had found the range of the beach and the off lying-ships, which had *accordingly withdrawn to the westward*. Rear-Admiral Wake-Walker asked for the balloons to be shot down, and aircraft came over for that purpose ; at times the balloons were hauled down—but they always re-appeared.[4]

---

[1] *A.L.C.8, A.L.C.15, Enterprise, Excellent's 35 ft. M/B, Excellent's A/A M/B, Golden Spray II, Princess Lily, St. Patrick,* and the Seaplane tender *243* and *A.M.C.3* ; the *Sea Falcon, Sunshine, Triton* and the *Two Rivers.*
[2] M.017978/41, p.21.
[3] Lt. Cdr. McClelland speaks of the final evacuation of A, B and C beaches La Panne, but this is evidently an error as the beaches were lettered from West to East (See Plan 3) and must therefore have been M, N and O Beaches.
[4] M.017978/41, p.16.

Work was commenced on a second lorry pier at La Panne by Lieut. Great-wood R.N.[1] and the 12th Lancers who had been marshalling the beaches for the past 24 hours[2].   Parties were organised to collect all the oars and boats that could be found, the *intention at the time*—about 1600—*being to recommence the embarkation of troops from La Panne at 2030* with two ships, when it was hoped the fire of the Nieuport battery would be less effective[3].

At about 1630, arrangements were made from La Panne direct with V.A. Dover for the embarkation of Lord Gort at about 1800 from a point 2 miles westward of La Panne, which Lt. Cdr. McClelland considered would be out of range of the Nieuport battery.   In the event, however, Lord Gort embarked in the *Hebe's* whaler nearer to La Panne.

At 2030 two ships arrived off La Panne[4], and the beaching craft there which were already filled put off.   No additional boats arrived, however, and the rate of embarkation was no more than 300 an hour ; indeed, as darkness set in, the rate fell to about 150 an hour.   With about 7,000 men awaiting embarkation before 0400 the next morning (when the beach would be exposed to gunfire, and might even be in the hands of the enemy) a rate of at least 1,000 an hour was necessary.   Urgent representations were made to V.A., Dover, and to ships in the vicinity for more boats, but none came, although at 2130 V.A., Dover, informed Rear-Admiral Wake-Walker that La Panne had reported 6,000 troops to clear urgently and that they lacked ships and boats[5].   It was probably, however, in response to this signal that at 2223 the *Keith* asked V.A., Dover, to tell S.N.O., Dunkirk, that troops must be moved down to Bray, as tows of boats got intercepted at Bray in the dark, with a resulting shortage of boats at La Panne.

During darkness hostile low-flying aircraft were patrolling continually over-head and bombing promptly all lights shown, which no doubt explains why Rear-Admiral Wake-Walker in the *Keith* did not see the pre-arranged shore lights.

By 2200 the situation at La Panne had become serious ; only about 600 troops had been embarked and the few boats available, which had to be handled and pulled in the darkness by troops inexperienced in this work, had dwindled to three.   At this time, as the telephone to Dover was still working, Lt. Cdr. McClelland destroyed the W/T set.

At about 2300 the situation was becoming critical, as troops for whom there were no boats were piling up on the beach, and the military withdrawal which would leave La Panne in no-man's-land by 0400 the following morning was in full swing.   To make matters worse the Nieuport battery opened a slow fire on the crowded beach, causing casualties with almost every shell.

Lt. Cdr. McClelland discussed the situation with the G.O.C., Major-General D. G. Johnson, V.C., D.S.O., M.C., Commanding the 4th Division, who in turn conferred with the Duty Captain at Dover, and it was finally decided to march the 6,000 men remaining at La Panne to Dunkirk, via Bray-Dunes, the decision being reached after Lt. Cdr. McClelland had made a personal reconnaissance right along the beaches, without finding any more ships or boats, and after he had informed the G.O.C. in reply to a direct question that he thought they would not arrive[5].

---

[1] Lt. Cdr. McClelland's report.   The name " Greatwood " is not in the May 1940 Navy List.

[2] S/Lt. E. C. Croswell R.N: (C.W.23187/40).

[3] Appendix Q.16.

[4] Probably the *Worcester* and *Hebe*.

[5] Appendix H.16.

Thereupon, at about 0050 on the 1st June Lt. Cdr. McClelland informed Dover that he was closing down the telephone line as the headquarters were now being abandoned.

While this decision was being arrived at further batteries had come into action on the town of La Panne, and by 0100 the rate of fire on the beach was increased. Lt. Cdr. McClelland says that he had by that time lost touch with Major-General Montgomery, who had left earlier and subsequently embarked in the *Codrington* at Dunkirk at 0525 on the 1st June.

By 0130 it was low water, and about half a mile walk to the end of the piers which were now high and dry. While walking there with the intention of assisting in the embarkation of the few men who had not been ordered to march to Dunkirk, Lt. Cdr. McClelland was twice knocked down by shell bursts ; a splinter smashed the box signalling lantern he was carrying, and another slightly injured his ankle. Several houses on the front were now blazing fiercely.

On reaching the embarkation point Lt. Cdr. McClelland was told that no boats had been in for over half an hour, and that the naval beach party had left—apparently in accordance with his orders that they were to leave in the last boat.[1] As will be seen later, the beach parties at Bray also embarked early on the 31st May. .

There being neither ships nor boats now at the beaches, Lt. Cdr. McClelland ordered a general retirement westward of all the groups on the beaches with the object of getting them inside the defended perimeter outside Bray-Dunes before 0400.

At 0200, two or three miles down the beach towards Bray, three ships[2] at anchor and some troops had been trying unsuccessfully to attract their attention by firing their rifles. Further on, as other large groups were waiting for boats, Lt. Cdr. McClelland decided to swim off and report on the situation. He managed to get close enough to the *Gossamer*, which was anchored 4 cables from the shore, to pick up a lifebelt on a line brought to him by one of the ship's company.

He was just able to gasp out his message to the Captain of the *Gossamer* before collapsing, but he had told of the 4th Division's change of plan and of the state of the beaches and had asked that Rear-Admiral Wake-Walker and Vice-Admiral Dover be informed. The former was evidently informed at 0215[3], and at 0235, the *Gossamer* signalled V.A. Dover that 6,000 British were marching from La Panne through Bray on Dunkirk[4].

Being very exhausted and no longer able to walk because of the pain from the wound in his ankle, Lt. Cdr. McClelland remained in the *Gossamer*.[5]

Sub.-Lieut. E. C. Croswell's report on La Panne confirms that of Lt. Cdr. McClelland. He says : " On Friday [31st May] embarkation at La Panne was slowed up as shelling caused some ships to move westward to Bray-Dunes. The rest camp in the rear of La Panne beach and a small arms ammunition hut were hit during bombing attacks which continued throughout Friday, and ships also suffered shell fire. . . . On Friday evening German gunners found the range of the beach and were aided by 2 observation balloons which we did not manage

---

[1] Lt. Cdr. McClelland's report (R.O.III, p.392).
[2] The *Codrington, Ivanhoe* and *Gossamer.*
[3] M.017978/41, p.21.
[4] Appendix H.20.
[5] Lt. Cdr. McClelland received a mention in despatches.

to destroy.   At 0200 Saturday [1st June] La Panne was abandoned as a place of embarkation".[1]

The following extract from *War Diary General Staff 4 Division*, dated the 1st June 1940[2], confirms the above accounts :

"[At La Panne] by 0100 hrs. not more than three to four hundred men of the Division out of eight thousand to be embarked had been put on transports.   A conference was called at Divisional H.Q. which had now opened in a house by the side of the beach where it was decided that it was useless to continue the embarkation from La Panne.   Motor Contact officers were sent out to inform Brigades that they were to proceed direct to Bray Dunes and Dunkerque Mole.   Whilst this conference was going on the beach was heavily shelled by 5.9's and a few casualties were sustained.   A Staff Officer was sent to warn the French Guards at the Frontier that 4 Division would be passing through them.   Another Staff Officer was sent to order the men on the beach to make their way along the beach either to Bray or Dunkerque.   From this moment H.Q. ceased to operate until it arrived at Dunkerque Mole.   Certain officers arrived at Dunkerque Mole as follows :—
GSO II, GSO III, and Camp Commandant at 0500 hrs. 1 June.   GOC, GSO I, AA and QMG, I.O., ADC, Motor Contact Officer at about 0700 hrs."

Captain R. Pim, R.N.V.R., Beach Master

In view of the foregoing outline of events at La Panne, it is necessary, in order to avoid confusion, to refer briefly to a report by Captain Pim who was sent over from the Admiralty to assist in speeding up the embarkation.

After visiting as many of the beaches as possible he assumed the duties of Beach Master (at Bray beach) and arranged to continue the organisation of ferrying boats until " all the troops on the beaches " were on board.   " I told them", he said, " that if anything went wrong during the night we would return at dawn".[3]

Later, Captain Pim stated : " All the troops that I could find were embarked by midnight and placed in ships which sailed for England.   Just before midnight I went along certain beaches to look for stragglers.   A Staff Officer informed me that no more troops would embark from these beaches[4] but that they would march to Dunkirk, as it was anticipated these beaches would be shelled and would probably be in German hands the following day."[5]   Captain Pim estimated that from pontoon bridges and beaches, approximately 5,000 troops were probably embarked.

Although his report is entitled " Final evacuation of troops from the beaches of La Panne and Bray", Captain Pim does not say that these 5,000 troops were embarked from La Panne, and it is evident from Rear-Admiral Wake-Walker's report, and particularly from Lt. Cdr. McClelland's report, and the War Diary of the 4th Division, that they were not embarked from La Panne.   Vice-Admiral Dover[6], however, assumes from Captain Pim's report that he worked at La Panne, the weight of evidence shows that he worked at Bray and immediately to the east and west of it.

During the night, Captain Pim found it necessary to shift his anchorage to the west, as shells meant for the beaches were ricocheting over the *Hilda*. Then, at 0315 on the 1st June, in accordance with his undertaking to the troops, Captain Pim " sent off all [his] boats. . . . to search the beaches, *starting from the western end of Bray-Dunes*".   During the next 3 hours, he says, only about 250

---

[1] C.W.23187/40.
[2] Provided by Lt. Col. H. F. Joslen, (Historical Section, War Cabinet).
[3] Capt. Pim's report (R.O. IV, p.52).
[4] Evidently the La Panne beaches.
[5] Capt. Pim's report (R.O. IV, P.52).
[6] D.R., p.20, para.61.

men were taken from the beach, apparently stragglers. A large rearguard party (probably troops of the 4th Division) marching along the beach decided to continue to Dunkirk.[1]

Bray Beach parties return to England

It was on this day that the majority of the beach parties returned to England. Captain Howson records that on the evening of the 30th May he had "learnt that the enemy were closing in and that it might be expected that the final evacuation would take place during the following day (31st May) or night at latest". As he had received orders that beach parties were not to be taken prisoner[2], and anticipated that very many troops would be left ashore, he deemed it undesirable for all naval personnel to embark "in the final rush". Accordingly he arranged that half the naval personnel should embark during the early hours of Friday (31st May)[3].

This arrangement to some extent accounts for V.A. Dover's 1229/31 to Rear-Admiral Wake-Walker saying that officers and men of beach parties had returned to Dover on instructions from Dunkirk, and that they must be retained to the last[4]; and his further signals notifying that more beach parties were being sent out with all despatch in the destroyer *Worcester*[5].

An account of the activities of the beach parties at Bray has been given by Lieutenants G. W. Vavasour and J. G. Wells, R.N. They were among the 12 officers and 60 ratings, who sailed from Dover in the *Esk* with Rear-Admiral Wake-Walker and Commodores Stephenson and Hallett on the 29th May (Page 49).

On the way over the 12 officers were divided into 3 groups of 4 officers, and to each of the 12 officers was allocated a party of 1 P.O., 1 Leading Seaman, 2 Able Seamen and a Signalman. Rear-Admiral Wake-Walker told the officers that on no account were their parties to be captured, and with this in mind, they were to re-embark when they thought fit.

On arrival off the various beaches at about 2330 on May 29th the *Esk* stopped off each and the 3 beach parties were landed in whalers; one party went to La Panne where Cdre. Stephenson was to be S.N.O., Afloat, off the beach[6], one went west of Bray, and the third went to Bray where Commodore Hallett was to be S.N.O., Afloat, off the beach. There is no report available of the activities of the first two parties.

The 4 officers in Cdre. Hallett's section were Lieuts. Vavasour, Wells Tibbits and Cameron, R.N., all of H.M.S. *Excellent*. Cdre. Hallett had previously explained to these officers that he himself would be afloat approximately in front of his sectiions (E, F, G and H) of the beach, and repeated the warning that the officers were to be the sole judges of when to evacuate the naval parties;

---

[1] Capt. Pim's report (R.O. IV, p.52), Italics not in original.
[2] Rear-Admiral Wake-Walker says that the V.A. Dover had stressed that Naval ratings (in beach parties) were not to risk being taken prisoner (M.017978/41, p.3).
[3] Capt. Howson's Report (R.O. IV, p.117).
[4] Appendix Q.12.
[5] Appendices Q.13 and Q.14.
[6] Lt. Vavasour's report, R.O.III, p.422. Lt Vavasour says that Cdre Stephenson was S.N.O., A.B.C.D. Sections. But the beaches had been lettered A to O, from west to east and so the La Panne beach was L.M.N.O. It was probably because of the almost invariable confusion about the lettering of the beaches that this method of designating beaches was changed by signal at 1906/29 (Appendix O.11), and the whole length was divided into 3 equal parts, referred to as Malo, Bray and La Panne, from west to east with a mile gap between each part.

moreover, if one party had to leave, it was to communicate along the whole beach so that all would have the warning[1].

On landing, the 4 section Lieutenants of the Bray party decided that all 4 sections, being small, should remain close together, and they took up a position covering a frontage, in all, of about 400 yards; they at once proceeded to organize 3 embarkation points. There were at first no signs of any soldiers but, within 2 minutes of landing, about 5,000 troops left their cover in the sand dunes and approached the boats. The troops were on the whole easy to control and implicity obeyed orders about boats given by the naval officers and ratings, except the orders to bring back the boats from ships to shore.

Evacuation in Commodore Hallett's section was very slow and Lieut. Vavasour says that by 0500 on the 30th May it is doubtful if 80 men were got off. A few boats appeared, were loaded and sent off; but when the troops reached a ship, they let the boats go adrift, as there were no boat-keepers.

At dawn Lieut. Vavasour contacted a headquarters[2] in one of the houses along the front at Bray. There he saw a Captain R.N. and 2 Commanders[3]. No suggestions or orders were issued from headquarters, says Lieut. Vavasour. One of the commanders, "who had come from Dunkirk", told him that the port was out of action, and the moles were in ruins.

Shortly after 0500 on the 30th May there was a destroyer and a minesweeper off Bray beach, but the boat situation had become acute and there were now about 15,000 troops on the beach. With the assistance of some senior Army Officers who by then had arrived, the troops were moved away from the water's edge and settled in the sands.

By 0600, a considerable number of collapsible boats had been collected from the Royal Engineers and these were loaded with 10 soldiers apiece and sent off. In the majority of cases, however, on arrival at the ships the boats were abandoned and, drifting to the east, came ashore abreast the French, who used them to go off to British ships. By 0700, there were no power boats at all, and whaler trips were very infrequent. The rate of evacuation continued to be very slow.

Meanwhile the "Captain R.N." (Captain Howson) had gone to La Panne and Lieut. Vavasour did not see him again.

By 0730 more ships had arrived and evacuation proceeded more quickly, as the beach parties had organised their own boat keepers. It was still, however, far from satisfactory. The troops found it difficult to get into the boats in the surf, and the beach parties had to wade out shoulder-deep to keep the boats stern-on to the beach.

Lieut. Vavasour and his party then boarded the *Anthony* to get a change of clothing, and while there obtained a motor boat which they manned for 12 hours until she broke down. They first proceeded to recover the majority of their lost boats, now in use by the French, and then organised a ferry service.

At 0900 contact was made with Commodore Hallett who was then in drifter. "I informed him of what I was doing" says Lieut. Vavasour. "He approved. He informed me that he was very short of coal. At approximately 0930 the Commodore steamed away to seaward. I did not see the Commodore again."

Lieut. Wells said: "We never saw him [the Commodore] at all as I believe his boat broke down, and he had to be towed clear of the danger area."

---

[1] Report by Lt. Vavasour (R.O.III, p.423).
[2] Probably the Corps Headquarters referred to by Capt. Howson (Section 158).
[3] Captain Howson R.N. and probably Cdrs. Otway-Ruthven and Gorton, or Richardson.

As to the method of embarking the troops, Lieut. Wells found that the best way to organise them into a long queue at each of the 3 embarkation points. The queues were 3 deep and were spaced out in groups of 10, this number being most suitable for the type of boat available. The following group could be used for shoving off a loaded boat, which took a good deal of moving at half tide owing to a bar running parallel to the sea. The Army pontoon boats proved most suitable, because of their draught, double-ended construction and general handiness.

The main difficulty, according to Lieut. Wells, lay in the insufficiency of naval boat keepers. As a rule the soldiers detailed to return the boats did not carry out orders and the beach parties had to swim or wade out for drifting boats, which continually delayed and slowed up the operation. Lieut. Wells considered that the troops could hardly be blamed as it was clearly a naval responsibility. More ratings were asked for from outlying ships, but none could be sent.

At 0930 on May 30th there was only one other motor boat working within 5 miles either side of Lieut. Vavasour's beach, i.e. G section. It was a destroyer's motor boat which, being aground when the destroyer sailed, had been left behind.

By about noon, all ships within sight from G beach had departed fully loaded. About an hour later a destroyer [the *Windsor*] anchored east of Bray, and as many boats as possible were towed out to her. Lieut. M. A. Hemans R.N., says Lieut. Vavasour closed the destroyer. On board her were two officers, Lieuts. Stubbs and Fletcher from the beach party which had gone to La Panne (under Cdre. Stephenson) who said they had been told to leave by their Commodore. Rear-Admiral Wake-Walker was on board the destroyer and he told Lieuts. Hemans and Vavasour to carry on with the boats.

At about 1300 some 10 trawlers, drifters and minesweepers began to arrive, and evacuation proceeded apace until 2000, in spite of there being only 3 motor boats for towing and ferrying. By 2000 all ships had left except the Special Service vessel *Royal Eagle*. By 2100, however, just after dark, many destroyers and minesweepers commenced to arrive.

Lieut. Vavasour went on board the *Royal Eagle* at about 2000 in response to a signal. While his motor boat was away collecting boat loads of troops for the *Royal Eagle* the former broke down and was picked up by a destroyer which was on the way to La Panne. That was the last Lieut. Vavasour saw of his party. He later got on board a minesweeper at 0100/31 and sailed for Harwich. Subsequently, on arrival at H.M.S. *Excellent* he found the remainder of Cdre. Hallett's lieutenants were back. They had been told, he says, to abandon the evacuation about midnight " by the S.N.O. of the beach—a Commander".

" I felt most limited in my activities," says Lieut. Vavasour, " by the very definite orders that I had received that on no account was the naval party to be left behind. No accurate information was available. . . . I was unable to obtain any information at all from any single one of the large number of ships to which I towed boats during the day and night". This is not surprising because in the circumstances, with the situation continually and rapidly changing, no one either ashore or afloat had any accurate information. Thus, for instance, the *Gossamer* which anchored one mile west of La Panne at 2207, had sent in the motor boat *Handy Billie* in charge of S/Lt. M. Phipps R.N. to search for troops. He found none, and received no answer to his hails. " Inside an hour, however, the situation had changed, and thousands were massing abreast the ship".[1]

---

[1] Report by *Gossamer* (R.O.I, p.264).

Lieut. Wells says that at 0100/31 he was informed that naval personnel would have to evacuate at dawn if the shelling continued. Some officers not in his original party had already left, and at 0300/31 he swam out to fetch a boat for the "Brigadier" [?Major General W. G. Holmes] in command of the 42nd Division, who was embarked at about 0330.

The shelling of the beach continued, and (says Lieut. Wells) "the order was passed from Headquarters that as the embarkation would probably be over at dawn the following day [1st June], all naval personnel were to embark forthwith". Lieut. Wells accordingly remained in the *Halcyon*, where he had taken the "Brigadier". The *Halcyon* arrived at Dover at 0845/31.

There is clearly some connection between the above "order from Headquarters" and Captain Howson's arrangement for embarking naval personnel during the early hours of the 31st May.

The only other account of the activities of the beach parties comes from Cdr. H. du P. Richardson, R.N., who worked with Lt. Cdr. D. B. Dowling, R.N., and a naval platoon at Malo beach from 2000 on May the 27th until the beach was cleared of troops at about noon on the 28th May.[1]

S.N.O. Dunkirk then ordered him to Bray beach to embark 5,000 troops, and he arrived there at about 1700 on the 28th May, with Cdr. Ken[2] [?Kerr] and 16 men. They found about 30,000 troops, stretching from Bray to the eastward, awaiting embarkation. Cdr. Richardson's beach party, as will be seen, also returned on the 31st May.

At 0130 on the 29th May a high wind got up which made beach embarkation almost impossible. Cdr. Richardson therefore sent off about 20,000 troops to Dunkirk in batches of 1000.

During the night of 29th/30th May another naval embarkation party arrived on the beach to the eastward[3], and this reduced the limits of Cdr. Richardson's beach.

Early on the morning of the 30th May Cdr. Richardson went to Brigade H.Q.[4] at Bray and suggested that piers be built by running lorries into the sea. This, he says, was quickly done and proved successful.

Between 1800 and 2000 on the 30th May the enemy directed accurate artillery fire on to the beach, and continued firing throughout the night. Cdr. Richardson's beach was completely evacuated by allied soldiers. "No boats", he says, "had now been in for 16 hours on our beach".

During the night of the 30th/31st May, the weather became bad once more, and a heavy surf was running. By about 0300 on the 31st May it was impossible to carry out embarkation from the beaches.

Cdr. Richardson's men were by now showing signs of extreme exhaustion, and as it was impossible to communicate with the S.N.O. he decided to take over a whaler they had salved and go to the nearest destroyer to report to the S.N.O.

They waited for high water, and at about 0730 put to sea. There was a very heavy surf running, and they had an uneven set of oars, rope crutches and only an oar to steer by. They approached 2 destroyers, but both got underway. Two other destroyers passed at about 7 cables, but paid no attention.

---

[1] Cdr. Richardson's report (R.O.III, p.367).
[2] There is no officer of this name in the May 1940 Navy List.
[3] Evidently the party landed at E.F.G.H., Cdre. Hallett's sections of the beach.
[4] These were probably the same H.Q. as those referred to by Capt. Howson as "Corps headquarters" (p. 59).

After about an hour the Margate life-boat, the *Lord Southborough*, appeared. All destroyers were now under way, and as the life-boat was returning to Margate the party went back in her[1]. She reached Margate at 1450 on May 31st.

Thus, by about 0830 on the 31st May all the beach parties of which there are any records had returned or were on their way to England.

Devonia is beached

At 1035 Rear-Admiral Wake-Walker had informed V.A. Dover that he would beach a ship in the hope of improving conditions for boat work, which was then being made difficult by a lop and he instructed Cdre. Stephenson accordingly. Cdre. Stephenson, then in the yacht *Bounty* off La Panne, boarded the minesweeper *Devonia* at 1600 and gave orders to beach the ship. The *Devonia*, already much damaged by near misses at 1230, was beached at full speed off La Panne, and at 1930, on account of the shelling and bombing, she was abandoned. Fortunately by 1700 the weather off the beaches had much improved.

Casualties to H.M. Ships

With the exception of the *Devonia* none of H.M. ships was lost on this day, but the following were slightly damaged: the *Vivacious* was damaged by a shell hit and had 3 dead and 12 wounded; the *Hebe* received slight damage from a near miss; the *Wolsey* was in collision with the P/V *Roebuck*; the *Impulsive* damaged a propeller on uncharted wreckage; the *Malcolm* was in collision with Dunkirk pier; and the *Scimitar* was in collision with the *Icarus* and later with a drifter[2].

Air patrols

During the 31st May Fighter Command carried out patrols, as on the 30th May, at an average strength of three to four squadrons. Eight patrols in all were flown, involving 289 sorties. The periods in the day when the Dunkirk area was not covered were 0620–0800, 0830–1110, 1510–1615, and 1745–1915[3].

Coastal Command patrolled the line North Goodwins—Gravelines—Ostend throughout the day, patrols being of one section strength, involving in all 37 sorties[4].

Shortly before 0930 the Air Ministry intercepted a meassage indicating that the enemy air force had been ordered not to attack the town or harbour of Dunkirk but to concentrate attacks on shipping at sea, or leaving the coast[3].

It was at about 1230 that, off La Panne, the *Devonia* received extensive damage to her hull from 4 near misses, but the first major attack on our ships occurred about 1415–1430 when one of our squadrons estimated the enemy strength as about 100 aircraft (bombers and fighters). Rear-Admiral Wake-Walker says, " a terrific air battle took place overhead and it seemed to go against us "[5]. Actually, we lost 9 aircraft and claimed 7 enemy shot down.[6]

Air attacks then followed at half-hourly intervals between 1530 and 1730, and at about 1717 the *Ivanhoe*, *Whitehall* and *Express* off Dunkirk harbour were attacked by about 50 bombers. The *Whitehall* received some damage and the *Express* slight damage from near misses. At this time also the *Hebe* was attacked off La Panne by 4 bombers and was damaged by near misses;

---

[1] Cdr. Richardson's report (R.O.III, p.370).
[2] Probably either the *Gervais Rentoul* or the *Eileen Emma* which both returned damaged as the result of collisions.
[3] R.A.F. Narrative, p.334.
[4] R.A.F. Narrative, p.336.
[5] M.017978/41, p.17.
[6] R.A.F. Narrative, p.335.

she shot down one Heinkel in flames.   Between 1630 and 1745 our air patrols encountered many enemy aircraft in mixed formations, the largest being a group of about thirty.   In this series of combats we lost 5 aircraft for 12 enemy definitely destroyed[1].   It was during this latter period that a squadron detailed to shoot down the enemy observation balloon failed to find it.   It was, said Rear-Admiral Wake-Walker, "at times hauled down but always re-appeared".

At 1800, when Lord Gort was due to embark, there were further air attacks which continued until 1930.

At 1920, off Dunkirk, the *Whitehall's* after group shot down a bomber. Between 1920 and 1930 our patrols were engaged with a formation of about 70 H.E.111's and M.E.109's.   In the encounter, Fighter Command lost 3 air-craft and claimed 10 bombers and 6 fighters definitely destroyed.   Some of the Hurricane pilots complained on their return that they had been shot at by the Spitfires[1].

At 2010 six Hurricanes trying to locate the observation balloon at Nieuport engaged about thirty M.E.109's, but no bombers were intercepted[1].

Final evacuation of B.E.F. expected on night 1st/2nd June

Meanwhile, at 1920, all ships in the Nore and Dover Commands were informed by the V.A., Dover, that the final evacuation of the B.E.F. was expected on the night 1st/2nd June, and that the evacuation of the French from Dunkirk and Malo beach would continue from the 1st June by both British and French ships[2].

At 2309 General Lloyd informed the D.M.O. of the new plan and stated that General Alexander had been placed in command of the final phase of the evacuation, that the composition of his force was not known, and that it was impossible now to state how long the French evacuation would take but that the Alexander force would remain till the last[3].

Meanwhile, no firm information could be obtained from the French on the following matters[4] :—

(i) the number of French troops to be evacuated ;

(ii) the nature and extent of French seaborne transport ;

(iii) the French military plan for the defence of the perimeter and the final withdrawal of French troops.

Embarkation reaches its zenith

The main features of the day had been :—

(a) the increased enemy artillery activity on Dunkirk, La Panne beach and the approach channels ;

(b) the change in the military plan as regards the locality and time of lifting the final contingents of the B.E.F. ;

(c) the set-back to beach evacuation that occurred during the choppy weather of the forenoon, followed by an excellent recovery in the after-noon and evening, when large numbers were lifted from the western beaches.

The rate of embarkation had, however, come up to expectations.   A total of 22,942 were lifted from the beaches and 45,072 from the harbour.   The grand total of 68,014 proved to be the highest daily total of the whole operation.

---

[1] R.A.F. Narrative, p.335.
[2] Appendix Q.19.
[3] Appendix Q.22.
[4] D.R. p.21, para. 63.

CHAPTER IX

SATURDAY, 1ST JUNE

GERMANS RENEW THEIR HEAVY AIR EFFORT

E-Boat activity : sinking of the *Stella Dorado* and *Argyllshire*

During the night of 31st May—1st June there was a recrudescence of enemy E-boat activity. After the torpedoing of the destroyers *Grafton* and *Wakeful* off Nieuport in the early hours of the 29th May M.T.B. patrols had been established during the dark hours to prevent enemy E-boats from using the inshore channels.

It was, however, in the less confined waters along Route Y that the enemy obtained their successes, despite intensive air and surface patrols. Route Y was patrolled that night by 2 corvettes and 6 trawlers, while Coastal Command provided 6 aircraft with bombs and parachute flares ; and owing to magnetic mines ships evacuating troops were given permission in the early hours of 1st June to use that route as well as Route X.

At 0230 on the 1st June the A/S trawler *Stella Dorado*, which 24 hours earlier had picked up 55 survivors from the *Siroco*, torpedoed by an E-boat near T buoy, was herself torpedoed in the same position and sunk whilst on patrol. About a quarter of an hour later the A/S trawler *Argyllshire*, on patrol in company with the *Lord Melchett* and *Stella Rigel* about 2 miles east of S buoy, commenced an attack on what appeared to be a submarine. Within 5 minutes she was struck by a torpedo fired by an E-Boat and sank immediately. Five survivors, including her Captain, Sub-Lieutenant J. S. Weddle, R.N.R., S.O. 11th A/S Striking Force, were picked up by the trawler *Malabar*.

At the time there were many trawlers and other small craft in the neighbourhood, and one of the two E-Boats responsible for these sinkings was reported to have been disguised as a sailing boat.

Final evacuation postponed

Already on the afternoon of the 31st May ships in Dunkirk road had come under fire from guns on shore at Mardyck, and early on 1st June it became evident that Major General Alexander's force could not be evacuated completely on the night of 1st/2nd June. At 0800, therefore, he agreed on a modified plan with Admiral Abrial and General Fagalde which involved holding his present line till midnight 1st/2nd June, so as to cover Dunkirk and to enable the French to evacuate as many of their troops as possible. Subsequently Major General Alexander was to withdraw to a bridgehead round Dunkirk with all available A/A and anti-tank guns and such troops as had not yet embarked.

Embarkations over Bray beaches

It was not only in Dunkirk roads that the ships had been under fire on the previous day ; off Bray they had the same experience. Troops were moving westward, and embarkation at La Panne was no longer possible. It was clear to Rear-Admiral Wake-Walker that beach work at Bray would be costly, and he so informed Vice-Admiral, Dover (0235/1), who concurred, whilst pointing out the necessity of using the beaches up to the last possible moment.

The Rear-Admiral, in the *Keith*, with the *Basilisk* for supporting fire against enemy tanks or lorries along the beach, was investigating the position to the east of Dunkirk.   As the light grew, at 0330, it was seen that the beach by La Panne was deserted.   The sea too, was empty, small boats had vanished under instructions to move westward to Dunkirk whilst those which were full were going back to England as intended.   However, ships were still loading off Bray and to the westward, though men were moving westward along the beaches.

The minesweeper *Speedwell* was anchored a little west of La Panne, using her motor boat and two whalers to ferry troops to the ship as the pontoon pier had been hit by shell fire.   She closed the shore at daylight, and at about 0500, shortly after low water, she grounded aft and continued thus to embark troops under machine-gun fire by enemy aircraft of the troops on shore, the boats, and the ship, until the minesweeper *Albury* towed her off.   She sailed at 0730 for Dunkirk.   On the way she took off 100 troops from the *Ivanhoe* which was damaged by a bomb as the *Speedwell* was steaming past her.   At Dunkirk she made up her number of troops to 972 and left for Dover at 0950 after being repeatedly but unsuccessfully bombed.   The minesweeper *Salamander* was anchored a mile east of Bray Dunes, similarly engaged in embarking troops with her boats, and she sailed for Dunkirk astern of the *Keith* and *Skipjack* soon after 0600.   At Dunkirk she came in for two air attacks in one of which, at about 0820, she was damaged by a near miss, but she reached Dover on one boiler at 1530 and disembarked 479 troops.   It was her last trip.   A mile east of Bray, too, the minesweeper *Sutton* embarked 453 troops from the beaches before sailing at 0600 for Dover.   She was bombed and machine-gunned, but the only man hit was one wounded soldier.   The minesweeper *Dundalk* was anchored nearer to La Panne, also embarking troops.   Having no motor boat, the *Speedwell* and *Salamander* both lent a hand to tow her whalers.   From 0500 onwards she was subjected to air attacks at regular intervals, and about 0800 she " decided to proceed to Margate," where she arrived at 1215 with 280 troops.   Still further east, the minesweeper *Halcyon* was anchored off La Panne embarking troops swimming off to the ship, paddling in rubber boats, and in her whalers, during which she had one officer (Lieut. N. Thurston, R.N.) mortally wounded and suffered some casualties amongst the crew from machine gunning by enemy aircraft.

Off Bray, the destroyer *Sabre* was embarking 451 troops and the minesweeper *Niger* 310, pressing into service carley floats and lifebelts with which men swam from the beach.   Daylight showed a minesweeper and a paddle minesweeper ashore, and the Rear-Admiral hailed a tug which was on its way homeward with soldiers on board, and told him to go in and try to tow off the minesweepers. However, the tugs had been sent over from England with pulling boats in tow and told to load up, and they regarded themselves as transports only, whereas Rear-Admiral Wake-Walker, who knew nothing of these instructions, naturally regarded them as tugs.   It was not until a gun was trained on the tug and an R.N.V.R. Sub.-Lieutenant put on board to take charge, that the master's anxiety to get away was overcome.

A welcome addition to the evacuation craft consisted of the first of a dozen Belgian fishing boats which now appeared on the scene from seaward down the Zyuidcoote Pass.[1]

Early liftings from Dunkirk

At 0241 Rear-Admiral Wake-Walker had given orders for all small craft to

---

[1] Probably the 10 Belgian trawlers from Brixham, referred to in Section 176.

move westward with boats in tow in the direction of Dunkirk, towards which the troops were now marching from La Panne.

The first loaded ship to leave Dunkirk seems to have been the *Whippingham*, in time of peace an Isle of Wight paddle ferry boat belonging to the Southern Railway. She had been embarking troops alongside the mole since 2200 on the previous day, and when she cast off at 0130 on 1st with 2,700 troops on board she was overladen and her sponsons were only about a foot above water. Disaster nearly overwhelmed her at the start, when she was straddled by shell fire and the troops rushed over to the port side, causing the ship to list 20°. Fortunately, the sea was calm. The chief mechanician (Ch. Mech. 2nd Cl. F. A. Ford) checked the rush, moved the troops back to starboard, and thereby probably saved the ship.

Another early sailer was the personnel vessel *Lady of Mann*, who proceeded at 0430 for Dover, with 1500 casualties. The hospital carriers *St. Andrew* and *St. Julien* disembarked in England this day 130 and 287 wounded, respectively, after which no more hospital ships brought wounded from Dunkirk. Space alongside the large-ship berths was too valuable to be occupied by hospital ships, and walking wounded went with the troops, whilst those that could not walk had to be left behind.

The personnel ship *Maid of Orleans* berthed at the East Mole at about 0330 and for 6 hours, most of the time under air attack, she acted as a floating stage for the embarkation of troops on board the destroyers *Icarus*, *Vanquisher* and *Windsor*, whose upper decks were far below the top of the mole. The pier was crowded and as many troops as possible were embarked over mess tables rigged across the " B " gun decks of inside ships to the outside vessel. The *Vanquisher* was the first of the three to leave, at 0630 with 1200 troops. An hour later the *Icarus* and *Windsor* sailed in company, with 1,114 and 493 troops respectively. Finally, at about 0900 the *Maid of Orleans* herself proceeded, during an air attack, with 1,856 troops, which, like the destroyers, she disembarked at Dover. In six trips, once being diverted without completing the trip and once returning on account of collision, the *Maid of Orleans* had transported in all 5,461 men ; but this was her last crossing, for when leaving Dover again for Dunkirk at 2030 that day she was rammed amidships by the destroyer *Worcester* returning from Dunkirk with manoeuvrability impaired through damage to propellers and rudder, caused by air attack at 1630 in which she had 6 men killed and 40 wounded, and shot down two enemy aircraft. No lives were lost in the collision, but the *Maid of Orleans* was too badly damaged to continue her voyage. For the *Worcester*, too, this was the final crossing : she had evacuated 4,545 troops in 6 trips.

Other destroyers were embarking troops at the same time alongside Dunkirk pier. The *Vivacious*, after being dive-bombed whilst waiting to enter harbour, went alongside at 0630, embarked 475 troops in a quarter of an hour, and sailed again for Dover at 0645. The *Winchelsea* was bombed at 0745 and again at 0830, but was not damaged, and she sailed at 0830 with 1150 troops on board.

Despite vicious air attacks, the embarkation of troops continued. The gunboat *Locust*, after embarking troops for four hours from Malo beach in her whalers, having no power boat, moved to Dunkirk at 0415 and took on board a further 500 at the east pier under air attack before sailing for Dover at 0610. The corvette *Kingfisher* left the east pier at 1130 with 210 troops and some wounded, embarked under almost continuous high level bombing.

There were times, however, during the day when the harbour was deserted.

When Rear-Admiral Wake-Walker left about 0930 to make contact with Vice-Admiral, Dover, all the ships which had not been sunk had gone. " At about 1800," he wrote, " the harbour was full of destroyers, sloops and minesweepers, many with the signs of their strenuous times upon them—bent bows, holes and the evidence cf bumps and collisions. Some were out of action altogether and all were enjoying the first few hours at rest in harbour that many of them had had for many days."[1]

Air Patrols

Consequent on the bombing of the day before, Rear-Admiral Wake-Walker had asked for fighter protection at dawn. As the morning mists and clouds dispersed many aircraft appeared on the scene, and fighters constantly came low over the ships. More often than not they were Spitfires, but the ships were not taking chances and nearly always opened fire indiscriminately on them. In order to stop the firing Rear-Admiral Wake-Walker hoisted 6 Flag—" Cease fire", and blew the syren to draw attention, in spite of which, however, the after machine gun of his own ship the *Keith* continued to fire regardless of the " cease fire " gong ; once firing started they could hear nothing.[2]

Route X to Dunkirk was patrolled during the early hours of daylight by the A.A. cruiser *Calcutta*, which sailed from Margate at 0315 with the corvettes *Mallow* and *Shearwater* and carried out a patrol between W and V buoys. The *Calcutta* was recalled to Sheerness at 0938 in readiness to perform the same service next night, and at 1015 she shot down a Heinkel which had bombed and damaged the *Mosquito* by a near miss 15 miles from Dover.

Fighter Command provided 8 patrols during the 1st June of an average strength of 3 to 4 squadrons. The main periods when no fighter protection was afforded were approximately 0730–0850, 1020–1120, 1120–1145, 1545–1615 and 1715–1845. Coastal Command continued to fly patrols of 3 aircraft over the North Goodwins—Gravelines—Ostend line throughout the day.

Enemy air attacks begin : *St. Fagan* sunk 0355.

Sporadic enemy air attacks began at early light. Ships alongside the mole reported being attacked at 0415 and 0500. This was before the first main R.A.F. air patrol appeared on the scene, for the R.A.F. had been asked to provide maximum protection from 0500 onwards.[3]

Before the first patrol appeared enemy aircraft claimed what was to prove the first of a long series of victims that day. The tug *St. Fagan* had towed over from Dover during the night three Thames barges. At about 0355, in the Dunkirk Channel, abreast the town the ship was hit by a bomb and practically disintegrated. Only two officers, including her Captain, Lieut.-Commander G. H. Warren, M.B.E., R.N., and 6 ratings, were saved out of a total complement of 25. They were picked up by the tug *Tanga* which had come over from Ramsgate with 6 boats in tow and had " hung off " outside Dunkirk most of the night waiting for troops to be brought out to her, and was then on her way home with 160 men on board and a motor-boat in tow.

Almost simultaneously with the withdrawal of our aircraft at 0730 a heavy dive bombing attack developed by a compact formation of some 30 or 40 Ju. 75s, causing the loss of the destroyers *Keith* and *Basilisk*, the minesweeper *Skipjack*, and the tug *St. Abbs*.

---

[1] *Report*, M.017978/41 p.29.
[2] M.017978/41, p.23.
[3] R.A.F. narrative.

The second series of attacks, which began at about 0906 and caused the loss of the *Havant*, coincided with the arrival of the third main R.A.F. patrol of the day. Coastal Command patrols were also over the ships, and at about 1015 one drove off a He. 111 which was about to attack two destroyers.

The third, a particularly heavy and prolonged enemy air attack, took place from about 1009 to 1120, at which latter time a patrol of 28 Hurricanes appeared and within ten minutes was engaged with an enemy force of 50 or 60 M. 109s and 110s. The presence of enemy bombers was also reported, but they were not engaged. They were responsible for sinking the French destroyer *Foudroyant*, the minesweeper *Brighton Queen*, personnel vessel *Scotia*, and damaging a second personnel vessel the *Prague*. A fourth air attack developed, at about 1230, during the Hurricanes' patrol. In this raid the corvette *King-fisher* received damage from a near miss which rendered her unseaworthy in heavy weather, and the gunboat *Mosquito* was sunk.

There was a lull after this and the next air attacks fortunately occurred at a time when the fifth R.A.F. patrol was operating, at 1500 and 1530, and a Coastal Command patrol was also on the spot; and no ship was damaged. Renewed attacks occurred at 1600–1630 in the very short interval before the sixth R.A.F. patrol came up, and it was in this raid that the paddle minesweeper *Westward-Ho*, sailing from Dunkirk with 900 French troops, and the destroyer *Worcester* were damaged, over 100 bombs being dropped near the latter ship When this was over, visibility had so far declined that at 1750 the paddle minesweeper *Princess Elizabeth*, trying to approach Bray beach, ran into fog and was compelled to return to Dover. The seventh R.A.F. patrol was troubled by poor visibility, and the eighth and last encountered no enemy at all. No bombing attacks were reported after 1840.

Five destroyers, a gunboat, two minesweepers, two personnel vessels, and two tugs were sunk or put out of action by the German bombers on this 1st June.

The weight of the enemy attacks may be gauged from the fact that over 1000 German bombing sorties were reported over the Dunkirk area during the day. Forty-three enemy aircraft were destroyed.

The first heavy air attack, 0730. *Keith*, *Skipjack* and *St. Abbs* sunk

The *Keith* and *Salamander* moved westward from the deserted eastern beaches. At 0737, off Bray, a large number of enemy bombers accompanied by fighters was seen approaching, and a dive-bombing attack was made on the *Keith*. The latter's manoeuvrability was restricted by shoals, magnetic mines and wrecks, but she was not hit. But a delay action bomb from a dive bomber exploded just astern of the ship and caused the steering wheel on the bridge to jam. Tiller flat steering was connected up and the ship was conned by telephone from the bridge. By this time all the *Keith's* 3-inch ammunition had been expended, and the only defence which the ship could put up was the passive one of continuing to turn in small circles at high speed in the restricted waters.

At about 0800 numerous dive-bombing attacks took place, and the *Keith* was hit or near missed on the starboard side. A large hole was blown in the side at the forward end of the starboard engine room below the water line, and the bulk-head between the engine room and the after boiler room was ruptured, flooding both spaces and killing Lieut. (E) W. H. Kenward, R.N. and several men. The boiler room shortly afterwards caught fire, possibly as the result of a further bomb hit.   It seems probable that serious damage was now caused to the port side by two further hits, for the ship took a heavy list to port, which increased until the upper deck was within a few inches of the water.   Steam was gradually lost and the ship stopped, with one anchor down.   Torpedoes were fired with no range on and all depth charges were set to safe and jettisoned.

As the ship was now settling, Rear-Admiral Wake-Walker transferred from the *Keith* to *M.T.B. 102* ; the order to abandon ship was given, and most of the men left her.   At this moment a further series of dive bombing attacks shook the ship with near misses which landed amongst the men in the water.

About 0830 the tug *St. Abbs* came alongside and assisted by the tug *Vincia* took off survivors and picked up men in the water.   The skoot *Hilda* rescued Lt. Gen. Laidsell, 2 officers, and 20 ratings.   The minesweeper *Salamander* rescued 7 ratings.   An unidentified grey yacht which was picking up survivors was bombed and sunk.   As late as 1100 men were still struggling in the oil slick, and the motor barge *Sherfield*, which had arrived off the coast with a small convoy of 2 X lighters and a motor launch, rescued 15.

At about 0940 aircraft again appeared, and the *Keith* was sunk in a salvo of bombs from about 50 of the enemy.   Three officers and 33 men were reported lost.

Ten minutes later the *St. Abbs*, by this time off Dunkirk, was hit by bombs and sank in 45 seconds.   Of the 135 officers, ratings and troops on board, 30 were left swimming in the water, including the Captain of the *Keith*, Capt. E. L. Berthon, D.S.C., R.N., who was saved.

Meanwhile the *Skipjack*, which had been busy off Malo embarking troops and fighting off continuous air attacks from 0530 which had reduced her ammunition supply to about 12 rounds a gun, was dive-bombed at 0845 by 10 aircraft and hit by 2 bombs.   A minute later 3 more bombs hit her.   She turned turtle and floated bottom upwards for about 2 minutes before finally sinking.   A few survivors were picked up by the *Hilda* and the *St. Abbs*. Nearly all the 275 troops on board were below decks and had no chance to escape. Enemy aircraft machine-gunned men in the water.

Ivanhoe damaged, *Basilisk* sunk.

Already, by this time, another destroyer had been put out of action.   At 0800 off Dunkirk harbour, the *Ivanhoe*, with 1,000 troops on board which she had embarked from La Panne, was dive-bombed and hit amidships.   Damage was severe and she had 26 killed and 30 wounded.   The troops and wounded were transferred to the *Havant*, the *Speedwell* and the yacht *Grive* ; and the *Ivanhoe*, assisted by the tug *Persia* and escorted by the War Dept. M. L. *Haig*, proceeded to Sheerness. While within a radius of 1 mile of No. 6 W buoy, 3 waves (each of 21 bombers) attacked the *Ivanhoe* and other vessels in that area for half an hour, but the *Ivanhoe* received no further damage.

At about the time that the *Keith* and *Ivanhoe* were under attack off Bray and Dunkirk, the *Basilisk* was also being bombed off La Panne.   Three attacks were made.   In the first attack one bomb exploded in No. 3 boiler room, cutting the main and auxiliary steam lines and putting all machinery out of action ; six other bombs exploded underneath the ship, causing the upper deck and the ship's sides to buckle.

Torpedoes and depth charges were jettisoned and at 0845 the ship was floating on an even keel.

An hour later, while efforts were being made by the French trawler *Jolie*

Mascotte to tow the *Basilisk*, the enemy returned to the attack but made no hits. The French trawler slipped the tow and moved off to a safer distance.

At noon bombers returned for a third time, diving to about 400 feet. Smothered by hits and near misses the *Basilisk* shuddered and heeled to starboard, righted herself momentarily, but sank in about 3 minutes, settling on the bottom on an even keel in some 4 fathoms. As soon as she was abandoned the *Whitehall* completed her destruction by gunfire and torpedoes.

The *Jolie Mascotte* picked up 6 officers and 71 ratings, the *Whitehall* 2 officers and 52 ratings. Other survivors got away in the motor boat and a whaler.

Second air attack, 0906 : sinking of the *Havant*

Meanwhile the *Havant*, after transferring 500 troops from the damaged *Ivanhoe*, proceeded down Dunkirk Channel. At 0906, at the western end of the channel, she was hit by 2 bombs which entered the starboard side of the engine room killing every one in it. A third bomb dropped 50 yards ahead and exploded as the *Havant* passed over it. Out of control and listing to port, the ship continued to steam ahead towards the sandbanks opposite Dunkirk. The engine room and No. 2 boiler room were on fire, there was a heavy escape of steam and all auxiliary machinery was out of action, resulting in a failure of the electric supply. It was impossible to enter the engine room, but Chief Stoker M. Gallon, in spite of the fire, let the steam out of the boilers and the ship was brought up in 4 fathoms by the starboard anchor.

The *Saltash* and *Grive* came alongside and the *Havant's* troops were transferred during almost continuous bombing. The *Saltash* took the *Havant* in tow, but further concussion from near misses increased considerably the destroyer's list to port, so the majority of her ship's company were transferred to the skoot *Aegir*. A bomb fell between the *Havant* and the *Saltash* followed by another close to the *Havant's* port quarter. By 1000 the list had increased and the decks were almost awash. "Abandon ship" was ordered, the tow was slipped and the remainder of the ship's company were transferred to the *Aegir*. At 1015 the *Havant* rolled over and sank. 1 officer and 7 men were killed, 25 wounded.

Third air attack, 1009. *Prague* damaged

The enemy air attacks had not been confined to ships off the beaches. At 1009 the personnel vessel *Prague*, which had embarked about 3000 French troops from Dunkirk harbour, was attacked by dive-bombers between W and V buoys and suffered severe damage astern from 3 near misses which put the starboard engine out of action.

The majority of the troops were transferred, whilst the ship continued to go ahead on the port engine, to the *Scimitar*, the minesweeper *Halcyon* and the paddle minesweeper *Queen of Thanet*, the later taking on board no less than 1,500 and the *Scimitar* 376 ; and at 1331 the tug *Lady Brassey* took the *Prague* in tow to the Downs, where the remaining troops were transferred to the trawlers *Olvina* and *Lady Philomena*. The *Prague* had ended her service in Operation "Dynamo", for to save her from sinking she was beached off Sandown Castle, Deal, at 1730 that day. In three trips, she had taken out from Dunkirk over 6,000 men.

Sinking of the *Foudroyant*

Before the morning was out yet a fourth destroyer, the French *Foudroyant*, was sunk by air attack. The ship had sailed from England at 0800. She reached the Dunkirk Channel, at the beginning of Route X, about 1030, during the third heavy air attack of the day, when she was hit by two consecutive salvos of bombs, blew up, and sank in 2½ minutes. A French trawler, herself damaged, picked up 137 of the *Foudroyant's* crew and transferred them to the trawler *Gara*; and the motor yacht *Naiad Errant* rescued about a score and put them on board a nearby French tug. Some were also picked up by the French minesweeping trawler *Bernadette*.

Brighton Queen and *Scotia* sunk

The paddle minesweeper *Brighton Queen* arrived at Dunkirk at 1035 on the 1st June, having for the last hour been under continuous enemy air attack which she successfully fought off with 12 pounder and Lewis gun. In little more than half an hour she took on board 700 French Moroccan troops and sailed for Margate.

The ship had barely rounded No. 5 buoy, off Mardyck, and entered the channel (Route X) when a formation of enemy dive bombers came out of a cloud and peeled off to attack. One bomb, estimated at 200 pounds, exploded very close on the starboard quarter, causing severe damage and a number of casualties. The ship began to settle at once, took a heavy list, and in five minutes filled and sank on an even keel in about 5 fathoms of water. The crew worked quickly and intelligently in getting life rafts and floating material over the side, and the French troops, despite the language difficulty, behaved steadily and intelligently though nearly half of them were killed by the explosion or drowned. The minesweeper *Saltash* was quickly alongside, rescued some 400 survivors, and landed them safely at Margate.

The main attack of the enemy formation was directed against the personnel ship *Scotia* (3,500 tons) which had left Dunkirk carrying 2,000 French troops very shortly after the *Brighton Queen*, and was now only 2 cables distant on her port bow. The enemy attacked in sections of 4 aircraft, two each with machine guns and bombs of small size. At least 4 of the latter hit the ship, which began to sink by the stern, and the order to abandon her was given. The *Scotia* heeled over until her forward funnel and mast were in the water. The enemy now made another attack on the sinking vessel, dropping 4 more bombs and machine gunning the men swimming and clinging to the wreckage. By this time, however, the destroyer *Esk* had come out from Dunkirk and drove off the enemy aircraft when they returned yet again. The destroyer put herself alongside the sinking *Scotia* and transferred nearly 1,000 of the troops, a fine feat, and the destroyer *Worcester* and other craft picked up several; but 28 of the *Scotia's* crew and an estimated 200 to 300 of the French troops were unfortunately lost.

Fourth air attack, 1230. Sinking of the *Mosquito*

Among the vessels which went to the assistance of the *Scotia* was the gunboat *Mosquito*, though she never reached her.

The *Mosquito* arrived off Dunkirk from the Downs at about 1230; she was attacked on the way over by a single dive bomber and was damaged by a near miss, but was able to continue on her course. Off Dunkirk she embarked some 30 French and Belgian troops from the motor boat *Rapid I*. Hearing that the *Scotia* was reported to be sinking at the west end of the channel, she proceeded towards the scene, followed by the *Rapid I*.

Almost immediately (about 1330) six or more of a flight of 20 Ju.87s attacked her from different directions, obtaining a direct hit and a near miss. With boiler and engine rooms badly holed, the steering gear jammed with the rudder hard over, the ship took a heavy list to port. The crew of the pom-pom were all killed or knocked out except Acting Leading Seaman Ronald Thirlwall, who, although shockingly badly wounded in at least four places, kept the one undamaged barrel firing until ammunition was exhausted. The 0.5″ gun aft was also kept in action by Able Seaman C. A. L. Hirschfield, who went aft and brought the gun into action single handed after all the crew were wounded. With water pouring into the ship, the *Mosquito* was abandoned, the survivors being picked up by the *Rapid* and two drifters. Among the killed was the executive officer Lieutenant A. H. Mainwaring, R.N.

Fifth and sixth air attacks, 1500 and 1610

Between 1230 and about 1500 there was a lull in the air attacks on shipping, and when attacks were renewed at the latter hour R.A.F. and Coastal Command patrols were operating and no damage occurred.

About 1600 the French minesweeping trawlers *Président Briand*, *Denis Papin*, *Moussaillon* and *Vénus*, were approaching Dunkirk after landing troops in England, when gunfire from a shore battery opposite 6 W buoy caused the two former, who were ahead, to turn back. Ten minutes later, a formation of 9 enemy aircraft dived on them, directing their bombs on the *Vénus* and the *Denis Papin*. The latter apparently sank immediately with total loss of her crew, and the *Vénus* in four minutes, after a direct hit. Whilst the other two trawlers were engaged in rescuing the survivors of the *Vénus*, the *Moussaillon* was hit and sank within a minute.

Losses from mines

On this black day mines were also taking their toll of shipping. Enemy aircraft had been mining the inshore channels during the night 31st May–1st June, and at 0313 Vice-Admiral Dover informed the Admiralty that he was allowing ships evacuating troops to use Route Y as well as Route X. In the early hours the corvette *Sheldrake* " after a night spent in dodging M.T.B. torpedoes ", was skilfully directed by aircraft to a position between the West Hinder and Kwint buoys, where she found wreckage with men clinging to it. This was the remains of the trawler *St. Achilleus* which had been mined on patrol. The *Sheldrake* rescued 11 men, but 4 of them died before they could be got to harbour. About the same time, i.e. at 0330, the little Thames Estuary cockle bawley boat *Renown* was blown to pieces with her crew of 3, on the way back from Dunkirk.

The third ship to be sunk on this day was the F.A.A. training yacht *Grive* a vessel which, on account of her untiring activity, could ill be spared. Having disembarked 374 troops at Dover at 0100 on the 1st June the *Grive* sailed again two hours later for Dunkirk without waiting to replenish ammunition, of which she had only 5 rounds per gun remaining. On the way in to the harbour she lent assistance to the *Ivanhoe* after the latter was bombed and damaged, went alongside the jetty and embarked troops under heavy bombing. At 0800 she left again. On the way out, she passed the sinking destroyer *Havant* with the *Ivanhoe's* troops and survivors of the crew on board ; these she transferred, and arrived at Dover with 785 persons about 1300. Three hours later, her indefatigable Captain (Capt. the Hon. L. J. O. Lambart, D.S.O., R.N. (Retired)) sailed once more for Dunkirk. But he never arrived, for at about 2230, when a mile or so outside the harbour, the *Grive* was blown to pieces by a mine. Nineteen survivors were picked up, but her Captain was not among them.

Loadings at Dunkirk during the day

In the space of a few hours the enemy had caused almost as much damage to shipping as during the whole of the previous 7 days. C.-in-C. Nore, concerned at the losses of destroyers, a type of vessel which was in all too short supply at any time, asked the Admiralty to give orders that they should be used only in positions where they could manoeuvre at high speed under bombing attack. In the short view, however, the effect on the evacuation of the loss of personnel vessels was perhaps equally serious. These ships possessed great carrying power; no other vessels could compare with them. Up to date the services of no less than 15 of them had been lost to the operation, 9 by sinking and 6 through serious damage.

Nevertheless, and despite the increasing difficulty of threading a way into Dunkirk through the growing number of wrecks, the supply of personnel vessels was maintained throughout the day, though not without a series of setbacks.

The *Côte d'Argent*, a French mail boat transferred to the orders of Vice-Admiral Dover, disembarked 1,000 troops from Dunkirk harbour on the 1st June, the *King George V* 700, the French vessel *Rouen* 800. The *St. Helier*. disembarked 1,250 troops at Dover in the morning and left again about 0930 At 1530 she entered Dunkirk harbour to embark wounded and troops, and was twice hit by shore batteries before sailing for Dover once more at 2230 with 1,334 troops.

The controlling organisation

The organisation which controlled the supply of shipping functioned in a room below Dover Castle, known as the " Dynamo Room " from the codeword of the Dunkirk operation. In charge was Captain M. M. Denny, R.N. With him there were 20 or more officers, soldiers, naval officers and Board of Trade and Sea Transport officials, and the work they did was marvellous. They were controlling, organizing, fuelling and supplying, not only men-of-war, but a variety of merchant vessels. Sometimes a merchant vessel would need a new crew to take her over to Dunkirk again, but within a few hours the Sea Transport Officer would get one and the ship would sail. At Ramsgate, the Nore, and various other places besides Dover, ships and boats were collected and organised, but the head and control of the whole was in this room, where they worked continuously and tirelessly against time day and night.[1]

Crews for the numerous small craft, working parties, and beach parties were provided by the Chatham Depot. The great majority of the small craft of the inshore flotillas were serviced and controlled by N.O.I.C. Ramsgate. At Harwich, an exceptional Naval and Military system was organised to assist those ships which called there to make a quick turn round by relieving the tired ships' companies of the work of cleaning and clearing their vessels.

NAVAL LOSSES OF THE DAY.
SUNK BY AIR ATTACK.

Destroyers—*Basilisk, Havant, Keith,* French *Foudroyant.*
Gunboat *Mosquito.*
Minesweepers *Brighton Queen, Skipjack.*
French Minesweeping Trawlers *Denis Papin, Moussaillon, Vénus.*
Personnel vessel *Scotia.*
Tugs *St. Abbs, St. Fagan.*
Barges *Lady Robinson, Doris.*

---

[1] *Report of R. A. Wake-Walker,* M 017978/41, p.27.

SUNK BY E-BOAT TORPEDOES.

Trawlers *Argyllshire, Stella Dorado.*

SUNK BY MINES.

Trawler *St. Achilleus,* small craft *Renown.*

SUNK BY GUNFIRE.

Drifter *Lord Cavan.*

SUNK BY COLLISION OR OTHER MISADVENTURE.

Drifters *Eileen Emma, Fair Breeze, Gervais Rentoul.*
Yachts *Amulree, Pellag II.*
Barges *Aidie, Barbara Jean, Duchess, Ethel Everard, Lark, Royalty.*
Small craft, number unknown.

DAMAGED BY AIR ATTACK.

Destroyers *Ivanhoe, Worcester.*
Minesweepers *Ross, Salamander, Westward-Ho.*
Corvette *Kingfisher.*
Personnel vessel *Prague.*

DAMAGED BY MINE.

Hospital carrier *St. David.*

DAMAGED BY GUNFIRE.

One trawler, name uncertain.

DAMAGED BY COLLISION OR GROUNDING

Destroyer *Vimy.*
Personnel vessel *Maid of Orleans.*

The evacuation figures for the day

Little ships added their quotas to those of the big ships, though not without casualties : they suffered heavy losses from collision or other misadventure, although in the circumstances it was not always possible to obtain details (See App. B.I.)

On this day there were lifted from the beaches and from Dunkirk harbour : by motor boats and the like 2334 persons, by hopper barges 1470, by tugs 736, by yachts 1,831, by skoots 3,170, of which almost all were from the beaches, by special service vessels 1,250, by drifters 2,968, and by trawlers 1,876 practically all of whom were lifted from Dunkirk harbour. French ships lifted 3,967, Belgian trawlers 402, and a Dutch yacht 114 ; all troops evacuated by foreign ships were embarked in Dunkirk harbour, none coming from the beaches.

Though losses of ships had been highest this day the total of troops lifted was the second highest of the operation, no less than 64,429 being landed in England. Of these, 47,081 had been embarked in Dunkirk harbour and 17,348 from the beaches.

CHAPTER X

THE NIGHT OF 1ST — 2ND JUNE AND

FROM DAYLIGHT TO DUSK ON 2ND

Situation ashore on evening of 1st (Plan 3)

During the 1st June heavy enemy attacks developed on the British sector of the line, and our forces had to give some ground. By nightfall, however, the enemy advance had been checked on a line Bergues–Uxem–Ghyvelde, thence due east of the frontier and along the frontier defences to the sea.

French troops were holding a line in rear of ours, and the British rearguard was to withdraw through this line which the French would continue to hold.

Two divisions of French Territorial troops reduced in strength, in addition to part of the British 1st Corps and rearguard of 4,000 men, still remained to be evacuated on the evening of the 1st. The War Office, aware that they were not in a position to judge the local situation, did not set a period to the evacuation but ordered Major-General Alexander to hold on as long as possible in order that the maximum number of French and British might be embarked. It was left to the General, in close co-operation with Admiral Abrial, to decide the moment when evacuation must come to an end.[1]

Plan for the night 1st–2nd June (See Plan 4)

Early in the afternoon of the 1st June the only remaining Route X came under the fire of German guns, and it was judged impossible to carry out any further evacuation by day. There was hope both at Dover and at the War Office that it would be possible to complete the evacuation of the B.E.F. during the dark hours of the night 1st/2nd June, by using both sides of Dunkirk harbour, pier and eastern beach. The War Office asked General Weygand to urge Admiral Abrial to co-operate in completing the evacuation of the French this night.

Evacuation was to be confined to the period between 2100 and 0330. It was estimated that British vessels could lift about 17,000 men, probably in the proportion 50 per cent British and 50 per cent French, during these hours, as follows :—(Appendix R8) :—(a) From the beach between Dunkirk and 1½ miles to the eastward between 2100/1 and 0300/2, 9,000 men. (b) At the East Pier between 2100/1 and 0330/1[2], 7,000 men. This time might be extended.

(c) On the east side inside the harbour, between 2200/1 and 0300/2, 1,000 men.

It was intended to withdraw all naval personnel this night[3].

All minesweepers, both fleet and paddle, and skoots and all small craft except certain flotillas specially organised, were to lift from the beach stretching eastward 1½ miles from Dunkirk, and it was hoped to employ here also about 100 French small beach fishing craft and drifters. Personnel ships up to 7 in

---

[1] *Report of Captain W. Tennant, S.N.O. Dunkirk*, Record Office Case 5458 Vol. 3, p.357.

[2] The originator's copy of this signal is (rather exceptionally) typed instead of being written by hand, and the time has been altered by the typewriter, either from 0300 to read 0330 or from 0330 to read 0300, though it is not possible to say with certainty which figure was intended. The time was received at the Admiralty at 0330, and Rear Admiral Wake-Walker in his *Report*, M.017978/41 p.32 says 0330 was intended.

[3] S.N.O. Dunkirk reported, however (Appendix R.24) that he did not receive the message giving details of the plan until 0430/2.

number and 8 destroyers were to enter Dunkirk harbour and go alongside the East Pier, where British troops were. Only by using this pier would it be possible to evacuate large numbers, and there was considerable apprehension lest the Germans should shell it heavily and damage it or render it impossible for ships to lie alongside. The pier had already been damaged by the armed boarding vessel *King Orry* when she secured alongside at 1730 on 29th May with her steering gear out of order and all instruments shattered by air attack, but the gap had been bridged. Drifters and other small craft were to be sent into the inner harbour at Dunkirk, to lift troops from the Quay Félix Faure, in the Tidal Harbour, the North Quay, in the shipyard, and the quay in the new outer harbour.

The French troops assembled on the west side of the harbour, and it was intended that French vessels, including torpedo boats, should serve the West Quay in the new outer harbour, whilst private small boats used the Quay Félix Faure.

Assembly of shipping

Early in the afternoon of the 1st June Vice-Admiral Dover recalled all destroyers to harbour : and minesweepers of the 1st, 4th, 5th and 6th M/S Flotillas were warned for duty : only ships having degaussing equipment were to sail. Five vessels, the *Sharpshooter, Albury, Kellett, Ross,* and *Leda* were unable to comply ; the compasses of another the *Pangbourne,* were unreliable, though her D.G. gear was functioning ; and in the event, she sailed, led by a Dutch skoot, though she was too late to go to the beaches, and accordingly proceeded along Route Y as far as T buoy, looking for any ships in need of assistance.

The destroyers designated Force K, were to proceed in pairs at hourly intervals to berth at the East Pier in Dunkirk harbour, returning to Dover when loaded. If there was no vacant berth at the pier when a pair of destroyers arrived, they were to assist at the beach instead. Four pairs were detailed, viz. the *Windsor* and *Icarus, Codrington* and *Sabre, Shikari* and *Esk, Winchelsea* and *Whitshed.* The *Esk,* however, which had been running almost continuously since 27th May, was unable to sail and was given 24 hours stand off.

Preparations to assemble the requisite small craft for working off the beach commenced early in the forenoon of 1st June, when a number of Senior Officers were despatched from Dover in fast motor boats to round up all stray motor boats in the Downs and along the routes, and direct them back in the evening to the beach 1½ miles east of Dunkirk. A flight of 30 motor boats and 34 lifeboats with 3 tugs, the last three large tugs left in London, was sent during the early hours of 1st June from London to Ramsgate where they were prepared for beach work, naval crews being placed in the lifeboats that lacked crews and extra towage provided. Motor boats were also sent from Harwich and Sheerness. A number of flotillas under Commodore A. H. Taylor and Captain the Hon. G. Frazer were re-organised for the night's effort.

Abandonment of daylight evacuations (Appendix R)

It was decided to abandon daylight evacuation after 1st June, because the scale of enemy air attack experienced on that day, and the fact that the Germans could by now command the newly swept central route at its point of junction with Dunkirk Roads by gunfire from the shore, rendered it too costly. Vice-Admiral Ramsay, when drawing up the plan for the night, intended sailings to cease at 0300 or 0330 ; and Captain Tennant at Dunkirk, who did not yet know of the plan arranged for the night, independently gave orders, in the late afternoon of the 1st June with General Alexander's concurrence, that no ships were to sail during daylight and that evacuation by transports was consequently to cease at 0300 on 2nd.   If the perimeter held, evacuation by the B.E.F. would be completed on the following night, by which time most of the French troops would also have been lifted.

The Admiralty, however, decided that, should it be possible to use any of the three channels during daylight hours, evacuation was to continue until 0700 and, if necessary also from 1730 on the 2nd June until dark provided daylight evacuation was then still possible.   Only between 0700 and 1730 on the 2nd there would be no sailings.   They intended to be the arbiters as to whether evacuation was possible in daylight as late as 0700.

At 2114, an hour and a half after the receipt of these instructions, Vice-Admiral Ramsay informed the Admiralty and all concerned at Dunkirk that, owing to casualties now being caused to shipping by heavy artillery, all ships had been ordered to withdraw before daylight on the 2nd.   The Vice-Admiral followed up this signal at 2329 by a message to the Admiralty giving in some detail the shipping situation as he knew it.   All three channels to Dunkirk, X, Y and Z were now under fire of German batteries, for traffic on the last remaining daylight route X, had had to be suspended on account of a new enemy battery which came into action that evening and was maintaining a heavy barrage[1].   Vice-Admiral Ramsay's information (not altogether correct) was that a total of 16 transports (personnel vessels invaluable in the work of evacuation) were now out of action, 8 being lost and 8 disabled, and that two of the sinkings had been caused by enemy shell fire on Route X.   It was now difficult to compel the crews of the remainder to face the conditions which existed.

This had been a day of very heavy naval sinkings coupled with losses of troops from drowning.   It is obvious that at some point losses incurred in continuing daylight evacuation would more than counterbalance the gains ; it seems clear that Vice-Admiral Ramsay considered that this point had now been reached, and, in accordance with the Admiralty's own direction sent to him earlier in the evening, he now informed them that any attempt to continue the evacuation in daylight was unwise and he asked permission to withdraw all his forces at 0300 until the following night.   In this, he told the admiralty, Major General Alexander concurred.

The Admiralty, however, were unwilling that evacuation should cease altogether at daylight and directed that it was to continue up to 0700, but only by destroyers unless further experience showed that enemy gunfire was rendering the channel prohibitively dangerous.

Danger to personnel ships

It is impossible to resist the conclusion that in the difficulty of obtaining accurate reports of conditions on the routes and estimating the true causes of the mounting losses of ships the danger from enemy shell fire was magnified in the minds of those at Dover.   By some means the planners had been informed that two personnel ships had already been sunk by shell fire in the fairway near No. 5 buoy.   Not only was this incorrect, but in point of fact no ship of any kind was lost from gunfire on the routes during the 1st June ; the only sinking by shell fire on that day was the drifter *Lord Cavan*, depot ship of S.N.O. Dunkirk hit as she quitted the pier at Dunkirk, whilst the only other ship to be hit was the personnel vessel *St. Helier*.   This ship arrived at

---

[1] The War Office 1330/1 reported : " Only remaining channel now coming under fire of German guns."

Dunkirk and entered harbour at 1530 on 1st June. Whilst there, she was twice hit by shore batteries, though damage was slight and there was only one light casualty. The ship lay alongside for 7 hours, embarking stretcher cases and troops and finally proceeded at 2230.

Amongst the various classes of ships none had suffered proportionately heavier losses than the personnel vessels to which Vice-Admiral Dover referred in his message to the Admiralty. Their crews had been doing magnificent work in the face of nerve-racking experiences. Up to date 8 of these ships had been sunk and 4 disabled. It was arranged that during this night's evacuation personnel ships in addition to destroyers were to berth at the East Pier in Dunkirk where they were to be given priority.

The danger of sending these valuable ships in to Dunkirk in daylight was too great, and after the 1st of June they were sent in only under cover of darkness, with a naval Lieutenant-Commander or Commander on board each ship as adviser to the Master and with crews stiffened by 10 seamen for handling the wires and going alongside under fire. It was hoped by these means not only to get the ships to sail to time but also to ensure that they would enter Dunkirk harbour and not linger outside awaiting a quiet interval, or return empty. To their credit it must be recorded that not all the personnel ships needed the moral support of naval ratings.

Air Operations, morning of 2nd June

The batteries which had brought Route X under fire were between Le Clipont, near Pointe de Gravelines (see *Plan 3*), and Les Huttes, about a mile north east of Gravelines ; they were attacked by the R.A.F. in 24 Blenheim sorties between first light and 0745 on the 2nd, the object of spreading the attack in this manner being to neutralise the batteries during the period of daylight evacuation. The Blenheims encountered much anti-aircraft fire, and though no aircraft were lost some were damaged and afterwards crash-landed on their airfields.

The Air Ministry were asked to provide strong continuous patrols over Dunkirk and the beaches from 0430 to 0830 on the 2nd June, with night fighter patrols during the hours of darkness. It was arranged that the fighter patrols should go out over the routes in use by our ships, and on the return journey fly low on the routes to give maximum protection to ships against low flying bomb and machine gun attacks. The concentration of fighter patrols in the dawn and dusk periods resulted in a great decrease in the total number of flying hours on the 2nd June (See Appendix C.)

The early morning was hazy, and the first two main R.A.F. patrols, both at four squadron strength, encountered no enemy aircraft and no ships reported being attacked during this period. The third patrol, the strongest yet flown, consisting of five full squadrons, which was over the Dunkirk area from 0745–0845, encountered very considerable enemy forces, and claimed to have shot down 18 enemy bombers and 10 fighters, themselves losing 7 Spitfires. Again, no reports of attacks came from the ships ; and as far as can be ascertained no attacks occurred until the *Calcutta*, patrolling near W buoy with the *Mallard* and *Shearwater*, was attacked at 1035 by 3 Ju. 88 which dived out of the sun and bombed her, causing slight damage from near misses. A Coastal patrol witnessed the incident and drove off the enemy. The French light cruiser *Epérvier* and destroyer *Léopard* were also on the patrol line, but they apparently left the patrol when bombing began at 1035 and up to 1442 when the *Calcutta* returned to Sheerness by orders of Vice-Admiral Dover, nothing more was seen

99

of them (Appendix J.7). Air protection by Coastal Command had been arranged from 0830 until 1100 on 2nd June, and Fighter Command patrols of three aircraft of Nos. 206, 235, 801 and 806 Squadrons operated under Coastal Command during these hours, to cover Route X.

Fifth column activities (Appendix H27-32)

On the 1st June there came to notice, for the first time during Operation "Dynamo", fifth column activities of the type of which the Germans made such effective use during the war.

At 2150 on the 1st the Minesweeper *Niger*, en route to Dunkirk with the *Sutton* in company, met a number of power boats and small boats returning empty, and orders were sent out from Dover to the destroyers of Force K and the minesweepers, to keep a look out and turn such boats back to their duty. Apparently it was at first believed at Dover that small boats were daunted by the severe conditions and enormous wastage on the French and Belgian coasts ; but a report came in from the S.N.T.O. Ramsgate during the evening that a fifth column skoot was going about the beaches at Dunkirk giving false information and orders to return. The first example to come to notice was at 1300 on the 1st when the skoot *Oranje*, off Dunkirk Channel, was informed by another skoot that evacuation from the beaches was complete, that there were already sufficient ships in Dunkirk Harbour, and that the *Oranje's* boats were not required. The *Oranje* remained where she was, however, in case the four boats she had towed over were needed, and until all ships in her neighbourhood turned for home about 1515, subsequent to air attack.

Although on the night of the 1st–2nd June the services of a number of small craft were lost to the coast, there actually were a sufficient number off the beaches to cope with the troops available.

Embarkation from the beaches

The first ships of the night flight to arrive off the beaches were minesweepers, which began to anchor off Malo about 2000 on 1st. Here there were already some 3 or 4 Thames barges, besides the paddle minesweeper *Medway Queen* which had arrived some four hours earlier and had been engaged in filling up with troops ever since. The skoot *Lena* had been there since 1300 on the 1st. embarking 340 B.E.F. and 6 French troops ; she was slightly damaged by air attack during the day, and sailed at 2145 for Ramsgate. By midnight on the 1st–3nd June there were anchored off the beaches the minesweepers *Marmion*, *Snaefell*, *Niger*, *Glen Avon*, *Emperor of India*, *Glen Gower* and *Lydd*, besides the personnel ship *Portsdown* and the special service vessel *Royal Eagle*. Loading was a slow process, for there were more ships lying off the beaches than could be loaded by the boats available. Only one ship finished in 3 hours, most of them taking nearly twice that length of time.

The *Emperor of India* was apparently the first ship to sail from Malo, at 0238, with 213 troops. She left behind her, abandoned on the beach, the R.N.L.I. motor lifeboat *Mary Scott* which had ferried troops and towed the *Emperor of India's* whalers from the shore until she broke down. The *Medway Queen* left at 0245, after nearly 11 hours at anchor during which the ship claimed to have shot down an enemy aircraft on the beach west of Dunkirk. She took 426 troops and some details, including 10 Spanish refugees rescued from an open boat, and the crews of two motor boats, one, the *Aura*, whose engines broke down after some hours of ferrying troops and towing, and another, with name unrecorded, like so many small craft which came to grief in the course of rendering valuable service in the operation. The *Glen Avon,* which sailed a quarter of an hour after the *Medway Queen,* also picked up 24 Spaniards, from the Dutch S.S. *Alphacca* ; it is not known how they came to be afloat, for the *Alphacca* was not sunk until 4 April 1942. The *Lydd* left at the same time as the *Medway Queen,* with 200 troops, but defective degaussing then necessitated putting an end to her service in Operation " Dynamo". The *Niger, Snaefell,* and *Royal Eagle* all sailed within half an hour of one another. The last ship to leave Malo beach was, by her own account, the *Glen Gower* at 0320, as day wa breaking, by which time it was low water. Her Captain, Acting Commander M. A. O. Biddulph, R.N., S.O. 8th M.S.F., reported that the embarkation had been very trying, for the enemy's gunfire during the night had been mainly directed at the beaches, which had been very heavily shelled[1], and the *Glen Gower* was continually under fire from guns and howitzers on shore from the time she anchored at 2355. " Sight and hearing were almost overwhelmed by the ruddy glow of flames, the flashes of gunfire, the shrieking of shells all around, and the noise of their explosion as they burst". When the *Glen Gower* sailed, with 435 troops, she had lost two of the boats (one from shrapnel hits) which she had brought from England to ferry troops from the beach to the ships, whilst a third was left aground.

Of all the minesweepers that left the beach this night only the *Snaefell* was filled to capacity.

Embarkations at Dunkirk

Although there were more ships than were required off the beaches there was plenty of room at the East Pier, and during the night Rear-Admiral Wake-Walker, who had come over from Dover and was afloat in *M.A/S.B.10,* diverted some of the redundant ships from Malo. He met the minesweeper *Sutton* at 2121 and sent her to load at the East Pier, where she embarked in about 1½ hours 725 troops, about a third of whom were French. The *Duchess of Fife* arrived off Malo at 2310, found no troops and was sent on to Dunkirk Pier where she embarked 550 men. The destroyer *Venomous* had come over to Malo with a beach party of 10 officers and 90 men ; no boats came off from the shore, and at 0200 Rear-Admiral Wake-Walker sent her to Dunkirk, where she took on board 632 troops and sailed for Dover about 0230. The paddle minesweeper *Marmion* was ordered into Dunkirk Harbour at 0200 cn 2nd, after waiting in the roads for four hours, and embarked 225 French troops. Ships were led into harbour and allocated to their berths by Commander Maund in a motor boat.

French troops, to the number of 285, were also embarked by the trawler (danlayer) *Strathelliot* alongside the inner jetty : amongst them was General Nicolle and his staff. The *Strathelliot* grounded outside the harbour on sailing at 0130 but got off undamaged, by her own efforts. Another small ship to get away early with French troops only on board was the skoot *Reiger* which left the jetty in the Nouvel Avant Port at 2215 on 1st after lifting 330 men in 45 minutes.

The first pair of destroyers to berth alongside the East Pier were the *Codrington* at 2300 and the *Sabre* a quarter of an hour later. The former embarked 878 troops, the latter 756 both ships taking only 45 minutes. The *Icarus* which left Dover with the *Windsor,* also berthed at 2300 and took on board 677 troops. On the way home, she was in collision with a trawler in Dunkirk Channel, and her further service in Operation " Dynamo " was cancelled.

---

[1] Report of R. A. Wake-Walker, M.017978/41, p.31.

The *Windsor* did some quick turns round. From the present night's work she returned to Dover with 493 troops, sailed again for Dunkirk and lifted a further 624 men which she disembarked at Dover, leaving about 1900. Before the day was out, she was once more alongside Dunkirk East Pier embarking troops, and she sailed at 0100 on 3rd June, loaded with 1,022 men.

As the *Esk* was unable to sail owing to exhaustion of her crew the *Shikari* proceeded alone. She berthed at Dunkirk at 0125 and left again at 0200 with 470 troops. When the first vessel of the last pair of destroyers, the *Whitshed* and *Winchelsea*, arrived at Dunkirk the East Pier was bare of troops ; but by using a loud hailer and making a search a total of 512 were collected. The *Winchelsea* disembarked 1,100 men at Dover.

On this night personnel vessels were not much in evidence at Dunkirk. The *Côte d'Argent* disembarked 1,250 troops in England on 2nd June, the *Newhaven* 716 at Dover at 1030. The *Royal Daffodil*, after bring turned back earlier in the day by a French destroyer, left Margate again at 2200 on the 1st and was back at 0600 on the 2nd with 1,500 troops. The *Manxman* did not arrive at Dunkirk until 0506 on the 2nd, long after daylight; she brought back 177 troops and disembarked them at Dover at 1043. The only other considerable lift from Dunkirk pier by a British ship on this night was by the 220 ton coaster *Seine*, which arrived at Dunkirk about 2000 and, after an air attack lasting about an hour, went alongside the pier and embarked 250 troops. After landing these at Ramsgate the crew, who had worked continuously for four days and nights, had their first night's sleep.

In addition to the large ships, tugs, skoots, drifters and all manner of small craft evacuated troops on this night. Some lay off and were loaded by smaller boats ferrying troops out to them, others went up harbour, past the large ship berths. Over 4,000 men were brought to England on the 2nd June in this way. Of these the skoot *Hondsrug* took 421 French and the skoot *Reiger* 330 French.

French embarkations

During the early part of the night 1st–2nd June French troops embarked as arranged at the West Pier, though none of the French torpedo boats which it was intended to employ disembarked troops in England.[1] Looking shoreward from the sea, the characteristic helmets of the endless line of French troops on the West Pier showed up against the glare of fires inland. The town and harbour lay under a pall of smoke. The minesweeping trawler *Chasse-Marée* lifted from the harbour 391 troops, the patrol vessel *Reine des Flots* 350, the cargo ship *Cap d'Antifer* 291, and trawlers and motor fishing vessels a further 548 ; all these were landed in England.

Four Belgian trawlers brought over 313 troops from Dunkirk on the 2nd June.

British Naval base party embarks, 0245/2

At 0200 on the 2nd Rear-Admiral Wake-Walker in *M.A/S.B.10* went up to the shore end of the East Pier at Dunkirk, to embark the base party as arranged. The party arrived and the M. A/S.B. sailed at 0245.

By this time it was beginning to get light, and although at one time there had been haze which had prevented some ships from arriving the morning was

---

[1] Rear-Admiral Wake-Walker in his *Report* M.017978/41 p.32 says, however, French T.B.'s. loaded on this night alongside the West quay.

now very clear and the Rear-Admiral decided to get the ships away at 0300 instead of 0330 as originally planned. The Admiralty orders that evacuation by personnel ships from Dunkirk Pier was to continue until 0700 did not apparently reach S.N.O. Dunkirk (Appendix R.20, 23) ; and it is to be presumed that Rear-Admiral Wake-Walker did not receive the orders which went out from the Admiralty at 0115/2, that destroyers were to continue the evacuation until 0700 (Appendix R.21). Although men were still coming down the pier, the Rear-Admiral was unwilling to run the risk of having ships sunk alongside and blocking the pier and harbour. Accordingly he told the ships to leave and himself followed out of harbour the last of them, apparently the destroyers *Winchelsea* and *Whitshed* about 0300.

British rearguard held up

Meanwhile, a most disquieting message had been received at Dover. At 0040 on the 2nd the *Lydd*, while embarking troops off Malo beach, was requested by the Brigadier of the brigade then embarking to transmit to Rear-Admiral Wake-Walker a message from Major General Alexander reporting that on account of French congestion on the mole at Dunkirk a considerable number of British troops were held up and further arrivals were still expected. It was essential that the rearguard of the B.E.F. should embark from the beaches east of the mole, where they were expected to arrive by 0230.

What had happened was, that French troops had cut into the flow of British making their way along the road to the East Pier, by a converging route; and both British and French troops were now being embarked at the pier.

Rear-Admiral Wake-Walker apparently never received the message and knew nothing of the state of affairs at the East Pier until he arrived there at 0200.

Vice-Admiral Dover, who received the message at 0200[1], at once sent orders to all destroyers of Force K still on the coast, the minesweepers, and the gunboat *Locust* which was off Bray supporting the evacuation by covering fire, to endeavour to embark the British rearguard from the beach, remaining after 0300 if necessary. The coding and transmission of the message took some time, and the orders apparently went out too late ; all ships had sailed, and the rearguard could not get away that night. Only the personnel vessel *Portsdown* was left on the coast. This was an undegaussed ship manned by a naval crew, which had anchored off Malo at 2205/1. After running to death her own two dinghies ferrying troops she got hold of a large motor boat, and she sailed about 0400. On the way home the ship collected further troops from a French vessel aground off Dunkirk, and from two further vessels encountered, and she eventually disembarked at Dover 168 British and 450 French.

Bombing of the hospital ships *Worthing* and *Paris*. (App. S)

There was a large number of wounded in Dunkirk because no hospital ships had sailed for 24 hours, orders having been given to evacuate fit men in preference, since, other considerations apart, embarking wounded would have taken up too much valuable time. The cessation of daylight sailings rendered it possible for hospital ships to occupy berths alongside, without detriment to the operation, and it was decided to get some of the wounded away in daytime in hospital ships, in the hope that the Germans would respect them.

In order to afford the enemy no excuse to attack a warning signal was sent

---

[1] *Dover Report*, p.27. The time of receipt on the flimsy of the decypher appears to be 0120.

en clair asking for hospital ships to be sent across and stating that for our part we should scrupulously observe the Geneva Convention.   Two hospital carriers were despatched from Dover, the *Worthing* at 1255 and the *Paris* at 1648, both clearly marked as hospital ships.   Neither of the two ever reached Dunkirk.

At 1433 the A/S trawler *Grimsby Town*, on patrol on Route X, reported that 12 aircraft bearing 90° South Foreland 27 miles (between V and W buoys) had bombed a hospital ship.   This was the *Worthing*.   Visibility was good. Nine bombs were dropped and the ship was machine gunned, she was slightly damaged by near misses and the *Calcutta* sent the corvette *Mallard* to stand by her.   The *Worthing* returned to harbour.

The *Paris*, after running into thick fog, was in clear visibility at about 1900, near W buoy, when two aircraft attacked her, near misses putting out of action her engines and extinguishing all lights.   About an hour later the ship was attacked again by 3 aircraft, and received further damage.   She was abandoned by all but the Captain and some of the officers, who were shortly afterwards taken off by a fast motor boat which also rescued men from some of the *Paris's* lifeboats that had been wrecked by bombing.   Three tugs, the *Sun XV*, *Sun IV* and *Lady Brassey* attempted to tow the ship; but at 0400 on 3rd June, after a further air attack, the *Paris* sank ¾ mile east of W. buoy.

Evacuation figures, 2nd June

A total of 26,256 men were landed in England on 2nd June, 19,561 from Dunkirk harbour and 6,695 from the beaches.   Of these totals, French ships working only from the harbour carried 1634, and Belgian trawlers carried 313. The accumulated total of men evacuated to this date was 285,305.

CHAPTER XI

THE NIGHT 2ND — 3RD JUNE

B.E.F. EVACUATED 2330/2

Plan for the night 2nd–3rd June

During the forenoon of the 2nd June considerable doubt existed at Dover as to the numbers remaining to be evacuated from Dunkirk. Captain Tennant thought that about 5,000 British and 30,000 French remained, but it was estimated at Dover, that in addition to the rearguard of 4,000, (who had been withdrawn according to plan, from the front line), a further 2,000 British troops might be found in Dunkirk; while the estimated number of French troops remaining increased during the forenoon from 25,000 quoted on the previous evening to figures in the region of 50,000 to 60,000. Admiral Nord himself estimated the French remaining to number 65,000 of which he hoped that 30,000 might be evacuated on the night 2nd–3rd and the remaining 35,000, who were holding the bridgeheads, on the following night.

Major-General Alexander intended that all British troops should be evacuated by 2400 on 2nd, and Captain Tennant asked for the maximum number of transports to be sent over. During the forenoon of the 2nd a joint Naval and Military conference was held at Dover, attended by Rear-Admiral Wake-Walker who came over from Dunkirk in the early hours, and by Commander J. C. Clouston, Pier Master at the East Pier, to devise a plan to accomplish this. The French Admiralty wished daylight evacuation to be resumed, but Vice-Admiral Ramsay refused to countenance it. The suspension of traffic in daylight hours had the advantage of enabling all transport resources to accumulate during the day and to be held available for a "massed descent" upon Dunkirk harbour during the night. By making provision for increased pier and berthing parties and control of traffic in the harbour channels by motor boats, it was hoped to berth all craft that were available between the hours of 2100 on 2nd and 0300 on 3rd.

At 1052 Vice-Admiral Dover made a signal to the destroyers and minesweepers, which practically amounted to a call for volunteers for the night's work (Appendix T.3) :—

"The final evacuation is staged for tonight, and the Nation looks to the Navy to see this through.
I want every ship to report as soon as possible whether she is fit to meet the call which has been made on our courage and endurance".

The replies showed that there was no lack of willing spirit. Ships were "fit and ready", "ready and anxious to carry out your orders", "ship unfit but . . . officers and ship's company are willing to serve in any capacity" : so the replies came in. Only the paddle minesweeper *Medway Queen*, which had returned to Ramsgate three hours earlier on her fifth evacuation trip, was unable to sail owing to the exhaustion of her crew, and was sent on to Dover where additional officers and crew were lent from the *Sandown*, which, like the destroyer *Javelin*, was not degaussed and was consequently forbidden to sail.

It was hoped to avoid on this night the situation which occurred on the previous night, when more ships could have used the pier had they been available, by working out a programme whereby personnel ships, destroyers, fleet minesweepers and paddle minesweepers were to come in at intervals of half an hour to different berths so that three or four ships should be alongside the East Pier continuously. Five inside berths were established, three large, A. B, and C at the outer end of the pier for destroyers and personnel vessels, and two smaller, D and E, at the inner end for minesweepers, all of which were to be kept constantly filled. If all inside berths were occupied a berth might be used on the east side of the pier, though this would not normally be filled.

A pier master (Commander E. R. Lewis, R.N. (Retd.)) was to direct the berthing, and ships were to be guided to their berths by motor boat, two of which were sent over in the afternoon. However, one of the two motor boats was sunk by air attack on the way across with Commander Clouston, and the other disabled. (See p.110).

Special brows and ladders were prepared at Dover, for even at high water the decks of all but the larger personnel ships were below the level of the footway of the pier; and ships were told to have boxes ready to form steps.

Thirteen destroyers were detailed to sail to arrive at Dunkirk at intervals of half an hour from 2100. Groups of minesweepers were to sail at intervals of an hour and a half from Margate, Sheerness, Dover, and Harwich respectively, commencing with the Margate contingent at 2100, and ships in each group were to stagger their time of arrival at Dunkirk.

In addition to the large ships, tugs, scoots, drifters and various small craft were to go over for the night's work, some to lie off and be loaded by smaller boats, and others to go right up the harbour, past the larger ships' berths.

Demolitions at Dunkirk (Operation X.D.(E)) (See Plan 4)

Now that the operation was drawing to a close it was time to carry out demolitions in the port. The Royal Naval demolition party, which arrived at Dunkirk on the 23rd May, had carried out the placing of demolition charges at the New Lock, the Trystram Lock, and the Guillain Lock in Dunkirk harbour, demolition of which had been agreed upon at an Anglo-French conference as a British responsibility. The French undertook to destroy Le Main Lock and all the pumping stations and the bridges over the locks and canals.

On the 2nd June Admiral Abrial decided to carry out the following modified programme of demolitions :—

New Lock—gates and bridge to be demolished ;

Trystram Lock—the two gates at the outer and inner ends to be demolished ;
Guillian Lock—the two northern gates to be demolished.

All bridges had to be left intact as large numbers of French troops were still withdrawing across them.

By now, however, two of the charges which were not under water and four primers had been exploded by bomb or shell fire ; they had been replaced and re-fuzed, but supplies of demolition stores were running short.

Demolitions were completed by 1400 on the 2nd June, except one depth charge at Guillain Lock which misfired. A second charge which was placed and primed also misfired ; and there remained now no further primers or fuzes.

Situation ashore

Although during the forenoon the military position had seemed critical, on the afternoon of the 2nd the S.N.O. Dunkirk hoped to get the troops away that night. The French were still maintaining the front line except for an area east of Bergues where the Germans had penetrated to a depth of two miles, to

Teteghem, on a front of two miles. The French intended to counter-attack at 1500 but in the event this was postponed until 2000 and when it took place some ground was regained. There was no movement in the port. Later Admiral Nord reported that Bergues was in the hands of the enemy, but they had not advanced beyond. Further attacks were expected by the French this day, when the situation regarding munitions might become critical.

Sailing of the night flight from England

The movement from England towards Dunkirk commenced at 1700. The armada consisted of 13 personnel vessels, 2 large store carriers, 11 destroyers, 5 paddle minesweepers, 9 fleet sweepers, 1 special service vessel, 9 drifters, 6 skoots, 2 armed yachts, 1 gunboat, a large number of tugs, lifeboats, etc., formed either in organised tows or proceeding individually. For various reasons, however, not all of these ships evacuated troops.[1]

The composition of the French contingent was not known at Dover. Actually, 3 French torpedo boats, two minesweeping trawlers, two patrol vessels, and 17 trawlers and motor fishing vessels landed troops in England on the 3rd June. One Belgian patrol boat and 16 or 17 trawlers brought troops.

B.E.F. evacuated, 2330/2

The first destroyers to reach Dunkirk were the *Sabre* and *Shikari*, which sailed together from Dover at 1845. As the latter ship rounded No. 6 W buoy enemy shore batteries opened fire, but caused no damage. Berthing was carried out by an officer with a loud speaker at the pier head. Both destroyers sailed again at 2200, the *Sabre* with 500 and the *Shikari* with 700 troops. The *Venomous*, which arrived at 2150, had difficulty in going alongside the East Pier. This was not a solid jetty, but was built of concrete piles through which the west-going tide set. This, coupled with a fresh easterly wind, made it very

---

[1] The following ships (other than those on patrol which picked up survivors and landed them) landed troops in England on 3rd June, (numbers in brackets) :–

BRITISH Destroyers – *Codrington* (44), *Esk* (500), *Sabre* (500), *Shikari* (700), *Vanquisher* (37), *Venomous* (1500), *Whitshed* (82), *Winchelsea* (152), *Windsor* (1022) ;
Gunboat *Locust* (800)
Minesweepers – *Albury* (200), *Duchess of Fife* (300), *Dundalk* (399), *Gossamer* (490), *Halcyon* (416), *Kellett* (364), *Marmion* (198), *Medway Queen* (481), *Niger* (430), *Oriole* (750), *Pangbourne* (47), *Speedwell* (300), *Westward-Ho* (48) ;
Special Service Ship *Golden Eagle* (1) ;
Drifters – *Forecast* (108), *Golden Sunbeam* (163), *Lord Howard* (100), *Midas* (43), *Netsukis* (119), *Starlight Rays* (319), *Ut Prosim* (49), *Yorkshire Lass* (103) ;
Trawler *Cayton Wyke* (300) ;
Skoot *Doggersbank* (50) ;
Yacht *Sargasso* (252) ;
Personnel ships – *Côte d'Argent* (955), *King George V* (1460), *Newhaven* (396), *Lady of Mann* (18), *Rouen* (1286), *Royal Sovereign* (1500), *St. Helier* (2000), *Tynwald* (1200) ; H.M.S. *Nelson's* M.B. (27) ;
Tugs – *St. Olaves* (200), *Sun X* (211), *Sun XI* (188), War Dept. M.Ls. (69) ;
Sailing barge *Glenway* (213)
R.N.L.I. Lifeboats *Cecil & Lilian Philpot* (51), *Michael Stephens* (52) :
3 motor boats and launches (300).

FRENCH Torpedo boats – *Bouclier* (340), *La Flore* (410) ;
Destroyer *Léopard* (19) ;
S/M Chaser 6 (50, apparently disembarked at Havre) ;
M/S trawlers – *Ste. Bernadette de Lourdes* (79), *Ste. Denise Louise* (78) ;
Patrol vessels – *Lucien Gougy* (78), *Reine des Flots* (500) ;
17 trawlers and M.F.V's. (1663).

BELGIAN Patrol boat *A.5* (229) ;
17 trawlers (1583).

difficult for ships to get alongside until the tide turned, about 2300. Rear-Admiral Wake-Walker, who was afloat in *M.A/S.B: 10* used the latter to push the *Venomous* in and tried to get other small craft to do likewise. The narrow harbour was now filled with numbers of small French craft of every sort, size and description. At this moment a defect developed in the *M.A/S.B's* clutch, apparently as the result of pushing the *Venomous* alongside, which prevented her from going astern and made turning a most hazardous adventure with boats of all sorts bearing down on her from both directions. The *Venomous* was away again in half an hour, with 1,500 troops, including Major-General Alexander and his staff who had been taken on board *M.A/S.B. 10* by Rear-Admiral Wake-Walker and transferred to the destroyer. The *Windsor*, too had difficulty in getting alongside but managed to clear the harbour with 1,022 troops, one minute before the next destroyer was due to enter. The stream of British troops was evidently diminishing in volume now, for the *Winchelsea*, which arrived at the pier at 2300, embarked only 152. The gunboat *Locust*, however, which sailed two minutes later, carried 800 troops, a proportion of whom were French.

Eight drifters disembarked 1,004 men in England, the *Starlight Rays* bringing 319 of these. The yacht *Sargasso* brought 252. Only two personnel vessels lifted British troops from the East Pier ; the *King George V* embarked 1,460 in 27 minutes and sailed at 2225 ; and the *St. Helier* embarked 2,000 and sailed at 2330 for England.

This completed the evacuation of the British rearguard.

At 2330 Captain Tennant made the welcome signal : " B.E.F. evacuated." He embarked in *M.T.B. 102*, together with the demolition party and left for Dover.

A pause in the embarkation

After the last of the B.E.F. were clear there was a long pause. French troops should have followed the British rearguard on the East Pier, but they did not appear. The West Quay, however, was crowded with French in their distinctive helmets, though there seemed a scarcity of ships on that side of the harbour. The personnel ship *Royal Sovereign*, which had been joined that afternoon by Commander L. P. Skipwith as adviser to the Master, Captain T. Aldis, went alongside the West Quay at 2130, " handled magnificently, turning and going alongside bows out", as Rear-Admiral Wake-Walker reported. She embarked 1,500 French troops and sailed at 2205 for Margate. The Rear-Admiral also sent the personnel ship *Rouen*, a French cross-channel steamer, to the West Quay. In getting away she got broadside on to the wind and grounded just to the westward of the quay, where she lay, on a falling tide, showing up clearly against an oil fuel fire behind her. A tug was sent to help her but drew too much water and could not get near. However, the ship remained unhit throughout the shelling, and she floated off with the next tide in daylight and reached England safely with 1,286 men.

Rear-Admiral Wake-Walker was unable to discover the reason for the cessation of the flow of French troops to the East Pier ; it was apparently caused by the necessity either of repelling a German attack or holding them up to make a counter-attack, for the counter-attack which was to have been made at 1500 to restore the line east of Bergues was postponed until 2000. With destroyers waiting to be filled the situation was most exasperating. Five destroyers had to be sent back to England for lack of troops to fill them. The *Vanquisher* was ordered to return to Dover to 0230, taking only 37 troops which she embarked from a small boat while lying off the harbour. The *Codrington* was also stopped off the harbour by orders at 0050 and had only 44 troops when she sailed at 0250. The *Express* entered the harbour at 0200, found the pier devoid of troops and was ordered by Rear-Admiral Wake-Walker to return to Dover with the *Codrington*. The *Whitshed* found no berth on arrival at 0030 and lay outside with orders to hail and stop other ships from entering. She sailed at 0245 with 82 men collected from small craft. Finally, the *Malcolm* was ordered back at 0248, empty. Thus five destroyer trips were wasted.

Only the minesweepers which berthed at the inner end of the East Pier after the British rearguard had embarked, managed to collect normal quotas from the trickle of French troops.

Dunkirk was the headquarters of a French Naval Command and there was always a considerable number of French marines in evidence. But after the British naval ratings left at 2300 there was difficulty in getting ships berthed, as the French did not replace them.

The *Albury* embarked 200 French troops, the *Duchess of Fife* 300, the *Dundalk* 399, the *Gossamer* 490, the *Halcyon* 416, the *Kellett* 350 French and 14 British, the *Marmion* 198, the *Medway Queen* 481, and the *Speedwell* 300. The *Niger* slipped at 0120 with 430 French troops. While turning an unknown French craft crossed her bows and was rammed, though apparently no damage was done to her. A few minutes later the Frenchman returned and rammed the *Niger*.

Personnel ships did well. The *Royal Sovereign* sailed at 2205 with 1500 troops, the *King George V* at 2225 with 1460, the *St. Helier* at 2330 with 2,000. The *Côte d'Argent* took 955 men, the *Newhaven* 396 French, the *Tynwald* 1,200, the *Rouen* 1,286 ; but the *Lady of Mann* was ordered back for lack of troops and took only 18 French embarked from a small boat.

Amongst the French ships the torpedo-boat *Bouclier* embarked 340 men and the *La Flore* 410. The patrol vessel *Reine des Flots* " embarked 500 troops during a violent bombardment " and also reported air attacks (from German strays returning no doubt), en route to England, for which she sailed from Dunkirk at 2300 on the 2nd. Seventeen French trawlers and motor fishing vessels brought off 1,662 troops and a Belgian patrol boat 229.

Summary of troops evacuated, night 2nd–3rd June

To Rear-Admiral Wake-Walker, who had worked out a programme by which 37,000 men could have been lifted, in addition to those that would get off in small craft, this had been a most disappointing night's work, owing to the long pause when the flow of men to the East Pier ceased for some hours after the British rearguard completed its embarkation, and the difficulty of getting ships berthed owing to the failure of the French to replace the British naval parties after these left Dunkirk. Between midnight on 2nd-3rd and 0300 on the 3rd a lifting capacity of about 10,000 men was left empty.

There were disembarked in England on 3rd June 26,700 troops. Of these, British ships lifted 21,671, French ships 3,216 and Belgian ships 1,812. The great majority of these, namely 24,830, were embarked in Dunkirk harbour, principally by ships berthed alongside, though a few were ferried to ships waiting outside the port. Most of the remainder were taken out of small craft by ships which were likely to reach England with greater expedition and certainty : many of these found in small craft had no doubt come off from the beaches.

At noon on the 3rd June the total of troops evacuated had reached 305,078. Of these 211,137 were British fit and 13,004 casualties. Allied fit numbered 79, 808 and casualties 1,129.

Naval losses 2nd June

The brightest feature of the night was that embarkation in the crowded harbour at Dunkirk had been carried out without disturbance by enemy action, and apart from one motor boat sunk off Malo, and losses off small craft from collision or other misadventure, sinkings were confined to the routes.

In marked contradistinction from the heavy losses of the 1st June only one ship was sunk by air attack on the 2nd. This was the fast motor boat *Seaplane Tender 243*, from Calshot R.A.F. station, which sailed from Dover for Dunkirk at 1500 with Commander J. C. Clouston, R.N., pier master of the mole, who was returning from discussing the situation with the staff at Dover, and a naval embarkation party ; she was in company with *S.T. 276*, the intention being that the two boats should be used as " runners " for Rear-Admiral Wake-Walker during the night's work. At 1855, about 6 miles from Gravelines, 4 enemy aircraft attacked *S.T. 243*, which received severe damage from a near miss and was abandoned in a sinking condition. Commander Clouston ordered *S.T. 276* to proceed as the enemy aircraft were still continuing to attack, and she subsequently arrived at Dunkirk though too badly damaged to be of service. Commander Clouston was seen later, drowned, and only one officer and one rating from *S.T. 243* were picked up and saved.

The transport *Royal Daffodil* nearing Dunkirk from England was attacked by aircraft about an hour after *S.T. 243*. The ship was holed but by shifting all movable gear to port and filling boats with water she was listed to bring the damage above water. The engineers, J. W. Coulthard and W. L. Evans kept the motors running although the water had risen in the engine room, and the ship returned to Margate under her own steam. Another personnel ship, the *Ben-My-Chree*, was in collision on the evening of the 2nd shortly after leaving Folkestone for Dunkirk, and took no further part in the operation.

Two further ships were sunk by mines on Route Y on the 2nd June, although it was at first thought they had been torpedoed. At about 1600 the trawlers *Blackburn Rovers* and *Westella* were on patrol near T buoy, when the former blew up on a mine and sank instantly. As the *Westella* closed the position, explosions from the *Blackburn Rovers'* depth charges lifted the ship out of the water and put her asdic installation and pumps out of action. About 40 minutes later the *Westella* was herself blown up by a mine between S and T buoys, and commenced to sink. Her depth charges were set to 'safe', and the trawlers *Saon* and *Grimsby Town* sank her and picked up her survivors and those of the *Blackburn Rovers*, some badly injured. (Appendix J.9, J.10).

Two other trawlers met with misadventure on the 2nd, but neither was sunk. Details are lacking but it is known that the *Spurs* and another trawler, probably either the *Kingston Alalite* or *Kingston Olivine*, were both damaged by gunfire. The *Spurs* was on the patrol line, and it is not known how she came close enough to the coast to be damaged by shore gunfire. Gunfire also sank the *Gallant's* motor boat off Malo at 0210.

Three Belgian trawlers were lost on th 2nd June, though no details are known. These were the *Getuigt Vor Christus*, the *O.L.V. van Vlaandaren*, and the *Sunny Isle*.

Air co-operation, night 2nd-3rd June

The R.A.F. flew a patrol over the approaches to Dunkirk from about 2010 to 2120 on the 2nd June, to clear the air for the night's work. No enemy air-craft were seen and no ships reported being attacked. Blenheims of No. 604 Squadron then continued to patrol singly over Dunkirk throughout the night.

Only on three occasions during the 2nd June were enemy aircraft formations reported, and R.A.F. fighters intercepted successfully on all three.

During the early morning hours of the 3rd June the R.A.F. carried out a series of attacks on the batteries near Pointe de Gravelines, to coincide with the evacuation effort. Eighteen Blenheims bombed from a low level (1,000–3,000 feet), but were unable to observe results.

By night, the policy was continued of directing a small proportion of our air effort to targets near the battlefront and the main weight against Germany ; and in conformity with this policy twelve Wellingtons attacked Bergues.

Blocking of Dunkirk Inner Harbour (Operation C.K.) (See Plan 4 and Appendix Z)

The blocking of the inner harbour at Dunkirk was under the command of Captain E. Dangerfield, R.N., and was carried out on two successive nights. The operation was first timed to be carried out on the night 1st–2nd June, but at 1808 on the 31st the Admiralty ordered its postponement.

On each night three blockships, escorted by a destroyer, an MA/S.B. and an M.T.B., were employed. The blockships assembled in the Downs, and (as usual) they were such crocks that one, the French built *Emerald Wings* (Govern-ment Yard, Cherbourg, 1920) broke down soon after leaving Portsmouth for the Downs and had to be towed back to harbour ; a second could not keep up with the convoy ; and a third, the *Moyle*, developed defects which, however, by dint of working on her all night, were remedied in time.

The ships finally employed on the night 2nd–3rd June were as follows :—

Vivacious (destroyer)
M.A/S.B. 7
M.T.B. 107

Blockships *Westcove* 2734 tons, built 1912
Edvard Nissen[1] 2062 tons, built 1921.
Holland Dutch M.V. 895 tons, built 1923.

Early on the 2nd of June Admiral Nord asked that the blockships might be sent over to arrive at the entrance to Dunkirk harbour at 0300 on the 3rd, the latest hour at which they could enter on that night, by which time it was hoped the evacuation would have been completed. During the afternoon of the 2nd however, the Admiralty received a message from the Admiral postponing the operation because the evacuation would not be completed that night. However, the Admiralty still hoped to complete the evacuation and ordered the block-ships to sail.

At 2030 on the 2nd the *Vivacious*, with Captain Dangerfield on board and with *M.T.B. 107* in tow and *M.A/S.B. 7* in company, sailed from the Downs, leading the three blockships, and proceeded to Dunkirk by Route Z. The *Holland*, unable to maintain the $7\frac{1}{2}$ knots speed of the convoy, was soon lost to sight astern. Nearing Dunkirk a tug (either the *Sun X, Sun XI* or *Foremost* 87), towing a very long line of boats, crossed her bows and still further delayed her, but she eventually made contact with *M.A/S.B. 7* and asked to be led into the harbour. The other two blockships had anchored at 0230, and a

---

[1] This is her correct name

quarter of an hour later they all three proceeded, with the *Holland* last in the line, to carry out their part in blocking the port. As they neared Dunkirk a " long line of destroyers came out " of the harbour. " Astern of them", stated the *Holland*, " there was a gap of over a mile and then a large and fast transport". *M.A/S.B. 7* led the *Holland* through the gap between the destroyer line and the transport. When the latter was 6 cables away, and steaming very fast with the first streaks of dawn behind her, the danger of collision became apparent, so the *Holland* sounded one blast and put her wheel hard astarboard. Lieutenant-Commander E. C. Coats, R.N., captain of the blockship, reported that the transport " had then only to alter course 5° to starboard to pass well clear. . . . However, she appeared to alter to port", with the result that she struck the *Holland* hard on the bridge and just before the boiler room bulkhead. The transport, which did not appear to have sustained much damage, backed out and carried on her way. The *Holland* had no buoyancy in hand, and, a few seconds before she was struck, her captain ordered " abandon ship", seeing that it was inevitable she would be rammed. The bows sunk at once and rested on the bottom, there being apparently only 8 feet of water under her keel ; the stern remained above water. Two seamen were crushed and seriously injured in the collision. *M.A/S.B. 7* took off the crew and transferred them to the *Vivacious*. The wreck of the *Holland* came within an ace of being rammed a second time, for two more ships, reported to be destroyers, passed and missed the *Holland*'s stern by no more than a few feet.[1]

At 0300 the blockship *Westcove* entered Dunkirk, followed ten minutes later by the *Edvard Nissen*. Both ships proceeded into the channel leading to the inner harbour. When in her allotted position the *Westcove* put her wheel hard astarboard to ram the Inner Western Jetty, but her bows struck mud about 50 feet from the pier, with the ship at an angle of about 30° across the channel. By going full speed ahead on the engines, the athwartship's angle was increased to 50°.

As the *Edvard Nissen* came in with the intention of ramming the East Pier she endeavoured to strike the *Westcove*'s stern a glancing blow in order to increase her angle to the channel before scuttling herself ; but underestimating the strength of the ebb stream she passed close under the *Westcove*'s stern, and rammed the East Pier abreast of the latter. Letting go an anchor, she applied full port helm with all engine power to increase the blocking angle. The *Westcove* now fired her scuttling charges, which probably owing to coal gas in the bunkers, caused a large column of flame and smoke to envelop the ship's stern. When this had dissipated, the crew, who had pulled clear in their boat, saw that the *Westcove* had slid off the sloping bank of the channel and was lying on an even keel in the line of the piers, almost in mid stream, thus causing a minimum of obstruction. Between the sterns of the two ships there was now a gap of 80 feet which was reduced to 50 feet by heaving on a hawser run by the *Edvard Nissen*'s motor boat from the ship's stern to the *Westcove*. No more could be done and the *Edvard Nissen* abandoned ship and fired her scuttling charges from the boat. *M.A/S.B. 7* took out both ship's crews to the *Vivacious*.

---

[1] No transport reported being in collision at this time and it has not been possible to identify any of the vessels concerned. The following destroyers and transports sailed from Dunkirk at the times given : destroyers – *Vanquisher* 0230, *Whitshed* 2045, *Malcolm* 0248, *Codrington* 0250 and *Express* 0250 ; transports – *Newhaven* (French 1,888 tons) 0245, *Tynwald* (British 2,376 tons) 0300, *Rouen* (French, 1,882 tons time not known but ship was in Dunkirk in the early hours of 3rd June), and *Côte d'Argent* (French 3,047 tons, time not known but ship landed troops at Dover on 3rd June.)

CHAPTER XII

THE FINAL NIGHT, 3RD — 4TH JUNE

Decision to terminate evacuation after night 3rd-4th June (Appendix V)

After the last ship quitted Dunkirk at daylight on 3rd June a large number of French troops still remained behind, and it was decided at Dover that the evacuation must continue.

There was no certainty that the coming night would see the end of the operation. Admiral Nord stated in a situation report timed 0403 June 3rd, that as enemy attacks were probable during the day the situation concerning munitions might become critical; but the message was much mutilated, and the possibility that exhaustion of ammunition might prevent the continuance of resistance after the night 3rd–4th June was apparently not taken into account at Dover.

Vice-Admiral Ramsay, who had no reliable information of the number of French troops still to be evacuated but was aware that the figure was considerable and conscious that it was his duty to our Allies to continue evacuation as long as any French troops offered themselves for embarkation, was faced with a situation with which the forces remaining at his disposal might, with the best will in the world, be unable to cope.

The operation which had been in progress for the past nine days was of a nature unprecedented in naval warfare, and imposed on the crews of ships engaged an unprecedented strain. Officers and men had not only to cope with the ordinary hazards of the war—such as bombing on an unparalleled scale, frequent shelling, constant working in mined waters, and rescue work under most unpleasant conditions—but were also exposed to the exhaustion produced through having their mess decks and every other available space in their ships constantly crowded with troops. This precluded rest for the watch below, the preparation and enjoyment of proper meals, and such meagre amenities as a small ship operating in face of the enemy could offer. Stokers suffered equally with the seamen because, owing to the physical exhaustion of boats' crews after hours of work, relief crews of stokers were frequently provided from amongst the many who volunteered.

Even as early as the 28th May the strain was beginning to tell. Lieutenant P. F. S. Gould, R.N. of *M.T.B. 16*, working off Bray Beach, reported: "Comparatively fresh appearance of troops. . . . contrasted increasingly as the evacuation progressed with the evidence of strain shown by ship's companies of H.M. ships"[1]. Exhaustion was particularly marked in the destroyer force, the remnants of which had been executing a series of round trips without intermission for several days. Some of the ships had been working off the coasts of France and the Low Countries for the two weeks preceding the beginning of Operation "Dynamo", engaged on various duties such as evacuating refugees and giving supporting fire to the army and evacuating Boulogne, work which had imposed an intense strain and resulted in heavy losses of ships and men. Vice-Admiral Ramsay consequently represented to the Admiralty that continuance after the night of 3rd–4th June of the demands made by the evacuation would subject a number of officers and men to a test that might be beyond the limit of human endurance, and he requested that fresh forces should be employed if evacuation continued after the coming night, any consequent delay being accepted.

[1] M.011883/40, p.38.

The Admiralty had already (2312/2) undertaken that ships would be provided and air protection continued for the evacuation of French troops on the night 3rd to 4th June, and they now urged the French Admiralty to complete the evacuation on this night.   To this the French agreed.

Plan for the night

For this last night it was decided to cut down by one hour the time for embarkation, and the maximum effort was to be made, with such ships as remained available, between the hours of 2230/3 and 0230/4.   From the East Pier, liftings were to be made by personnel vessels, destroyers, and paddle minesweepers; ships were to be sent to the entire length of the pier as fast as they could be received, and it was estimated that accommodation would thus be provided for 14,000 men.   Drifters and small craft were to go right up to the quays and docks of the inner harbour.   French ships, for which no numbers could be estimated, were to be responsible for evacuation from Malo beach, the Quai Félix Faure, and the New Avant Port (West Pier); from the latter pier the remaining British ships (minesweepers other than paddle, corvettes and skoots) would also lift troops, to the number of 5,000.   The gunboat *Locust* was to remain outside and receive loads ferried out to her by small boats.

It was intended to employ on the work a force of 9 personnel vessels, 9 destroyers (all that were available), 4 paddle minesweepers, 7 fleet minesweepers, 9 drifters, the *Locust*, 2 corvettes, 4 French torpedo boats, and a number of organised motor boats flotillas including lifeboats from Ramsgate and Dover, together with a large number of French and Belgian fishing vessels.   Eleven small French ships and 3 small tugs left Cherbourg for Dover on the night 2nd–3rd June; Le Havre was scheduled to send 8 trawlers, 2 minesweepers, 1 tug, and 20 small dinghies; and Fécamp sent 14 trawlers.[1]

During the afternoon of the 3rd the French authorities transmitted the figure of French troops still remaining in Dunkirk.   This was about 30,000, a proportion of whom belonged to other than combatant units.   The total capacity of the lifting force, if used to the full, was 30,000, but this was about 5,000 more than the facilities within the port would permit of being embarked in 4 hours, even if the French troops moved with the greatest rapidity at all points of embarkation.   On previous occasions there had been some instances of difficulty in persuading French troops to embark otherwise than as complete units. Vice-Admiral Ramsay consequently impressed on the French liaison officers the necessity of speed, and he added a number of French officers and ratings to the augmented pier parties which were despatched to Dunkirk at 2200, in

---

[1] The following ships landed troops in England on 4th June (numbers landed in brackets):
British – destroyers *Express* (611), *Malcolm* (736), *Sabre* (592), *Shikari* (383), *Vanquisher* (414), *Venomous* (1200), *Whitshed* (444); Corvettes *Guillemot* (460), *Kingfisher* (200, transferred to trawler off Dunkirk on account of collision damage).; Gunboat *Locust* (196); Minesweepers *Albury* (400), *Halcyon* (501), *Kellett* (30), *Leda* (500), *Medway Queen* (266), *Princess Elizabeth* (329), *Queen of Thanet* (150), *Speedwell* (396); Trawler *Saturn* (418); Drifters *Forecast* (123), "*L.H.W.D.*" (90); Skoots *Bornrif* (96), *Hondsrug* (308), *Pascholl* (255), *Ruja* (300); Yacht *Gulzar* (140); Personnel vessels *Autocarrier* (712), *Canterbury* (659), *Côte d'Argent* (1349), *King George V* (817), *Lady of Mann* (1244), *Newhaven* (729), *Princess Maud* (1270), *Royal Sovereign* (took the place of *Manxman* which refused to sail) (1350), *Tynwald* (3000); Tugs *Racia* (123), *Sun XV* (31), *Tanga* (37); War Dept. M.Ls. *Pigeon* (23), *Swallow* (23); Sailing Barge *Beatrice Maud* (did not reach England until 5th June) (260); R.N.L.I. lifeboats *Edward Z. Dresden* (50), *Greater London* (48); Motor boats and launches *Bonny Heather* (210), *Diana Mary* (28), *Elizabeth Green* (10), *Meuse* (50), *Nayland* (55), *Walker II* (76).   French – 5 Torpedo boats (1416), 2 S/M chasers (127), 3 M/S trawlers (355), 3 patrol vessels (836), 13 trawlers and M.F.Vs. 1104.   Belgian – Tug *Coliath* (183), 5 trawlers (554).

advance of the evacuation force.   Captain de Revoir, the French Naval Attaché, also crossed over to assist.

There were still many British wounded in Dunkirk, and Admiral Nord was asked to make special arranagements to evacuate as many as possible in return for the effort the British were making on behalf of the French Army.

Air Protection

Coastal Command were to provide protection for shipping between Dover and Dunkirk during the period from 1930 on the 3rd until dark.

Fighter Command was to maintain a continuous patrol by one Blenheim over the Dunkirk area during the dark hours.   Fighter protection over the Dunkirk area and shipping in the Channel was arranged for first light, the intention being that Fighter Command should patrol from 0345 to 0600 on June 4th, and Coastal Command from 0600 to 0800.   The execution of the first part of this programme was hindered, and that of the second part prohibited by fog which, however, no doubt supplied an even more thorough form of protection for the ships.

From 0430 to 0615 four Spitfires squadrons were on the line, but encountered no enemy aircraft.   Fog rendered their landing in England difficult on their return.   Hurricane squadrons continued the patrol, reaching the Dunkirk area about 0530 : again no enemy aircraft were encountered, and again great difficulty was experienced in landing, one squadron losing 4 aircraft.   With this unfortunate anti-climax, the fighter patrols over Dunkirk came to an end.

The scene at Dunkirk 2200, 3rd June

Movements from England of the 50 or so ships and numerous small craft for the night's evacuation commenced according to plan.   Rear-Admiral Wake-Walker, who had come over to Dover earlier in the day for consultation, returned to Dunkirk, arriving at 2200 in *M.T.B. 102* "to find the harbour swarming with French fishing craft and vessels of all sorts.   They were yelling and crowding alongside the East Pier which was already thick with French troops.   At one time it looked as if they would get in the way of the transports and destroyers which were on their way, but I managed to get them to go on up the inner harbour and out of the way in time."[1]

" The congestion", said Lieutenant J. N. Wise, R.N.V.R., one of the officers of the skoot *Pascholl* which arrived at Dunkirk at 2300, " was chaotic, ships going astern into others coming ahead. French destroyers shrieking on their sirens, small craft nipping here and there, rendering the exit most dangerous."

The numerous wrecks in the harbour and its approaches increased the difficulty and danger of entering.   In addition to old wrecks marked on the charts there were now a dozen or more new ones, 3 to the west, and 9 to the east, half of them in the fairway ;   and more wrecks lay in the harbour.   One lay alongside the East Pier ;   there was a wrecked trawler off the end of the piling on the west side of the Channel leading up harbour and blockships in the Channel, though luckily the tide was high.

Off the Thanet Coast and in mid-Channel there was thick fog (the *Royal Sovereign*, 40 minutes out from Margate, reported visibility nil), though the ships were spared this added difficulty at Dunkirk where a fresh easterly wind was blowing and there was a choppy sea at the entrance.

[1] M.017978/41 *Report of R. A. Wake-Walker*, p.37.

Casualties from collison and grounding

It was under conditions such as these that the corvette *Kingfisher*, which had embarked 200 French troops at the West Pier between 2255 and 2319, was rammed when just clear of the harbour entrance by the French trawler *Edmond René*; her port bow, 20 feet from the stern, was opened up to the water line, cutting her degaussing circuits. The collision caused the two ships to swing alongside one another, and the troops trans-shipped to the trawler, which was undamaged. The *Kingfisher*, making a little water, proceeded towards England at 7 knots, eventually joining company with the minesweeper *Leda*, another collision casualty.

The *Leda*, having embarked 484 French troops, had pushed off from the West Pier about an hour after the *Kingfisher*. At 0300, on the way back to Margate, the ship ran into the prevailing fog, and off the Goodwin Light Buoy she ran down the Belgian trawler *Maréchal Foch*. The *Leda's* bows were damaged, and for a while the minesweeper *Albury*, which had sailed from the West Pier at about the same time as the *Leda*, with 400 troops, stood by her; but the *Leda's* forward bulkhead held, so the ship continued on her way to Margate, escorted for a while by the *Kellett* until the latter had to break off to assist a ship in greater trouble and left her with the *Kingfisher* as companion in misfortune. The fog was thick at Margate, and in the roads the *Kingfisher* was rammed once more, the personnel vessel *King George V* hitting her on the starboard bow, though only minor damage was caused.

Meanwhile, the *Maréchal Foch* had sunk. In economy of operation this Belgian trawler seems to have been unequalled, for despite the fact that her entire complement consisted only of the Master, Captain P. Lusyne, and one man, (F. Decoster), she had embarked no less than 300 troops. To accomplish this, the ship had lain alongside the quay at Dunkirk since the 2nd of June, for she had grounded on the falling tide and did not get away until the night of the 3rd–4th. It is satisfactory to know that the Captain and his crew were picked up and landed at Dover; but half of the 300 troops she was carrying were drowned. The French M.T.B. *V.T.B 25* which was bringing Admiral Abrial from Dunkirk picked up some but was hampered by a propeller disabled by wreckage, and some were rescued by the destroyer *Malcolm*, which left Dunkirk at 0245 and reported picking up, in fog near the North Goodwin, survivors of an unknown "schuyt" which had been sunk in collision with a minesweeper.

Another ship that grounded in Dunkirk and was lost in consequence, was the Skoot *Lena*. This vessel had sailed from England at 1530 on the 3rd June, in company with four other skoots, the *Pascholl* (S.O.), *Hondsrug*, *Bornrif*, and *Reiger*. The latter ran aground on the Quern Sand soon after leaving Ramsgate, and was left behind. Going alongside the " middle pier of Avant Port " at Dunkirk (probably the West Quay or Guiding Jetty, or possibly the Inner Western Pier) the *Lena* grounded at about 2300. A tug was asked for, but none was available and attempts made to tow her off by the *Bornrif* and a British drifter were unsuccessful. At 1045 on the 4th June, two hours after high water, orders having been given that no further embarkation was to take place after daylight, it was decided to abandon ship. Part of the crew embarked in a British drifter, part in a French drifter, and the remainder, including the officers, were ferried to the *Locust* outside the harbour.

It was presumably owing to difficulty of communication that no tug was forthcoming to tow off the *Lena*, for within a few minutes of her grounding a considerable convoy of tugs arrived off the entrance to the harbour. At 1700 on the 3rd the tugs *Sun IV*, *Tanga*, *Sun XV*, and *Racia*, towing between them 14 motor boats, sailed from Ramsgate to Dunkirk. Two of the motor boats, were abandoned on the way across : the *Thark* with foul propeller and rudder, the *Santosy* on account of water in the petrol ; while the *Diana Mary* was abandoned at Dunkirk with engine trouble (though she eventually returned to Dover with 28 troops), and the barge of the Admiral Superintendent, Portsmouth, piled up on some submerged masonry in Dunkirk harbour and was abandoned. After waiting off Dunkirk since 2300 on the 3rd, the four tugs were ordered at about 0200 on the 4th to go alongside the (East) Pier and embark as many troops as possible, and by the time they were " ordered to clear out " they had collected 203 between them. Of the 14 motor boats which started from Ramsgate with the tugs only 5 or 6 found their way back ; all the remainder were abandoned for one reason or another.

Embarkations at the West Pier (see Plan 4)

Owing to confusion of nomenclature it is impossible in every case to specify definitely at which of the west piers or jetties the ships (other than destroyers and personnel vessels which berthed at the east pier) embarked their troops. In the western part of the port, reading from west to east, were (1) the West Pier (termed western jetty in the Sailing Directions), (2) the West Quay or Guiding Jetty, and (3) the Inner Western Pier (the inner or old western jetty of the Sailing Directions). Of the other three skoots that came over with the *Lena*, the *Bornrif* stated that she embarked 96 troops at the " West Mole" between 2230 on the 3rd and 0100 on the 4th, and the *Hondsrug* 308 at the " West Pier " between 2245 and 0000 ; while the *Pascholl*, which had been commanded by four different captains in 8 days, does not specify from which part of the port she lifted the 255 troops with which she sailed at 0030. Another skoot, the *Rina*, which had spent 24 hours at Dunkirk, sailed about this time with 300 troops.

The corvette *Guillemot*, which had come over with the *Kingfisher*, went to the " Western mole " and secured ahead of the minesweeper *Speedwell* at 2355, leaving again at 0154 with French troops " embarked to capacity " (460). This was her first and only trip, her previous service having been as base ship at Margate. The *Speedwell* which had berthed nearly an hour earlier than the *Guillemot*, took off 396 French troops, and the *Halcyon*, which had sailed from Dover in her company, 501.

The minesweeper *Kellett* grounded forward against the western breakwater on a falling tide when she attempted to go alongside at 0100. It was an anxious moment, for almost simultaneously there same a report that 6 enemy T.B.Ds. were proceeding south-westward from off Ostend ; but the motor lifeboat *Greater London* towed the *Kellett's* stern away from the wall and enabled her to back away. She embarked a few troops from motor boats and sailed for Margate at 0220 by orders of Rear-Admiral Wake-Walker, for the West Pier was occupied and it would be some time before she could be loaded, and the Rear-Admiral feared that so slow a ship might not be able to reach England while our fighter patrols were operating. Two of the personnel ships were sent by Rear-Admiral Wake-Walker to the West Pier instead of to the East Pier, since the former was continuously crowded with French troops, whereas at the East Pier there were gaps in the flow of men. One of the two, the *Royal Sovereign*, embarked 1,350 men and sailed " overladen ", half an hour after she should have been clear.

Among the many ships and craft of which few or no details are recorded were the trawler *Saturn* which brought 418 troops to England, and the yacht *Gulzar* which brought 140. An unknown drifter brought 90, and 260 troops boarded the sailing barge *Beatrice Maud*, while she was lying at Dunkirk abandoned by her crew, and were picked up in mid-Channel and towed to Dover by a destroyer on the 5th June.

The *Leda* paid tribute in her report to the excellent arrangements at West Pier for the embarkation on this night. Commander H. R. Troup R.N., on the staff of Rear-Admiral A. H. Taylor, "Dynamo" Maintenance Officer, assumed charge at the Centre Pier at 2230, making ships fast, finding out the number of men they could take and then getting the French officers to assist him to embark the troops quickly. Commander Troup estimated that he embarked at least 10,000 troops.

Embarkations at the East Pier

Meanwhile, there had been some heavy liftings of troops from the East Pier despite a hold up which threw out the programme of ships entering the harbour and caused great congestion in the entrance. The flow of French troops to the East Pier was better than on the preceding night, though there were some bad pauses.

The first ship to arrive off the pier was the destroyer *Whitshed* at 2215, with Commander H. J. Buchanan, R.A.N. and pier party on board. In consequence of the fresh easterly wind and the westgoing tide the ship could not get alongside the East Pier, where there was nobody who could be persuaded to take a line. However, after disembarking part of her pier party into Rear-Admiral Wake-Walker's M.T.B. for transfer to the pier, she got her bows alongside the personnel ship *Autocarrier* and her stern alongside the *Sabre* and commenced embarking troops. The *Sabre* had been working since 30th May with a compass damaged and rendered unreliable by a shell splinter, and had been led across by the *Venomous*. She got away from the East Pier at 0025 with 592 troops and followed other ships towards England until they were lost to sight near U buoy at the south end of the South Falls. This was within hearing of the North Goodwin Light Vessel, which the *Sabre* located by sound, subsequently proceeding from buoy to buoy until she reached Dover at 0500.

When the *Autocarrier* left in her turn at 0035 she carried 712 French troops. The *Canterbury* left ten minutes later with 659, while the *Côte d'Argent* had shoved off from the pier five minutes earlier with 1,349 troops. After these three practically simultaneous sailings of personnel ships some time elapsed before another bunch got away. The *Princess Maud* had berthed at the extreme end of the pier, and sailed at 0150 with 1,270 troops and "dogs of all kinds" that managed to get aboard. The *Lady of Mann* which berthed about the time when the first three personnel vessels left, took 1,244 troops at 0200. The *Tynwald* seems to have been the last to leave the East Pier. She sailed at 0305 with the record lift, only equalled by the *Scotia* on 29th May, of 3,000 French troops : in 4 trips she had evacuated 8,953 men. With a single exception all destroyers had now gone ; the *Malcolm* went at 0245 with 736 troops, *Vanquisher* at 0240 with 414, and the *Venomous*, which had arrived at 0245 to find the harbour very congested and was ordered to wait outside until 0130, took out no less than 1,200 troops. In four days the *Venomous* had made 5 trips, evacuating 4,410 men in all.

The British pier party was taken off by the destroyer *Express* which, owing to fog, did not arrive at Dunkirk until 0230 on the 4th. She left half an hour later, having embarked 611 troops.

The *Locust* also, after embarking troops ferried out to her from 2300, came alongside the East Pier at 0225, and when she sailed ten minutes later had on board 196 troops.

Mining of the *Emile Deschamps*

The personnel vessel *King George V* which left the East Pier about 0300 with 817 troops, ran into thick fog off the English coast. About 0615, near the Elbow Buoy 2½ miles east of the North Foreland, she passed a "small French naval vessel." Suddenly there was a heavy explosion astern of her, and within a minute the vessel had sunk.

The small French ship was the Fleet Auxiliary *Emile Deschamps* which had sailed from Dunkirk for England at about 2100 on 3rd June, crowded with troops and refugees. About 0558 the minesweeper *Albury*, 5 cables ahead of her, gave her a course for the North Goodwin Light Vessel, which the French ship had missed. A quarter of an hour later the *Emile Deschamps* struck the magnetic mine which sank her.

Several vessels were near and hastened to rescue the survivors. The fire-float *Massey Shaw*, on passage from Ramsgate to London, was only 200 yards away at the time and picked up 40, reported to be all sailors, which she transferred to the *Albury*. The *King George V* lowered four boats and picked up 67. The minesweeper *Kellett*, called up by signal from the *Albury*, rescued some very badly injured people as did also H.M.S. *Nelson's* motor boat, whose log contains the apparently, but no doubt unintentionally, casual entry: "2400. L/Sea. Eggington lost overboard with candle-lantern." Fog came down again as the rescue operations were completed. Among the survivors landed at Margate were 7 French women and a boy.

Blocking Operation repeated night 3rd-4th June

Owing to the failure of the blocking operation of the previous night to close the port, the Admiralty, during the forenoon of the 3rd June, ordered it to be repeated on this night with Admiral Abrial's concurrence. Captain E. Dangerfield, R.N. was again in charge. The ships employed were as follows :—

destroyer :	*Shikari* ;
coastal craft :	*M. A./S. B. 10*,
	M.T.B. 107 ;
blockships :	*Gourko*, 1975 tons, built 1911,
	Moyle, 1761 tons, built 1907,
	Pacifico, 687 tons, built 1905.

The force sailed from the Downs at 2030 on the 3rd by Route Z, *M.T.B. 107* being in tow of the *Shikari*, and anchored at 0130 on the 4th between No. 14 W and 16 W buoys, near the entrance to Dunkirk harbour.

At 0230 Captain Dangerfield, who had transferred to *M. A./S. B. 10* ordered the ships to weigh and the *Shikari* proceeded to lead them to the entrance. The *Gourko's* anchor was barely aweigh when a violent explosion occurred aft, caused, it is reported, by a magnetic mine, although the ship was degaussed and had been wiped in Chatham Dockyard as recently as the 31st May. The *Gourko* began to sink rapidly and was ordered to be abandoned. She sank stern first in 3 minutes. *M. A./S. B. 10* took off 9 survivors and transferred them to the *Shikari*. *M.T.B. 107* rescued 7 others, some of them from the water. One of the crew was missing, and 8 were wounded.

Meanwhile, the other two blockships carried on with the operation. The

119

Moyle rammed the Inner Western Pier abreast the wreck of the *Westcove* and scuttled herself. As she sank, she slid off the bank towards the centre of the channel, as the *Westcove* had done, and finally settled at a slight angle to the line of the channel, her after part being against the *Westcove*.

The *Pacifico* decided to scuttle in the position allotted to the *Gourko*. Her intention was to proceed between and beyond the wrecks of the *Edvard Nissen* and *Westcove* and then drift down between them broadside on. However, the strong current defeated this manoeuvre, so the *Pacifico* rammed the *Westcove* abreast her after hold, dropped anchor into her and secured the cable. The stern then swung over to port towards the *Edvard Nissen*, but, after a certain point, would not turn further owing to the tide race between the two ships. Orders were then given for the scuttling of the *Pacifico* ; As in the case of the *Westcove*, this was accompanied by a considerable sheet of flame, probably due in this instance to oil fuel vapour.

The time now was about 0330 and at this juncture shelling recommenced. One shell hit the pier, causing many casualties, for there were still some 200 French troops on the East Pier. General Bathelemy, Commander of the Flanders Garrison, who was taken off by the *Shikari*, stated that 12,000 French troops still remained in Dunkirk. The *Shikari* carried 383 when she sailed from Dunkirk at 0340 by orders of Captain Dangerfield ; she was the last ship to leave. Apart from an air attack, which caused no damage, her passage home was uneventful.

An M.T.B. had been detailed to evacuate Admiral Abrial but the latter could not be found, and as a matter of fact he was brought out from Dunkirk in a French M.T.B. *V.T.B. 25.* Near the North Goodwin Light Vessel the vessel's propeller became disabled by wreckage, and the *Malcolm* towed her to Dover about 0600.

On the conclusion of the blocking operation there remained a gap of about 100 to 120 feet unobstructed on the west side of the channel. Part of this gap was, however, shoal water, because of the shelving bank.

Disembarkation figures, 4th June

There were landed in England on 4th June 26,175 persons, of which British ships had evacuated 21,600, French 3,838, and Belgian 737. These figures included a number of survivors, both troops and ships' crews, from sunken ships and some refugees. It was recorded that 622 of the total were evacuated from the beaches, but it is doubtful whether any of these were actually evacuated from the beaches, for the figure includes many such as the 43 French troops landed by the *Pangbourne*, who were taken from a French vessel (probably the mail packet *Rouen*) which had run aground on a sand bank : the 260 brought over by the *Beatrice Maud*: a number (apparently 210) recorded as evacuated from the beaches and landed in England but actually ferried from Dunkirk pier to various transports, by the motor launch *Bonny Heather*.

Operation " Dynamo " completed, 1423/4th June

When the *Shikari* sailed, the enemy were reported to be only 3 miles away. Ammunition in Dunkirk was exhausted, and the troops remaining consisted principally of non-combatant units. Accordingly, Admiral Nord agreed that the operation should be considered as terminated. The fleet of rescue ships was dispersed at 1030.

The decision to terminate the operation was agreed to by the French

Admiralty, and at 1423 on the 4th June a message went out from the Admiralty: " Operation Dynamo now completed."

Vice-Admiral Ramsay was aware that the aftermath of the operation would probably be a number of open boats, barges and so forth drifting about in the Channel with troops on board. Air reconnaissances were accordingly carried out on the 4th and 5th. On the 4th a transport was reported lying on its side between Dunkirk and Gravelines and a barge was sighted east of the Goodwins with survivors on board. Two M.T.B.s. despatched by C.-in-C. Nore searched for the transport without success.

Air reconnaissance was carried out on the morning of the 5th but nothing was reported. However, an R.A.F. speedboat carried out a sweep south of a line Goodwins – Boulogne and recovered 33 French troops and two naval ratings. During the day, patrols picked up French troops and brought them in to Dover, Margate and Ramsgate ; and troops also arrived in French and Belgian trawlers. It is reported that in all about 1,100 men were brought in during the 5th June.

CHAPTER XIII

ANALYSIS OF THE OPERATION

Inadequate planning

Operation "Dynamo" was an improvisation, in which the initiative of those taking part largely took the place of planning. Events on the Continent developed so swiftly and unexpectedly that lack of time prevented any but the most meagre preparation for what proved to be a far more extensive operation than was anticipated.

The problem of evacuating large numbers of British troops from the Continent was not mooted until the 19th May, seven days before the operation commenced; and even at that date it was considered unlikely that it would actually be undertaken. As late as the 24th May it was still uncertain whether the British Expeditionary Force would be evacuated.

Two days later, when the Admiralty ordered the operation to commence, the military situation was thought to have deteriorated so rapidly that a lift of no more than 45,000 troops within a period of 48 hours was considered possible, after which the evacuation would have to be terminated on account of enemy action.

In the event, seven times as many men were evacuated, and the operation continued for 9 days.

The organisation was built up as the evacuation proceeded. A Maintenance Officer to take charge of the small craft was appointed on the 27th May, the day after the beginning of the operation. S.N.O. Dunkirk assumed duty at 1900 on the same day, and S.N.O. Afloat off the beaches two days later. It was not, however, until the 30th May that an S.N.O. arrived to take charge off the French–Belgian coast, together with an N.O.I.C. Beaches and two Commodores to take charge off shore. How great was the effect of these appointments, will be shown in due course in the analysis of the evacuation figures.

The arrival of beaching craft at the beaches was unnecessarily delayed on the 28th and 29th May, owing to the Admiralty (and the majority of the Naval Authorities who provided craft), directing them to Dover instead of the Downs, as had been requested by Vice-Admiral Ramsay.

Lack of Signal Communications

Difficulties and confusion were caused throughout the operation owing to the absence of efficient signalling arrangements, both locally between Dunkirk and the beaches and between Dunkirk and Dover. The equipment taken by the signal party which proceeded from England to Dunkirk on 27th was inadequate either for inter-communication between the beaches or from the beaches to Dunkirk.

The naval beach parties, as might have been expected, used their ingenuity to improvise local inter-communication arrangements but it was not until the 30th May that a naval wireless set capable of communicating with

England was sent to Dunkirk; until then messages had either to be sent through the French station in an unsuitable code, or fortuitously via any destroyer which might be lying alongside, necessitating a messenger forcing his way along the narrow crowded footway of the pier.

In the absence of efficient communication it was impossible to distribute ships to the best advantage off the beaches or between Dunkirk harbour and the beaches; whilst the uncertainty as to whether the harbour was blocked on the 29th May was responsible for a reduction of 10,000 men in the possible lift during the night 29th–30th.

Air Co-operation

There is no doubt that the R.A.F. carried out, as far as their available resources permitted, all the tasks which they were asked by the Navy to undertake. The odds at which our airmen fought were very long, four or five to one. Formations of single squadron strength or less would boldly attack German groups of forty or fifty machines, usually with success out of all proportion to the odds against them. It was a direct test of British against German quality.

Numbers did not, however, permit of a continuous patrol being maintained over the scene, though ' the whole Metropolitan Air Force, our last sacred reserve, was used. Sometimes the fighter pilots made four sorties a day'.[1] Unfortunately, the troops on the beaches and on Dunkirk piers saw but little of the fighting in the air, for much of the weight of the effort of the Royal Air Force was directed against objectives far inland, to prevent or break up enemy raids before these reached the beaches and ships. It was the ships that took the brunt of the German attack. Galling though it was to our troops to be bombed and machine gunned with little or no opportunity to defend themselves their losses, grievous enough, were yet never of such severity as to jeopardise the entire operation, as did the losses of ships. However, the system of co-operation in force at that early date, which did not permit of direct contact with R.A.F. operational units allocated for duty with the Naval Command, rendered difficult complete co-ordination of effort with naval requirements on the spot.

Evacuation figures analysed[2]

In analysing the evacuation figures it is necessary to consider separately the rates of lift from day to day and the daily total figures of troops lifted. The former naturally affected the latter ; but the days which showed the best rates of lift were not necessarily those giving the highest evacuation total, since circumstances affected the two sets of figures differently and factors which affected one set often had no effect whatever on the other.

The following table shows the number of men from the beaches and the harbour landed daily in England by British ships, and the number of round trips undertaken. Evacuations of wounded by hospital carriers have been omitted, as have also the liftings from the beaches on 3rd and 4th of June, which were largely fortuitous.

---

[1] Churchill, *The Second World War Vol. II.*
[2] The figures employed in this analysis are those of H.S./T.S.D. The total differs by **397** (= 0.0013%) from the military figure. *See* Note to Tables 1–3 which will be found before the appendices at the end of this book.

LANDINGS IN ENGLAND BY BRITISH SHIPS

	FROM BEACHES					FROM HARBOUR				
	LARGE VESSELS[1]		SMALL CRAFT		TOTAL Daily lift	LARGE VESSELS[1]		SMALL CRAFT		TOTAL Daily lift
	Trips	Average lift (men)	Trips	Average lift (men)		Trips	Average lift (men)	Trips	Average lift (men)	
(1)	(2)	(3)	(4)	(5)	(6)	(7)	(8)	(9)	(10)	(11)
Date										
May 27th	—	—	—	—	—	7[2]	1,001	—	—	7,011
28th	13	318	12	95	5,930	17	698	—	—	11,874
29th	34	391	3	(insufficient trips to strike an average)	13,746	37	763	—	—	28,225
30th	55	491	19	40	29,512	21	614	28	129	19,491
31st	50	376	44	73	22,942	46	652	21	46	40,281
June 1st	47	260	44	53	17,314	48	484	37	116	42,181
2nd	19	276	20	73	6,695	24	688	19	93	17,614
3rd	—	—	—	—	—	28	656	19	103	19,530
4th	—	—	—	—	—	31	630	13	57	20,518
Total	218	352	142	67	96,130	259	689	137	90	206,725

Note: Tables 1–3 giving the figures of embarkation from Dunkirk will be found facing page 210.

It will be seen that the average lift per trip from the harbour was nearly double that from the beaches : 396 vessels evacuated 206,725 men from the harbour while 360 vessels evacuated 96,139 from the beaches, i.e., 10 per cent more vessels evacuated $2\frac{1}{8}$ times as many troops. Against this must be set the fact that the number of large ships engaged in lifting from the harbour was slightly greater than the number that embarked troops from the beaches, viz. 259 against 218 ; the number of small vessels was approximately equal in each case.

---

[1] For the purposes of this Table " Large vessels " are those whose average lift was over 200 men.

[2] 5 personnel vessels and 2 armed boarding vessels capable of very high lifts.

The following table shows the difference in average lift per type of vessel from beaches and harbour respectively:

LIFT PER SHIP

TYPE OF SHIP	AVERAGE LIFT PER TRIP FROM	
	Beaches	Harbour
Personnel vessels	488	1,054
Destroyers	504	751
Minesweepers	358	432
Skoots	280	290
Drifters	140	156
Small Craft .... (excluding drifters)	90	116

It will be seen that the average lift of all vessels was larger from the harbour than from the beaches, and that the difference decreased with the size of vessel. The difference was most marked in the case of personnel vessels, which were civilian manned and consequently less efficient in boat work.

The average lift of all types of ship and the time spent in collecting the load at beaches and in harbour respectively was as follows :—

AVERAGE LIFT PER TRIP :
    from beaches   344
    from harbour   529

AVERAGE NO. OF MINUTES SPENT :
    at beaches   345
    in harbour   117

i.e. one man per minute was lifted from the beaches as against 4.5 men per minute from the harbour.

The average lifts and number of minutes required by large ships to load at beaches and harbour, respectively, from day to day are shown in the following table. Data of waiting times for small craft are incomplete and consequently reliable figures cannot be given ; much time was occupied by small craft in ferrying troops to larger ships.

FIGURES FOR LARGE SHIPS

	BEACHES			HARBOUR			
DATE	RATE OF LIFT (men minutes)	AVERAGE Lift (men)	Waiting time (minutes)	RATE OF LIFT (men : minutes)	AVERAGE Lift (men)	Waiting time (minutes)	
(1)	(2)	(3)	(4)	(5)	(6)	(7)	
28 May	1 : 1	318	312	5.2 : 1	698	133	Arrival
29 ,,	1.1 : 1	391	358	5.7 : 1	763	133	of
30 ,,	1.4 : 1	491	356	5.2 : 1	614	118	ships
31 ,,	1.2 : 1	376	315	5.0 : 1	652	129	not
1 June	0.6 : 1	260	447	3.4 : 1	484	140	planned
2 ,,	1 : 1	276	284	10.3 : 1	688	67	Arrival
3 ,,	— —	—	—	7.0 : 1	656	94	of ships
4 ,,	—	—	—	5.2 : 1	630	122	planned
Average	1 : 1	352	345	5.5 : 1	648	117	
Estimated norm.	1.1 : 1	345	315	5.2 : 1	650	125	

The variations in the daily figures are believed to have been influenced by the factors recorded in the following paragraphs.

28TH MAY. *Beaches.* Although the rate of lift was average (1 : 1), and the average waiting time corresponded to the estimated norm, the number of men lifted per trip was below normal. This was probably due to shortage of beaching boats. Destroyers, which made 8 of the 13 trips, were new to the work and their lift per trip was only 356 as against a destroyer aveage of 504 over the whole operation. The *Calcutta's* lift was reduced by the large number of wounded (cot cases) which she embarked.

HARBOUR. Although the average lift was above normal, the long waiting time reduced the men : minutes ratio to the estimated norm for the operation. The figures of waiting time are not, however, entirely satisfactory ; only 10 ships provided data, three of which waited for periods greatly in excess of the average.

HARBOUR. The increase in average lift without corresponding rise in waiting time is accounted for by the great increase in the number of personnel ships employed and the average lifts made by them on this day. The average lift per personnel ship, which on the 28th May was only 552, rose to 1,520 today.

30TH MAY. *Beaches.* The increase of 25 per cent in the figure for average lift without corresponding rise in waiting time, resulting in the highest men : minutes ratio achieved at the beaches during the operation, is believed to have been due to :—

> (a) better organisation consequent upon the arrival of R.A. Dover as S.N.O. on the French coast and of Captain Howson as N.O.I.C. Beaches, together with the employment of two Commodores to take charge off shore at La Panne and Bray ; (b) better discipline amongst the troops on the beaches ; (c) employment as beaching craft of the A.L.Cs. which began to arrive on the 29th, and the arrival of 12 motor boats for retrieving abandoned pulling boats ; (d) absence of enemy air attacks.

Harbour. Although the rate of lift deviated little from the average, both lift and waiting time declined. This was probably the effect of the disastrous air attacks of the previous day on shipping, which resulted in only one destroyer at a time being allowed to enter Dunkirk during the forenoon and early afternoon and perhaps engendered a feeling of insecurity and a wish to get the ships away as quickly as possible.[1]

31ST MAY. *Beaches.* A considerable reduction in average waiting time and a slight rise above normal in average lift gave a rate of lift slightly better than normal. This was due probably to the fact that greater numbers of beaching boats were available. Although during the forenoon conditions on the beaches were very bad they improved greatly during the afternoon and evening. On the beaches, after 1600, the piers of pontoons were largely responsible for the rapid evacuation of troops.

Harbour. Lift was average, but waiting time was high and reduced the men : minutes rate of lift. No valid reason for this can be discovered, and it should be noted that all the figures agree closely with the estimated norm.

---

[1] This belief is based on the final sentence in Situation Report by S.N.O. Dunkirk timed 0943 : " The moment bombing starts all must shove off "; and on the signal at 0950 : " If this weather persists I want a ship every half hour," which would seem to imply that the single destroyer allowed to enter would remain alongside for only half an hour.

1ST JUNE. *Beaches.* The climax of boat shortage occurred on this day, and " increasing enemy air attack caused continual interruptions of embarkation on the beaches and in Dunkirk " (*D.R.* p. 25). The disastrous figures reflect the serious situation that developed on the beaches about 2030 on the 31st May, when the rate of embarkation fell to about 150 an hour owing to shortage of boats.

Harbour. The interruptions caused by air attacks and shelling undoubtedly accounted partly for the poor rate of lift. A further factor was the berthing of destroyers two or three deep at the East Pier. It is true that some destroyers filled up in less than an hour : the *Vivacious*, for example, out of 35 minutes spent in Dunkirk, was alongside the East Pier for only 15 minutes, during which time she took on board 475 men ; and the *Shikari* needed only 20 minutes to embark 623 troops. On the other hand, owing to the state of the tide, the personnel vessel *Maid of Orleans* spent $5\frac{1}{2}$ hours at the East Pier acting as a floating pontoon for destroyers, while the outermost destroyer, the *Windsor*, spent nearly 15 hours alongside.

2ND JUNE. No daylight evacuations took place after the 1st June, all took place at night.

Beaches. The average lift and waiting time were both much below normal. There were more ships lying off the beaches than could be loaded by the boats available ; consequently, scarcely a single ship left with a full load of troops. The rate of lift, however, was average.

Harbour. The night of the 1st–2nd June saw the introduction of planned arrival and berthing of ships at Dunkirk. This resulted in a marked improvement in the average lift, which was almost the best of the entire operation.

3RD JUNE. The increase in average time spent at Dunkirk during the night of the 2nd–3rd June over the previous night was probably accounted for by the difficulties experienced by ships in going alongside the East Pier. The figure was worsened by the fact that, owing to the cessation of the flow of French troops to the East Pier after the embarkation of the British rearguard at 2330 on the 2nd, five destroyers had to be sent back to England practically empty.

4th JUNE. Owing to chaotic conditions in Dunkirk harbour time waiting to berth averaged no less than 100 minutes. Pauses in the flow of French troops to the piers, and the impossibility of inducing them to embark in quick and orderly manner (which latter factor had also operated on the previous night) sufficed to depress the rate of lift from the high averages of the two previous nights, to the norm for the operation.

Discipline

No instances of naval indiscipline came to light. But in an operation where the level of initiative was very high an unaccountably heavy wastage of small boats occurred from lack of boatkeepers. There were undoubtedly instances where small boats which were brought off from shore to ship manned only by troops, drifted away and were lost after the troops climbed out of them, owing to the omission to put boatkeepers into them.

The state of discipline of the troops had a direct bearing on the rate of embarkation. In the early stages of the operation the troops on the beaches were mainly rear units and indiscipline occurred. The arrival of combatant units soon put an end to this : meanwhile it was effectively dealt with by the British Naval officers and men of the beach parties.

In the early stages the French troops were at a disadvantage as compared with the British in being disorganised and unofficered. Due allowance must be made for the demoralising position in which they found themselves. The language difficulty and the particular system of discipline which rendered the French soldier unwilling to be separated from the remainder of his unit, together with perhaps a lack of sea sense, resulted in the embarkation of French troops being consistently slower than British.

Many reports, however, bear tribute to the discipline of the French troops when properly led ; and it seems fitting to take a last look at them as seen by Commander H. R. Troup, who constituted himself piermaster at the Centre Pier on the final night :—

> "I would like to put on record the wonderful discipline of the French troops when the last ship left about 0300 [on 4th June].
> About 1,000 men stood to attention four deep about half way along the pier, the General and his staff about 30 feet away ; and after having faced the troops, whose faces were indiscernable in the dawn light, the flames behind them showing up their steel helmets, the officers clicked their heels, saluted and then turned about and came down to the boat with me and we left at 0320."[1]

The operation was at an end.

---

[1] Commander Troup's Report, R.O. II, p.369.

APPENDIX A

LIST OF SHIPS WHICH TOOK PART IN OPERATION " DYNAMO "
AND
NUMBERS OF TROOPS TRANSPORTED

NOTE.—The following list of ships which took part in Operation " Dynamo " has been compiled after critical examination of every available source of information. It differs from *The final list of British Ships*, M.020721 of 25th October 1940 accompanying V. A. Dover's *Report on Operation " Dynamo "* M.011883 of 18th June 1940, in 320 entries.

Part I. British Ships

	FLOTILLA	TROOPS TRANSPORTED
A.A. CRUISER		
Calcutta		1,856
(Capt. D. M. Lees, R.N.)		
DESTROYERS—41, of which 6 were sunk		
Anthony	16th	3,107
(Lt. Cdr. N. V. Thew, R.N.)		
Basilisk[1]	Nore Command	1,115
(Cdr. M. Richmond, O.B.E., R.N.)		
Codrington	Capt. (D) 1	5,677
(Capt. (D) G. F. Stevens-Guille, D.S.O., O.B.E., R.N.)		
Esk	20th	3,904
(Lt. Cdr. R. J. H. Couch, R.N.)		
Express	Capt (D) 20	2,795
(Capt. (D) J. G. Bickford, D.S.C., R.N.)		
Gallant	1st	1,880
(Lt. Cdr. C. P. F. Brown, R.N.)		
Grafton[1]	1st	860
(Cdr. C. E. C. Robinson, R.N.) (killed)		
(Lieut. H. C. J. McRea, R.N.)		
Grenade[1]	Nore Command	1,000
(Cdr. R. C. Boyle, R.N.)		
Greyhound	1st	1,360
(Cdr. W. R. Marshall-A'Deane, R.N.)		
Harvester	9th	3,191
(Lt. Cdr. M. Thornton, R.N.)		
Havant[1]	9th	2,432
(Lt. Cdr. A. F. Burnell-Nugent, D.S.C., R.N.)		
Icarus	20th	4,704
(Lt. Cdr. C. D. Maud, R.N.)		
Impulsive	20th	2,919
(Lt. Cdr. W. S. Thomas, R.N.)		
Intrepid	20th	661
(Cdr. R. C. Gordon, R.N.)		
Ivanhoe	20th	1,904
(Cdr. P. H. Hadow, R.N.)		
Jackal	1st	—
(Cdr. T. M. Napier, R.N.)		
Jaguar	1st	700
(Lt. Cdr. J. F. W. Hine, R.N.)		
Javelin	1st	1,400
(Cdr. A. F. Pugsley, R.N.)		
Keith[1]	Capt. (D) 19	1,200
(Capt. (D) E. L. Berthon, D.S.C., R.N.)		
Mackay	11th	581
(Cdr. G. H. Stokes, R.N.)		
Malcolm	Capt. (D) 16	5,851
(Capt. (D) T. E. Halsey, R.N.)		
Montrose	17th	925
(Cdr. C. R. L. Parry, R.N.)		

[1] Sunk.

	FLOTILLA	TROOPS TRANSPORTED
DESTROYERS (*contd.*)		
Sabre	16th	5,765
(Cdr. B. Dean, R.N. (Retd.))		
Saladin	11th	—
(Lt. Cdr. L. J. Dover, R.N.)		
Scimitar	16th	2,711
(Lieut. R. D. Franks, O.B.E., R.N.)		
Shikari	16th	3,589
(Lt. Cdr. H. N. A. Richardson, R.N.)		
Vanquisher	11th	3,941
(Lt. Cdr. C. B. Alers-Hankey, R.N.) (relieved sick)		
(Lt. Cdr. W. C. Bushell, R.N.)		
Vega	Nore Command	34
(Cdr. C. I. Horton, R.N.)		
Venomous	16th (Attached	4,410
(Lt. Cdr. J. E. H. McBeath, R.N.)	Dover Command)	
Verity	Nore Command	504
(Lt. Cdr. A. R. M. Black, R.N.) (wounded)		
(Lieut. E. L. Jones, R.N.)		
Vimy	Nore Command	2,976
(Lt. Cdr. R. G. K. Knowling, R.N.) (missing)		
(Lieut. A. P. W. Northey, R.N.) (temporarily)		
(Lt. Cdr. M. W. E. Wentworth, R.N.)		
Vivacious	Nore Command	1,999
(Lt. Cdr. F. R. W. Parish, R.N.) (relieved—sick)		
(Cdr. E. F. V. Dechaineux, R.A.N.)		
Wakeful[1]	17th	639
(Cdr. R. L. Fisher, R.N.)		
Whitehall	11th	3,453
(Lt. Cdr. A. B. Russell, R.N.)		
Whitshed	19th	1,038
(Cdr. E. R. Condor, R.N.)		
Wild Swan		12
(Lt. Cdr. J. L. Younghusband, R.N.)		
Winchelsea	11th	4,957
(Lt. Cdr. W. A. F. Hawkins, R.N.)		
Windsor	Nore Command	3,991
(Lt. Cdr. P. D. H. R. Pelly, R.N.)		
Wolfhound	Nore Command	130
(Lt. Cdr. J. W. McCoy, D.S.C., R.N.)		
Wolsey	Attached Dover	3,337
(Lt. Cdr. C. H. Campbell, R.N.)	Command	
Worcester	11th	4,545
(J. H. Allison, R.N.)		
	Total	96,197
CORVETTES. Total 6		
Guillemot		460
(Lt. Cdr. H. M. Darell-Brown, R.N.)		
Kingfisher		640
(Lt. Cdr. G. A. M. V. Harrison, R.N.)		
Mallard		—
(Cdr. The Hon. V. M. Wyndham-Quin, R.N.)		
Shearwater		—
(Lt. Cdr. P. F. Powlett, R.N.)		
Sheldrake		—
(Lt. Cdr. A. E. T. Christie, R.N.)		
Widgeon		—
(Lt. Cdr. R. Frederick, R.N.)		
	Total	1,100

[1] Sunk.

	FLOTILLA	TROOPS TRANSPORTED
SLOOP		
Bideford		436
(Lt. Cdr. J. H. Lewes, R.N.)		
GUNBOATS. Total 2, of which 1 was sunk.		
Locust		2,329
(Lieut. A. N. P. Costobadie, R.N.)		
Mosquito[1]		1,183
(Lieut. D. H. P. Gardiner, R.N.)		
	Total	3,512

	FLOTILLA	TROOPS TRANSPORTED
MINESWEEPERS—36, of which 5 were lost.		
Albury	5th	1,536
(Lt. Cdr. C. H. Corbet-Singleton, R.N.)		
Brighton Belle[1]	10th	Nil
(Lieut. L. K. Perrin, R.N.V.R.)		
Brighton Queen[1]	7th	160
(Ty. Lieut. A. Stubbs, R.N.R.)		
Devonia[2]	7th	Nil
(Ty. Lt. J. Brotchie, R.N.V.R.)		
Duchess of Fife	12th	1,801
(Ty. Lt. J. N. Anderson, R.N.R.)		
Dundalk	4th	1,129
(Lt. Cdr. F. A. J. Kirkpatrick, R.N. (retd.))		
Emperor of India	10th	642
(Ty. Lieut. C. Pawley, R.N.R.)		
Fitzroy	4th	867
(Lt. Cdr. R. A. Forbes, R.N.)		
Glen Avon	8th	888
(Ty. Lieut. B. H. Loynes, R.N.R.)		
Glen Gower	8th (S.O.)	1,235
(Actg. Cdr. M. A. O. Biddulph, R.N., S.O. 8th M.S.F.)		
Gossamer	5th (S.O.)	3,169
(Cdr. R. C. V. Ross, R.N., S.O. 5th M.S.F.)		
Gracie Fields[1]	10th	281
(Ty. Lt. N. Larkin, R.N.R.)		
(Ty. Lt. A. C. Weeks, R.N.V.R.)		
Halcyon	6th	2,271
(Lt. Cdr. J. M. S. Cox, D.S.C., R.N.)		
(Cdr. E. P. Hinton, M.V.O., R.N.)		
Hebe	1st	1,140
(Lt. Cdr. J. B. G. Temple, R.N.)		
Kellett	5th	1,456
(Cdr. R. C. Haskett-Smith, R.N.)		
Leda	5th	2,848
(Lt. Cdr. H. Unwin, R.N.)		
Lydd	5th	1,502
(Lt. Cdr. R. C. D. Haig, R.N.)		
Marmion	12th	713
(Ty. Lt. H. C. Gaffney, R.N.V.R.)		
Medway Queen	10th	3,064
(Lieut. A. T. Cook, R.N.R.)		
Niger	4th	1,245
(Cdr. St. J. Cronyn, R.N., S.O., 4th M.S.F.)		
Oriole	12th	2,587
(Ty. Lieut. E. L. Davies, R.N.V.R.)		
Pangbourne	5th	1,020
(Actg. Cdr. F. Douglas-Watson, R.N.)		

[1] Sunk.
[2] Beached and lost.

	FLOTILLA	TROOPS TRANSPORTED
MINESWEEPERS (*contd.*)		
Plinlimmon	7th	900
(Lt. G. P. Baker, R.N.V.R.)		
Princess Elizabeth	10th	1,673
(Lt. C. J. Carp, R.N.V.R.)		
Queen of Thanet	7th (S.O.)	2,500
(Actg. Ty. Cdr. S. P. Herival, R.N.V.R.) (S.O. 7th M.S.F.)		
Ross	5th	1,096
(Actg. C. O. Lt. K. A. Gadd, R.N.R. (injured) (Cdr. J. P. Apps, R.N. (Retd.))		
Salamander	4th	1,161
(Lieut. Cdr. L. J. S. Ede, R.N.)		
Saltash	5th	800
(Lt. Cdr. T. R. Fowke, R.N.)		
Sandown	10th (S.O.)	1,861
(Actg. Cdr. K. M. Greig, R.N., S.O., 10th M.S.F.)		
Sharpshooter	1st	373
(Lieut. A. E. Doran, R.N.)		
Skipjack[1]	6th	865
(Lieut. Cdr. F. B. Proudfoot, R.N. (retd.))		
Snaefell	8th	981
(Ty. Lieut. F. Brett, R.N.V.R.)		
Speedwell	6th	1,668
(Lt. Cdr. F. R. G. Maunsell, R.N. (Retd.))		
Sutton	4th (S.O.)	1,371
(Actg. Cdr. G. M. Temple, R.N., S.O. 4th M.S.F.)		
Waverley[1]	12th (S.O.)	Nil
(Ty. Lieut. S. F. Harmer-Elliott, R.N.V.R.) (Actg. S.O., 12th M.S.F.)		
Westward Ho	7th	1,686
(Ty. Lieut. A. L. Braithwaite, R.N.V.R.)		
	Total	46,434

	TROOPS TRANSPORTED
TRAWLERS. Total 52, of which 12 were lost.	
Amethyst	—
Comdr. (*Act.*) R. C. Stokes, R.N.[3]	
Arctic Pioneer	—
(Lt. R. A. D. Cambridge, R.N.R.)	
Argyllshire[1]	—
(S/Lt. J. S. Weddle, R.N.R.) (S.O. 11th A/S Striking Force)	
Arley	135
(Skr. Lt. G. W. Robinson, R.D., R.N.R.)	
Blackburn Rovers[1]	—
(Cdr. R. W. English, R.N.) (Skipper W. Martin, R.N.R.)	
Brock	6
(S/Lt. K. H. G. Roberts, R.N.V.R.) (Skipper Jappy)	
Calvi[1]	—
(Skipper B. D. Spindler, R.N.R.)	
Cape Argona	—
(Lt. K. J. Lee, R.N.V.R.)	
Cayton Wyke	605[2]
(Comdr. R. H. B. Hammond-Chambers, R.N. (Ret.))[3]	
Clythness	150
(Skipper E. G. Catchpole, R.N.R.)[3]	
Comfort[1]	—
(Skipper J. D. Mair, R.N.R.)	
Dhoon	130

[1] Sunk.
[2] Including 300 in a barge which was picked up.
[3] Name taken from *The Navy List for June* 1940.

	TROOPS TRANSPORTED
TRAWLERS (*contd.*)	
Spurs	—
(Skipper H. H. Jarvis, R.N.R.)[1]	
Edwina	120
(Skipper P. Bedford (?))	
Evelyn Rose	130
(Tempy-Skipper (F.R.) A. J. Lewis)[3]	
Fyldea	180
(Lieut. R. Bill, R.N., Asst. to Cdr. M/S Dover)	
(Lieut. J. K. M. Warde, R.N.V.R., Unit Officer)	
(Skipper G. Whamond)	
Gava	502
(Lieut. F. J. Jordan, R.N.R.) (Skipper Day, R.N.R.)	
Grimsby Town	—
(Lieut. W. C. Riley, R.N.V.R.)[3]	
Inverforth	—
(Lt. Cdr. A. A. Martin, R.N.R. (Group Officer)).	
Jacinta	—
Jasper	—
(Lieut. A. Johnson, R.N.V.R.)[3]	
John Cattling	77
(Ty. Lt. G. St. C. Rideal, R.N.V.R.)	
(Ty. Skipper G. W. Aldan, R.N.R.)	
Kingston Alalite	—
(Ch. Skipper A. H. Foster, R.N.R.)[3]	
Kingston Andalusite	—
(Skipper J. Bruce (*Act.*) R.N.R.)[3]	
Kingston Galena	—
(S/Lt. J. L. Pringle, R.N.V.R.)	
Kingston Olivine	—
(Lieut. G. W. Gregorie, R.N.R.)[3]	
Lady Philomena	—
(Skipper J. Hodson, R.N.R.)[3]	
Lord Grey	400
(Ty. Lt. J. A. Simson, R.N.V.R.)	
Proby. Skipper W. J. Tiller, R.N.R.)	
Lord Inchcape	240
(S/L S. J. Longsdon, R.N.V.R.) (Unit Officer)	
Lord Melchett	—
(Skipper R. C. Raylor, R.N.R.)	
(Group Officer Lt. W. H. Ward, R.N.V.R.)	
Malabar	26
Nautilus[1]	—
(Lieut. W. E. Gelling, R.N.R.) (Skipr. R. Maclean, R.N.R.)	
Ocean Reward[1]	—
Olvina	347
(S/Lt. J. H. Cooper, R.N.V.R.) (Unit Officer, 40th A/S Group)	
Our Bairns	200
(Skipper J. H. Miller)	
Polly Johnson[1]	—
(Skipper Lieut. L. Lake, R.D., R.N.R.)	
Relonzo	—
(Skipper Slater)	
Restrivo	—
(Tempy.-Skipper J. Fountain, R.N.R.)[3]	
St. Achilleus[1]	—
(Ty. Lt. H. A. Gellett, R.N.V.R.) (S.O. 11th A/S Group)	
Saon	359
(Lt. Com. A. G. G. Webb, R.N. (*Ret.*))[3]	
Sphene	—
(Skipper C. Pennington, R.N.R.)	
Saturn	1,177
(Ty. Skipper H. C. Watson, R.N.R.)	

[1] Sunk.
[3] Name taken from *The Navy List for June* 1940.

	TROOPS TRANSPORTED
TRAWLERS *(contd.)*	
Stella Dorado[1]	55
(Skipper W. H. Burgess, R.N.R.)[3]	
Stella Rigel	—
(Skipper L. P. Keable, R.N.R.)	
(Unit Officer S/Lt. J. W. Wykeham, R.N.V.R.)	
Strathelliot	339
(S/Lt. W. E. Mercer, R.N.V.R.)	
Tankerton Towers	50
(Skipper J. Hannaford)	
Thomas Bartlett[1]	—
(Skipper J. J. Tomlinson, R.N.R.)	
Thuringia[1]	—
(Ch. Skipper D. W. L. Simpson, D.S.C., D.S.M., R.N.R.)	
Topaze	118
(Lt. Cdr. J. N. Hambly, M.B.E., R.N., S.O. 40th A/S Group)	
Velia	—
(Skipper J. Clarkson)	
Viviana	—
(Skipper G. L. Olesen)	
Westella[1]	—
(Chief Skipper A. Gove, R.N.R.)	
Wolves	50
(Skipper J. D. Fowler, R.N.R.	
Skipper W. S. Flowers, R.N.R.)[3]	
Total	5,396

DRIFTERS. Total 61, of which 5 were lost.	
Alcmaria	32
(Skipper A. C. Offord, R.N.R.)[3]	
Ben & Lucy	100
(Captain W. A. Watling, R.N.R., Skipper)	
(Actg. Lt. F. G. M. Iles, R.N.V.R. Unit Officer)	
Boy Roy[1]	—
(Ty. Skipper E. F. Dettman, R.N.R.)	
Dorienta	65
(Skipper W. F. Reynolds, R.N.R.)	
Eileen Emma	114
(Tempy. Skipper B. E. S. Smith, R.N.R.)[3]	
Fair Breeze[1]	316
(Lt. Cdr. A. R. W. Sayle, R.N.R.)	
Feasible	—
(Skipper C. C. Findlay, R.N.R.)[3]	
Fidget	568
Fisher Boy	777
(Ty. Skipper G. W. Brown, R.N.R.)	
Forecast	353
(Lt. T. P. Graham, R.N.R., Unit Officer)	
Genius	109
(Skipper G. H. Green, R.N.R.)[3]	
Gervais Rentoul	57
(Tempy.-Skipper J. H. Burgess, R.N.R.[3]	
Girl Gladys	249
(Tempy.-Skipper F. L. Strowger, R.N.R.[3]	
Girl Pamela[1]	51
(Ty. Skipper G. Sanson, R.N.R.)	
Golden Gift	273
(Ty. Skipper G. S. Sampson)	
Golden Sunbeam	397
(Skipper W. C. F. Chaney)	

[1] Sunk.
[3] Name taken from *The Navy List for June* 1940.

	TROOPS TRANSPORTED
DRIFTERS (contd.)	
Gula	110
(Tempy.-Skipper A. W. West, R.N.R.)[3]	
Jacketa	651
(Ty. Skipper D. Tause, R.N.R.)	
Jackeve	120
(Skipper C. E. F. Reynolds, R.N.R.)	
Jeannie MacIntosh	Not known
(Skipper J. W. Nicholson, R.N.R.)[3]	
John & Norah	61
(Skipper R. A. Sims, R.N.R.)[3]	
Kindred Star	——
(T. W. Sheridan, Tempy. Skip. R.N.R.)	
(G. Corney, Temp. Skipper, R.N.R.)	
(Lieut. A. J. Dunbar, R.N.V.R., Unit Officer)	
Lord Barham	388
(Tempy.-Skipper J. Masterton, R.N.R.)[3]	
Lord Cavan[1]	——
(Ty. Skipper J. H. Muggridge, R.N.R.)	
Lord Collingwood	332
Lord Hood	——
(Skipper J. W. Lawn, R.N.R.)[3]	
Lord Howard	379
(Tempy-Skipper D. Davidson, R.N.R.)[3]	
Lord Howe	277
(Skipper W. H. Pollock)	
Lord Keith	323
(R. Pye, Master)	
Lord Rodney	Not known
(R. Durrant, Master)	
Lord St. Vincent	150
L.H.W.D.	90
Mare	219
(Skipper A. H. W. Pendle, R.N.R.)	
(Group Offr. Cdr. J. W. D. Powell, D.S.C.(Bar), R.N.R.)	
Midas	360
(Skipper H. Holden, R.N.R.)	
Monarda	190
(Lieut. P. T. Lovelock, R.N.V.R.)	
Netsukis	483
(Tempy.-Skipper A. V. Muffett, R.N.V.R.)[3]	
Ocean Breeze	259
(Lieut. V. A. de Mauny, R.N.) (Skipper Bailey (?))	
Overfall	Not known
(Tempy.-Skipper D. Miller, R.N.R.)[3]	
Paxton[1]	——
(Lt. Cdr. R. M. Prior, R.N.) (Skipper A. M. Lovis, R.N.R.)	
Reed	Not known
(Skipper G. Hatton, R.N.R.)[3]	
Renascent	260
(Skipper R. E. Hannaford, R.N.R.)	
Rewga	162
(Tempy.-Skipper J. W. Macanley, R.N.R.)[3]	
Rig	60
(Skipper E. Beckham, R.N.R.)	
Robert Cliff	——
Sarah Hyde	100
(Skipper H. G. Meen, R.N.R.)	
(Unit Officer Lt. J. I. Cruickshank, R.N.V.R.)	
Shipmates	196
(Ty. Skipper H. E. Ward)	
Silver Dawn	694
(Skipper S. A. White, R.N.R.)	

[1] Sunk.
[3] Name taken from *The Navy List for June* 1940.

TROOPS
TRANSPORTED

DRIFTERS (*contd.*)

Starlight Rays	610
(Skipper, A. Buchan, R.N.R.)	
(Lt. W. R. Hutcheson, R.N.V.R.)	
Strive	243
(Skipper H. A. Catchpole, R.N.R.)	
Swift Wing	Not known
(Tempy.-Skipper G. Frosdick, R.N.R.)[3]	
Taransay	162
(Tempy.-Skipper G. S. Peek, R.N.R.)[3]	
The Boys	—
(Skipper A. Buchan, R.N.R.)	
Thomsons	—
(Skipper S. J. A. Drake, R.N.R.)	
Three Kings	350
(Skipper G. W. Smith, R.N.R.) (Skipper A. V. Long, R.N.R.)	
Thrifty	—
(Tempy.-Skipper G. Corney, R.N.R.)[3]	
Torbay II	302
(Tempy.-Skipper W. B. Jenner, R.N.R.)[3]	
Tweenways	126
(Skipper E. Fawcett, R.N.R.)	
Unicity	225
(Skipper W. A. George, R.N.R.)	
Ut Prosim	457
(Skipper W. Reaich, R.N.R.)[3]	
Yorkshire Lass	469
(Ty. Lieut. E. H. G. Hope, R.N.V.R.)	
(S/Lt. M. A. A. Chodzko, R.N.V.R.)	
Young Mon	120
(Tempy.-Skipper A. W. Lockwood, R.N.R.)[3]	
Total	12,370

SPECIAL SERVICE VESSELS. Total of 3, of which 1 was lost.

Crested Eagle[1]	—
(Tempy. Lt. Cdr. B. R. Booth, R.N.R.)	
Golden Eagle	1,751
(Lt. Cdr. C.O.)	
(Lt. W. L. Lucas, R.N.R. (navigator))	
(Lt. J. C. Newman, M.B.E., R.N.V.R., in command)	
Royal Eagle	2,657
(Cdr. E. C. Cordeaux, M.B., M.R.C.S., L.R.C.P., R.N.) (sick)	
(Ty. Lr. Cdr. E. F. A. Farrow, R.N.R.)	
Total	4,408

M.A./S.B.'s ETC. Total 7.

*M.A/S.B.*5	—
(Lieut. E. M. Thorpe, R.N.)[3]	
*M.A/S.B.*6	26
(Lieut. W. G. Everitt, R.N.)	
*M.A/S.B.*7	38
(S/Lt. A. Ecclestone, R.N.)	
*M.A/S.B.*9	—
*M.A/S.B.*10	—
(Lieut. R. G. H. G. Eyre, R.N.)	

[1] Sunk.
[3] Name taken from *The Navy List for June* 1940.

TROOPS
TRANSPORTED

M.A./S.B.'s ETC. (*contd.*)

M.L.100 . . . . . .   — — —
  (Lieut. W. L. Stephens, R.N.V.R.)
D.C./M.B.   15
  (Lieut. E. F. Hamilton-Meikle, R.N.)

                           Total   79

M.T.B.'s. Total 6.

M.T.B.16 . . . .   — — —
  (Lieut. P. F. S. Gould, R.N.)
M.T.B.22 . . . .   — —
M.T.B.67 . . . .   — —
  (Lieut. C. C. Anderson, R.N.)
M.T.B.68 . . . .   — —
  (Lieut. R. K. L. Walker, R.N.V.R.)
M.T.B.102   20
  (Lieut. C. W. S. Dreyer, R.N.)
M.T.B.107 . . . . . .   — — —
  (Lieut. J. Cameron, R.N.V.R.)

                           Total   20

ARMED BOARDING VESSELS. Total 3, of which 1 was sunk.

King Orry[1]   1,131
  (Cdr. J. Elliott, R.D., R.N.R.)
Lormont   1,083
  (Lt. Cdr. W. S. Smithies, R.N.)
Mona's Isle   2,634
  (Cdr. J. C. K. Dowding, R.D., R.N.R.)

                           Total   4,848

SKOOTS (i.e. ex-DUTCH SCHUITS or coasters). Total 40, of
    which 4 were lost.
Where lying 22nd May (in brackets).

Abel Tasman (London)   220
  (Lt. Cdr. T. G. P. Crick, R.N.)   (wounded)
  (Lieut. C. E. S. B. St. G. Beal, R.N.) (from *Kaap Falga* 28/5/40)
Aegir (London)   835
  (Lieut. W. B. Whitworth, R.N.)
Alice[2] (Poole) . . . . .   —
  (Lieut. H. M. Slater, R.N.)
Amazone (Poole)   549
  (Lt. Cdr. L. H. Phillips, R.N.)
Antje (London)   450
  (Lt. M. Buist, R.N.)
Atlantic (Poole)   590
  (Lt. Cdr. L. E. Fordham, R.N.R.)
Bart (London) . . . . .   —
  (Lieut. E. G. Ball, R.N. (Retd.)
Bornrif (London)   146
  (Lieut. A. N. Blundell, R.N.R.)
Brandaris (London) . . .   330
  (Cdr. C. Euman, R.N. (Retd.))
Caribia (London)   701
  (Lt. M. G. Morais, R.N.R.)
  (Lt. G. H. Williams, R.N.R. (as from 29th May)
Delta (London)   503
  (Lt. Cdr. D. F. Lawrence, R.N. (retd.).
Deneb (London)   100
Despatch II (Poole) . . .   428
  (Lt. Cdr. F. E. Wilmot-Sitwell, R.N. (Retd.))

---

[1] Sunk.   [2] Lost.
[3] Name taken from *The Navy List for June* 1940.

TROOPS
TRANSPORTED

SKOOTS (contd.)

Doggersbank (London)	800
(Lieut. D. T. McBarnet, R.N.)	
Fredanja (Poole)	850
(Lt. Cdr. K. W. Stewart, R.N. (Retd.))	
Frisco (Poole)	1,002
Gorecht (London)	47
(S/Lt. D. M. Edwards, R.N.R.)	
Hebe II (Poole)	515
(Lt. Cdr. J. B. G. Temple, R.N.)	
Hilda (London)	835
(Lieut. A. Gray, R.N.)	
Hondsrug (London)	1,453
(Lieut. F. T. Renny, R.N.R.)	
Horst[1] (Poole)	1,150
(Lt. Cdr. G. E. Fardell, R.N.) (Lt. T. E. Sargent, R.N.R.)	
Jaba (Poole)	469
Jutland (London)	505
(Lieut. G. L. Barwell, R.N. (Retd.))	
(Relieved, 30 May, re-assumed command 31st May)	
(Lt. Cdr. W. R. T. Clements, R.N.R.) (30th-31st May)	
Kaap Falga (Poole)	5
(Lieut. C. E. S. B. St. G. Beal, R.N.)	
(Lieut. H. F. Wykeham-Martin, R.N., 28/5/40)	
Lena[1] (London)	996
(Lt. Cdr. R. P. C. Hawkins, R.N. (Retd.))	
Oranje (London)	605
(Lieut. H. T. Crispin, R.N.)	
Pacific (Poole)	945
(Lt. Cdr. C. J. Skrine, R.N.)	
Pascholl (Poole)	695
(Lieut. T. Johnston, R.N.)	
(Relieved and appointed i/c *Portsdown*)	
(Lieut. J. N. Wise, R.N.V.R.)	
(Cdr. C. E. Hammond, D.S.O., D.S.C., R.N.) (Retd.) (i/c Group)	
Patria (London)	1,400
(Lt. Cdr. N. L. J. Pisani, D.S.C., R.N. (Retd.))	
Reiger (London)	592
(Lieut. A. Tyson, R.N.)	
Rian (Poole)	257
(Lt. Cdr. J. I. Miller, D.S.O. R.N. (Reported)[2]	
Rika (London)	495
(Lt. Cdr. J. J. Youngs, R.N.R.)	
Ruja (Poole)	300
(Lt. H. R. Webber, R.N.)	
San Antonio (Poole)	484
(Lt. Cdr. G. V. Legassick, R.N.R.)	
Sursum-Corda[1] (Poole)	370
(Lieut. C. L. G. Philpotts, R.N.)	
Tilly (London)	602
(Lt. Cdr. W. R. T. Clements, R.N.R.)	
(Lt. Cdr. C. M. Ramus, R.N.R.)	
Tiny (Poole)	261
(Lt. Cdr. J. M. D. Hunter, R.N.) (Lt. Martin, R.N.)	
Twente (London)	1,139
(Lt. Cdr. H. G. Boys-Smith, R.N.R. to 30th May) (Lt. A. W. McMullen R.N.R.)	
Vrede (London)	473
(Lt. Cdr. R. T. Lampard, R.N.)	
Zeus (Poole)	601
(Lt. Cdr. C. B. Hoggan, R.D., R.N.R.)	
Total	22,698

[1] Lost.
[2] There was no officer of this name in the *Navy List*.

TROOPS
TRANSPORTED

YACHTS. Total 26, of which 3 were lost.

Ahola	5
(Lt. J. F. Alexander, R.N.V.R.)	
Alouette II	175
(S/Lt. R. E. Lee, R.N.V.R., Unit Officer)	
Amulree[1]	—
(S/Lt. G. P. Probert, R.N.V.R.)	
Ankh	—
(Lt. C. C. Bone, R.N.V.R., Senior Officer, Inner Patrol)	
Aronia	42
(Lieut. J. S. Roe, R.N.V.R.)	
Bounty	—
(Lt. C. A. Lundy, R.N.V.R.)	
Bystander	99
(S/Lt. H. J. B. Barge, R.N.V.R.)	
Caleta	35
(S/Lt. J. F. Dunning, R.N.V.R.)	
Caryanda	—
(Lt. D. A. L. Kings, R.N.V.R.)	
Chico	317
(S/Lt. J. Mason, R.N.V.R.)	
Christobel II	33
(Lieut. H. E. Wigfull, R.N.V.R.)	
Conidaw	80
(Skipper R. G. Snelgrove)	
Eilla II	—
(Lt. E. H. Batt, R.N.V.R.)	
Erica	—
Glagla	—
(S/Lt. J. A. Dow, R.N.V.R.)	
Grive[1]	1,484
(Capt. the Hon. L. J. O. Lambart, D.S.O., R.N. (Retd.)[3]	
Gulzar	814
(Ty. Lt. C. V. Brammall, R.N.R.)	
Lahloo	15
Laroc	147
(Capt. G. B. Butler, (Master/Owner)	
Llanthony	280
(S/Lt. R. W. Timbrell, R.N.)	
Noneta	—
(S/Lt. A. J. Potter-Irwin, R.N.V.R.)	
Pellag II[2]	—
(Lieut. F. W. R. Martino, R.N.V.R.)	
Sargasso	605
(Lt. C. C. L. Gaussen, R.N.V.R.)	
Seriola	—
(Lieut. D. A. Dawson, R.N.V.R.)	
Tarret	550
Thele	—
(Lt. H. M. Glassborow, R.N.V.R.)	
Total	**4,681**

PERSONNEL SHIPS. Total 45 (including 3 store ships and 2 motor vessels) of which 8 were sunk.

Archangel	—
Auto Carrier	712
(Capt. C. M. Masters, Master)	
Beal (M/V)	364
(J. W. Liley, Master)	

---

[1] Sunk. [2] Abandoned.

[3] Ty. Lieut. C. E. West, R.N.R. is shown in the *Navy List* as Captain of the *Grive*, but the operative command seems to have been with Capt. Lambart at the time of "Dynamo". Lieut. West was not on board when the ship was sunk, Capt. Lambart having persuaded him to land at Dover at 1300 on 1st June, to recuperate.

	TROOPS TRANSPORTED
PERSONNEL SHIPS (*contd.*)	
Ben-My-Chree	4,095
(Capt. G. Woods, Master)	
Biarritz	—
(Capt. W. H. Baker, Master)	
Bullfinch (M/V) .	600
Canterbury	4,416
(Capt. C. Hancock, Master)	
City of Christchurch .	—
(Capt. A. W. Wooster, O.B.E.)	
Clan Macalister[1] .	1
(Capt. R. W. Mackie, Master)	
Côte d'Argent[2] .	5,754
Dorrien Rose (store ship) .	1,494
(Capt. W. Thompson, Master)	
Fenella[1] . . .	—
(Capt. W. Gubbon, Master)	
Foam Queen .	98
(Capt. A. T. Mastin, Master)	
Hythe (coaster) .	749
(R. W. Morford, Master)	
Killarney . . .	900
(Capt. R. Hughes, Master)	
King George V .	4,300
(Capt. R. M. Maclean, Master)	
Lady of Mann .	4,262
(Capt. T. C. Woods, Master)	
Levenwood (store ship) .	60
(Capt. W. O. Young, Master)	
Lochgarry	1,001
(Capt. E. Mackinnon, Master)	
Lorina[1] . .	—
(Capt. A. Light, Master)	
Maid of Orleans .	5,461
(Capt. A. E. Larkins, Master) (Sick)	
(Capt. G. D. Walker, Master)	
Malines . . .	1,500
(Capt. G. Mallory, Master) (quitted Opn. Dynamo 2 June)	
Manxman .	2,394
(Capt. P. B. Cowley, Master) (disembarked 2 June)	
Mona's Queen[1] . . .	1,200
(Capt. R. Duggan, Master) (Capt. A. Holkham, Master)	
Nephrite (store ship) .	504
(Capt. C. G. West, O.B.E., Master)	
Newhaven[2] . .	1,841
(Lt. Cdr. L. H. Phillips, R.N.,) (———? Master)	
Ngaroma .	100
(Capt. J. W. Dickinson, Master)	
Normania[1]	—
(Capt. M. C. Whiting, Master)	
Portsdown .	618
(S/Lt. R. H. Church, R.N.R.)	
Prague .	3,039
(Capt. C. R. Baxter, Master)	
Princess Maud .	1,270
(Capt. H. Clark, Master)	
Queen of the Channel[1] .	—
(Capt. W. J. O'Dell, Master)	
Roebuck	500
(Capt. W. Y. Larbalestier, Master)	
Rouen[2] . .	2,886
Royal Daffodil .	7,552
(Capt. G. Johnson, Master)	

[1] Sunk.   [2] Former French mail packet.

TROOPS
TRANSPORTED

PERSONNEL SHIPS (*contd.*)

Royal Sovereign	6,772
(Capt. T. Aldis, Master)	
St. Helier	6,584
(Capt. R. R. Pitman, Master)	
St. Seiriol	672
(Capt. R. D. Dobb, Master)	
(Lieut. A. R. MacKewn, R.N.R.)	
Scotia[1]	3,000
(Capt H. W. Hughes, Master)	
Scottish Co-operator	525
(Capt. T. S. Robertson, Master)	
Sequacity (M/V)[1]	—
(Capt. J. Macdonald)	
Tynwald	8,953
(Capt. J. H. Whiteway, Master)	
(Capt. W. A. Qualtrough, Master) (relieved 2 June)	
Whippingham	2,700
(Lieut. E. Reed, R.N.R.)	
Whitstable	14
(Capt. W. Baxter, Master)	
Yewdale (tramp)	890
(Capt. E. Jones)	
Total	**87,810**

HOSPITAL CARRIERS. Total 8, of which 1 was sunk.

Dinard	374
(Mr. J. W. A. Jones, Master)	
Isle of Guernsey	836
(Capt. E. L. Hill, Master)	
Isle of Thanet	—
(Capt. A. J. Hammond, Master)	
Paris[1]	630
(Capt. E. A. Biles, Master)	
St. Andrew	130
(Capt. H. C. Bond, Master)	
St. David	149
(Capt. C. Joy, Master) (Sick)	
(Capt. B. H. Mendus, Master)	
St. Julien	287
(Capt. L. T. Richardson, Master)	
Worthing	600
(Capt. C. G. G. Munton, Master)	
Total	**3,006**

NAVAL M/Bs. Total 12, of which 6 were sunk.

Admiral Superintendent, Portsmouth's barge[1]	—
Dolphin's power boat	—
(S/Lt. E. J. Cornish-Bowden, R.N.)	
Excellent's (A/A) M/B[1]	. . .
(S/Lt. A. W. M. Matthew, R.N.)	
Excellent's 35 M/B[1]	. . .
(L/Sea. H. H. Dixon and a crew of four)	
40 ft. Ship's M/B	—
(Lt. E. F. Hamilton-Meikle, R.N.)	
Gallant's M/B[1]	—
Naval Steam Pinnace[1]	—
(S/Lt. T. E. Goodman, R.N.V.R.)	
Nelson's M/B	55
(Lieut. H. L. Holman, R.N.V.R.)	

[1] Sunk.

141

	TROOPS TRANSPORTED
NAVAL M/Bs (*contd.*)	
Nelson's Picket boat	16
(Actg. S/Lt. J. M. Campbell, R.N.)	
Vernon's Pinnace (V.4)	Not known
V.A. Dover's barge[1] . .	—
(Act. S/Lt. C. E. S. Beale, R.N.)	
Vernon I, M/B	25
(S/Lt. G. A. Gabbett-Mulhallen, R.N.)	
Total	96

BLOCKSHIPS.   Total 6, of which 2 were lost en route.

Edvard Nissen	
(Lt. E. J. King-Wood, R.N.R.)	
Gourko[2]	
(Cdr. A. V. Hemming, R.N.)	
Holland[2]	
(Lt. Cdr. E. C. Coats, R.N.)	
Moyle	
(Lt. Cdr. R. H. D. Lane, R.N.)	
Pacifico	
(Lt. Cdr. G. H. F. Owles, R.N.)	
Westcove	
(Lt. Cdr. A. M. McKillop, R.N.)	

TUGS.   Total 40[3] of which 3 were sunk.

C.9. (*West Acre*)	23
(J. Treleaven, Master)	
Cervia	30
(W. H. Simmons, Master)	
Challenge	
Contest	—
(H. J. Bates, Master)	
Crested Cock	—
(T. Hills, Master)	
Doria	90
(A. W. Mastin, Master)	
Dromedary	—
(S/Lt. T. Lawrie, R.N.V.R.)	
Duke	44
(B. P. Mansfield, Captain)	
Empire Henchman	—
(J. (?) E. Fishe, (?Fisher), Master)	
Fabia	—
(F. Smith, Master)	
Fairplay I	—
(S. Wright and G. Finch)	
Foremost 22	30
(C. Fieldgate, Master) (Sick)	
(F. M. Holden, Actg. Master)	
Foremost 87	100
(J. Fryer, Master)	
Fossa[1]	—
(S/Lt. M. H. B. Solomon, R.N.V.R.)	
Gondia	14
(C. Pratt, Master)	
Java	270
(W. Jones, Master)	
Kenia	—
(W. Hoiles, Master)	

[1] Sunk.   [2] Sunk en route.

[3] The following 6 tugs performed harbour duties only : *Betty, C. 11, Hibernia, Simla, Vesta* and *Watercock*.

	TROOPS TRANSPORTED
TUGS (*contd.*)	
Lady Brassey	—
(F. J. Hopgood, Master)	
Ocean Cock	—
(A. V. Mastin, Master)	
Persia	27
(H. Aldrich, Master)	
Prima	75
(J. B. Morran, Master)	
Prince	—
(J. Benson, Master)	
Princess	—
(J. Wallis, Master)	
Racia	423
(A. C. Addison, Master)	
St. Abbs[1]	—
(Lieut. T. E. Brooker, R.N., Retd.)	
St. Clears	70
(W. J. Penney, Master)	
St. Fagan[1]	—
(Lt. Cdr. G. H. Warren, M.B.E., R.N.)	
St. Olaves	200
(Skipper H. Forrester, R.N.R.)	
Sultan	193
Sun	175
(Cdr. E. K. Le Mesurier, M.V.O., R.N.)	
Sun III	148
(F. W. Russell, Master)	
Sun IV	236
(Mr. C. G. Alexander, Master)	
Sun V	—
(W. H. Mastin, Master)	
Sun VII	—
(G. Cawsey, Master)	
Sun VIII	120
(S. Smith, Master)	
Sun X	211
(W. A. Fothergill, Master)	
Sun XI	188
(J. R. Lukes, Master	
Sun XII	—
(A. V. Mee, Master)	
Sun XV	106
(J. J. Belton, Master)	
Tanga	367
(H. P. Gouge, Master)	
Vincia	24
(A. V. Hoiles, Master)	
Total	3,164

LANDING CRAFT
Total 13, of which 8 were lost

A.L.C. 3	20
A.L.C. 4[2]	—
A.L.C. 5	—
(Cdr. R. A. Cassidi, R.N. in command of 8 A.L.Cs. in *Clan Macalister*)	
A.L.C. 8[2]	10
A.L.C. 10	—
(S/Lt. E. R. Ponsonby, R.N.V.R.)	
A.L.C. 15[2]	—
(S/Lt. G. B. Eyre, R.N.V.R.)	

[1] Sunk.   [2] Lost

	TROOPS TRANSPORTED
LANDING CRAFT (contd.)	
A.L.C. 16[1]	25
(S/Lt. R. O. Wilcoxon, R.N.V.R.)	
A.L.C. 17	—
A.L.C. 18[1]	—
M.L.C. 12[1]	—
(P/O Brinton, Coxswain)	
M.L.C. 17[1]	—
(L/S A. Coleman, Coxswain)	
M.L.C. 21	63
(S/Lt. Towers, R.N. (?R.N.V.R.))	
M.L.C. 22[1]	—
C.P.O. H. Mitten)	
Total	**118**

WAR DEPARTMENT M/Ls. Total 8.

Grouse	35
(W. T. Mason, Mate i/c)	
Haig	60
(Lt. Cdr. N. L. J. Pisani, D.S.C., R.N., Retd.)	
(Cdr. H. R. Troup, R.N.)	
Kestrel	55
(Lt. Cdr. H. G. Boys-Smith, R.N.R.) (transferred to Dutch *M* 74 1st June)	
(A. E. Cains, Mate)	
Marlborough	146
(J. Matthews, Master (1st 3 trips))	
(S/Lt. R. W. D. Don, D.S.C., R.N.)	
Pigeon	60
(S/Lt. G. A. Gabbett-Mulhallen, R.N.)	
Swallow	68
(Lt. Col. R. L. Hutchins, M.C., Gren. Guards)	
(S/Lt. W. R. Williams, R.N.)	
Vulture	86
(L. C. Bell, Mate i/c)	
Wolfe	69
(E. L. Beard, Master)	
Total	**579**

R.A.F. SEAPLANE TENDERS. Total 6, of which 3 were lost.

S.T. 243[1]	None reported
(Cdr. J. C. Clouston, R.N., drowned)	
(Pilot Officer C. Collings, R.A.F.)	
S.T. 254[1]	None reported
S.T. 276	None reported
(S/Lt. R. Wake, R.N.)	
(Corpl. Flowers, R.A.F., Coxswain)	
S.T. 291	None reported
A.M.C. 3[1]	None reported
High Speed Launch 120	None reported

DOCKYARD LIGHTERS. Total 8, of which 2 were lost.

X. 95 (Chatham. N.S. Dept.)	—
X. 149[2] (Sheerness)	—
X. 209 (Royal Clarence Yard, Gosport, (Victg. Dept.))	
(S/Lt. W. R. Williams, R.N.)	
(Capt. R. G. Banks, Actg. Master)	67

---

[1] Lost.   [2] Reported sunk.

TROOPS
TRANSPORTED

DOCKYARD LIGHTERS (*contd.*)

X. 213[2] (Chatham)	——
X. 217 (Chatham. N.S. Dept.)	200
(S/Lt. R. A. W. Pool, R.N.)	
Y.C. 63	106
Y.C. 71. (Late *A.S. 28*) (Chatham N.S. Dept.) . . .	Not known
Y.C. 72 (Late *A.S. 29*) (Chatham N.S. Dept.) . . .	45
(Lieut. Mortimer, R.N.R.) (P/O G. Senior, Coxswain)	
Total	418

STEAM HOPPER BARGES.   Total 7[3]

Foremost 101	70
(W. E. Llewellyn, Master)	
Foremost 102	206
(Actg. S/Lt. H. Martin, R.N.) (W. C. Attwaters, Master)	
Gallion's Reach	123
(S/Lt. F. N. F. Johnstone, R.N.) (J. F. Mason, Master)	
Lady Southborough	350
(Capt. A. M. Poole, Master)	
Queen's Channel[3]	141
(J. L. Bunt, Master)	
W. 24	980
(Capt. H. F. Boyce, Master)	
W. 26	296
(Capt. W. J. Allen, Master)	
Total	2,166

AUXILIARY BARGES   Total 8, of which 1 was lost.

Cabby	——
Lady Rosebery[1]	——
(W. F. Ellis, Master)	
Lady Sheila[4]	300
(G. H. E. Brooks, Master)	
Pudge	——
(Mr. W. Watson, Master)	
Seine	793
(Mr. C. V. Cogger, Master)	
Sherfield[6]	74
(S/Lt. J. D. F. Kealey, R.N.)	
Thyra	19
Mr. E. W. Filley, Master)	
Viking	70
(S/Lt. T. R. Rumbold, R.N.V.R.) (D. Gregory, Master)	
Total	1,256

SAILING BARGES.   Total 25, of which 9 were lost.

Ada Mary	——
Aidie[1]	——
(H. Potter, Master)	
Barbara Jean[1]	——
(C. Webb, Master)	
Beatrice Maud	260
(L. Horlock, Master)	
Burton	——

[1] Lost.   [2] Reported Sunk.
[3] Two others, the *James 67* and the *W.95* stood by at Ramsgate.
[3] Erroneously referred to in official reports as the " *Queensland*".
[4] A motor coaster.

	TROOPS TRANSPORTED
SAILING BARGES (*contd.*)	
Claud (water boat)[1]	—
Doris[1]	—
(F. Finbow, Master)	
Duchess[1]	—
(H. J. Wildish, Master)	
Ena	100
(A. G. Page, Master)	
Ethel Everard[1]	—
(T. Willis, Master)	
F.W. 23 (dumb)	13
Glenway	213
(W. H. Easter, Master)	
H.A.C.	100
(R. H. Scott, Master)	
Haste Away	—
Lark[1]	—
(R. H. Scott, Master)	
Monarch	—
Queen	—
Queen Alexandria	—
Royalty[1]	—
(H. Miller, Master)	
Sark (dumb)	—
Shannon	—
Shetland (dumb)	—
Spurgeon	—
(— Haisman, Master)	
Tollesbury	200
(R. Webb, Master)	
Warrior[1]	—
Total	886

LIFE BOATS

Total 19, R.N.L.I. life boats[2], of which 1 was lost.	
Abdy Beauclerk	—
Cecil & Lilian Philpott	51
(A/B W. J. Morris, Coxn.	
Charles Cooper Henderson	—
Charles Dibdin	—
Cyril & Lilian Bishop	—
(Actg. P.O. W. H. Adkin)	
Edward Z, Dresden	50
(Lt. Cdr. R. W. Faulkner, R.N.R. (?Retd.))	
E.M.E.D.	39
(Lieut. R. H. Mead, R.N.V.R., died)	
(P.O. Tel. W. H. Cooley)	
Greater London	48
(S/Lt. W. D. F. Claydon, R.N.R.)	
Guide of Dunkirk[3]	—
(S/Lt. R. H. C. Amos, R.N.V.R.)	
(S/Lt. R. H. Wallace, R.N.V.R.)	
Jane Holland	
(Sto. J. Strangeways) (Sto. A. H. Shaw)	
(S/Lt. E. R. Ponsonby, R.N.V.R.)	
Lord Southborough	17
(E. Parker, Coxswain)	

[1] Lost.

[2] The reserve life boat *Agnes Cross* carried out duties at Dover. She did not go to Dunkirk.

[3] At the same time of Dunkirk evacuation, this boat had just been built and had not yet been named.

TROOPS
TRANSPORTED

LIFE BOATS (contd.)

Louise Stephens	**49**
Lucy Lavers .	—
(S/Lt. T. W. Betts, R.N.V.R.)	
Mary Scott	—
Michael Stephens	**52**
(S/Lt M. J. R. Yeatman, R.N.V.R.)	
Prudential	**17**
(H. P. C. Knight, Coxswain)	
Rosa Wood & Phyllis Lunn	—
The Viscountess Wakefield [1]	—
Thomas Kirk Wright	—
(L/Sea. H. Huntington)	

                                       Total   **323**

MOTOR BOATS, LAUNCHES AND VESSELS.

Total 202, of which **78** were lost.

Advance	—
(C. P. Dick, Owner, Skipper)	
Adventuress	**85**
Albatross [1]	—
Aljanov [1]	—
Aloha-Oe [1]	—
Ambleve [1] [2]	—
(S/Lt. R. E. Blows, R.N.V.R.)	
Andora	**23**
(L/Sea. H. Cook, Coxswain) (S/Lt. E. T. Garside, R.N.V.R.)	
Angler II	Not known
Anne	—
Aura [1]	—
(S/Lt. M. A. Chodzko, R.N.V.R.)	
Balquhain	**54**
(S/Lt. B. D. O. MacIntyre, R.N.)	
Bat	**116**
(J. T. Butchers, Capt.)	
Bee	**15**
(W. C. Trowbridge, Capt.)	
Belfast	**61**
Black Arrow [1]	—
Blackpool	**250**
Bluebird	—
(S/Lt. G. B. Eyre, R.N.V.R.)	
Bobeli [1]	—
(S/Lt. W. G. H. Bonham, R.N.)	
Bonnibell [1]	—
(Sto. 1st Cl. G. H. Rose)	
Bonny Heather	**420**
(Lieut. C. W. Read, D.S.C., R.N.R.)	
Britannia	—
(S/Lt. S. D. Ward, R.N.V.R.)	
Brittanic	**65**
Bullpup [1]	not known
Cairngorm	not known
Canvey Queen [1]	—
Chamois	—
(A. E. Brown, Capt.) (L. Church, Engr.)	
Chantecler	**30**
(S/Lt. T. K. Edge-Partington, R.N.)	
Commodore [1]	—
(S/Lt. Thompson, R.N.R.)	

[1] Lost.
[2] Ex-Belgian canal boat.

TROOPS
TRANSPORTED

MOTOR BOATS, LAUNCHES AND VESSELS (*contd.*)

Constant Nymph . . .	—
(Dr. B. A. Smith, Owner/Skipper)	
Cordelia . . .	—
(S/Lt. C. A. Thompson, R.N.V.R.)	
Court Belle II[1] . . .	—
Cyb[1] . . .	—
Dab II . . .	—
(Lieut. R. W. Thomson, R.N.V.R.)	
Defender . . .	60
(Skpr. E. A. Turnnidge)	
Diana Mary . . .	28
Dreadnought II[1] . . .	—
Dreadnought III[1] . . .	—
Eastbourne Belle . . .	—
Elizabeth Green . . .	10
(S/Lt. E. T. Garside, R.N.V.R.)	
Eastbourne Queen[1] . . .	—
Empress[1] . . .	—
(S/Lt. T. W. Betts, R.N.V.R.)	
Enchantress[1] . . .	—
Encore . . .	44
(Lt. Cdr. Wilson,)	
Endeavour . . .	—
(Skpr. F. C. Halls)	
Enterprise[1] . . .	—
Escaut[1] [2] . . .	—
Eskburn . . .	27
Eve[1] . . .	—
(L/Sea. N. Furse, R.N.R.)	
Ferry Nymph . . .	44
Fervent . . .	—
(Lt. Cdr. W. R. T. Clements, R.N.R.)	
Fishbourne (I.O.W. Ferry)	
Forty Two . . .	—
(Lieut. R. Nimmo, R.N.R.)	
Frightened Lady[1] . . .	—
(S/Lt. S. C. Allen, R.N.V.R.)	
Gavine[3] . . .	—
Gay Crusader . . .	—
(S/Lt. T. H. Rodgers, R.N.V.R.)	
Gipsy King . . .	—
(A. Betts) (H. Brown) (F. Hook, Deal boatman)	
Glitter II . . .	—
(Actg. S/Lt. J. W. S. Culham, R.N.)	
Golden Lily . . .	
Golden Spray II[1] . . .	—
(J. O'Neill and N. Cohen, Deal boatmen)	
(A. C. Crowthall, a Lloyd's official)	
Gondolier King . . .	—
Gondolier Queen . . .	—
Good Hope[1] . . .	—
Grace Darling IV[1] . . .	—
Gwen Eagle[1] . . .	—
Halfway . . .	140
Handy Billy[1] . . .	—
(S/Lt. M. Phipps, R.N.)	
Hanora[1] . . .	—
(S/Lt. C. Minchin, R.N.)	
Hound . . .	98
(H. W. Knight, Capt.)	

---

[1] Lost.

[2] Ex-Belgian canal boat.

[3] Recorded as sunk in Home Waters apparently subsequent to Operation " Dynamo."

TROOPS
TRANSPORTED

MOTOR BOATS, LAUNCHES AND VESSELS (contd.)

Idaho	—
Iolanthe	35
Iote[1]	—
(S/Lt. R. H. C. Amos, R.N.V.R.)	
Island Queen[3]	—
Johanna	10
(S/Lt. A. Carew-Hunt, R.N.)	
Jong	—
(S/Lt. I. F. S. Smith, R.N.V.R.)	
Josephine I[1]	—
Kayell	70
(J. H. Crook, Skipper)	
Kestrel	50
(W. W. Cribbens, Skipper)	
Kingsgate	910
Kit Cat	—
(S/Lt. D. C. Williams, R.N.V.R.)	
Lady Cable	40
(Lieut. B. S. Fidler, R.N.V.R.)	
(Actg. S/Lt. G. A. Cadell, R.N. (Retd.))	
Lady Haig	—
Lansdowne[1]	—
(S/Lt. E. A. E. Cornish, R.N.V.R.)	
Letitia (Bawley boat)	—
(A. J. Dench, Skipper)	
Letitia[1] (M/B)	—
(S/Lt. B. D. O. MacIntyre, R.N.)	
Little Ann[1]	—
(Mr. A. D. Divine)	
Luisiana	20
Madame Sans Gene[1]	—
(S/Lt. K. Adderley, R.N.V.R.)	
Madame Pompadour	—
(Lt. Cdr. Faulkner, R.N.V.R. (Retd.))	
(Mr. Morley Lawson, Engr.)	
Maid of Honour[1]	—
Ma Joie[1]	—
(G. Harvey, Skpr.)	
Maldon Annie IV[1]	—
(S/Lt. T. Lawrie, R.N.V.R.)	
Margherita[1]	—
Marsayru	19
(Mr. G. D. Olivier, Skipper, 31st May)	
(S/Lt. T. E. Godman, R.N.V.R., 1st-2nd June)	
Mary Rose[1]	—
(S/Lt. H. McClelland, R.N.V.R.)	
Mary Spearing[1]	—
(S/Lt. W. G. M. Christian, R.N.V.R.)	
Mary Spearing II	15
(S/Lt. W. G. M. Spearing, R.N.V.R.)	
Massey Shaw (fire float)	106
(Sub. Officer A. J. May)	
Matilda	Not known
Mayspear	15
Meander	—
(Skipper G. W. Halliday, R.N.R.)	
Mermaiden	25
(Actg. S/Lt. C. E. S. Beale, R.N.)	
(P/O F. J. Norton, R.F.R.)	
Meuse[2]	50

[1] Lost.
[3] Sunk off **Folkestone** on 14th July, by aircraft.
[2] Ex-Belgian Canal boat.

TROOPS
TRANSPORTED

MOTOR BOATS, LAUNCHES AND VESSELS (contd.)

M.F.H.	87
(W. H. Smith, Capt.)	
Minikoi[1]	—
(S/Lt. R. E. Blows, R.N.V.R.)	
Minoru II[1]	—
Minotaur	—
(T. Towndrow, Skipper)	
Minwood	51
Mivasol[1]	—
Moss Rose[1]	—
Murious	—
Naiad Errant	8
(A. B. S. Palmer, i/c)	
Nanette II	30
Nayland	83
Nemo IV[1]	—
New Britannic	83
(W. Matthews, Cox.)	
New Prince of Wales[1]	—
(S/Lt. P. H. E. Bennett, R.N.)	
New White Heather[1]	—
Offemia	50
Patricia (T.H.V.)	—
Pauleter	400
(Sto. D. T. Banks)	
Peggy IV[1]	—
(S. H. Hughes, Skipper)	
Pioneer[1]	—
Princess Freda	—
(S/Lt. E. S. Forman, R.N.V.R.)	
Princess Lily	—
(Prob. Ty. S/Lt. K. E. A. Bayley, R.N.V.R.)	
Princess Maud	—
Provider	Not known
(F. Hannaford, Skipper)	
Queen Boadicea II	
(Lieut. J. S. Seal, R.N.R.) (Capt. J. Whittaker)	
Queen of England[1]	—
Quest	—
Quicksilver	20
(S/Lt. D. L. Satterford. R.N.) (L/Sea. T. Phillips)	18
Quisisana	28
(S/Lt. A. J. Weaver, R.N.V.R.)	
Rapid I	
(S/Lt. J. C. Clarke, R.N.V.R.)	
Reda	44
(S/Lt. P. Snow, R.N.) (P.O. R. W. Rawlings, Motorman)	
Reliance	80
(Skpr. A. Legget)	
Renown[1]	—
(Skpr. W. H. Noakes)	
Resolute	40
(Skpr. H. D. Osborne)	
Roberta[1]	—
Rocinante[1]	—
Rosabelle[1]	—
Rose Marie	Not known
St. Patrick[1]	—
Sambre[2]	Not known
Santosy[1]	—
(Actg. S/Lt. J. M. Chappell, R.N.)	
Saviour	22

[1] Lost.
[2] Ex-Belgian canal boat.

	TROOPS TRANSPORTED
MOTOR BOATS, LAUNCHES AND VESSELS (*contd.*)	
Sea Falcon[1]	—
(L/Sea. A. Westbrook)	
Sceneshifter[1]	—
Sea Foam	—
Seamew[1]	—
Sea Roamer	2
(Lieut. J. Bald, R.N.V.R.)	
Seasalter	70
(L. W. Salmon, Skipper)	
Semois[1] [2]	—
Shamrock[1]	—
(A. Barrell, Owner, Skipper)	
Silicia	314
Silver Foam	—
Silver Moon	—
(Actg. S/Lt. B. D. O. MacIntyre, R.N.)	
Silver Queen[1]	100
(S/Lt. ?)	
(A.B. P. T. Sullivan, C/JX 147897)	
Silvery Breeze	—
Singapore	5
(S/Lt. J. W. Pratt, R.N.V.R.)	
Singapore II	—
(S/Lt. F. E. Greenfell, R.N.V.R.)	
Skylark I	—
(S/Lt. E. C. B. Mares, R.N.V.R.)	
(S/Lt. H. McClelland, R.N.V.R.)	
Skylark II	—
Skylark III[1]	—
Skylark III	—
(Sto. G. Bramhall)	
Skylark LL. III[1]	—
Skylark III(S.M.281.II)[1]	—
Skylark 6	—
(Cadet Rating, G. R. Prince)	
Skylark (Southend)	50
(P.O. R. A. Smith, R.F.R. and crew of 5)	
Skylark	—
(S/Lt. M. J. R. Yeatman, R.N.V.R.)	
Small Viking	62
Southend Britannia	—
(Lieut. G. L. Norton, R.N.V.R.)	
Southern Queen	—
(S/Lt. B. G. P. de Mattos, R.N.V.R.)	
Southern Queen (P.L.17)[1]	—
Spinaway	—
Stonehaven[1]	—
Summer Maid (P.E. 42)	—
Sundowner	122
(Cdr. G. H. Lightoller, D.S.C., R.N.R., (Retd.) owner-Skipper)	
Sunshine[1]	—
Surrey	—
Tenias	100
Thark	—
(S/Lt. A. Carew-Hunt, R.N.)	
Thetis[1]	—
(T. Towndrow, Scoutmaster, Mortlake Sea Scouts)	
Thorneycroft M/B	Not known
Thyforsa	66
Tigris I	—
(H. Hastings, Owner, Skipper)	
Triton[1]	—
(Lieut. R. H. Irving, R.N.R.)	

[1] Lost.

[2] Ex-Belgian canal boat.

TROOPS
TRANSPORTED

MOTOR BOATS, LAUNCHES AND VESSELS (contd.)

Two Rivers[1]	—
(P/O G. B. Thomas, R.N.R., Coxswain)	
Vanguard	20
(A. Grimwade, Skipper)	
Vanitee[1]	—
Venture[1]	—
Vera	30
Viewfinder[1]	—
(S/Lt. F. N. Dann, R.N.V.R.)	
Walker I	29
(A. Cadman, Cox)	
Walker II	76
(P. King, Cox)	
Wave Queen[3]	—
Westerley[1]	—
White Bear	—
(Comd. Gnr. E. Deacon, R.N.)	
White Heather	—
(Lt. Seal ?)	
White Wing	6
(S/Lt. A. S. Mullins, R.N.R.)	
Willie & Alice	—
Windsong	—
(T. H. Falkingham, Skipper) (A. Barden (Engine man))	
Wings of the Morning	—
(R. E. Button, Skipper) (S/Lt. T. Lawrie, R.N.V.R.)	
Yser[1] [2]	Not known
(S/Lt. R. W. D. Don, D.S.C., R.N.) (P/O W. H. Atkin)	
Total	5,031

LIFE BOATS.   Total 56, of which 39 were lost.

OWNER	LIFE BOAT	NUMBER LOST
Blue Star Line . . .	Four	4
B.I.S.N. Co. Ltd. . .	Ten	10
Butchers . . .	Two (M.L/B)	—
Can. Pac. S.S. Co. .	*Beaverdale*	—
Englis & Mills .. .	Four (ex-*Dunbar Castle*) . .	4
Englis & Mills . .	One (ex-*Lolworth*) . .	1
Englis & Mills . .	One (*Parales*) . . .	1
—	Two (ex-*Flandres*) . .	2
Houlder Bros. & Co. .	Four (ex-*Upway Grange*) .	1
Orient Line . .	*Orient IV* (M.L/B) . .	—
P. and O. S.N. Co. .	" G "	—
P. and O. S.N. Co. .	Fifteen	10
Ropner Shipping Co. .	One (ex-*Hawnby*) . .	1
	Four (ex-*Roslin Castle*) . .	2
Royal Mail Line . .	Five	3

WHERRIES, PUNTS AND BOATS.   Total 16, all of which were lost.

Annee (wherry)	*Edina* (wherry)
Carama (punt)	*Lark* (punt)
Clara Belle (wherry)	*Medora* (wherry)
Dinky (10 ft. boat)	*Miranda* No. 58 (boat)
Doris (wherry)	*Sarah & Emily* (boat)
Dumpling (boat)	*Viking III* (dinghy)

---

[1] Lost.

[2] Ex-Belgian canal boat.

[3] Returned to England in sinking condition.

Part II. List of French Ships

	TROOPS TRANSPORTED
TORPEDO BOATS AND DESTROYERS.	
Total 14, of which 3 were sunk.	
Bouclier	1,725
(Capt. de frégate de la Fournière, Commanding 14th Div. Torpedo boats)	
Bourrasque[1]	——
(Capt. de frégate R. Fouque, Commanding 4th Div. Torpedo boats)	
Branlebas	1,120
(Capt. de corvette de Cacqueray)	
Cyclone[2]	460
, (Capt. de vaisseau U. de Portzampare, Capt. (D) 2nd Flotilla)	
Epervier (light cruiser)	——
Foudroyant[1] [2]	1,250
(Capt. de corvette Fontaine)	
La Flore	761
(Capt. de corvette Roussel de Courcy)	
Léopard[2]	19
(Capt. de frégate C. Loisel)	
L'Incomprise	——
(Capt. de corvette Gras)	
Mistral[2]	4
(Capt. de corvette Lavene) (Lieut. de vaisseau Guillanton)	
Siroco[1] [2]	509
(Capt. de corvette de Toulouse-Lautrec-Montfa)	
T.112[3]	117
T.113[3]	275
T.143[3]	406
	Total 6,646
DESPATCH VESSELS (*Avisos*). Total 5.	
Amiens	——
(Capt. de corvette Monick)	
Amiral Mouchez	——
Arras	600
Belfort (aircraft tender)	400
(Capt. de corvette L. Viel)	
Savorgnan de Brazza (A/A ship)	——
	Total 1,000
MINESWEEPERS (*Avisos-draguers*). Total 2.	
Commandant Delage	807
(Capt. de corvette Froget)	
L'Impétueuse	1,231
(Capt. de corvette Bachy)	
	Total 2,038
SUBMARINE CHASERS (*chasseurs*). Total 5.	
Chasseur 5	20
(Lieut. de vaisseau Detroyat)	
Chasseur 6	50
(Enseigne de vaisseau Desmoutis)	
Chasseur 7	39
Chasseur 11	88
(Enseigne de vaisseau Montillier)	
Chasseur 42	6
(Premier Maître Timonier Y. Jule)	
	Total 203

[1] Sunk.

[2] Destroyer.

[3] Probably the pendant ; the name of the ship is not known.

TROOPS
TRANSPORTED

M.T.Bs. (*Vedettes torpilleurs*).   Total 2.

V.T.B. 25	—
V.T.B. 26	Not known

MINESWEEPING TRAWLERS.   Total 13 of which 5 were sunk.

Angèle Marie	199
Bernadette	
(Maître Principal de Manoeuvre P. Stohlberger.)	
Chasse-Marée	947
(Lieut. de vaisseau Y. Drogou)	
Denis Papin[1] (A.D. 48)	405
(Lieut. de vaisseau J. F. Raquez, S.O. 2nd Section)	
Joseph Marie[1]	—
(A. Le Calvez, Maître de Manoeuvre)	
La Majo[1]	—
Louise Marie	57
Moussaillon[1]	309
Président Briand (L.R. 33146)	283
(Lieut. de vaisseau(?) Le Talaer)	
Ste. Bernadette de Lourdes	79
Ste. Denise (D. 618)	108
(Pilote P. Raoult, Commanding the 102nd Section)	
Ste. Elizabeth (A.D. 385)[2]	60
(Enseigne de vaisseau Vergonzanc, S.O. 156th Section)	
Vénus[1] (A.D. 76)	218
(Enseigne de vaisseau de R. Rosec.)	

Total 2,665

PATROL VESSELS (*patrouilleurs*).   Total 7.

André Louis	549
(Lieut. de vaisseau Aubert)	
Cerons (escort vessel)	—
Diligente	346
La Nantaise	15
(Lieut. de vaisseau Jaume)	
Lucien Gougy	282
(Lieut. de vaisseau Foignet)	
Reine Des Flots	1,312
(Enseigne de vaisseau Le Bitoux)	
Sauternes (escort vessel)	—

Total 2,504

CARGO SHIPS[3].   Total 12, of which 2 were sunk.

Cap d'Antifer	291
Cap Tafalneh	—
Cérès	—
Douaisien[1]	—
Emma	29
Fronsac	500
François Tixier	—
Ingénieur Cachin	601
Margaux	369
Monique Schiaffino	—
Normanville	500
St. Camille[1]	—

Total 2,290

[1] Sunk.

[2] Reg. No. C.1478.

[3] The French mail packets *Côte d'Argent*, *Côte d'Azure*, *Newhaven* and *Rouen* were transferred to the orders of V.A. Dover, and were employed side by side with British personnel vessels.   With the exception of the *Côte d'Azure* which was sunk before the commencement of Op. Dynamo, they are shown in the list of *British* ships.

	TROOPS TRANSPORTED
TRAWLERS AND M.F.Vs. Total 59 of which at least 3 were sunk.	
(Reg. No., if any, in brackets)	
Alfred Paul	50
André Marcel	50
Angelus de la Mer	17
(B. 1339)	
Antoinette Michel	93
(C. 1376)	
Ave Maria Gratia Plena	**111**
(C. 1298)	
Barbe Auguste	65
(D. 812)	
Blei Mor	[2]
(L. 3126)	
Caporal Peugeot	105
(Maître Josselin)	
Ciel de France	108
(C. 5598)	
Credo	53
(DG. 924)	
Du Guesclin	18
(DG. 910)	
Duperre	307
Edmond René	210
Emile Deschamps[1]	—
Etoile Polaire	[2]
(L. 4125)	
Gabrielle Georges	[2]
(Not known)	
Gaston Rivier	100
(Officier des equipages H. Wallyn)	
Henriette	[2]
Jean Bart	208
(Doublecourt, Skipper)	
Jean Ribault	100
(Premier-Maître Dupiénois)	
Jeanne Antoine	[2]
(Not known)	
Jésus Flagelle	98
(B. 1853)	
Jeune France	186
(Di. 1213)	
Jolie Mascotte	[2]
(C. 1347)	
Joseph Marcel	150
La Colombe	111
(C. 1322)	
La Mouette	53
(C. 1441)	
Lauritz	[2]
(DG. 574)	
Les Trois Cousins	48
(DG. 350)	
Lutteur (tug)	308
Marcel Paul	[2]
(C. 5530)	
Margaux	[2]
(D. 692)	
Maria Elena	120
(Enseigne de vaisseau Fatout)	
Marie	100
(Enseigne de vaisseau J. Aguttes, Patron Leprêtre)	

---

[1] Sunk.

TRAWLERS AND M.F.Vs. (contd.)	TROOPS TRANSPORTED
Mimi Pierrot (L. 3968)	(²)
Monique Camille .	302
Nôtre Dame de la Salette (B. 1832)	48
Nôtre Dame des Miracles (Di. 1194)	50
Noune (DG. 694)	66
Patrie .	659
Pierre[1] (Patron P. Elran)	—
Pierre et Marie . (Enseigne de vaisseau Royer in charge of the convoy)	393
Reine Amélie (DG. 668)	48
Rose Effeuillée (C. 2716)	65
Saint Cyr (L. 4183)	(²)
Saint François de Salles (B. 1738)	31
Saint Michel (B. 1388)	(²)
Saint Pierre IV (C. 1418) (Enseigne de vaisseau E. Le Coniat)	(²)
Saint Saulve (B. 1581)	45
Saint Sophie (DG. 715)	66
Ste. Germaine (B. 1790)	34
Ste. Isabelle . (Patron Boudard)	—
Ste. Marie Protégez Nous (B. 1510)	30
Ste. Thérèse de L'Enfant Jésus (DG. 230)	(²)
Soizic . (L. 4107)	16
Stella Maris .	1
Surcouf (DG. 921)	17
Thérèse Louis (B. 1741)	174
Yvonne et Moabe[1] . (Not known)	(²)

Total recorded 4,814

Part III. List of Belgian Ships.

TRAWLERS, *unless otherwise stated.* Total 45 ships. Four of them were sunk.	
A.5 (Patrol boat) . (Lieut. J. D'Hauwer, Belgian Navy)	229
Abel Dewulf (N. 58) .	17
Alex Rachel (H. 23) .	25
Aline-Bertha-Antoinette (Z. 26) .	93

[1] Sunk.

	TROOPS TRANSPORTED
TRAWLERS (*contd.*)	
André Lucienne (N. 53)	18
Anna (N. 38)	97
Anna Léopold (H. 76)	289
Anna-Marguerite (Z. 2)	(²)
Buffalo Bill (Z. 4)	(²)
Constant Léopold (Z. 35)	43
Cor Jésu (O. 227)	191
(Capt. J. Delbal, Master)	
De Ruyter (Z. 25)	84
Elona-Constance (Z. 6)	(²)
Frieda (H. 13)	150
Gaby (O. 87)	(²)
Georges Edouard (O. 86)	401
(Capt. M. Coppin, Master) (Master of the Belgian S.S *.Julia*)	
Gerard-Léon (H. 64)	(²)
Getuigt vor Christus (N. 59)[1]	—
Gilda (H. 77)	120
Gods Genade (H. 75)	100
Goliath (tug)	183
Graaf van Vlaanderen (O. 92)	(²)
Guido Gazelle (O. 225)	145
(Capt. R. Lusyne, Master)	
Gustaaf (Z. 31)	(²)
Henri (Z. 40)	33
Indépendence (O. 308)	(²)
Irma (Z. 71)	54
Irma-Germaine (Z. 3)	(²)
John (O. 210)	(²)
Jonge Jan (O. 200)	215
(M. Nys, Master)	
Louise-Irène (H. 80)	(²)
Lydie Suzanne (Z. 50)	416
(G. F. Ragaert, Master)	
Madeleine Kamiel (H. 81)	90
Maréchal Foch (O. 274)[1]	—
(Capt. P. Lusyne, Master)	
Navis-Maria (H. 51)	44
O.L.V. van Vlaanderen (N. 49)[1]	—
Onder Ons (O. 318)	139
Pharailde (H. 42)	
Prins Boudewijn (O. 153)	138
(Kolb-Bernard, Second-Maître de Manoeuvre, Commanding Convoy No. 7)	
Raphael-Raymonde (H. 43)	(²)
Rockall (O. 323)	150
Sunny Isle (H. 5)[1]	—
Victor-Erna (H. 63)	(²)
Yvonne (Z. 41)	(²)
Zwaluw (Z. 11)	(²)
Total	3,464

Part IV. List of Polish Ships.

Blyskawica (destroyer)	—

[1] Sunk.
[2] Not known.

Part V. List of Dutch Ships.

Demok I (yacht)   214
M.74 (motor boat) . . . .   —
   (Lt. Cdr. H. G. Boys-Smith, R.N.R. from *Kestrel* 1st June)
   (L/Sea. R. W. Legg, Coxswain)

Part VI. List of Norwegian Ships.

S.S. *Hird*   3,500
   (Capt. A. M. Fredhjem)

APPENDIX B

NAMED SHIPS AND VESSELS LOST AND DAMAGED DURING OPERATION " DYNAMO "

(Dates in brackets)

Note : Large numbers of unnamed boats were also lost and damaged.

Part I. Ships and vessels lost

BY AIR ATTACK

DESTROYERS
Basilisk (1/6)
Grenade (29/5)
Havant (1/6)
Keith (1/6)

GUNBOAT
Mosquito (1/6)

A.B./V.
King Orry (30/5)

MINESWEEPERS
Brighton Queen (1/6)
Devonia (31/5)
Gracie Fields (30/5)
Skipjack (1/6)
Waverley (29/5)

TRAWLERS
Calvi (29/5)
Nautilus (29/5)
Polly Johnson (29/5)

DRIFTERS
Boy Roy (27/5)
Paxton (27/5)

PERSONNEL VESSELS
Clan Macalister (29/5)
Crested Eagle (sp. S/V) (29/5)
Fenella (29/5)
Lorina (29/5)
Normania (29/5)
Queen of the Channel (28/5)
Scotia (1/6)

HOSPITAL CARRIER
Paris (3/6)

SEAPLANE TENDER
S.T. 243 (2/6)

MOTOR LIGHTERS
X.149 (31/5)
X.213 (31/5)

LANDING CRAFT
A.L.C. 16 (29/5)

TUGS
St. Abbs (1/6)
St. Fagan (1/6)

BARGES
Lady Rosebery (1/6)
Doris (1/6)

SMALL CRAFT
Commodore (31/5)
Mirasol (1)
Southern Queen (P.L.17) (1)

BY TORPEDOES (E-BOATS)

DESTROYERS
Grafton (29/5)
Wakeful (29/5)

TRAWLERS
Argyllshire (1/6)
Stella Dorado (1/6)

¹ Date not known.

BY MINES

TRAWLERS
Blackburn Rovers (2/6)
St. Achilleus (1/6)
Thuringia (28/5)
Westella (2/6)

PERSONNEL VESSEL
Mona's Queen (29/5)

YACHT
Grive (1/6)

SMALL CRAFT
Renown (1/6)

BLOCKSHIP
Gourko (4/6)

BY GUNFIRE (SHORE)

DRIFTER
Lord Cavan (1/6)

SKOOT
Horst (31/5)

PERSONNEL VESSEL
Sequacity (27/5)

SMALL CRAFT
Gallant's Motor Boat (2/6)
New Prince of Wales (31/5)

BY COLLISION OR OTHER MISADVENTURE

MINESWEEPER
Brighton Belle (28/5)

TRAWLERS
Comfort (29/5)
Thomas Bartlett
    (28/5) ([1])

DRIFTERS
Eileen Emma (1/6)
Fair Breeze (1/6)
Gervais Rentoul (1/6)
Girl Pamela
    (night 28/29 May)

SKOOTS
Alice (28/5)
Lena (4/6)
Sursum-Corda (31/5)

YACHT
Amulree (1/6)
Pellag II (1/6)

EXN. SERV. V.
Ocean Reward (28/5)

BLOCKSHIP
Holland (3/6)

TUG
Fossa (2/6)

SEAPLANE TENDERS
S.T.243 (31/5)
S.T. 254 (31/5)
A.M.C. 3 (31/5)

SMALL CRAFT

Albatross[2]
Aljanor[2]
Aloa-Oe[2]
Ambleve (30/5)
Aura (2/6)[3]
Black Arrow (29/30 May)
Bobeli (2/6)
Bonnibell (2/6)
Bullpup[4]
Canvey Queen (30/5)
Court Belle[2]
Cyb[2]
Dreadnought II[2]
Frightened Lady[3] [4]
Golden Spray II (31/5)
Good Hope[2]
Grace Darling IV[2]
Gwen Eagle[2]
Handy Billy[2]

Hanora[3] [4]
Iote (1/6)
Island Queen[2]
Josephine I[2]
Lansdowne (1/6)[3]
Letitia (M/B) (4/6)
Little Ann[2]
Madame Sans Gêne (4/6)
Maid of Honour[3]
Ma Foie (30/5)
Maldon Annie IV (31/5)
Margherita[3]
Mary Rose (31/5)
Mary Spearing[4]
Minikoi (29/5)
Minoru II[2]
Pioneer[2]
Queen of England (29/5)
Roberta[2]

Rocinante[5] [6]
Rosabelle[2]
St. Patrick (31/5)
Santosy (3/6)[3]
Scene Shifter (29/6)
Sea Falcon (31/5)
Seamew[2]
Semois[2]
Shamrock (30/5)
Silver Queen (30/5)[1]
Skylark III
    (S.M.281. II)[2]
Skylark L.L.III[2]
Stonehaven[2]
Sunshine (31/5)[3]
Thetis (2/6)[3]
Triton (31/5)[3]
Two Rivers (31/5)[1]
Vanitee[2]

---

[1] Blew up on Allied minefield.
[2] Date and cause of loss not known.
[3] Abandoned.
[4] Date of loss not known.
[5] Cause of loss not known.
[6] Returned from Dunkirk damaged beyond repair.

BY COLLISION OR OTHER MISADVENTURE (*contd.*)

SMALL CRAFT (*contd.*)

Dreadnought III[1]
Eastbourne Queen (1/6)
Empress (1/6)[2]
Enchantress[1]
Enterprise (31/5)
Escaut[1]
Eve[4]

Moss Rose[1]
Nemo IV[1]
New White Heather[1]
Peggy IV[4]
Princess Lily (31/5)

Venture[1]
Viewfinder (31/5)
Viscountess Wakefield (31/5)[2]
Wave Queen (5/6)[5]
Westerley (1/6)[2]
Yser[1]

WHERRIES, PUNTS, BOATS
Aimée (wherry)[1]
Carama (punt) (30/5)
Clara Belle (wherry)[1]
Dinky (10 ft. boat)[1]
Doris (wherry)[1]
Dumpling (boat)[1]
Edina (wherry)[1]
Lark (punt)[1]
Medora (wherry)[1]
Miranda (No. 58)[1]
Sarah & Emily (boat)[1]
Viking III (dinghy)[1]

BARGES
Aidie (1/6)[2]
Barbara Jean (1/6)[2]
Claude[3]
Duchess (1/6)[2]
Ethel Everard (1/6)[2]
Lark (1/6)[2]
Royalty (1/6)[2]
Warrior[2][4]

LANDING CRAFT
A.L.C.4 (29/5)
A.L.C.8 (31/5)[2]
A.L.C.15 (31/5)
A.L.C.18 (29/5)
M.L.C.12 (2/6)[2]
M.L.C.17 (3/6)[2]
M.L.C.22 (2/6)[2]

Part II. Ships and vessels damaged

BY AIR ATTACK

DESTROYERS
Anthony (30/5)
Gallant (29/5)
Greyhound (29/5)
Intrepid (29/5)
Ivanhoe (1/6)
Jaguar (29/5)
Sabre (30/5)
Saladin (29/5)
Vivacious (31/5)
Windsor (28/5)
Wolfhound (27/5)
Worcester (1/6)

A. A. CRUISER
Calcutta (2/6)

SLOOP
Bideford (29/5)

A.B/V
Mona's Isle (27/5)

MINESWEEPERS
Hebe (31/5)
Pangbourne (29/5)
Ross (1/6)
Salamander (1/6)
Westward-Ho (1/6)

PERSONNEL VESSELS
Canterbury (29/5)
Prague (1/6)
Royal Daffodil (2/6)

HOSPITAL CARRIERS
Isle of Guernsey (29/5)
St. Julien (29/5)
Worthing (2/6)

BY GUNFIRE

PERSONNEL VESSELS
Biarritz (27/5)
Princess Maud (30/5)

TRAWLERS
"Kingston" (2/6)[6]
Spurs (2/6)

A.B/V.
King Orry (27/5)

---

[1] Date and cause of loss not known.
[2] Abandoned.
[3] Water-boat. Date and cause of loss not known.
[4] Date of Loss not known.
[5] Returned to England in sinking condition.
[6] Probably either the *Kingston Alalite* or the *Kingston Olivine*.

BY MINE

HOSPITAL CARRIER
St. David (1/6)

BY COLLISION OR GROUNDING

DESTROYERS	MINESWEEPERS	PERSONNEL VESSELS
Icarus (2/6)	*Leda* (4/6)	*Ben-my-Chree* (2/6)
Impulsive (31/5)	*Sharpshooter* (30/5)	*Maid of Orleans* (1/6)
Mackay (29/5)		*Roebuck* (31/5)
Montrose (29/5)		
Vimy (1/6)	HOSPITAL CARRIER	
Whitehall (31/5)		
Wolsey (31/5)	*Isle of Thanet* (28/5)	

Part III. French Ships Sunk during Operation " Dynamo "

NAME	TYPE	HOW SUNK	DATE
Bourrasque	Torpedo boat	Shell fire	30/5
Foudroyant	Destroyer	Air attack	1/6
Siroco	Destroyer	E.-Boat	31/5
Denis Papin	M/S trawler	Air attack	1/6
Joseph Marie	M/S trawler	Air attack	29/5
La Majo	M/S trawler	Air attack	29/5
Moussaillon	M/S trawler	Air attack	1/6
Vénus	M/S trawler	Air attack	1/6
Douaisien	Cargo ship	Not known	Not known
St. Camille	Cargo ship	Not known	Not known
Emile Deschamps	Fleet auxiliary	Mine	4/6
Pierre	Trawler	Shell fire	31/5
Yvonne St. Moabe	Not known	Air attack	1/6

Part IV. Belgian Ships Sunk during Operation " Dynamo "

Belgian Ships etc.

Getuigt Vor Christus	Trawler	Not known	2/6
Maréchal Foch	Trawler	Collision	4/6
O. L. V. Van Vlaandaren	Trawler	Not known	2/6
Sunny Isle	Trawler	Not known	2/6

APPENDIX C
No. 11 GROUP FIGHTER PATROLS — DUNKIRK AREA

DATE	PATROLS	TOTAL FLYING HOURS DAILY	ENEMY AIRCRAFT DESTROYED	ENEMY AIRCRAFT DRIVEN DOWN
26/5	22	480	30	20
27/5	23	536	48	32
28/5	11	576	20	6
29/5	9	674	78	8
30/5	9	704	—	—
31/5	8	490	36	4
1/6	8	558	69	—
2/6	4	231	16	6
3/6	4	339	—	—
4/6	3	234	—	—
Total flying hours		4,822		

APPENDIX D

SIGNALS RE BUILD-UP OF DESTROYERS
BETWEEN 27th MAY AND 1st JUNE

Note (i)   The 213 signals in Appendices D to Z have been collated from the copies of some 2,500 "Dynamo" signals in *Admiralty Record Office Enclosure Box No. 370* which accompanies *Admiralty Record Office Case 5458.*

Note (ii)   15 destroyers from the Nore Command, 10 from the Western Approaches Command, 10 from the Portsmouth Command, and 6 of the Dover Command, —a total of 41 British destroyers—were employed in Operation Dynamo.

Monday, 27th May

1. VICE-ADMIRAL, DOVER to ADMIRALTY (R) C.-in-C. Nore
    Request Dover Forces may be strengthened forthwith by six additional destroyers but not at the expense of Nore Command.

    1036/27

2. ADMIRALTY to C.-in-C. WESTERN APPROACHES, C.-in-C. PORTSMOUTH (R) Vice-Admiral Dover, C.-in-C. Nore, C.-in-C. Home Fleet, F.O.I.C. Humber, R.A Dover.
    Request four destroyers from Western Approaches and two from Portsmouth be sailed for Dover as soon as possible. . . .

    1317/27

3. VICE-ADMIRAL, DOVER to *Grafton* (R) S.O. 10th M.S.F., *Greyhound, Calcutta.*
    Close beach in vicinity of La Panne at 0100 and send in boats for British troops. You should withdraw at your discretion and anyhow not later than 0330. Paddle minesweepers and small craft will be in vicinity. Acknowledge.

    2054/27

    [V.A. Dover informed (between 2015 and 2055/27) that embarkation was only possible from the beaches, and that evacuation on the night of 28th-29th May was problematical (see Apps. M.3 and M.4)].

4. VICE-ADMIRAL, DOVER to *Grafton, Greyhound, Blyskawica*[1] (R) S.O. 10th M.S.F.
    Close the beach at La Panne at 0100 tomorrow Tuesday and embark all possible British troops using your boats. This is our last chance of saving them.

    2127/27

4a.   [1] The Polish destroyer *Blyskawica* was not in company but she replied at 2242/27 :
    " We have two pulling boats only. Can accommodate 3 in each ".

Monday, 27th May

5. VICE-ADMIRAL, DOVER to *Gallant, Vivacious, Windsor, Vimy, Calcutta, Anthony, Impulsive.*
    Close beaches one to three miles east of Dunkirk with utmost despatch and embark all possible British troops using your own boats. This is our last chance of saving them. *Maid of Orleans, Lormont,* 17 drifters and other craft will be operating.

    2142/27

6. VICE-ADMIRAL, DOVER to *Wolfhound, Wolsey.*
    17 drifters arriving Dunkirk tonight
    Direct to beaches as necessary.

    2158/27

7. VICE-ADMIRAL, DOVER to *Vimy.*
    Close the beaches one to three miles east of Dunkirk at 0100 tomorrow Tuesday and embark all possible British troops using your boats. This is our last chance of saving them.

    2238/27

8. VICE-ADMIRAL, DOVER to *Sabre*

Last chance of saving B.E.F. is tonight.   Proceed with all despatch to beach one to three miles east of Dunkirk and embark troops using own boats.   Route from Dover is by No. 6 Calais buoy, south of Dunkerque B.W. buoy and French coastal route.   Return by Zuydcoote Pass Q.Z.F.3. and Q.Z.S.60.   Other British ships will be off the beach.   You should leave at your discretion and anyhow not later than 0330.

2305/27

SIGNALS RE BUILD UP OF DESTROYERS

Thursday, 30th May

9. VICE-ADMIRAL, DOVER to ADMIRALTY, C.IN-C. NORE

Dover 30th May, departures: *Javelin, Impulsive, Havant, Harvester, Icarus, Intrepid, Ivanhoe*, at 0515, for Sheerness.

0538/30

Note : This followed a decision to withdraw the 7 modern destroyers from Operation Dynamo.

10. C.-IN-C. NORE to *Harvester, Havant, Ivanhoe, Impulsive, Icarus, Intrepid* (R) C.S. S/H, V.A. Dover.

Raise steam forthwith and proceed to Dunkirk by Route X for X-ray.

1531/30

Note : The decision to withdraw the modern destroyers was revoked.

11. ADMIRALTY to C.-IN-C. NORE (R) *Ajax, Hotspur*, V.A. Dover, *Lynx*

A spare destroyers crew is to be sent to Dover as soon as possible to provide temporary reliefs in crews of destroyers operating off Belgian coast. . . .

2341/30

APPENDIX E

SIGNALS RE BUILD-UP OF MINESWEEPERS

Note : 36 minesweepers took part in Operation Dynamo and were drawn from the following flotillas : 1st, 4th, 5th, 6th, 7th, 8th, 10th, and 12th.

Sunday, 26th May

1. ADMIRALTY to C.IN-C. HOME FLEET, (R) A.C.O.S., V.A. Dover, M/S 1, M/S 6

Owing to casualties, 6 M.S.F. at Dover has been reduced to two effective ships. Oil-burning fleet sweepers are urgently required there to maintain channel for communication with B.E.F.

Request two ships of 1st M.S.F. may be spared from your command and sailed to join 6 M.S.F. at Dover forthwith[1].

1833/26

[1] *Hebe* and *Sharpshooter* arrived Dover 1723/28.

Monday, 27th May

2. C.-IN-C. NORE to VICE-ADMIRAL, DOVER

5th M.S.F. can sail from Harwich at daylight.
Would they be of use to you at Dunkirk.

2345/27

Reply

3. No thank you very much.

0044/28

Tuesday, 28th May

Note : Admiralty message 1063/28 [not available] ordered the 7th and 8th M/S Flotillas (which were at Rosyth) to Harwich, under the orders of the Vice-Admiral, Dover.

4. C.-IN-C. NORE to F.O.I.C. HARWICH, (R) V.A. Dover, Admiralty

12th M.S.F. is to proceed to arrive off La Panne at 2200 today, Tuesday. . . .
5th M.S.F. is to proceed to arrive off beach between Zuydcoote and Malo-les-Bains at 2200 today Tuesday. . . .

0939/28
T.O.R. 1036

5. VICE-ADMIRAL, DOVER to *Emperor of India, Princess Elizabeth* [10th M.S.F.] (R) C.M.S.
Emperor of India is to proceed direct over minefield to La Panne to embark troops.

Princess Elizabeth is to proceed over minefields to Dunkirk keeping well clear to northward of Gravelines Point where enemy batteries may be in place. Then embark troops. Return route to be at your discretion depending on the state of the tide.

1607/28

APPENDIX F

SIGNALS RE BUILD-UP OF SKOOTS

22nd May

F.1. ADMIRALTY to C.-IN-C. PORTSMOUTH, (R) F.O.I.C. Portland, F.O.I.C. Southampton, V.A. Dover

From the following list of Dutch coasters lying in Poole, four empty and of about 200-300 tons, are to be sent immediately to New Docks, Southampton, where they will be loaded with military supplies. These will be manned by naval crews after arrival at Southampton, and will work under the War Office.

2. As many of the remainder as are in light condition will be taken over and manned by naval crews and when ready will be at the disposal of V.A. Dover.

3. C.-in-C. Portsmouth, is requested to arrange for the organisation and assembly of these vessels reporting names of vessels as they became ready for service.

4. Arrangements are being made for sets of charts to be sent to Portsmouth Chart Depot.

5. Further signal will be made regarding provision of naval personnel and disposal of Dutch crews on taking over.

6. It is a matter of great importance that these vessels should be got ready for service as soon as possible.

7.	*Despatch II*	*Horst*	*Jaba*
	Brem[1]	*Sursum Corda*	*Ruja*
	Boekelo[1]	*Abel Tasman*	*Java*
	Hebenobel[1]	*Kaapfalga*	*Friso*
	Virgo[1]	*Alice*	*Dourswold*[1]
	Aldo[1]	*Fredanja*	
	Nottingham[1]	*Hebe II*	

1703/22

F.2. ADMIRALTY to C.-IN-C. NORE (R) F.O.I.C. London, V.A. Dover

1. From the following list of Dutch coasters lying in the Port of London, four in ballast and of about 200-300 tons, are to be sent immediately to Victualling Wharf Deptford to load military supplies. These will be manned by naval crews after arrival at Deptford, and will work under the War Office.

2. As many of the remainder which [?as] are in light condition are to be taken over and manned by naval crews.

3. C.-in-C. Nore is requested to arrange for the organisation and assembly of these vessels which when ready will be placed at the disposal of V.A. Dover.

4. Names of ships to be reported as they became ready for service.

5. Arrangements are being made for sets of charts to be sent to Chart Depot Sheerness.

6. Further signal will be made re dispoasl of Dutch crews and provision of personnel for manning.

---

[1] Was not available.

7. It is a matter of great importance that these ships should be got **ready as** soon as possible.

8.

Twente	*Brabant*[1]	*Bart*
Tilly	*Antje*	*Hondsrug*
Brandaris	*Reiger*	*Delta*
Lena	*Princess Juliana*	*Borneo*[1]
Caribia	*Oranje*	*Liberty*[1]
Vrede	*Gorecht*	*Bernina*[1]
Rika	*Fiducia*[1]	*Limburg*[1]
Patria	*Junior*[1]	*Bornrif*
Amstelroom[1]	*Deneb*	*Martha*[1]
Express[1]	*Mercurius*[1]	*Aegir*
Jutland		

1704/22

F.3. ADMIRALTY to VICE-ADMIRAL, DOVER, C.-IN-C. NORE, C.-IN-C. PORTSMOUTH, (R) F.O.I.C. London, F.O.I.C. Southampton, F.O.I.C. Portland
Admiralty 1703/22 and 1704/22 to certain addressees only. The operation for which these ships are being prepared will be known as Dynamo.

1944/22

APPENDIX G

SIGNALS RE LACK OF SMALL CRAFT

Sunday, 26th May

1. ADMIRALTY to A/S CHATHAM, A/S PORTSMOUTH, (R) C.-IN-C. Nore, C.-IN-C. Portsmouth, V.A. Dover
Investigate and report how many cutters and whalers can be made available for immediate service under V.A. Dover.

2028/26

2. ADMIRALTY to C.-IN-C. PORTSMOUTH, VICE-ADMIRAL, DOVER (R) Combrax Portsmouth, Commandant 1st D.C. Fort Cumberland
8 A.L.C's. with crews complete are available and will be embarked in S.S. *Clan Macalister* at Southampton a.m. 27th May. . . .

2337/26

Monday, 27th May

3. (ADMIRALTY) D.S.V.P. to COMMODORE, SHEERNESS (R) C.-in-C. Nore V.A. Dover
About 40 motor launches have been ordered to Sheerness of which **30** should arrive at daylight tomorrow Tuesday. The rest during the day. These **will be** manned on arrival at Sheerness . . . . Request you will inform V.A. Dover when boats are ready for service.

2035/27

Tuesday, 28th May

Note : [At 0436. S.N.O. Dunkirk asked for all vessels to be sent alongside east pier.]

4. VICE-ADMIRAL, DOVER to S.N.O. DUNKIRK (R) Fighter Command
Further destroyers and small craft are being sent now to Dunkirk.

0630/28

SIGNALS RE BUILD-UP OF SMALL CRAFT

5. N.O.I.C RAMSGATE to VICE ADMIRAL, DOVER
1st Mine Recovery Flotilla vessels *Lord Cavan, Fidget, Jacketa, Silver Dawn* and *Fisher Boy.* Tug *Java.* Drifters *Lord Collingwood, Lord Rodney, Lord Keith, Lord St. Vincent.* Motor boats *New Brittanic, Walker I, Walker II, Angler, Nayland,* sailed Ramsgate for Dunkirk.

1550/28

---

[1] Was not available.

6. **D.M.O.[1] to Vice-Admiral, Dover (R) C.-in-C. Nore, N.O.I.C. Ramsgate, Admiralty**

18 motor boats and 17 whalers left Sheerness for Dover between 1830 and 1900 escorted by trawler *Asama*.

1916/28

7. **Vice-Admiral, Dover to C.-in-C. Nore (R) Admiralty**

Request you will send every available shallow draft power boat capable of ferrying from beaches to ships, direct to ships lying off beaches to eastward of Dunkirk stocked with fuel and provisions for 2 days.

2002/28

8. **(Admiralty) D.S.V.P. to C.-in-C. Nore, S.N.O. Dover, S.N.O. Sheerness**

Additional motor boats up to a possible 40 are being sent from Thames to Dover to arrive before tomorrow night 29th.

Some boats will come by lorries direct to Dover. 12 crews are being sent to Dover and 20 to Sheerness to await arrival of boats. Runner crews take boats to Sheerness but will not proceed further.

2031/28

9. **N.C.S.O. Thames to Commodore Sheerness, C.-in-C. Nore, Vice-Admiral, Dover, N.O.I.C. Ramsgate**

All small craft are being route-ed direct to beaches east of Dunkirk provided they have charts, food, fuel, etc. If not complete they will be sent to Sheerness first.

2301/28

Wednesday, 29th May

10. **Admiralty to Commodore in Charge, Sheerness (R) C.-in-C. Nore V.A. Dover, N.O.I.C. Ramsgate**

All motor boats being prepared for service under V.A. Dover are to be sent immediately they are ready to Ramsgate where they will recieve orders from the Naval-Officer-in-Charge.

0120/29

11. *Wolfhound* **to Vice-Admiral, Dover**

Have you any orders for fleet of motor boats now tied up alongside *Wolfhound*.

0224/29

Reply

12. Make utmost endeavour to hasten departure of motor boats to La Panne beach.

0256/29

13. **(Admiralty) D.S.V.P. to C's-in-C. Portsmouth, Nore, S.N.O.'s Yarmouth, New-haven, Vice-Admiral, Dover.**

Officers from S.V.P. are proceeding to requisition suitable motor boats reported to S.V.P. under Emergency Statute[2] and otherwise, for immediate service on coast from Portsmouth to Yarmouth.

In all about 140 are anticipated of which 40 have already been requisitioned in the Thames Estuary for special service and ordered to Dover.

It is requested that boats when collected are placed under control until their crews arrive as follows :

Area 1—Lymington to Littlehampton including I.O.W. assembling at Hamble.

Area 2—Littlehampton to Rye, assembling at Newhaven.

Area 3—Brightlingsea to Harwich, assembling at Harwich.

Area 4—Southwold to Gt. Yarmouth, assembling at Yarmouth.

0940/29

---

[1] Dynamo Maintenance Officer (Admiral Taylor) at Sheerness.

[2] This emergency statute was *Statutory Order No.* 718, dated 10th May, 1940, entitled *Small Craft (Information) Order*, 1940. It was issued at the request, on 16th April 1940, of Admiral Sir Lionel Preston, Director of the Small Vessels Pool, Admiralty, in view of the probable requirements for small motor craft.

The order, briefly, called on all owners of self-propelled craft between 30 and 100 feet in length, to send particulars of their craft to the Admiralty within 14 days. The Order was published in the press in the usual way, and on 14th May it was broadcast on the B.B.C. At the time of the conception and issue of the Order, however, there was clearly no question of a possible evacuation from the Continent.

14 ADMIRALTY to C.-in-C. PORTSMOUTH, C.-in.-C. NORE (R) V.A. Dover, N.O.I.C. Ramsgate, Cdr. i/c Sheerness.

Investigate as a matter of urgency provision of additional small craft which can be made available within 48 hours from all ports in your command for Operation Dynamo including X-lighters and other self-propelled lighters. Any available in Portsmouth Command to be sent to Dover forthwith.[2] Those in Nore Command to be sent to Ramsgate. V.A. Dover to be kept informed.

All craft are to be provided with charts and if necessary manned by naval crews. S.T.O.'s have been informed and have full requisitioning powers.

1115/29

15. (ADMIRALTY) D.S.V.P. to C.-in-C. Portsmouth, Nore, Vice-Admiral, Dover (R), N.O.I.C. Ramsgate, C.S. Sheerness, S.N.O. Yarmouth, S.N.O. Newhaven.

My 0940/29 and Admiralty 1115/29 :

Officers of S.V.P. now in area mentioned have been ordered to co-operate with your organisations.

They are to supply records from S.V.P. of boats available, and to send boats as ordered in Admiralty 1115/29 and not repetition not as in my 0940/29.

1130/30

16. ADMIRALTY to VICE-ADMIRAL, DOVER (R) C.-in-C. NORE.

20 Thames barges in tow of 5 tugs expected to arrive Ramsgate 1700 today May 29th. . . It is for consideration that they be used as piers.

1255/29

17. VICE-ADMIRAL, DOVER to *Hebe* for CAPTAIN BUSH

20 Thames barges in tow are being sent. Can they be usefully used as piers for loading troops at points on the beaches or do you consider they would be more usefully employed for ferrying troops. . . .

1456/29

18. C.-in-C. NORE to A/S CHATHAM, COMMODORE IN CHARGE, Sheerness, D.M.O. (R), N.O.I.C. Ramsgate.

All available X-lighters which can be released without disorganising dockyards are to be sent to Ramsgate forthwith. . . .

1210/29

19. VICE-ADMIRAL, DOVER to C.-in-C. PORTSMOUTH

All small craft should be route-ed direct to Ramsgate and not repeat not to Dover.

1618/29

Thursday, 30th May

20. C.-in-C. PORTSMOUTH to ADMIRALTY, N.O.I.C. Ramsgate, Vice-Admiral, Dover

Small craft for Belgium operations due Ramsgate approximately as follows :

0600   3 fast M/B's.
0700   Dutch *Mok I*.
0900   2 fast paddle steamers, 1 M/B, 1 Picket boat.
1000   H.M.S. *Dwarf*, tug *Grappler* towing lighter and launches, tug *Emprise* towing launch, and 2 coaling tugs.
1100   3 Hopper barges.
1200   2 picket boats, 1 diesel boat.
1300   2 small cargo carriers, 1 launch, 1 small tug.
1400   1 Dutch M/B and 2 M/B's.
1500   2 I.O.W. car ferries and 2 drifters.
1600   1 small tug towing launch.
1900   5 Hoppers.
2400   2 launches.

All above times are 30th May. No ships are degaussed.

0005/30

21. VICE-ADMIRAL, DOVER to *Hebe*.

Rear-Admiral [Dover] from 1st Sea Lord.

Report conditions on beaches and whether boats are distributed to best advantage.

1019/30

---

[2] See Appendix G.22.

22. **REAR-ADMIRAL, DOVER to ADMIRALTY for 1ST SEA LORD**
Your 1019. Beaches crowded. Hardly any ships are here for loading. Request destroyers and sloops.... Until more small boats [?are available for ferrying] strongly of opinion .... essential to concentrate on evacuating from Dunkirk itself.

1107/30

23. **ADMIRALTY to F.O. DOVER STRAITS (R) V.A. Dover**
Understand pulling boats are weak link please confirm. Every step is being taken to send as many as possible.

1141/30

24. **ADMIRAL TAYLOR, SHEERNESS to D.S.V.P. (R) D. of S.T.**
Thames river steamers have no condensers and cannot run on sea water. Request no more be sent.

1150/30

25. **ADMIRALTY to VICE-ADMIRAL, DOVER, N.O.I.C. RAMSGATE**
War Office have placed seven 30-knot motor launches at your disposal and are sending them to Ramsgate today Thursday. Naval crews are being sent to man them.
Names of launches : *Marlborough, Wolfe, Grouse, Kestrel, Vulture, Swallow, Pidgeon.*

1336/30

and later
26. .... Add to list of fast military launches Haig....

1882/30

27. **C.-in-C. PORTSMOUTH to ADMIRALTY, N.O.I.C. Ramsgate, VICE-ADMIRAL, Dover.**
Small craft due Ramsgate approx. as follows :
1900/30 Power boat R.F.A. 115 (?)
2100/30 Fast motor boat, Admiral's barge and Examination Serv. Vessel *Llanthony.*
0100/31 F.A.A. Tender *Ocean Rover* and hopper *Foremost* 102.
0880/31 Car Ferry *Fishbourne* (previously reported but delayed.)
1000/31 One self-propelled lighter.
1300/31 One self-propelled lighter and steam pinnace...

1852/30

28. **F.O.I.C. LONDON to C.-in-C. NORE, VICE-ADMIRAL, DOVER, N.O.I.C. RAMSGATE, N.O.I.C. SOUTHEND, ADMIRALTY.**
23 merchant ships motor-lifeboats and 46 rowing ditto in tow of six tugs leaving Tilbury from now till complete, manned by volunteers and naval ratings
On arrival Southend they will be route-ed immediately to Ramsgate where first tow should arrive about 0600 Friday [31st May]....

1900/30

Friday, 31st May

29. **VICE-ADMIRAL, DOVER to C.-in-C. NORE, F.O.I.C. HARWICH, Admiralty, R.A. Dover, N.O.I.C. Ramsgate.**
Boat convoy for last flight of B.E.F. departs Ramsgate 1300 Friday 31st for Dunkirk via Route X. Anticipate time of return to Dover and Sheerness 1000 Saturday 1st June. Request all available M.T.B.'s may escort this convoy for as much of the outward passage as possible and for the whole of the return passage.
Anticipated speed of advance outward bound six knots.

0459/31

30. **VICE-ADMIRAL, DOVER to M.A/S.B.'s *06, 07,* M.T.B.'s *68, 102* (R) R.A. Dover**
M.A/S.B.'s are to rendezvous off Ramsgate at 1200 Friday 31st May with boat convoy to Dunkirk, and escort on outward passage also on return passage, sailing about 0300, Sat. 1st June for Dover.
Off Dunkirk beaches, M.A./S.B.'s and available M.T.B.'s are to embark, under the direction of R.A. Dover, the C.-in-C., B.E.F., and Staff.
M.T.B.'s report when ready to sail.

0736/31

Friday, 31st May—*contd.*

31. C.-in-C. Nore to N.C.S.O. Southend, F.O.I.C. London, F.O.I.C. Harwich, Commodore in Charge, Sheerness (R) Admiralty, D.M.O. Sheerness, V.A. Dover, N.O.I.C. Ramsgate

No more small craft are to be sailed for Ramsgate until further orders. They are to be kept at immediate notice at the places where they now are.

1825/31

32. Vice-Admiral, Dover to Admiralty (R) N.O.I.C. Ramsgate, C.-in-C. Nore, F.O.I.C. London.

For Admiral Preston.

In view of alteration of plan request 30 motor boats and a number of pulling boats up to 40 may be sent to Ramsgate forthwith. Please advise expected time of arrival.

2031/31

33. F.O.I.C. London to Vice-Admiral, Dover (R) C.-in-C. Nore, N.O.I.C. Ramsgate, Admiralty, N.C.S.O. Thames.

V.A. Dover 2031/31. 30 motor boats sailed ; expect to arrive Ramsgate 1100. And 40 lifeboats with 3 tugs should arrive noon 1st June. Crews for lifeboats will be required to join at Ramsgate.

2330/31

Saturday, 1st June

34. Admiralty to F.O.I.C. Harwich (R) Cdre. i/c Sheerness, V.A. Dover, N.O.I.C. Ramsgate

All motor boats from Burnham if still detained at Harwich and any others available are to be sent at once direct to Ramsgate for operation Dynamo.

0947/1

APPENDIX H

SIGNALS RE LACK OF SMALL CRAFT

Tuesday, 28th May

1. *Wakeful* to Vice-Admiral, Dover

Plenty of troops few boats. Conditions good alongside Dunkirk east pier protected by smoke.

0507/28

2. *Calcutta* to Vice-Admiral, Dover (R) S.N.O. Dunkirk

.... Conditions for embarkation at La Panne are very bad owing to heavy surf but may improve with rising tide. Have already lost one and possibly both my whalers.

2225/28

Wednesday, 29th May

3. *Leda* to Vice-Admiral, Dover

Message from Brigadier-General i/c of embarkation.

Present rate of embarkation from shore to ship quite inadequate. Beach bombed throughout the day.

0210/29

4. D.16 [*Malcolm*] to Vice-Admiral, Dover

Destroyers motor boats are inadequate to deal with number on beaches.

More boats urgently needed.

Weather is now difficult for boat work.

0428/29

5. *Calcutta* to Vice-Admiral, Dover

Evacuation at La Panne being seriously delayed by lack of boats. ...

0805/29

6. M.S. 10 to Vice-Admiral, Dover

Motor landing craft urgently required

Bray strong tide.

1455/29

Thursday, 30th May

7. S.N.O. AFLOAT to VICE-ADMIRAL, DOVER
   There is a serious shortage of ships and boats.
   I have no destroyers.

0039/30

8. V.C.I.G.S. to VICE-ADMIRAL, DOVER
   Beaches well organised. Troops in good heart. There has been no bombing
   since dark. There is still a great shortage of small craft which are urgently required.

T.O.R.0044/30

9. REAR-ADMIRAL IN CHARGE BASE to VICE-ADMIRAL, DOVER
   Beaches are filling up rapidly. More ships and boats are an essential requirement.

0744/30

10. REAR-ADMIRAL IN CHARGE, BASE to VICE-ADMIRAL, DOVER
    Can you .... send over 5 ships life boats with skeleton crews to work from
    beach .... as soon as possible.

0916/30

Friday, 31st May

11. REAR-ADMIRAL, DOVER to VICE-ADMIRAL, DOVER (R) Admiralty
    Urgent need for boats particularly power boats still paramount at La Panne and
    Bray. Presence of motor boats will be decisive in final evacuation. Request I be
    informed of action taken on this signal.

0045/31

12. *Icarus* to VICE-ADMIRAL, DOVER
    Situation at Bray impossible. No power boats ?evacuation 10 an hour. At
    least 2,000 men still ashore. Troops being bombed and shelled. Dunkirk being
    bombed continually. If no power boats become available propose withdraw at
    dawn.

0047/31

13. COLONEL HUTCHISON, *Impulsive*, to ADMIRALTY (R) V.A. Dover
    Conditions ideal at present for embarkation but pulling cutters urgently required
    also more power boats.

0945/31

14. ADMIRALTY to VICE-ADMIRAL, DOVER (R) C.-in-C. Portsmouth, C.-in-C. Nore.
    War Office request maximum possible number of Carley floats and similar devices
    be left lying on beaches together with paddles after other craft have withdrawn.

1152/31

15. REAR-ADMIRAL, DOVER to VICE-ADMIRAL, DOVER
    Boats not yet arrived. Most available vessels are evacuating from Dunkirk.
    Minesweepers will not be here in time. I will do what I can.

1736/31

16. VICE-ADMIRAL, DOVER to REAR-ADMIRAL, DOVER
    La Panne reports 6,000 troops to clear urgently and they lack boats and ships.

2130/31

Saturday, 1st June

17. *Gossamer* to VICE-ADMIRAL, DOVER.
    Troops arriving now. Send more boats.

0132/1

18. VICE-ADMIRAL, DOVER to *Niger, Gossamer, Halcyon*.
    Use own boats. Utmost despatch essential.

0204/1

Reply from *Gossamer*.
19. Your 0204. Hardly any boats available.

0226/1

20. *Gossamer* to VICE-ADMIRAL, DOVER
    6,000 British marching from La Panne through Bray on Dunkirk.

                                                   0235/1

21. *Gossamer* to VICE-ADMIRAL, DOVER
    We must have more boats west of La Panne.

                                                   0243/1

22. VICE-ADMIRAL, DOVER to *Gossamer*
    It is now impracticable to send more boats. You must do your utmost with yours

                                                   0334/1

23. *Niger* to VICE-ADMIRAL, DOVER, REAR-ADMIRAL, DOVER
    Situation on beaches is critical. Third Division marching to Dunkirk. More
    boats urgently required.

                                                   0345/1

24. *Gossamer* to VICE-ADMIRAL, DOVER
    Thousands more (?moving) from La Panne westward. No boats.

                                                   0358/1

25. GENERAL WHITAKER to GENERAL DILL, WAR OFFICE
    Absolutely essential provide many more small boats with motor boats to tow if
    grave losses are to be avoided and remainder B.E.F. cleared. Matter utmost
    urgency.

                                                   0430/1

26. REAR-ADMIRAL, DOVER to VICE-ADMIRAL, DOVER
    All craft used for towing boats have returned in the night. They must be sent
    back.

                                                   0611/1

27. *Niger* to VICE-ADMIRAL, DOVER
    Number of towing and small boats are returning empty. Warn following ships
    to stop them.

                                                 2150/1

28. VICE-ADMIRAL, DOVER to FORCE K AND MINESWEEPERS (R) Admiralty
    Reported that number of towing and small boats are returning empty. Essential
    to arrest this. Keep good lookout and force them back.

                                               2201/1

29. VICE-ADMIRAL, DOVER to ADMIRALTY
    Owing to severe conditions and enormous wastage on Dunkirk coast, small boat
    flotillas, vital for beach work, can no longer be relied upon even in fair weather.
    Information just received that at least two such flotillas have turned back tonight
    Saturday.

                                               2328/1

30. VICE-ADMIRAL, DOVER to FORCE K AND MINESWEEPERS (R) Admiralty
    False information and orders to return are being given to our inshore units by 5th
    Column scoots or other vessels. Endeavour to keep our small vessels to their duty
    on the coast.

                                             2335/1

Sunday, 2nd June

31. ADMIRALTY (D.N.I.) to VICE-ADMIRAL, DOVER
    Your 2335/1 : Please supply any information regarding the ships suspected of
    5th Column activities.

                                             1834/2

Monday, 3rd June

32. VICE-ADMIRAL, DOVER to ADMIRALTY
    Your 1834/2. Following is information to date :

    On the morning of the 1st June it was reported that a number of small craft had
    left Dunkirk beaches. An M.T.B. was sent out to round them up and send them
    back. A signal was intercepted from *Leda* en route to Dunkirk saying that she had
    met boats returning, and she was ordered to send them back.

During the evening of the 1st June a report was recieved from S.N.T.O. Margate to the effect that a skoot was going along the beaches at Dunkirk telling boats to return to England.

The *Antje* was hailed and told to return. A warship was in the vicinity, and *Antje* intended to get confirmation from her, when the troop carrier *Scotia* was sunk close to her; so *Antje* filled up with survivors and returned. It is understood that skoot *Oranje* with boats in tow was told to return to England and complied.[1]

In view of these reports, message 2335/1 was sent out. On an earlier occasion another skoot was informed that Dunkirk was in German hands. It has not been possible to get confirmation of these details.

2332/3

APPENDIX J

SIGNALS RE PATROLS IN THE NORTH SEA SOUTH AND ON THE ROUTES TO DUNKIRK

Sunday, 26th May

1. ADMIRALTY to C.-IN-C. NORE, (R) V.A. Dover, F.O.I.C. Harwich, F.O.I.C. Humber

All available forces are to be used for covering operation Dynamo tonight Sunday.

1937/26

2. *Widgeon* to C.-IN-C. NORE

Siroco was torpedoed by *2 M.T.B.'s*

0200/31

Saturday, 1st June

3. *Malabar* to ANY-BRITISH MAN-OF-WAR

Argyllshire sunk by torpedo. Survivors report submarine submerged before explosion 2 miles ? S buoy.

0310/1

4. *Kingston Galena* to VICE-ADMIRAL, DOVER (R) Capt. A.P.
Stella Dorado torpedoed. Picked up 5 survivors, 1 badly injured. Proceeding to Dover.

0430/1

5. VICE-ADMIRAL, DOVER to SHIPS & AUTHORITIES NORE & DOVER COMMAND

Magnetic mines reported to have been laid vicinity of buoy F.G. on route X.

2310/1

Sunday, 2nd June

6. VICE-ADMIRAL, DOVER to *Epervier* (R) *Léopard, Savorgnan de Brazza.*

Three aux. patrol vessels reported out of action at 1214 B.S.T. in position 090° N. Goodwin L.V. 8 miles. Caused by shell fire. *Vanquisher* left Dover 1305 B.S.T. to investigate and report.

1315/2

7. VICE-ADMIRAL, DOVER to *Calcutta*, (R) C.-in-C. Nore, Admiralty, *Savorgnan de Brazza*

Return to Sheerness and revert to 1 hours notice for steam. An exactly similar patrol to that carried out today Sunday is to be carried out tomorrow Monday, provided C.-in-C. Nore can provide a screen. Inform the French vessels on your patrol line.

1247/2

---

[1] A skoot informed *Oranje* that beach evacuation was complete, that there were already sufficient ships in Dunkirk harbour and that *Oranje's* tow of 4 boats, was not required. About an hour later the *Oranje* did in fact return to England.

8. *Calcutta* to VICE-ADMIRAL, DOVER

> Your 1274. French ships apparently left patrol when bombing started at 1035 as I have not seen them since.
>
> 1442/2

9. *Saon* to CAPTAIN A.P.

> *Blackburn Rovers* struck by torpedo. Going to her assistance.
>
> 1618/2

10. *Saon* to VICE-ADMIRAL, DOVER
    Westella torpedoed.
    My posisition 51° 20′ N., 02° 7′ c.

> 1639/2

Monday, 3rd June

11. VICE-ADMIRAL, DOVER to C.-IN-C. NORE (R) Admiralty, *Calcutta*

> As withdrawal from Dunkirk tonight 3rd/4th is planned for 0230 instead of 0300, do not propose to employ *Calcutta* as A/A escort.
>
> 1419/3

APPENDIX K

SIGNALS RE ROUTES TO DUNKIRK

27th May

1. VICE-ADMIRAL, DOVER to SHIPS OPERATING UNDER ORDERS OF VICE-ADMIRAL, DOVER

> Routes to Dunkerque are as follows :
> *Route Z*, via No. 6 Calais bell buoy and south of Dunkirk AW buoy.
> *Route Y*, via Downs, West Hinder, North Channel and West Deep, Q.Z.S.80 and 60.
>
> *Route X*, via Downs from North Goodwin 115 degrees, 24.5 miles to light buoy, F.G., and thence 164 degrees to No. 6 W buoy. New light buoys[1] are 115 degrees 7.8, 15.0, and 22.3 miles from N. Goodwin.
>
> *Route X* may be used in emergency when state of tide permits, or when ordered.
> *Route Z* should only be used at night.
> *Route Y* is in general use.
>
> 1107/28
>
> [1] i.e. " U ", " V " and " W " buoys.

2. VICE-ADMIRAL, DOVER to SHIPS OPERATING UNDER ORDER OF VICE-ADMIRAL, DOVER

> My 1107. Add to Route Z :
> " passing south of chartered position of Dyck Light Vessel ".
>
> 2006/28

29th May

3. VICE-ADMIRAL, DOVER to SHIPS AND AUTHORITIES, NORE AND DOVER COMMANDS

> *Route Y* is to be amended to run from Middelkerke Bank buoy 320 degrees 9½ miles to position north of Dyck whistle buoy. Transports are to be instructed accordingly as opportunity offers.
>
> 0631/29

1st June

4. VICE-ADMIRAL, DOVER to ADMIRALTY

> Owing to magnetic mines ships evacuating troops may be using Route Y as well as Route X. Request Fighter and Coastal Command be informed.
>
> 0313/1

5. VICE-ADMIRAL, DOVER to ADMIRALTY

  . . . . . Channels to Dunkirk now all under fire of German batteries. New battery came into action this evening suspending traffic on only remaining daylight route, namely X, maintaining heavy barrage . . . .

                 2329/1

2nd June

6. *Venomous* to VICE-ADMIRAL, DOVER

  Dunkirk approach channel is under fire from the shore guns.

                 2110/2

3rd June

7. VICE-ADMIRAL, DOVER to SHIPS & AUTHORITIES NORE & DOVER COMMANDS

  Route X. From F.G. buoy steer 172 degrees for No. 3 W buoy and thence keep close to Southern channel buoys.

                 1635/3

APPENDIX L

SIGNALS RE REQUESTS FOR FIGHTER COVERS

Monday, 27th May

1. B.N.L.O. DUNKIRK to VICE-ADMIRAL, DOVER

  Pass to War Office from O.C. Dunkirk :
  Complete fighter protection over Dunkirk now essential if a serious disaster is to be avoided.

                 1655/27

2. AIR LIAISON DUNKIRK to FIGHTER COMMAND (R) Air Ministry

  Unless fighter protection is provided continually from dawn tomorrow result will be very serious. Embarkation on beach east of 892 [?] Dunkirk.

                 2350/27

Tuesday, 28th May

3. (C.A.S.[1]) AIR MINISTRY to FIGHTER COMMAND, COASTAL COMMAND etc.
  Today is likely to be the most critical day ever experienced by the British Army. The extreme gravity of the situation should be explained to all units. I am confident that all ranks will appreciate that it is the duty of the R.A.F. to make their greatest effort today to assist their comrades of both the Army and Navy.

                 0125/28

   [1] Chief of the Air Staff.

4. B.N.L.O. DUNKIRK to VICE-ADMIRAL, DOVER

  Continuous bombing and machine gunning on beaches. Only maximum air protection can alleviate situation at dawn.

                 0225/28

5. VICE-ADMIRAL, DOVER to COASTAL COMMAND, FIGHTER COMMAND, (R) 16 Group, 11 Group, Dover Forces, Admiralty, Air Ministry

  Request maximum fighter protection throughout today 28th as follows :

  Suggest *Coastal Command* patrol line Ostend to Nord and Sandettie Bank. *Fighter Command*, Dunkirk and adjacent beaches. *Skuas* from Detling are patrolling line North Goodwin to Nieuport from 0800 to 1300.

                 0855/28

6. ADMIRALTY to VICE-ADMIRAL, DOVER

The Air Ministry are fully in the picture as to requirements at Dunkirk and are doing all they possible can.   If any particular requirements turn up, such as group of ships being attacked, report to Admiralty as soon as possible.

1240/28

7. VICE-ADMIRAL, DOVER to S.N.O. DUNKIRK

Can personnel ships still go alongside Dunkirk.

1135/28

Reply
8. B.L.O., C.-IN-C. NORTHERN NAVAL FORCES to VICE-ADMIRAL, DOVER

Your 1135.   Yes when fighters are actually keeping off bombers.

1337/28

APPENDIX M
SIGNALS RE EVACUATION 26TH AND 27TH MAY
(Additional to those in Appendices D to L)

26th May
1. ADMIRALTY to VICE-ADMIRAL, DOVER C.-IN-C. NORE, C.-IN-C. PORTSMOUTH

Operation Dynamo is to commence.

1857/26

2. ADMIRALTY to C.-IN-C. NORE, VICE-ADMIRAL, DOVER, C.-IN-C. PORTSMOUTH, B.N.L.O. MARCEAU, B.N.L.O. DUNKIRK

Captain W. G. Tennant has been appointed S.N.O. Dunkirk.   He will proceed to take up his duties tomorrow Monday, May 27th.

2321/26

27th May
3. S.N.O. DUNKIRK to VICE-ADMIRAL, DOVER (R) Admiralty

Port continuously bombed all day and on fire.   Embarkation possible only from beaches east of harbour A.B.C.D.[1]

Send all ships and passenger ships there to anchor.   Am ordering *Wolfhound* to load there and sail.

T.O.O. 2005/27
T.O.R. 2025

4. S.N.O. DUNKIRK to VICE-ADMIRAL, DOVER

Please send every available craft east of Dunkirk immediately.   Evacuation tomorrow night is problematical.

T.O.O. 1958/27
R.O.T. 2055

[Here see Apps. D3 to D8].

---

[1] *Note :* See p. 23, footnote[1].

APPENDIX N
SIGNALS RE EVACUATION ON 28th MAY
AND NIGHT OF 28th–29th MAY
(Additional to those in Appendices D to L)

28th May

1. VICE-ADMIRAL, DOVER to S.N.O. DUNKIRK

   Report now and every hour the approx. number of men waiting to be embarked from Dunkirk.
   Acknowledge.

   0758/28

2. S.N.O. DUNKIRK to N.O.I.C. DOVER

   Your 0758. There are at present 2,000 men on Dunkirk beach, and 7,000 men on sand dunes for whom I have had no ships. They are now in need of water which Army cannot supply. Unlimited numbers are falling back on this area and situation in present circumstances will shortly become desperate.

   I am doing my best to keep you informed but shall be unable to report hourly.

   0935/28

3. VICE-ADMIRAL, DOVER to S.N.O. DUNKIRK

   Your 0935. Steady transport by 15 destroyers[1] will continue by day, spread evenly between beaches.

   Maximum effort by every type of craft from all beaches and from Dunkirk if practicable is intended for 2200 tonight.

   1140/28

   [1] 16 destroyers were evacuating troops from Dunkirk and the beaches on 28th May.

APPENDIX O
SIGNALS RE EVACUATION 29th MAY
(Additional to those in Appendices D to L, and in Appendix Y)

Wednesday, 29th May

1. VICE-ADMIRAL, DOVER to S.N.O. DUNKIRK (R) Admiralty

   Owing to surf on beach most important move as many troops as possible from La Panne and Bray to Dunkirk.

   0431/29

2. S.N.O. DUNKIRK to VICE-ADMIRAL, DOVER (R) Admiralty

   No enemy interference at present. Embarkation going at 2,000 an hour. This can be kept up provided supply transport is maintained.

   Swell prevents use beach ; all ships to Dunkirk.

   Any air attack would be disastrous. Maximum fighter protection essential. Passenger transport, inflammable loaded, mined and sunk about 2 miles east Dunkirk pier light.

   0709/29

3. S.N.O. DUNKIRK to VICE-ADMIRAL, DOVER (R) Admiralty

   Embarkation is going on well ; enemy is leaving us alone. The situation ashore is obscure and ominous.

I have sent Capt. Bush by M.T.B. with an appreciation.

There is little food or water in Dunkirk.   This should be sent as soon as possible. . . .
Armies are quite unable to help or organise anything.   Keep on sending any ships. . . .
A good medical officer with staff should be despatched. . . .

1001/29

4. ADMIRALTY to VICE-ADMIRAL, DOVER C.-IN-C. PORTSMOUTH

Rear-Admiral Wake-Walker has been appointed as R.A., Dover for command
of seagoing ships and vessels off the Belgian coast, and is to hoist his flag in such
ship as V.A. Dover shall direct.

1748/29

5. VICE-ADMIRAL, DOVER to SHIPS & AUTHORITIES NORE & DOVER (R) Admiralty
C.-in-C. Portsmouth, C.-in-C. Nore

My 1748/29[1], 1321/29 and 1832/29 to *Hebe* only :

Authority for operation Dynamo under V.A. Dover is as follows :

R.A. Wake-Walker has been appointed as R.A. Dover for command of seagoing
ships and vessels off the Belgian coast.

R.A. Dover has hoisted his flag in *Hebe*.   Captain Tennant has been appointed
as S.N.O. Dunkirk and is responsible under R.A. Dover for all shore organisation.

1328/30

6. ADMIRALTY to SHIPS & AUTHORITIES IN AREA A (R) C.-IN-C. Portsmouth C.-IN-C. W.A.

During present operations on Belgian coast where many small craft are present,
destroyers are not repetition not to stop to render assistance to ships in distress.

1105/29

7. *Ivanhoe* to VICE-ADMIRAL, DOVER

From S.N.O. Dunkirk—enemy shelling pier with shore batteries from S.E.
Request bombers to counter.   Vital.

1105/29

and later

8. B.N.L.O., C.-IN-C. NORTHERN NAVAL FORCES to VICE-ADMIRAL, DOVER

My . . . . 1105 cancel request.   Consider possible retaliation would be to our disadvantage.

1200/29

SIGNALS RE EVACUATION 29TH MAY

9. MAJOR GENERAL LLOYD to MAJOR GENERAL DEWING, D.M.O., WAR OFFICE

Morale of troops landing is remarkably high partly no doubt due to arrival home.
Approximately half armed.   Percentage of officers small.   All drawn from units
promiscuously, mostly Third Corps . . . .

1204/29

10. VICE-ADMIRAL, DOVER to GENERAL LINDSELL [Q.M.G.], S.N.O. DUNKIRK

Stores and supply craft have had to return undischarged owing to lack of assistance from shore.

Must press you to organise parties for unloading purposes ; Naval beach parties
will indicate when and where required.

1432/29

---

[1] V.A. Dover's 1748/29 cannot be traced.   Probably Admiralty Message
1748/29 (see Appendix O, 9c) is meant.

11. VICE-ADMIRAL, DOVER to S.N.O. DUNKIRK (R) Admiralty[1]

Evacuation of British troops to continue at maximum speed during the night. If adequate supply of personnel vessels cannot be maintained to Dunkirk east pier destroyers will be sent there as well. All other craft except hospital carriers to embark from beach which is extended from one mile east of Dunkirk to one mile east of La Panne. Whole length is divided into 3 equal parts referred to as La Panne, Bray, Malo, from east to west with a mile gap between each part. La Panne and Bray have troop concentration points each end and in middle ; Malo at each end. These points should be tended by inshore craft. Pass this message by V/S to ships not equipped W/T as opportunity offers.

1906/29

12. S.N.O. DUNKIRK to VICE-ADMIRAL, DOVER

[Your 2057] No. Hope to get a good move on tonight but it is doubtful if much more can be done in daylight hours.

2150/29

Note.—The authority for the above signal is S.N.O. Dunkirk's Report (R.O.III, p. 350). V.A. Dover's 2057 is not available. It asked whether the harbour was blocked.

APPENDIX P

SIGNALS RE EVACUATION ON 30th MAY

(Additional to those in Appendices D, E, G—L, and Y)

30th May

1. MILITARY DUNKIRK to VICE-ADMIRAL, DOVER (R) War Office

Great opportunity missed during night when only 3 drifters arrived. No water or food yet provided on Dunkirk beach for large number of troops. Sporadic bombing.

0755/30

2. B.N.L.O. to N.O.I.C. DOVER

From S.N.O. Dunkirk.

. . . . Have sent [Captain] Howson take charge La Panne beach under G.H.Q. . . . .

T.O.R. 0835/30

3. S.N.O. DUNKIRK to VICE-ADMIRAL, DOVER

Troops are concentrated in unlimited numbers just east of Dunkirk beach, on Bray beach, and at La Panne. Please do your best to distribute . . . .

0930/30

4. S.N.O. DUNKIRK to VICE-ADMIRAL, DOVER

. . . . I have no M.T.B. and can only communicate with U.K. by French W/T station or when destroyers are in sight. If conditions remain as at present a destroyer alongside continuously for embarkation would be a magnificent help. The moment bombing starts all must shove off.

0943/30

5. S.N.O. DUNKIRK to VICE-ADMIRAL, DOVER

If this weather persists I want a ship every half hour.

0950/30

---

[1] *Note :* This signal is not available but the text of it, as above, is quoted verbatim in D.R., page 10, para. 32.

APPENDIX Q

SIGNALS RE EVACUATION ON 31st MAY AND NIGHT OF 31st MAY 1st JUNE

Friday, 31st May

1. VICE-ADMIRAL to *Gossamer, Leda, Speedwell, Halcyon, Skipjack, Salamander, Niger, Ross, Albury, Kellett, Fitzroy, Sutton, Saltash, Lydd, Dundalk,* (R) C.-in-C. Nore, F.O.I.C. Harwich.

Ships addressed are grouped as follows for special embarkation today Friday.

Group one. *Gossamer, Leda, Ross, Albury.*
Group two. *Halcyon, Skipjack, Speedwell, Dundalk.*
Group three. *Niger, Salamander, Fitzroy, Sutton.*
Spare. *Kellett, Saltash, Lydd.*

Each ship is to adjust programme forthwith as necessary to rendezvous empty with Senior Officers of groups at W buoy . . . . at 2200/31. Object final evacuation of covering force of five thousand troops.

Execution. Groups are to proceed so as to arrive off beach eastward of Dunkirk in following positions vide chart 1872 as close as possible to the shore at 2400/31.

Group One. Bray Dunes Hotel, 5 cables apart.
Group Two. La Panne light $4\frac{1}{2}$ cables apart.
Group Three. *Niger, Salamander,* Rosendael.
          Fitzroy, Sutton, battery longitude 02° 27′ E.
          Kellet, Saltash, spare ship between Groups One and Three and Groups One and Two respectively. *Lydd* is to make rendezvous, and if not required to complete Groups, to lie off Braye.

Troops will be brought off in three flights by waiting motor boats commencing at 0130 or earlier. Maximum speed of embarkation essential. Seven ocean tugs will lie to seaward of minesweepers to take overflow but maximum loading of ships is necessary to ensure complete evacuation. Group One is to return to Sheerness, Groups Two and Three to Dover. Spare ship to Harwich. Acknowledge.
                                                                                  0400/31

Note : The above signal was amended later—see Appendix Q.18.

2. S.N.O. DUNKIRK to VICE-ADMIRAL, DOVER

Every available ship will be required at Dunkirk during next 2 hours to evacuate rest of Army.
                                                                                  0445/31

3. REAR-ADMIRAL, DOVER to VICE-ADMIRAL, DOVER

Conditions on beach bad. On-shore wind. Whalers capsized.
                                                                                  0651/31

4. VICE-ADMIRAL, DOVER to ADMIRAL [LANDRIAU], *Savorgnan de Brazza*

Request you will send in all your available destroyers and ships to Dunkirk and to beaches at once.
                                                                                  0819/31

5. ADMIRAL [LANDRIAU] to VICE-ADMIRAL, DOVER

C.-in-C. Dover from French Admiral, Pas de Calais :

This night and tomorrow I continue maximum effort. I request support of aviation on Dunkirk tomorrow as today.
                                                                      T.O.R. 2104/31

6. REAR-ADMIRAL, DOVER to VICE-ADMIRAL, DOVER (R) Admiralty

Majority of boats are broached to and have no crews. Conditions on beach are very bad owing to freshening on-shore wind. Only small numbers are being embarked even in daylight. Under present conditions any large scale embarkation from beach is quite impracticable. Motor boats cannot get close in. Consider only hope of embarking any number is at Dunkirk. Will attempt to beach ship to form a lee to try to improve conditions.

1035/31

7. S.N.O. DUNKIRK to VICE-ADMIRAL, DOVER

Your 0855. We have been continuously and heavily bombarded and they are gradually finding the range of our loading berth. I would rather only enter ships which are necessary for the flow of troops.

1044/31

8. REAR-ADMIRAL, DOVER to VICE-ADMIRAL, DOVER

Dunkirk our only real hope. Can guns shelling pier from westward be bombed and silenced.

1105/31

9. VICE-ADMIRAL, DOVER to *Saltash, Queen of Thanet, Westward Ho, Devonia, Plinlimmon, Brighton Queen, Niger, Dundalk, Fitzroy, Speedwell,* N.O.I.C. Margate, C.S. Sheerness.

Ships carrying out Sheerness—La Panne ferry are now to run to Dunkerque beach and Margate instead. This service is to be maintained as long as possible while conforming to my 0400/31 [i.e. Appendix Q.1.].

1114/31

SIGNALS RE EVACUATION ON 31st MAY AND NIGHT OF 31st MAY—1st JUNE

10. ADMIRALTY to REAR-ADMIRAL, DOVER (R) V.A. Dover, S.N.O. Dunkirk

A paddle minesweeper suggests that much time could be saved if she puts her bows ashore on rising tide and she is then used as a bridge for deeper draught ships coming to her stern.

1134/31

11. VICE-ADMIRAL, DOVER to REAR-ADMIRAL, DOVER

Admiralty's 1134 :
Act on this if you judge conditions suitable.[1]

1151/31

12. VICE-ADMIRAL, DOVER to REAR-ADMIRAL, DOVER (R) S.N.O. Dunkirk

Officers and men of beach parties have returned to Dover under intructions from Dunkirk. All repeat all beach parties must be retained to the last.

1229/31

13. VICE-ADMIRAL, DOVER to *Worcester*

Embark beach parties and proceed when ready by Route X with all despatch. Land them as allocated and then continue evacuation from La Panne.

1308/31

14. VICE-ADMIRAL, DOVER to REAR-ADMIRAL, DOVER

Fresh beach parties are being sent in *Worcester* and have been allocated to beaches.

1405/31

---

[1] *Note :* The minesweeper *Devonia* was beached at about 1600.

15. VICE-ADMIRAL, DOVER to DESTROYERS (R) R.A. Dover

When there is room in Dunkirk harbour destroyers are to enter there in preference to beaches. R.A. Dover pass to S.N.O. Dunkirk.

1910/31

16. VICE-ADMIRAL, DOVER to REAR-ADMIRAL, DOVER (R) S.N.O. Dunkirk

Army wish to recommence evacuation at 2030. Instruct boats and ships to close beaches at this time.

1640/31

17. REAR-ADMIRAL, DOVER to VICE-ADMIRAL, DOVER

Weather off beaches now good. Many more boats should come into use again as tide rises. General movement of troops to westward towards Dunkirk. No petrol supply yet and many motor boats are getting short off La Panne and Bray. Movement from Dunkirk continues. Great air activity.

1707/31

Note : Actually, drifters with petrol arrived at 1815/31.

18. VICE-ADMIRAL, DOVER to *Gossamer, Halcyon, Niger, Lydd*

My 0400/31 [i.e. Appendix Q.1]. Cancel words " final " and " covering ". Cancel positions off beaches. Embarkation will take place from beach between long. 02° 29′ E., and long. 02° 36′ E.[1] Ships are to be evenly spread along this beach in order of Groups from east to west, Two, One, Three. First flight will leave beach at 0030 repetition 0030. *Lydd* take place of *Saltash.* Senior officers of Groups pass to remaining ships and acknowledge.

1904/31

[1] *Note :* Between Zuydcoote Sanatorium and 1 mile east of La Panne.

[See also next signal].

19. VICE-ADMIRAL, DOVER to SHIPS & AUTHORITIES NORE & DOVER COMMANDS

Military now desire that tonight's special evacuation should take place from beaches covered by 1 and 2 [?Groups] starting at 0030/1. Groups should be closed up to conform to this. Embark naval personnel from beaches 1 and 2 if practicable. Embarkation of French will continue tomorrow Saturday from the harbour and from Malo beach by British and French Ships. The final evacuation of the B.E.F. is is expected on the night 1st/2nd June. R.A. Dover acknowledge.

1920/31

20. D.19 [*Keith*] to VICE-ADMIRAL, DOVER

V.A. Dover, Captain Tennant, from R.A. Dover. Impossible to embark except Dunkirk and beaches immediately east.

1929/31

21. S.N.O. DUNKIRK to VICE-ADMIRAL, DOVER

No ships for the French and us. Please despatch.

2235/31

22. GENERAL LLOYD to DIRECTOR OF MILITARY OPERATIONS

Following is new plan :
General Alexander has been placed in command of final phase of evacuation. Composition of force not known. Tonight, the special transport force designed for lifting last flight of 4,000 is being concentrated on 2 eastern beaches. Tomorrow efforts are to be concentrated on French evacuation. It is impossible now to say how long this will take, but Alexander Force remains till last. V.A. Dover will provide maximum capacity for Alexander on beach just east of Dunkirk on night 1st/2nd June, or later if necessary ; details being arranged between Admiral Wake-Walker and Alexander. Naval Liaison Officer is being provided at Alexander's H.Q.

2309/31

APPENDIX R

SIGNALS RE EVACUATION ON 1st JUNE
AND NIGHT OF 1st-2nd JUNE

Saturday, 1st June

1. REAR-ADMIRAL, DOVER to VICE-ADMIRAL, DOVER

    Parachute mines are being dropped all over west of Bray. Request sweep of Dunkirk road.

    0047/1

2. REAR-ADMIRAL, DOVER to VICE-ADMIRAL, DOVER (R) Admiralty

    Yesterday ships off Bray were under fire. Today's shorter front will bring dangerous area westward. For this reason, and mining, consider any beach work too costly and evacuation must be confined to Dunkirk. Small craft will be moved westward at dawn.

    0235/1

3. VICE-ADMIRAL, DOVER to REAR-ADMIRAL, DOVER (R) *Halcyon, Skipjack, Speedwell, Sharpshooter*

    Troops from La Panne now marching towards Dunkirk. Act accordingly.

    0306/1

4. VICE-ADMIRAL, DOVER to REAR-ADMIRAL, DOVER

    We must take full advantage of low visibility to use beaches. Keep me informed on this point.

    0630/1

5. VICE-ADMIRAL, DOVER to GENERAL ALEXANDER, DUNKIRK (R) R.A. Dover, S.N.O. Dunkirk

    On the likely assumption that complete evacuation will be ordered tonight the problem of transport makes it essential to use both sides of harbour, pier and eastern beach.

    I am planning on these lines and for evacuation to start at 2200/1.

    0951/1 (as amended by 1044/1)

6. VICE-ADMIRAL, DOVER to DESTROYERS

    All destroyers are to return to harbour forthwith.

    1345/1

7. VICE-ADMIRAL, DOVER to C.-IN-C. NORE, N.O.I.C. HARWICH, COMMODORE in CHARGE, SHEERNESS, N.O.I.C. RAMSGATE, 1st, 4th, 5th, 6th M/S Flotillas

    All available ships operating under V.A. Dover of the minesweeping flotillas addressed, are required to assist in evacuation tonight Saturday.

    Ships to sail to arrive off the beach between Dunkirk and a point 1½ miles east, at 2200/1. Ships which have not D.G. equipment are not to sail. Ships report forthwith whether they can comply.

    1510/1

8. VICE-ADMIRAL, DOVER to GENERAL ALEXANDER, S.N.O. DUNKIRK. C.-IN-C. NORTHERN NAVAL FORCES (R) Admiralty

    Evacuation will take place tonight Saturday from

    (A) Beach betwween Dunkirk and 1½ miles to the eastward, between 2100/1 and 0300/2, for 9,000 men.

    (B) East Pier, between 2100/1 and 0330/2, for 7,000 men.

    (C) East side inside harbour, between 2200/1 and 0300/2, for 1,000 men.

All **naval** personnel are to be withdrawn this Saturday night.

Reference (B), time of termination of this evacuation may be extended and will be signalled.

1609/1

9. VICE-ADMIRAL, DOVER to DESTROYERS

Following destroyers are required for duty tonight.
Remainder revert to 2½ hours notice for steam :
Esk, Codrington, Icarus, Windsor, Venomous, Winchelsea, Whitshed, Sabre, Shikari.

1711/1

and later

10. Destroyers named in my 1711 will be addressed Force K.

1745/1

SIGNALS RE EVACUATION ON 1st JUNE AND NIGHT OF 1st/2nd JUNE

11. S.N.O. DUNKIRK to VICE-ADMIRAL, DOVER

Things are getting very hot for ships.   Over 100 bombers on ships near here since 0530.   Many casualties.

Have directed that no ships sail during daylight.   Evacuation by transports therefore ceases at 0300.   If perimeter holds, will complete evacuation tomorrow Sunday night, including most French.   General concurs.

1754/1

12. VICE-ADMIRAL, DOVER to FORCE K (R) R.A. Dover

Destroyers are to proceed in pairs at hourly intervals to berth on east pier Dunkirk harbour, returning to Dover when loaded.

If no vacant berth, V.A. Dover and next pair to be informed, and the destroyers to assist at beach instead.

The personnel vessels will also be berthing at east pier and have priority.

Destroyers to leave Dunkirk vicinity not later than 0300/2, Route X.   Route Z may be used during dark.

First pair to arrive Dunkirk 2200.

Pairs : *Windsor, Icarus.*
   Codrington, Sabre.
   Shikari, Esk.
   Winchelsea, Whitshed.

Caution is necessary owing to wrecks in Dunkirk harbour.

1810/1

13. VICE-ADMIRAL, DOVER to REAR-ADMIRAL, DOVER (R) S.N.O. Dunkirk

Enemy **action** bombing and shell fire make it impossible for personnel ships enter harbour in **daylight.**

1859/1

14. AIR MINISTRY to FIGHTER COMMAND, BOMBER COMMAND, COASTAL COMMAND, BACK C. B.E.F., WAR OFFICE, ADMIRALTY, VICE-ADMIRAL, DOVER

Confirming conversation between C.-in-C. and D.H.O.X. 153 1/6.

Situation at Dunkirk.
Two divisions French territorials reduced strength still to be evacuated.   Evacuation will continue in **any event** until tomorrow morning.   Strong continuous patrols should therefore be carried out over Dunkirk and beaches from 0430 to 0830 hours 2/6.

Last boat in the morning will leave Dunkirk before 0700 hours. If part of garrison still remains evacuation will recommence in the evening. If so, strong continuous patrols should be carried out over area from 1700 to 2100 hours, when operations will terminate night 1st/2nd June. Night fighters should patrol same area during hours of darkness. Fighter patrols should be routed out over area in which our ships are working between N. Foreland and Dunkirk, and on return journey should fly low on the same routeing to give vessels maximum protection against low flying bomb and machine gun attack.

1930/1

15. ADMIRALTY to REAR-ADMIRAL, DOVER STRAITS, S.N.O. DUNKIRK (R) V.A. Dover

    (A) Should there be a channel which it is possible to use during daylight hours, it is intended that evacuation from Dunkirk should proceed continuously from 2130 tonight Saturday until 0700 tomorrow Sunday.

    (B) Continuous air protection will be provided from daylight tomorrow Sunday until 0830 by fighters, and from 0830 until 1100 by Coastal Command.

    (C) It will be decided tomorrow Sunday forenoon in the light of the naval and military situation as to whether evacuation is to continue tomorrow Sunday night.

    (D) It may also be necessary to carry out evacuation from 1730 tomorrow Sunday until dark, should evacuation in daylight still be possible.

    (E) From the above it will be seen that there will be no ships proceeding to Dunkirk between 0700 and 1730 tomorrow Sunday.

    (F) Request you will inform Admiral Abrial and General Alexander of the above arrangements.

    (G) Should it be impossible to use any of the 3 Channels from Dunkirk owing to shell (R) shell fire from coast batteries you are to inform Admiralty . . . .

T.O.D. 2021/1

16. ADMIRALTY to VICE-ADMIRAL, DOVER

    (a) Embarkation of troops from Dunkirk is to proceed continuously from 2130 today Saturday until 0700 tomorrow Sunday.

    (b) Strong and continuous fighter protection will be provided from 0430 until 0830 tomorrow Sunday.

    (c) Protection by Coastal Command will be provided from 0830 until 1100.

    (d) It is hoped that the evacuation may be completed tonight but should this not be possible, you should be prepared for further evacuation tomorrow Sunday night.

    (e) It may be necessary to carry out evacuation from 1730 tomorrow Sunday in addition to the night evacuation.

    (f) Should it be decided that the conditions are such that evacuation cannot be carried out between 0300 tomorrow Sunday and 0700 tomorrow Sunday, you will be informed.

T.O.D. 2025/1
T.O.R. 2044/1

17. VICE-ADMIRAL, DOVER to S.N.O. DUNKIRK

Evacuation tonight Saturday from west end of beach and from harbour only, to cease at 0300.

Can embark about 9,000 from beach if weather remains calm. Lighters and destroyers will enter harbour.

2045/1

18. VICE-ADMIRAL, DOVER to ADMIRALTY, C.-IN-C. NORTHERN NAVAL FORCES
GENERAL ALEXANDER, S.N.O. DUNKIRK

My 1609/1 [Appx. R.8] and S.N.O. Dunkirk 1754/1 [Appx. R.11] :

Casualties to shipping are now being caused by heavy artillery. All shipping
has been ordered to withdraw before daylight tomorrow Sunday.

2214/1

19. VICE-ADMIRAL, DOVER to ADMIRALTY

A.M. 2025/1 [Appx. R.16] paras. (a) to (f), S.N.O. Dunkirk 1754/1 stating
General concurs that evacuation for transports is to cease at 0300 :
Channels to Dunkirk now all under fire of German batteries. New battery came
into action this evening, suspending traffic on only remaining daylight route,
namely X, maintaining heavy barrage, sinking transports *Mona's Queen* and
Brighton Queen[1] and a trawler in the fairway near No. 5 buoy.

French destroyer nearby turned back *Royal Daffodil* and " Royal Scot " [?*Royal
Sovereign*]. Eight transports have now been lost and eight disabled. Crews of
others difficult to keep on service.

The above facts coupled with recent naval losses and also military losses by
drowning have convinced me that any attempt to continue evacuation during the
day is unwise. Permission is therefore requested in accordance with A.M. 2021/1
[Appx. R.15] para. (G) to withdraw all forces at 0300 until the following night.

2329/1

Sunday, 2nd June

20. VICE-ADMIRAL, DOVER to S.N.O. DUNKIRK
Admiralty has directed that evacuation by personnel steamers from Dunkirk
pier shall continue until 0700.

0055/2

21. ADMIRALTY to VICE-ADMIRAL, DOVER (R) R.A. Dover Straits, S.N.O. Dunkirk

Your 2329/1 :
(a) Evacuation up to 0700 in accordance with Admiralty telegram 2025/1 to
    V.A. Dover, and 2021/1 to R.A. Dover Straits and S.N.O. Dunkirk, is to be
    carried out using destroyers only.

(b) Destroyers to be ready to open fire on any batteries.

(c) If further experience shows that the channel is prohibitively dangerous due
    to gunfire, evacuation by day is to cease and Admiralty informed immediately.

0115/2

22. VICE-ADMIRAL, DOVER to FORCE K
Evacuation by destroyers is to continue until 0700 from Dunkirk harbour. Transports are to leave Dunkirk at 0300. Destroyers inform transports. Fire of shore
batteries should be returned.

0125/2

23. *Winchelsea* to VICE-ADMIRAL, DOVER

Your 0055 and your 1729/1 not passed to S.N.O. Dunkirk.

0416/2

24. S.N.O. DUNKIRK to VICE-ADMIRAL, DOVER (R) Admiralty, War Office

Your 1609/1/6 [Appendix R.8] not received until 0430. Large proportion naval
personnel evacuated. Estimated approximately 20,000 British and French evacuated, greater (proportion ?) being French.

---

[1] No transports were sunk by gunfire on 1st June. The *Mona's Queen* was sunk
by magnetic mine on 29th May ; the A.B/V *Mona's Isle* was straddled by shore
guns on 1st June and sustained some damage. The minesweeper *Brighton Queen*
was sunk by aircraft on 1st June. The minesweeper *Sandown* came under fire of
Nieuport guns on 31st May.

There remain to be evacuated night 2/3 probably 5,000 British and approximately 30,000 French.

Request more transport for tomorrow's operation than was provided for tonight. Request . . . M.A/S . . . boats. Sappers, General, S.N.O. and remainder naval personnel (will leave ?) 2300 hours.

T.O.R. 0704/2

25. GENERAL LLOYD to WAR OFFICE M.O.4

Information is difficult to obtain and often contradictory. General Martel reports little pressure on his front yesterday but there is less reliable evidence to show that pressure on some points elsewhere was severe.

Most personnel evacuated last night were from pier. Shell fire on beach was apparently bad as have been given names of 3 officers killed there.

Estimated numbers so far reported landed Dover and Ramsgate since midnight 10,600 of which about 1/3 French.

Three personnel ships and many smaller craft not reported 0800 hours.

Numbers remaining 458 area impossible estimate. Might be in region 2,000 British.

0815/2

APPENDIX S

SIGNALS RE DELIBERATE ATTACKS ON HOSPITAL SHIPS ON 2nd JUNE

Sunday, 2nd June

1. DUNKIRK to DOVER W/T [Sent *en clair*]

Wounded situation acute. Hospital ships should enter during day.

Geneva Convention will be honourably observed. It is felt that the enemy will refrain from attack.

0730/2

2. VICE-ADMIRAL, DOVER to ADMIRALTY

Hospital carriers *Worthing* and *Paris* have been deliberately bombed and severely damaged today by Germans in circumstances admitting of no mistake of their identity.

2016/2

APPENDIX T

SIGNALS RE THE EVACUATION OF THE BRITISH REAR GUARD ON NIGHT 2nd/3rd JUNE

Sunday, 2nd June

1. H.M.S. LYDD to REAR-ADMIRAL (R) V.A. Dover, Force K, Minesweepers

Brigadier tells me that C.-in-C. says it is essential that rear guard B.E.F. embarks from beaches east of mole on account of French congestion on mole. Considerable number of British troops still on mole. Military are (? expecting) further arrivals there. Rear guard expects to arrive on beach by 0230.

0040/2

2. S.N.O. DUNKIRK to VICE-ADMIRAL, DOVER (R) War Office
. . . About 5,000 British remain . . . Sporting chance of embarking tonight. Maximum number of fast motor boats at 2130 at inner end of long pier would assist.

T.O.R. 0830/2

3. VICE-ADMIRAL, DOVER to DESTROYERS AND MINESWEEPERS

The final evacuation is staged for tonight, and the Nation looks to the Navy to see this through.

I want every ship to report as soon as possible whether she is fit to meet the call which has been made on our courage and endurance.

1052/2

4. VICE-ADMIRAL, DOVER to DESTROYERS, PADDLE SWEEPERS, PERSONNEL VESSELS (R) S.N.O. Dunkirk

Evacuation tonight 2nd June will be from Dunkirk harbour, ships berthing on east pier.

Following berths established if required (?) from north to south :

Berth A : from lighthouse to trawler wreck.
  ,,   B : from wreck to gap in pier.
  ,,   C : from gap in wall to hut at end of pier.
Berths
D & E : smaller berths extending to the inner end of pier.

In addition, berth on east side of east pier.   This berth will not normally be used unless all inside berths are occupied.

Pier master will direct berthing from east pier, and ships entering will be guided by a motor boat.

Ships are to work special brows and ladders which will be supplied at Dover, and have boxes ready to form steps . . . . Intention is to keep berths A to E constantly filled.

1430/2

5. VICE-ADMIRAL, DOVER to DESTROYERS

My 1430/2.   Destroyers are to sail to arrive at Dunkirk as follows :
2100—*Shikari* and *Sabre.*
2130—*Venomous.*
2200—*Windsor.*
2230—*Icarus.*
2300—*Winchelsea.*
2330—*Esk.*
2400—*Vanquisher.*
0030—*Codrington.*
0100—*Express.*
0130—*Vivacious*[1].
0200—*Whitshed.*
0230—*Malcolm.*

Acknowledge.

1715/2

SIGNALS RE THE EVACUATION OF THE BRITISH REAR GUARD ON NIGHT
2ND/3RD JUNE

Sunday, 2nd June—contd.

6. VICE-ADMIRAL, DOVER to MINESWEEPERS (R) C.-in-C. Nore, F.O.I.C. Harwich, Cdre. i/c Sheerness

Ships evacuating tonight Sunday are to sail to arrive off Dunkirk as follows :

From Margate : 2100 to 2230.
From Sheerness : 2230 to 2359.
From Dover : 0001 to 0130.
From Harwich : 0130 to 0200.

---

[1] *Vivacious* had, however, been detailed to take part in a blocking operation.

Times of arrival of ships in each group to be staggered.

Ships to berth at inner end of eastern arm as directed by traffic control motor boat. Red Very's light stops entry. Green Very's light allows entry.

1548/2

7. S.N.O. Dunkirk to Vice-Admiral, Dover (R) Admiralty

B.E.F. evacuated. Returning now.

2330/2

APPENDIX U

SIGNALS RE EVACUATION ON 3rd JUNE

Monday, 3rd June

1. Air Ministry to Fighter Command, Coastal Command, Back Violet, V.A. Dover (R) Admiralty, War Office

X.334 3/6.

This signals confirms arrangements made by telephone for providing fighter protection for Dunkirk and shipping in evacuation over the period 1930 hours 3rd June to 0800 hours 4th June.

Coastal Command to provide protection for shipping between Dover and Dunkirk during period 1930 hours till dark.

Fighter Command to maintain continuous patrol—strength one Blenheim fighter—over Dunkirk area during hours of darkness.

Fighter protection to be provided over Dunkirk area and shipping in the channel from 0430 hours to 0800 hours 4th June, protection to be provided by Fighter Command followed by Coastal Command; times to be concerted with C-in-C. concerned by Back Violet.

1850/3

APPENDIX V

SIGNAL RE THE DECISION TO TERMINATE THE EVACUATION AFTER THE NIGHT OF 3rd-4th JUNE

Monday, 3rd June

1. Vice-Admiral, Dover to Admiralty (R) C.-in-C. Nore

After nine days of operations of a nature unprecedented in naval warfare, which followed on two weeks of intense strain, commanding officers, officers and ships companies are at the end of their tether.

I therefore view a continuance of the demands made by evacuation with the utmost concern as likely to strain to breaking point the endurance of officers and men.

I should fail in my duty did I not represent to Their Lordships the existence of this state of affairs in the ships under my command, and I consider it would be unfortunate, after the magnificent manner in which officers and men of the surviving ships have faced heavy loss and responded to every call made upon them, that they should be subjected to a test which I feel may be beyond the limit of human endurance.

If therefore evacuation has to be continued after tonight I would emphasise in the strongest possible manner that fresh forces should be used for these operations, and any consequent delay in their execution should be accepted.

1344/3

2. ADMIRALTY (1ST SEA LORD) to B.N.L.O. MARCEAU (R) V.A. Dover

    Pass to Admiral Darlan from 1st Sea Lord.

    I urge most strongly that evacuation be completed tonight, as after nine days of continuous work of this nature officers and men of both H.M. Ships and merchant ships are completely exhausted. Request early confirmation that evacuation will be completed tonight, and number to be evacuated.

1512/3

3. B.N.L.O. MARCEAU to ADMIRALTY (1ST SEA LORD), VICE-ADMIRAL, DOVER

    French Admiralty agree that evacuation should be terminated tonight, if possible, and estimate approximately 30,000 men remaining.

    In French opinion, only competent authorities are now Admiral Abrial and V.A. Dover.

    Captain de Revoir[1], and officer from V.A. Dover are en route Dunkirk to inform Admiral Abrial of plans for termination evacuation. These officers should keep V.A. Dover informed of numbers involved as French Admiralty unable to communicate Dunkirk.

1651/3

APPENDIX W

SIGNALS RE THE BUILD-UP OF SHIPS FOR THE NIGHT OF 3rd/4th JUNE

I. DESTROYERS

Monday, 3rd June

1. VICE-ADMIRAL, DOVER to DESTROYERS, MINESWEEPERS, AUXILIARY VESSELS

    I hoped and believed that last night would see us through but the French who were covering the retirement of the British rearguard had to repel a strong German attack and so were unable to send their troops to the pier in time to be embarked.

    We cannot leave our Allies in the lurch and I must call on all officers and men detailed for further evacuation tonight to let the world see that we never let down our ally.

    The approach will be made later and the retirement earlier. The night protection of our fighters which stopped all bombing of the harbour last night will be repeated.

1009/3

    [Here see Appendices Y.18, Y.19 and Y.22.]

V. DISPOSITION OF SHIPS

2. VICE-ADMIRAL, DOVER to FORCE K, MINESWEEPERS, *Locust, Guillemot, Kingfisher*

    Dunkirk evacuation tonight Monday.

From East Pier	by personnel vessels, destroyers and paddle minesweepers.
From West pier *New outer port*	by other minesweepers, corvettes, skoots and French vessels.
Inner harbour	Drifters and small craft.

    All ships to leave by 0230/4. *Locust* will remain outside entrance receiving loads ferried out by small boats. Tugs will be available outside Dunkirk.

1440/3

---

    [1] French Naval Attaché.

APPENDIX X

SIGNALS RE EVACUATION ON 4th JUNE

Tuesday, 4th June

1. ADMIRALTY to C.-IN-C. HOME FLEET, VICE-ADMIRAL, DOVER, V.A.S., C.-IN-C. ROSYTH, C.-IN-C. NORE, C.-IN-C. PORTSMOUTH, C.-IN-C. WESTERN APPROACHES, C.S.2, C.S.

Operation Dynamo now completed.

1423/4

APPENDIX Y

SIGNALS RE THE EVACUATION OF FRENCH AND BELGIAN TROOPS

Wednesday, 29th May

1. ADMIRALTY to VICE-ADMIRAL, DOVER (R) N.O.I.C. Ramsgate

There are a certain number of Belgian troops at La Panne who ask permission to embark in British ships in order to join Allies. As we are using Belgian ships and crews for our own embarkation this request must be acceded to and instructions should be given accordingly.

1347/29

2. S.N.O. DUNKIRK to VICE-ADMIRAL, DOVER (R) Admiralty

Bombing of beaches and Dunkirk pier has now commenced without opposition from fighters. If they hit Dunkirk pier embarkation will become very jammed. Beach at La Panne covered with troops congregating in large numbers. Very slow emarkbation taking place from eastern beach. The French staff at Dunkirk feel strongly that they are defending Dunkirk for us to evacuate which is largely true...

1358/29

Note : The above signal was made by S.N.O. Dunkirk when he was in the *Express* off La Panne.

Friday, 31st May

3. ADMIRALTY to VICE-ADMIRAL, DOVER, REAR-ADMIRAL, DOVER STRAITS, S.N.O. Dunkirk.

The policy of H.M. Govt. is that both British and French troops be given equal opportunities for being evacuated in British ships and boats.

0104/31

4. S.N.O. DUNKIRK to VICE-ADMIRAL, DOVER (R) Admiralty, R.A. Dover

Am now receiving a number of Frenchmen. I have at present raised no objection to their embarking in British ships and am allowing them to do so.

0638/31

Saturday, 1st June

5. SECRETARY OF STATE FOR WAR to C.-IN-C. 1ST CORPS

You will appreciate importance from point of view of future Anglo-French relations embarking as large a proportion of French as is humanly possible today. I am sure that we can count upon you to help us in this.

0131/1

6. War Office to Madelon (R) British Commander, Dunkirk

> Following for General Weygand from C.I.G.S.

> All evidence, naval and military, shows that every effort must be made to complete evacuation tonight. Strongly urge that Admiral Abrial be instructed to co-operate in this effort in the interest of our two Armies.

> Only remaining channel now coming under fire of German guns, which will put an end to all evacuation by day indefinitely.
>
>   1330/1

7. C.I.G.S. to S.N.O. Dunkirk

> Following for General Alexander.

> We do not order any fixed moment for evacuation. You are to hold on as long as possible in order that the maximum number of French and British may be evacuated. Impossible from here to judge local situation. In close co-operation with Admiral Abrial you must act in this matter on your own judgement.
>
>   1729/1

8. S.N.O. Dunkirk to Vice-Admiral, Dover For C.I.G.S.

> Ref. 1858 from C.I.G.S.

> Withdrawal now proceeding according to plan. Shall have certain reserves here tomorrow to assist French. Intend to complete evacuation tomorrow by midnight.
>
>   2315/1

SIGNALS RE THE EVACUATION OF FRENCH AND BELGIAN TROOPS

9. S.N.O. Dunkirk to Vice-Admiral, Dover (R) Admiralty

> Reference S.N.O.'s 2315 from General [Alexander] ;
> Request again maximum number transports for British and French at 2130 June 2nd.

> It is intended that all British shall be evacuated by midnight. Request M.A/S.B. if possible for General at 2300.
>
>   0400/2

Sunday, 2nd June

10. French Admiral Pas De Calais to Admiral, C.-in-C. Dover

> Message received *Savorgnan* :

> Received new orders from French Admiralty to try resume evacuation by daytime. I ask opinion Admiral Dunkirk. Do you intend to operate by daytime as well as night.
>
>   0525/2

11. Vice-Admiral, Dover to French Admiral Pas De Calais (Pass via *Savorgnan*)

> Your 0525. No. By night only.
>
>   0811/2

12. Vice-Admiral, Dover to S.N.O. Dunkirk, Admiral Du Nord (R) Admiralty

> Following are the arrangements for final evacuation British and French tonight Sunday.

> Maximum numbers of transports, destroyers and minesweepers will be employed to evacuate from pier and harbour ; the first ships arriving at 2100 the remainder following at close intervals. In addition French are making own arrangements for embarking from beach and west pier in new harbour.

Transport for General will be sent as you asked for.

Arrange for Lewis to direct ships at entrance again. Clouston[1] is coming over as pier master with details of plan. Good luck to you all.

1251/2

13. S.N.O. to Vice-Admiral, Dover (R) War Office

French still maintain front line except for front east of Bergues where the Germans have penetrated 2 miles on a 2 mile front. Counter attack being made at 1500. In port, no movement. Present situation hopeful.

1538/2

and later

14.   Military situation : French counter-attack postponed until 2000. Remainder of front quiet. Bombers will probably be (playing ?) evening (hymn ?).

1840/2

15. Admiral Nord to Admiral Dover

Part One. If during night of 2nd/3rd June 30,000 men can be evacuated, I hope to be able to try on the night of 3rd/4th June to withdraw the 35,000 men who are defending the bridgehead.

Part Two. In order to embark these troops quickly after retirement, numerous boats will be required along east pier, Embecquetage, and Quai Felix Faure ; also boats and small craft to embark 6,000 men on the beach between Malo-les-Bains and Malo Terminus.

Part Three. This evening all British officers will leave Dunkirk but the help of British naval Officers will be essential during the night of 3rd/4th June to direct British ships.

Part Four. If this programme could be carried out, the blocking of harbour could take place at the end of the night of 3rd/4th June.[2] I will keep you and Rear-Admiral Dover Straits advised of my intentions.

Part Five. I shall require help of British fast motor boats to assist in the conduct of operations of evacuation, a great number of French fast motor boats being damaged.

1610/1

16. S.N.O. Dunkirk to Vice-Admiral, Dover

Have promised French I will press for shipping for them tomorrow night when they hope to evacuate 15,000. Reply Admiral Nord.

1735/2

17. War Ofice to General Alexander (R) S.N.O. Dunkirk

Understand from French that another night will be required to complete the evacuation altogether. If British troops are entirely evacuated tonight, conclude this is with concurrence of Admiral Nord.

2037/2

Monday, 3rd June

18. Rear-Admiral, Dover in *M.A/S.B.10* to Vice-Admiral, Dover

Four ships now alongside east pier but no French troops.

0030/3

[Here see Appendix Y.22].

---

[1] *Seaplane tender 243,* in which Cdr. Clouston was taking passage, was bombed en route and sunk. Cdr. J. C. Clouston, R.N., was lost.
[2] See Appendix Z.3.

19. REAR-ADMIRAL, DOVER to VICE-ADMIRAL, DOVER

Plenty of **ships cannot get troops.**

0115/3

and later

20. Ships in harbour will not be filled by 0300. Am returning to Dover. Waiting outside.

0200/3

21. CAPTAIN D.20 [*Express*] to VICE-ADMIRAL, DOVER

Ordered to return. No troops.

0250/3

22. ADMIRAL NORD to ADMIRAL LANDRIAU, Pass to Admiral Dover

2140/2/6.
Primo. Enemy attacked yesterday from East Berghes [?Bergues] and again today and advanced as far as Teteghen.
We have counter-attacked and regained ground. Counter-attack will continue tomorrow.

Secundo. On bridgehead partial attack has been repulsed.

Tertio. Enemy has occupied Berghes [?Bergues] without advancing further.

Quarto. General Jansenne killed.

Quinto. Last British elements have embarked.

Sexto. As attacks most probable today, situation concerning munitions may become critical and may oblige evacuation troops to which (group undeciphered) embarkation of all advanced troops (group undeciphered) and obtainable.

Note : The above signal was timed 2140/2/6, and was passed to V.A. Dover, with the following addition.

Admiral Landriau understands that this attack explains delay in bringing French troops to the pier.

French destroyers *Bouclier* and *Flore* delayed for one hour forty. Admiral Landriau begs on account of delay to send if possible more fighters this morning.

0403/3/6

[Here see Appendix W.1].

23. VICE-ADMIRAL, DOVER to ADMIRAL NORD (R) French Admiral in harbour

My intentions for tonight 3rd/4th are to provide a maximum effort with available remaining ships between 2230/3 and 0230/4.

We shall send ships to entire length of eastern pier as fast as possible capable of accommodation for 14,000 men. We will assist with ships at the western pier in the Avant Port to the extent of accommodation for 5,000 men. In addition, French ships will be responsible for evacuation from the Malo beach, Quai Felix Faure, and the New Avant Port for which I cannot estimate numbers.

I will land officers and men on the eastern pier. A British M.T.B. will be at your disposal from 2200.

I would be deeply grateful if special arrangements could be made to evacuate as many British wounded as possible in return for the British effort on behalf of the French Army.

1108/3

193

APPENDIX Z

SIGNALS RE OPERATION C.K. —
THE BLOCKING OF DUNKIRK INNER HARBOUR

Sunday, 2nd June

1. S.N.O. DUNKIRK to VICE-ADMIRAL, DOVER

Admiral Nord requests that blockships will arrive at entrance at 0300 tomorrow night. He will signal if their placing is to be postponed.

0405/2

2. ADMIRALTY to VICE-ADMIRAL, DOVER, REAR-ADMIRAL, DOVER STRAITS, S.N.O. DUNKIRK

My 1600/31st May, not to S.N.O. Dunkirk. Operation is to be carried out, forces sailing from the Downs about 1900 today Sunday. E.T.A. Dunkirk roads 0200 3rd June.

Final order to block is to be given by Captain Dangerfield who will enter Dunkirk ahead of forces and consult with Admiral Nord as necessary.

Owing to the tide, blockships cannot enter Dunkirk harbour after 0300 on night 2nd/3rd June.

1300/2

3. ADMIRALTY to S.N.O. DUNKIRK (R) V.A. Dover, R.A. Dover Straits

French now state that following has been received from Admiral Nord.

" Evacuation will not be completed during the night of 2nd/3rd. Blocking of Dunkirk must not take place for the moment".

We hope, however, to complete evacuation tonight and blockships are being sent. Captain Dangerfield has orders to proceed to Dunkirk in advance of blockships and get in touch with Admiral Nord and arrange time of blocking with him.

1552/2

[Here see Appendix Y.15].

Monday, 3rd June

4. *Vivacious* to ADMIRALTY (R) VICE-ADMIRAL, DOVER

Operation C.K. completed. Two blockships[1] sunk between breakwater, but regret obstruction of channel not achieved.

T.O.R. 0445/3

[1] The two blockships were the *Westcove* and *Edvard Nissen*. The third blockship, the *Holland*, was lost en route.

5. ADMIRALTY to VICE-ADMIRAL, DOVER, REAR-ADMIRAL, DOVER STRAITS

My 1300/2 [Appx. Z.2]. Operation is to be repeated tonight June 3rd, forces sailing from the downs about 2000 today Monday. E.T.A. Dunkirk roads 0130/4.

1158/3

RESTRICTED

INDEX

References are to pages.

Fighter Command. *See* Royal Air Force.
Fisher, Cdr. R. L., 36-7.
Fisher Boy, 32*n*, 51*n*.
Fitzroy, 31, 54*n*.
Fletcher, Lt., 81.
Fog, 115, 118-9.
Folkestone, mined, 38.
Force K, 97.
Ford, Ch. Mech. F. A., saves *Whippingham*, 87.
Ford R.N.A. Station, 71*n*
Forecast, 23*n*, 107*n*, 114*n*.
Foremost 87, 71*n*, 111.
Foremost 101, 72*n*.
Foremost 102, 71*n*.
Foudroyant, 62*n*, 91-2 (sunk).
Fouque, Capt. de Freg. R., 62.
Franklyn, Maj.-Gen. H. E., 6.
Frazer, Capt. Hon. G., 97.
Fredanja, 29*n*.
French Navy.   Failure to supply pier parties, 109.
French ships arrive, 35, 62.
French troops : evacuation begins, 35 ; rush boats, 45, 51, 53 ; organised evacuation not
    begun, 54 ; to embark equally with British, 56, 68 ; lack of information from, 84 ;
    uncertainty as to numbers, 105 ; pause in embarkation, 108 ; slow to embark, 128 ;
    12,000 left, 120 ; discipline, 128.
Friso, 29*n*, 31*n*.
Fyldea, 13*n*, 39, 40*n*, 44.

Gallant, 23, 24*n*, 27, 32, 39 (damaged), 55*n* ; her motor boat, 110.
Gallion's Reach, 72*n*.
Gallon, Ch. Stkr. M., 91.
Gandell, Cdre., W. P., P.S.T.O. French Ports, 13.
Gara, 92.
Genius, 71*n*.
Georges, General, 1.
Gerard Léon, 73.
Gervais Rentoul, 83*n* (damaged), 95 (sunk).
Getuigt vor Christus, lost, 110.
Gipsy King, 72*n*.
Girl Gladys, 23*n*, 62.
Girl Pamela, 23*n*, 55 (sunk).
Glagla, 71*n*, 74.
Glen Avon, 60*n*, 100-1.
Glen Gower, 60*n*, 100-1.
Glenway, 71*n*, 107*n*.
Glitter II, 31*n*, 53 (towed to England).
Godman, S/Lt., T. E., R.N.V.R., 72.
Golden Eagle, 42, 107*n*.
Golden Gift, 23*n*.
Golden Lily, 54, 60*n*.
Golden Spray II, 72*n*, 75*n*.
Golden Sunbeam, 23*n*, 47*n*, 62, 107*n*.
Goliath, 114.
Gort, Lord : faces possibility of evacuation, 4 ; proposal to counter attack, 5, 11, 14, 27 ;
    directed to execute Weygand Plan, 10 ; delays enemy, 26 ; moves H.Q. to La Panne,
    26 ; refuses to be evacuated, 47 ; orders piers to be built, 47 ; plans for final phase,
    56 ; hands over command and embarks, 66, 76 ; staff embarking, 67.
Gorton, Cdr. H. G., 49, 80*n*.
Gossamer, 28*n*, 33, 36, 75, 77, 81, 107*n*, 109.
Gould, Lieut. P. F. S., 113.
Gourko, 119-20.
Gracie Fields, 23*n*, 27, 41-2 (abandoned), 47*n*.
Grafton, 13 (bombards Calais) ; in **Dynamo**, **23**, **27**, **31**, **37-8** (sunk), 55*n*, 85.
Gravelines, evacuated, 18.
Gravesend, sends small craft, 61.
Greater London, 117.

NOTE TO TABLES 1–3

DISEMBARKATION FIGURES

1. There is a discrepancy of 397 between the military figure of troops disembarked in the U.K. during the period of Operation "Dynamo", 27th May—4th June, 308,491 (*c*), and the figure computed by H.S./T.S.D., 308,888 (*f*).

War Office figure (A.G. Stats.) 20 May—4 June	336,427 (*a*)
Subtract figure of pre-"Dynamo" disembarkations (20—26 May), to equate with naval period ...	27,936 (*b*)
	308,491 (*c*)
H.S./T.S.D. figure 27 May—4 June	338,226 (*d*)
Subtract figures for troops disembarked from French (22,160), Belgian (3,464), Dutch (214), and Norwegian (3,500) ships which are apparently not included in the military figure (*a*) ...	29,338 (*e*)
	308,888 (*f*)

2. H.S./T.S.D. figures (*d*) (*e*) are based on check of all ships' reports (British, French, Belgian, Dutch, Norwegian), but the unduly high percentage of round figures in the reports leads to the conclusion that some of these figures are approximate. The comparable figure to (*d*) in the Despatch of Vice-Admiral Dover, M.011883/40, Appendix III, is 338,682 (*g*), but it is there noted (p. 55) that the List is not necessarily complete and the numbers shown against each vessel are often approximate only.

3. The Dover Report, M.011883/40, Appendix IV and V also gives figures based on the daily disembarkations at ports in the U.K. from 27th May to 5th June as follows :—

Accumulated total excluding ambulance traffic ...	309,682 (*h*)
Subtract troops disembarked on 5th June	1,096 (*i*)
	308,586 (*j*)
Add Hospital carriers and ambulance train totals ...	6,981 (*k*)
Add French troops disembarked in U.K. from French ships	20,525 (*l*)
	336,092 (*m*)

(The disembarkations from Belgian, Dutch and Norwegian vessels are presumed to be included in (*l*)).

4. The Admiralty in a message V.C.N.S. 251300B May, 1943, to B.A.D. Washington for 1st S.L. (*War Diary*) gave sets of figures as follows :—

V.A. Dover's figures—British troops		193,568 (*n*)
Allied troops		123,095 (*o*)
	TOTAL	316,663 (*p*)
Lord Gort's figures—British troops		224,585 (*q*)
Allied troops		112,546 (*r*)
		337,131 (*s*)

(The following corrections apparently need to be applied to (*p*) and (*s*) in order to equate them with one another and with (*c*) and (*f*).

V.A. Dover's figure	316,663 (*p*)
Subtract hospital carrier and ambulance traffic ...	6,981 (*i*)
	309,682 (*h*)
Subtract troops disembarked on 5th June	1,096 (*i*)
	308,586 (*j*)
Lord Gort's figure	337,131 (*s*)
Subtract pre-Dynamo date figure	27,936 (*b*)
	309,195 (*t*)

which compares with 308,491 (*c*) and 308,888 (*f*)).

5. The total figure of troops disembarked from British ships in ports in the United Kingdom during the period of Operation Dynamo, as given by the War Office (A.G. Stats.) viz. 308,491 (*c*) is considered the most nearly correct. It differs from the total computed by H.S./T.S.D. by 397 (=0.0013%).

210

TABLES

TABLE 1

AN ANALYSIS OF THE ALLIED SHIPS WHICH TOOK PART IN OPERATION DYNAMO, AND OF THE RECORDED NUMBERS OF TROOPS LIFTED BY THEM FROM DUNKIRK HARBOUR AND THE BEACHES.

Table I

	British Ships employed in Dynamo					Troops landed in England		
	Evacuating troops	Patrols and other duties	Total	Lost	Put out of action[1]	From the Beaches	From the Harbour	Total
Cruiser	1	–	1	–	–	1,856	–	1,856
Destroyers	39	2	41	6	17	25,901	70,296	96,197
Sloop	1	–	1	–	1	436	–	436
Corvettes	2	4	6	–	1	271	829	1,100
Gunboats	2	–	2	1	–	2,046	1,466	3,512
Minesweepers	36	–	36	5	8	28,705	17,729	46,434
Trawlers	26	26	52	12	3	1,515	3,881	5,396
Drifters	51	10	61	5	3	6,271	6,099	12,370
Special Service Vessels	3	–	3	1	–	3,507	901	4,408
M.A./S.Bs., M.T.Bs. etc.	4	9	13	–	–	26	73	99
Armed Boarding Vessels	3	–	3	1	–	–	4,848	4,848
Skoots	39	1	40	4	4	15,414	7,284	22,698
Yachts	26	–	26	3	3	745	3,936	4,681
Personnel Vessels	45	–	45	8	3	5,087	82,723	87,810
Hospital Carriers	8	–	8	1	2	–	3,006	3,006
Naval M/Bs	12	–	12	6	1	2	94	96
Tugs	22	18	40	3	3	1,654	1,510	3,164
Landing Craft	13	–	13	8	5	118	–	118
War Dept. M/Ls	8	–	8	–	3	200	379	579
Dockyard Lighters	8	–	8	2	–	418	–	418
Steam Hopper Barges	7	–	7	1	–	890	1,276	2,166
Auxiliary Barges, etc.	8	–	8	–	–	706	550	1,256
Sailing Barges	25	–	25	9	–	886	–	886
R.N.L.I. lifeboats	19	–	19	1	–	172	151	323
M/Bs, M/Ls. etc.	203	–	203	81	–	1,928	3,103	5,031
Blockships	–	6	6	2[2]	–	–	–	–
Seaplane tenders	6	–	6	3	–	–	–	–
Life-boats	56	–	56	39	–	–	–	–
Wherries, punts and dinghies	16	–	16	16	–	–	–	–
Totals	689	76	765	218	57	98,754	210,134	308,888

[1] By enemy action, by collision or by grounding.

[2] Sunk en route.

TABLE 1 (continued)

AN ANALYSIS OF THE ALLIED SHIPS WHICH TOOK PART IN OPERATION DYNAMO, AND OF THE RECORDED NUMBERS OF TROOPS LIFTED BY THEM FROM DUNKIRK HARBOUR AND THE BEACHES.

French Ships in Dynamo

Destroyers		2	2	3	1	–	19³ / 6,627	6,646
Torpedo Boats	12	–	12	–	–	–	1,000	1,000
Sloops	2	3	5	–	–	–	2,038	2,038
Minesweeping sloops	2	–	2	–	1	6	197	203
Submarine chasers	5	–	5	–	2	–	–	–
M.T.Bs.	2	–	2	–	–	–	–	–
Minesweeping trawlers	13	2	13	5	–	–	2,665	2,665
Patrol vessels	5	4	7	–	–	–	2,504	2,504
Cargo ships	8	–	12	2	–	–	2,290	2,290
Trawlers and M.F.Vs.	59	–	59	3	–	1	4,813	4,814
Totals	108	11	119	13	4	7	22,153	22,160

Belgian Ships Employed in Dynamo

Patrol boat	1	–	1	–	–	–	229	229
Tug	1	–	1	–	–	–	183	183
Trawlers	43	–	43	4	–	–	3,052	3,052
Totals	45	–	45	4	–	–	3,464	3,464

Polish Ship Employed in Dynamo

Destroyer	1	1	1	–	–	–	–	–

Dutch Ship Employed in Dynamo

Yacht	1	–	1	–	–	–	214	214
M/L	1	–	1	–	–	–	–	–
Totals	2	–	2	–	–	–	214	214

Norwegian Ship Employed in Dynamo

Freighter	1	–	1	–	–	–	3,500	3,500

³ Picked up from a damaged M/L.

TABLE 2

AN ANALYSIS OF THE RECORDED NUMBERS OF TROOPS LIFTED DAILY FROM DUNKIRK HARBOUR AND THE BEACHES.

BRITISH SHIPS	27TH MAY			28TH MAY			29TH MAY			Grand Total
	Beaches	Harbour	Total	Beaches	Harbour	Total	Beaches	Harbour	Total	
Cruiser				656		656	1,200		1,200	
Destroyers		12	12	2,849	8,986	11,835	6,596	6,705	13,301	
Sloop										
Corvettes										
Gunboats										
Minesweepers				1,082		1,082	3,099	1,953	5,052	
Trawlers...								90	90	
Drifters				1,138		1,138	458		458	
Special Service Vessels										
M.A./S.Bs., M.T.Bs., etc. ...										
Armed Boarding Vessels ...		2,551	2,551		1,083	1,083				
Skoots				5	150	155	1,593	2,757	4,350	
Yachts										
Personal Vessels		4,460	4,460	200	1,655	1,855	800	16,720	17,520	
Hospital Carriers		646	646					833	833	
Naval M/Bs.										
Tugs...										
Landing Craft										
War Dept. M/Ls.										
Dockyard lighters										
Steam Hopper Barges										
Auxiliary barges, etc.										

	27th May			28th May			29th May		
	Beaches	Harbour	Total	Beaches	Harbour	Total	Beaches	Harbour	Total
Sailing barges									
R.N.L.I. life-boat									
M/Bs, M/Ls, etc.									
TOTALS FOR THE DAY		7,669	7,669	5,930	11,874	17,804	13,746	29,058	42,804
FRENCH SHIPS									
Torpedo boats and destroyers								460	460
Sloops									
Minesweeping sloops								520	520
Submarine chasers							6	20	26
Minesweeping trawlers									
Patrol vessels									
Cargo ships									
Trawlers and M.F.Vs.									
TOTALS FOR THE DAY							6	1,000	1,006
BELGIAN SHIPS									
Patrol boat									
Tug									
Trawlers									
TOTALS FOR THE DAY									
DUTCH SHIPS									
Yacht									
TOTALS FOR THE DAY									
NORWEGIAN SHIPS									
Freighter								3,500	3,500
TOTAL FOR THE DAY								3,500	3,500[1]
GRAND TOTAL	—	7,669	7,669	5,930	11,874	17,804	13,572	33,558	47,310

[1] Not mentioned in the Dover report

TABLE 2 (cont.)

AN ANALYSIS OF THE RECORDED NUMBERS OF TROOPS LIFTED DAILY FROM DUNKIRK HARBOUR AND THE BEACHES.

BRITISH SHIPS	30TH MAY			31ST MAY			1ST JUNE			Grand Total
	Beaches	Harbour	Total	Beaches	Harbour	Total	Beaches	Harbour	Total	
Cruiser										
Destroyers	7,968	10,862	18,830	16,613	6,221	22,834	1,244	13,044	14,288	
Sloop				436		436				
Corvettes				271		271		369	369	
Gunboats	563		563	620		620	770	470	1240	
Minesweepers	7,455	570	8,025	5,335	2,000	7,335	7,333	5,086	12,819	
Trawlers	404	674	1,078	399		399	157	1,629	1,786	
Drifters	1,655	804	2,459	1,483	1,447	2,930	1,279	1,689	2,968	
Special Service Vessels	1,200		1,200	1,831		1,831	350	900	1,250	
M.A./S.Bs., M.T.Bs., etc.		53	53		20	20	2		2	
Armed Boarding Vessels										
Skoots	6,651	662	7,313	3,940	1,664	5,604	2,829	341	3,170	
Yachts		1,222	1,222	690	301	991	55	1,776	1,831	
Personal Vessels	3,232	3,190	6,422	74	17,404	17,478	145	14,390	14,535	
Hospital Carriers		490	490		620	620		417	417	
Naval M/Bs.					16	16				
Tugs	190	207	397	187	32	219	541	195	736	
Landing Craft	55		55							
War Dept. M/Ls.				140	180	320	60	84	144	
Dockyard lighters				67		67	245		245	
Steam Hopper Barges					696	696	890	580	1,470	
Auxiliary barges, etc.				363	300	663	269		269	

	30TH MAY			31ST MAY			1ST JUNE		
	Beaches	Harbour	Total	Beaches	Harbour	Total	Beaches	Harbour	Total
Sailing barges … … … …				13		13	200		200
R.N.L.I. life-boat … … …				17		17		17	17
M/Bs, M/Ls, etc. … … …	139	950	1,089	463		463	562	1,628	2,190
TOTALS FOR THE DAY … …	29,512	19,684	49,196	22,942	40,901	63,843	17,348	42,598	59,946
FRENCH SHIPS									
Torpedo boats and destroyers		2,043	2,043		1,007	1,007		951	951
Sloops … … … … …		1,000	1,000						
Minesweeping sloops … …		581	581		937	937			
Submarine chasers … …									
Minesweeping trawlers … …		405	405		612	612		720	720
Patrol vessels … … …		15	15		346	346		379	379
Cargo ships … … … …					969	969		1,001	1,001
Trawlers and M.F.Vs. … …		483	483		100	100		916	916
TOTALS FOR THE DAY … …		4,527	4,527		3,971	3,971		3,967	3,967
BELGIAN SHIPS									
Patrol boat … … … …									
Tug … … … … … …									
Trawlers … … … … …		100	100		100	100		402	402
TOTALS FOR THE DAY … …		100	100		100	100		402	402
DUTCH SHIPS									
Yacht … … … … … …					100	100		114	114
TOTALS FOR THE DAY … …					100	100		114	114
NORWEGIAN SHIPS									
Freighter … … … … …								3,500	3,500
TOTAL FOR THE DAY … …								3,500	3,500[1]
GRAND TOTAL … … … …	29,512	24,311	53,823	22,942	45,072	68,014	17,348	47,081	64,429

TABLE 2 (cont.)

AN ANALYSIS OF THE RECORDED NUMBERS OF TROOPS LIFTED DAILY FROM DUNKIRK HARBOUR AND THE BEACHES.

BRITISH SHIPS	2ND JUNE			3RD JUNE			4TH JUNE			Grand Total
	Beaches	Harbour	Total	Beaches	Harbour	Total	Beaches	Harbour	Total	
Cruiser										1,856
Destroyers	512	5,630	6,142	119	4,418	4,537		4,418	4,418	96,197
Sloop										436
Corvettes				0		0		460	460	1,100
Gunboats	93		93		800	800		196	196	3,512
Minesweepers	3,106	1,970	5,076	845	3,578	4,423	50	2,572	2,622	46,434
Trawlers...	165	1,042	1,207	300	118	418		418	418	5,396
Drifters	258	942	1,200		1,004	1,004		213	213	12,370
Special Service Vessels ...	126		126		1	1				4,408
M.A./S.Bs., M.T.Bs., etc. ...	24		24							99
Armed Boarding Vessels ...		1,214	1,214							4,848
Skoots	346	751	1,097	50		50		959	959	22,698
Yachts		245	245		252	252		140	140	4,681
Personal Vessels	618	4,977	5,595	18	8,797	8,815		11,130	11,130	87,810
Hospital Carriers										3,006
Naval M/Bs.		47	47	2	25	27		6	6	96
Tugs	413	502	915	311	383	694	12	191	203	3,164
Landing Craft	63		63							118
War Dept. M/Ls.					69	69		46	46	579
Dockyard lighters	106		106							418
Steam Hopper Barges ...										2,166
Auxiliary barges, etc. ...	74	250	324							1,256

	2ND JUNE			3RD JUNE			4TH JUNE			Grand Total
	Beaches	Harbour	Total	Beaches	Harbour	Total	Beaches	Harbour	Total	
Sailing barges	200		200	213		213	260		260	886
R.N.L.I. life-boat	88		88		103	103	50	48	98	323
M/Bs, M/Ls, etc.	503	44	547	11	300	311	250	181	431	5,031
TOTALS FOR THE DAY	6,695	17,614	24,309	1,869	19,848	21,717	622	20,978	21,600	308,888
FRENCH SHIPS										
Torpedo boats and destroyers					769	769		1,416	1,416	6,646
Sloops										1,000
Minesweeping sloops										2,038
Submarine chasers					50	50		127	127	203
Minesweeping trawlers		416	416		157	157		355	355	2,665
Patrol vessels		350	350		578	578		836	836	2,504
Cargo ships		320	320							2,290
Trawlers and M.F.Vs.		548	548	1	1,662	1,663		1,104	1,104	4,814
TOTALS FOR THE DAY		1,634	1,634	1	3,216	3,217		3,838	3,838	22,160
BELGIAN SHIPS										
Patrol boat					229	229				229
Tug								183	183	183
Trawlers		313	313		1,583	1,583		554	554	3,052
TOTALS FOR THE DAY		313	313		1,812	1,812		737	737	3,464
DUTCH SHIPS										
Yacht										214
TOTALS FOR THE DAY					0	0		0	0	214
NORWEGIAN SHIPS										
Freighter										3,500
TOTAL FOR THE DAY										3,500
GRAND TOTAL	6,695	19,561	26,256	1,870	24,876	26,746	622	25,553	26,175	338,226

TABLE 3

TROOP AND SHIP SUMMARIES

(a)

Nationality	Evacuating troops	On patrol, etc.	TOTAL	Lost	Put out of action
SHIPS TAKING PART—SUMMARY					
British	689	76	765	218	57
French	108	11	119	13	4
Belgian	45	—	45	4	—
Polish	—	1	1	—	—
Dutch	2	—	2	1	—
Norwegian	1	—	1	—	—
TOTAL	845	88	933	236	61

(b)

Nationality of ships	From the beaches	From the Harbour	TOTAL
ALLIED SHIPS—SUMMARY OF TROOPS TRANSPORTED			
British	98,754	210,134	308,888
French	7	22,153	22,160
Belgian	—	3,464	3,464
Polish	—	—	—
Dutch	—	214	214
Norwegian	—	3,500	3,500
TOTAL	98,761	239,465	338,226

(c)

Date	From the Beaches	From the Harbour	TOTAL	Accumulated Total
DISEMBARKATIONS—SUMMARY				
26th May	Nil	Nil	Nil	
27th May	Nil	7,669	7,669	7,669
28th May	5,930	11,874	17,804	25,473
29th May	13,752	33,558	47,310	72,783
30th May	29,512	24,311	53,823	126,606
31st May	22,942	45,072	68,014	194,620
1st June	17,348	47,081	64,429	259,049
2nd June	6,695	19,561	26,256	285,305
3rd June	1,870	24,876	26,746	312,051
4th June	622	25,553	26,175	338,226
GRAND TOTAL	98,780	239,446	338,226	

PLANS

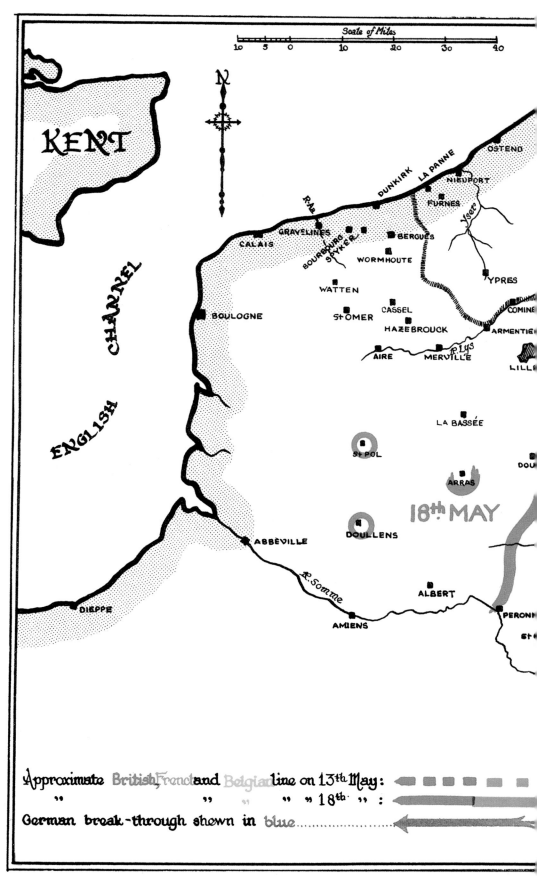

Scale of Miles
10 5 0   10   20   30   40

N

KENT

ENGLISH CHANNEL

OSTEND
DUNKIRK   LA PANNE
NIEUPORT
R.Aa   FURNES
GRAVELINES
BOURBOURG SPYKER   BERGUES
CALAIS   Yser
WORMHOUTE
WATTEN   YPRES
BOULOGNE   St OMER   CASSEL
HAZEBROUCK   COMINES
AIRE   MERVILLE   ARMENTIÈ
R.Lys   LILLE

LA BASSÉE

St POL
ARRAS   DOU
18ᵗʰ MAY

DOULLENS

ABBÈVILLE

R.Somme   ALBERT
DIEPPE   PERONN
AMIENS   St

Approximate British, French and Belgian line on 13ᵗʰ May :
  „   „   „   „ „ 18ᵗʰ „ :
German break-through shewn in blue.........

C.B.H. 16675 - Wt.41534 - Dd. D.8100 - 625 - 6/49

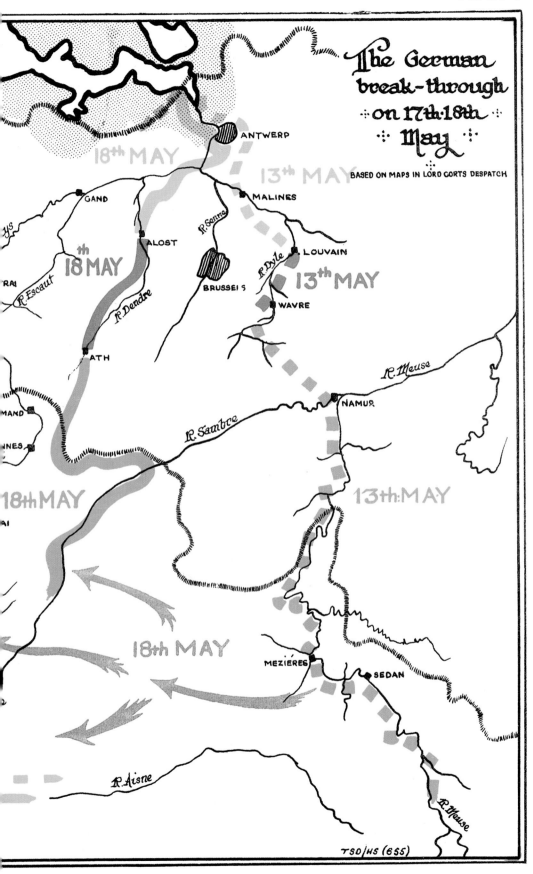

The German
break-through
∴ on 17th·18th ∴
∴ May ∴
∴
BASED ON MAPS IN LORD GORTS DESPATCH

18ᵗʰ MAY

13ᵗʰ MAY

ANTWERP

MALINES

GAND

R.Senne

ALOST

R.Dyle

LOUVAIN

th
18 MAY

BRUSSELS

WAVRE

13ᵗʰ MAY

R.Escaut

R.Dendre

R.Meuse

ATH

MAND

R.Sambce

NAMUR

NES

13th·MAY

18th MAY

18th MAY

MEZIÉRES

SEDAN

R.Aisne

R.Meuse

TSD/HS (655)

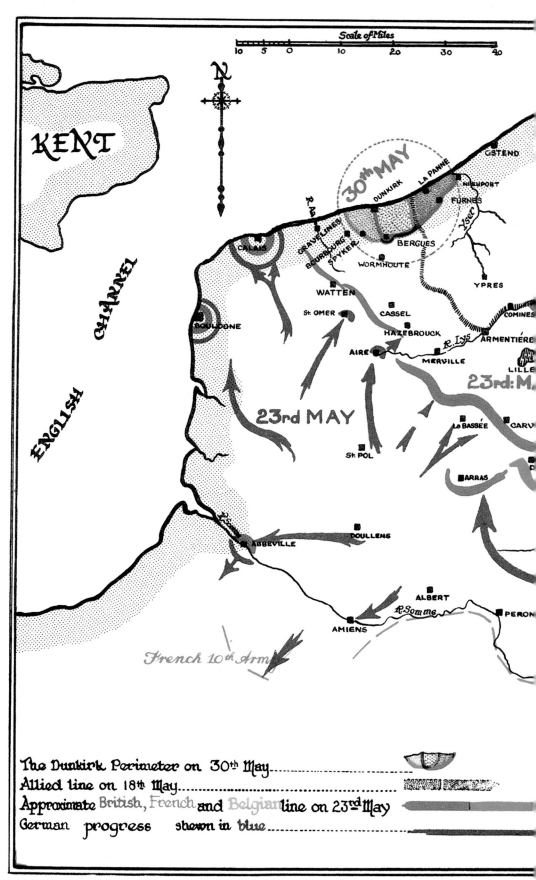

Scale of Miles

KENT

ENGLISH CHANNEL

R. Aa

R.Aa

CALAIS

GRAVELINES

BOURBOURG

SPYKER

DUNKIRK

LA PANNE

NIEUPORT

FURNES

OSTEND

30th MAY

BERGUES

WORMHOUTE

YSER

YPRES

WATTEN

COMINES

St OMER

CASSEL

HAZEBROUCK

R.LYS

ARMENTIÉRE

BOULOGNE

AIRE

MERVILLE

LILLE

23rd: M.

23rd MAY

La BASSÉE

CARV

St. POL

ARRAS

D

DOULLENS

ABBEVILLE

ALBERT

PERON

R.Somme

AMIENS

French 10th Army

The Dunkirk Perimeter on 30th May.....................

Allied line on 18th May.............................

Approximate British, French and Belgian line on 23rd May

German progress shown in blue.......................

C.B.H. 16675

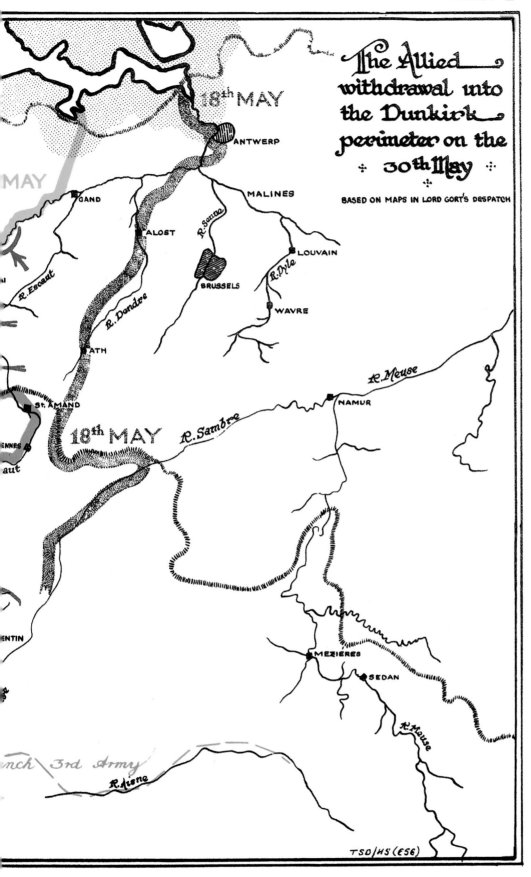

The Allied withdrawal into the Dunkirk perimeter on the ⁘ 30th May ⁘

⁘

BASED ON MAPS IN LORD GORT'S DESPATCH

18th MAY

18th MAY

ANTWERP

MALINES

GAND

ALOST

R. Senne

LOUVAIN

R. Dyle

BRUSSELS

WAVRE

R. Escaut

R. Dendre

ATH

St. AMAND

R. Meuse

NAMUR

R. Sambre

R. Meuse

MEZIERES

SEDAN

R. Meuse

...nch 3rd Army

R. Aisne

ENNES

aut

...ENTIN

TSD/HS(E56)

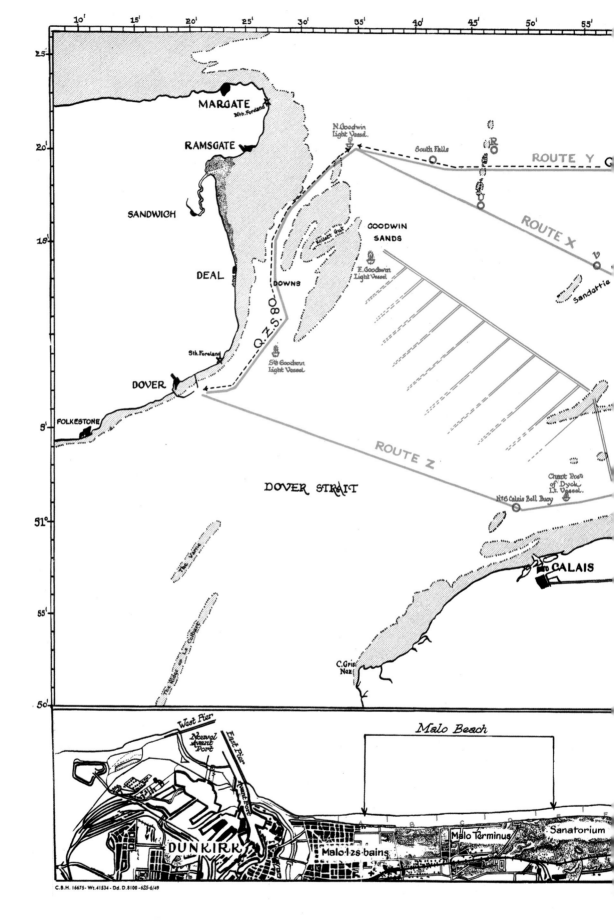

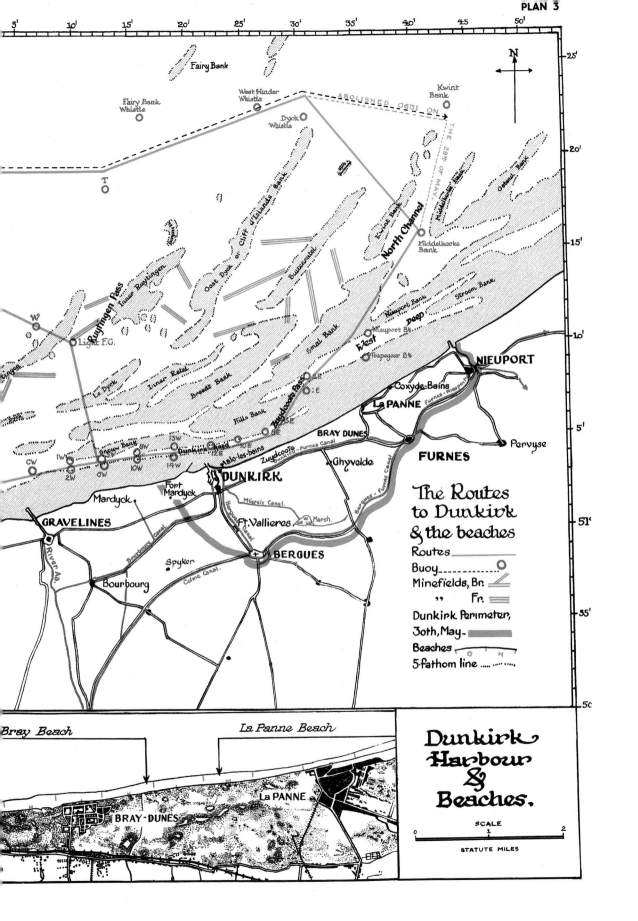

The Routes
to Dunkirk
& the beaches

Routes ——————
Buoy ———————— ○
Minefields, Br.
   "   Fr.
Dunkirk Perimeter,
30th, May.
Beaches
5-fathom line ....

Dunkirk
Harbour
&
Beaches.

SCALE

0   1   2

STATUTE MILES

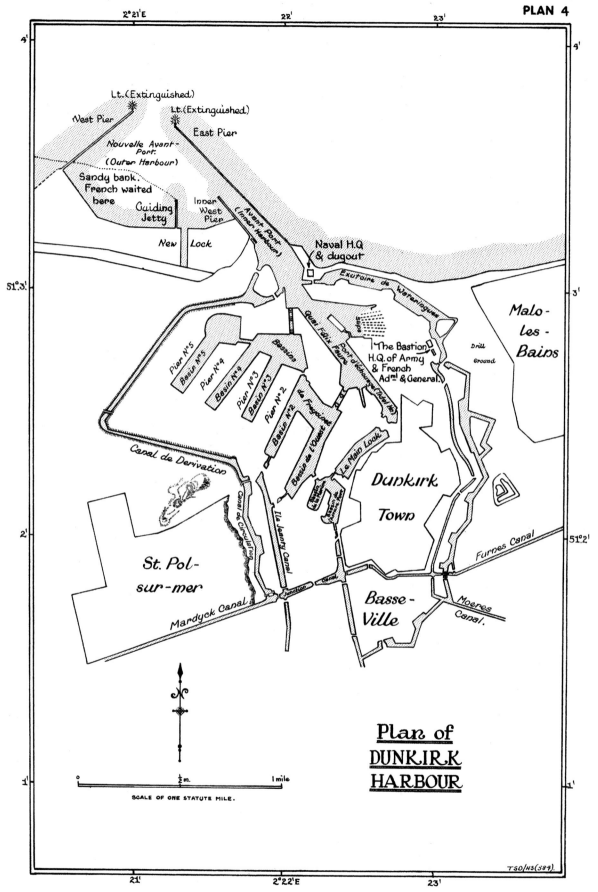

Plan of
DUNKIRK
HARBOUR